PILGRIM FELLOWSHIP OF FAITH

Joseph Cardinal Ratzinger

Pilgrim Fellowship of Faith

THE CHURCH AS COMMUNION

Presented by
the Association of the Former Students of
Joseph Cardinal Ratzinger
in celebration of his
seventy-fifth birthday

Edited by
Stephan Otto Horn
and
Vinzenz Pfnür

TRANSLATED BY HENRY TAYLOR

IGNATIUS PRESS   SAN FRANCISCO

Title of the German original:
Weg Gemeinschaft des Glaubens: Kirche als Communio
© 2002 by Sankt Ulrich Verlag GmbH, Augsburg

© 2005 by Ignatius Press, San Francisco
All rights reserved
ISBN 0–89870–963–6
Library of Congress Control Number 2004114955

Printed in the United States of America ∞

CONTENTS

INTRODUCTION

On the sixteenth of April this year [2002], Joseph Cardinal Ratzinger will have completed seventy-five years of his life. For his sixtieth birthday, the association of his former students published a comprehensive two-volume *Festschrift* under the title of *Weisheit Gottes—Weisheit der Welt*, in which seventy-seven authors from the sphere of the theologian Joseph Ratzinger's academic teaching witnessed to their indebtedness.[1]

For his seventieth birthday, the association of former students published a collection of texts from four decades, under the title *Vom Wiederauffinden der Mitte: Grundorientierungen*.[2] In doing so, they wanted to "open an initial perspective on the basic positions of the theological approach of Joseph Cardinal Ratzinger" and to "offer an introduction to some important subject areas in which the theological contribution of Ratzinger is of continuing relevance and significance".[3]

The present volume reinforces this aspect of relevance to the Church.

These three *Festschriften* reflect the path traveled by the man whose life they celebrate, from academic teaching to official

---

[1] *Weisheit Gottes—Weisheit der Welt: Festschrift für Joseph Kardinal Ratzinger zum 60. Geburtstag* [Wisdom of God—Wisdom of the world: Essays in honor of Joseph Cardinal Ratzinger on his sixtieth birthday], ed. on behalf of the association of his former pupils by W. Baier, S. Horn, V. Pfnür, C. Schönborn, L. Weimer, and S. Wiedenhofer (St. Ottilien, 1987).

[2] *Vom Wiederauffinden der Mitte: Grundorientierungen: Texte aus vier Jahrzehnten* [Rediscovering the center: Basic orientations: Texts from four decades], published by the association of former pupils, ed. S. Horn, V. Pfnür, V. Twomey, S. Wiedenhofer, and J. Zöhrer, 2nd ed. (Freiburg, Basel, and Vienna, 1998).

[3] Ibid., p. 11.

responsibility in relation to the whole Church. Joseph Ratzinger had indeed as a young man, just a few years after his qualifying as a professor, helped determine, in a decisive though still often underrated way, the course and the statements of the Second Vatican Council through his activity as a theological advisor, and yet research and teaching were still his main field of activity. For the bishop, and even more for the Prefect of the Congregation for the Doctrine of the Faith, there has been only a very limited place for specialized research and no leisure for the writing of a theological *Summa*. The main task has been responsibility to the Church as a whole. Thus, the pieces offered in this present volume are signposts, in the light of the Second Vatican Council, for the current situation in theology and the Church. They are a call to respond to the challenge of the truth and not to lose sight of the overall view.

This is true first of all of the *depth dimension of the whole, "the whole of our being"* (see below, p. 293), which cannot be reduced to what is demonstrable on the basis of a mechanistic and materialistic view of the world.

It is a matter of keeping what is earthly and human so that it is transparent toward the truly fundamental reality, the divine reality that opens itself to us through Christ in the Holy Spirit.

For theology this means, over and beyond the detailed questions of the separate disciplines and the working methods they apply, not to overlook the most important thing, the Christian faith as "being touched by God and witnessing to him". This is especially important for the interpretation of the Bible. Exegetes are called upon to examine their philosophical presuppositions and to be open to a hermeneutic of belief, so that "the most profound meaning of the Word" may be "grasped when we move beyond what is merely written" (see below, p. 34).

This also applies to the *view of the Church.* As a sacrament, as the Body opened up for us on the Cross, as the People of God, who live on the Body of Christ and thus become the body of Christ, as the Bride—sanctified by Christ despite all human guilt, she is more than what is accessible to purely sociological perspectives.

This existing sacramental reality of the Church is "not the result of adding together individual churches that already exist" (see below, p. 249); rather, she is ontologically prior to these. Hence, universality is a constitutive endowment of the Church. Even though the Eucharist, in which Christ builds up the Church as his body, takes place in practice only at a particular place, "yet [it] is at the same time universal, because there is only one Christ and only one body of Christ" (see below, pp. 131–32). "The indivisible presence of one and the same Lord, who is also the Word of the Father, therefore presumes that each individual congregation stands within the *one* and *whole* body of Christ; that is the only way they can celebrate the Eucharist" (see below, pp. 88–89). The emphasis on the ontological priority of the universal Church before the particular Churches is "not a declaration in favor of any particular form of distribution of responsibility within the Church, not a declaration that the local Church of Rome should seek to acquire as many privileges as possible. That kind of interpretation completely misjudges the level of the question. Anyone who always just turns straight to the question of the distribution of power has utterly missed the mystery of the Church" (see below, p. 239). Even Cardinal Ratzinger does not dispute that there "may be an extravagant and excessive Roman centralization, which then has to be identified as such and corrected" (see p. 133), but the alternative cannot be "a Church reduced to purely local ministries and the neighborly existence of congregations" (see below, p. 202, n. 20); it is, rather, a matter of the Eucharist being "for each local Church the point at which people are drawn into the one Christ", "the process of all communicants becoming one in that universal communion which binds together heaven and earth; the living and the dead; past, present, and future; and opens up toward eternity" (see below, pp. 142–43). That means, among other things, that "there are no foreigners in the Church; everyone is at home everywhere, and not just a visitor. It is always the one Church, one and the same. Anyone baptized in Berlin is just as much at home in the Church in Rome or in New York or in Kinshasa or in Bangalore or wherever he may be as in the Church where he was baptized. He does not need to report his move; it is all the one Church" (see below, p. 142).

Reference to *the whole in its depth dimension*, as against too superficial a view of reality and especially of the Church, and to *the whole in its universal dimension*, as against too particularist a view of reality and especially of the Church, is thus the main thread running through this volume. It begins with taking as a point of reference that greater reality with which faith and theology have to do, and in the succeeding articles it gives this concrete form under the theme of *communion*, fellowship. The Church draws her life from the fact that there is an ultimate, imperishable fellowship, that the Absolute is not an impersonal cosmic law but is a living, personal community opened up for man. The Church "draws her life from the Logos having become flesh, from the truth having become a way" (see below, p. 264). "The Church is not there for her own sake" (see below, pp. 128–29). For the priest, who puts his whole life at the service of communion, this means "that he does not talk of his own volition; rather, he makes himself the voice of Christ, so as to make room for the Logos himself and, through fellowship with the human Jesus, to draw people into fellowship with the living God" (see below, p. 160). Fellowship in and of the body of Christ then also means "fellowship with one another. This of its very nature includes mutual acceptance, giving and receiving on both sides, and readiness to share one's goods" (see below, p. 69).

The Eucharist, as "the enduring presence of the divine and human love of Jesus Christ, which is always the source and origin of the Church and without which she would founder, would be overcome by the gates of hell", is "also always the channel open from the man Jesus to the people who are his 'members', themselves becoming a Eucharist and thereby themselves a 'heart' and a 'love' for the Church." The Eucharist is thus in a more profound sense the origin of mission, which is "constantly. . . nourished from a deeper center" (see below, p. 122). The struggle on a practical level to transplant Church fellowship is manifest in the "Church movements" that are mainly organized on the level of the universal Church. Communion also includes the cleansing of conscience by recognizing the guilt that the Church has taken on herself.

One particular field of work of Christian communion is the realm of ecumenism. We find here in the writings of Joseph Ratzinger, from the beginning, two lines of thought and expression that are complementary: first, the striving to propagate Church fellowship in practical ways and, then, the knowledge of the merely relative value of such efforts, in view of the deeper fellowship that already exists, beyond the propagation and extension of canonical legality. These lines are already to be found in the preconciliar period. Thus, in 1961, in the article on "Protestantism" in the RGG, Ratzinger affirms the constitutive Church membership of all those baptized outside the Catholic Church and also the "existence of ecclesial elements" and "a certain presence of the reality of the Church" in Protestantism. On the other hand, with regard to overcoming the problem on the level of theological arguments, "some caution is appropriate, in that a complete reduction to systematic terms is impossible on either side, because happily, on both sides, faithfulness to the truth was stronger than the impulse to systematize".[4] Personal friendships with the man who was later chairman on the Orthodox side of the Joint International Commission for theological dialogue between the Roman Catholic Church and the Orthodox Church, Archbishop Stylianos Harkianakis of Australia,[5] and with Damaskinos Papandreou, later Metropolitan of Switzerland (see below, p. 217), both important for the relations between the Roman Catholic Church and the Greek Orthodox Church, likewise date from the time before the Council. In regard to the Lutheran side of things, we must point out his important change of direction, to the effect that the Catholic "should not" bet on "the disintegration of the Creed and on decay of Church elements in the Protestant sphere", "but, quite the contrary, on the strengthening of confessional ties and of ecclesial reality".[6] Finally, it is not least thanks to the good relationship between the Bishop of Munich and the Provincial Bishop of the Evangelical Lutheran Church in Bavaria, Johannes Hanselmann (see below, p. 242), that the *Joint Declaration on the*

---

[4] J. Ratzinger, "Protestantismus: III. Beurteilung vom Standpunkt des Katholizismus" [Protestantism: III. Assessment from the Catholic point of view] in *Religion in Geschichte und Gegenwart*, 3rd ed., vol. 5 (1961), 663–66.

[5] See the first document, issued in Munich in 1982, in the preparation of which Cardinal Ratzinger took a substantial part: "Das Geheimnis der Kirche und der Eucharistie im Licht des Geheimnisses der Heiligen Dreifaltigkeit" [The mystery of the Church and the Eucharist in the light of the mystery of the Holy Trinity], *Dokumente wachsender Übereinstimmung* [Documents of growth in agreement], vol. 2, ed. H. Meyer et al. (Paderborn and Frankfurt am Main, 1992), pp. 526–41.

[6] J. Ratzinger, "Prognosen für die Zukunft des Ökumenismus" [Prognosis for the future of ecumenism], in Ratzinger, *Vom Wiederauffindung der Mitte*, pp. 192f.

Doctrine of Justification was adapted ecclesially along with the *Official Common Statement*.[7]

We hope that the exchange of letters with Metropolitan Damaskinos Papandreou and Provincial Bishop Hanselmann, reprinted in this book, may also help to make the discussion about *Communionis notio* and about *Dominus Iesus* more objective and encourage readiness to grasp the central message and concerns of these texts.

The final piece, "The Church on the Threshold of the Third Millennium", sums up the task of the pilgrim fellowship of the Church: "The Church is there so that God, the living God, may be made known—so that man may learn to live with God, live in his sight and in fellowship with him" (see below, p. 286).

The theme of this presentation volume, *Pilgrim Fellowship of Faith: The Church as Communion*, is beautifully expressed in the depiction of Pentecost from the Codex Egberti (fol. 103): the fellowship with the apostles, directed toward the nations, which is called into being with the Pentecost event, has in its midst the "common life" (*communis vita*), the divine wellspring of life, together with the Bread of Life.

We would like first of all to thank our contact in Rome, ever ready to help, Monsignor Dr. Josef Clemens, and Frau Birgit Wansing, who has taken care of the bibliography for the last ten years, together with Professor Dr. Gunther Franz, of Trier, for his friendly and most helpful support with the reproduction of the Pentecost illustration from the Codex

---

[7] Lutheran World Federation and Joint Council, *Gemeinsame Erklärung zur Rechtfertigungslehre: Gemeinsame offizielle Feststellung:Anhang (Annex) zur Gemeinsamen offiziellen Feststellung* [Joint declaration on the doctrine of justification: Official common statement: Annex to the official common statement] (Paderborn and Frankfurt am Main, 1999).

Egberti (fol. 103) from the Stadtbibliothek in Trier. Not least we would thank the Sankt Ulrich Verlag for giving high priority to the typesetting.[8]

---

[8] These last acknowledgments pertain to the 2002 German edition of this work.—ED.

Faith and Theology

Address on the occasion of the conferring
of an honorary doctorate in theology
by the Theological Faculty of Wrocław / Breslau

I should like to express my humble thanks to the Chancellor of the Theological Faculty of Wrocław, Cardinal Henryk Roman Gulbinowicz, and to the Theological Faculty of Wrocław for conferring upon me the rank of honorary doctor of theology. It is an honor and a joy to me that I am now privileged to wear the doctoral cap of two Polish faculties of theology—those of Lublin and Wrocław—and that I have thus close academic relations with the land in which our Holy Father was born, grew up, received his theological training, and for a long time was himself active in teaching theology. It is an old academic tradition for one's thanks for the conferring of a doctorate to be expressed in a lecture in which the recipient of that honor tries to show that he has, indeed, something to say in his discipline. So as not to prolong this morning's ceremonies beyond reasonable length, I should like to do this in the form of a *lectio brevis*.

I have been thinking about what subject would be suitable for this occasion. The thought might perhaps suggest itself, at this time when there is heated dispute about the declaration *Dominus Iesus*, that I should talk about that document. Yet after some reflection, it occurred to me that at this particular moment I ought not to mix my official position as Prefect of the Congregation for the Doctrine of the Faith with my personal affairs, such as the award of an honorary doctorate. It thus seemed more appropriate to me to choose a somewhat more general theme, one that is the starting point of all theological work and is naturally among the preliminary questions faced by the Congregation for the Faith, to wit, the **relationship between faith and theology**. I certainly need not emphasize that I am far from being able to treat this extensive subject exhaustively, a subject that has repeatedly occupied the greatest theologians of every era; I should just like to try to single out one aspect that seems important to me.

The word *Glaube* [faith, belief] has in German, and no doubt in other languages, two quite different meanings. There is the everyday meaning that people usually associate with the word. Someone says, for instance: I believe the weather will be fine tomorrow. Or, I believe that this or that piece of news is not true. Here the word "believe" is the equivalent of *think*; it expresses an imperfect form of perception. People talk of believing when the status of knowing has not been reached. Many people probably think that this meaning of "believing" is also applicable in the realm of religion, so that the contents of the Christian faith are an imperfect, preliminary stage of knowledge. When we say, "I believe in God", this, they think, is just an expression of our not knowing anything definite about the matter. If this were so, then theology would be a rather strange discipline—indeed, the concept of an academic discipline dealing with faith would actually be a contradiction in itself. For how could one construct a real academic discipline upon suppositions? In reality, for the believing Christian the words "I believe" articulate **a particular kind of certainty**—one that is in many respects a higher degree of certainty than that of science yet one that does indeed carry within it the dynamic of "shadow and image", the dynamic of the "not yet".

As I was preparing for this lecture and reflecting on the problems of the quite odd relationship of **certainty** and risk that is inherent in the Christian act of faith, a little incident, which happened quite a few years ago, came to mind. I had been invited to speak at the Waldensian faculty in Rome. A discussion followed my lecture, which had concerned this very problem of the darkness and light of faith. A student raised the question of whether doubt was not the absolute condition for faith and was therefore always present within faith. It was not in fact completely clear to me exactly what the student meant, but he was probably trying to express the idea that faith never reaches complete certainty, just as a renunciation of faith cannot be sure of itself. All faith would in the end be a "perhaps"; I recalled Martin Buber's well-known story about Rabbi Levi Yitzhak of Berditschev and the way he countered the learned advocate of enlightenment with the words: "Yet perhaps it is true." [1] This "perhaps" broke down the other man's opposition; it appears to be faith's strength, but it would of course also be its weakness.

Is it really only perhaps? If the forms of verification of modern natural science were the only way in which man could arrive at any certainty, then faith would indeed have to be classified in the realm of mere "perhaps" and to be constantly fused with doubt, to be virtually identical with it. But just as a person becomes certain of another's love without being able to subject it to the methods of scientific experiment, so in the contact between God and man there is a certainty of a quite different kind from the certainty of objectivizing thought. We live faith, not as a hypothesis, but

---

[1] Martin Buber, *Werke*, vol. 3: *Schriften zum Chassidismus* [Writings on Hasidism] (Munich and Heidelberg, 1963), p. 348.

as the **certainty on which our life is based**. If two people regard their love merely as a hypothesis that is constantly in need of new verification, they destroy love in that way. It is contradicted in its essence if one tries to make it something one can grasp in one's hand. By then it has already been destroyed. Perhaps so many relationships break down today because we are aware of the certainty only of the verified hypothesis and do not admit the ultimate validity of anything not scientifically proved. Thus, the essential phenomena of human life escape us, with their quite different kind of certainty, which is in truth far higher. God, most of all, cannot be objectified as if he were a thing on a lower level than we are, which we could squeeze into our hand or into our apparatus. Yet his light is able, as Bonaventure says, "to stabilize our emotions and to enlighten our intellect".[2]

Belief is not at all mere opinion, as we express it in the sentence, "I believe the weather will be fine tomorrow." It is not doubt; rather, it is certainty that God has shown himself and has opened up for us the view of truth itself. Yet here arises the contrary objection, which Heidegger and Jaspers have insistently formulated. They say: *Faith excludes philosophy, real research into and seeking for ultimate realities. For faith supposes it knows all that already. Its certainty leaves no place for questions.* Anyone who believes has already failed as a philosopher, says Jaspers, for all the questioning is merely apparent; it has to come up in the end with the answer that has already been given. A theology that was based upon mere opinion could not be scholarly or scientific, as we have already said. Jaspers' argument takes the opposite approach. Theology, he says,

---

[2] *Sent.*, l. 3, d. 23, a. 1, q. 5, concl.: "Nam ipsa fides secundum essentiam suam aliquid respicit ex parte *intellectus* et aliquid ex parte *affectus*. Habet enim *affectum stabilire* et *intellectum illuminare*" (St. Bonaventure, *Opera omnia*, vol. 3 [Quarrachi, 1887], p. 484).

cannot be a genuine scholarly discipline since it argues only in appearance, having its results already given in advance. Many objections against theology doubtless do arise from this notion, and many rebellions against the teaching office, within theology, presuppose a similar kind of argument, in more moderate form.

Thus, a twofold problem seems to loom before theology: if faith basically never gets beyond doubt, then it offers no foothold for serious scholarly thought. If it is offering only ready-made certainties, then it seems equally to exclude the movement of thought. At this point it becomes clear that the two opposing positions ultimately originate in the same model of thinking, because both are obviously aware of only a single form of certainty and never have the quite specific anthropological structure of faith in their view. When you begin to understand that structure, it also becomes clear why the Christian faith produced theology and did so necessarily. The nature of theology can be understood only on the basis of the nature of faith. If we analyze these interconnections, then it becomes clear what is really at the heart of the two positions we have mentioned.

I do not know whether, in the short time I am allowing myself, I shall be able to some extent to make clear at least the direction in which the answers become accessible. I should like to try to do so by starting from a very dense passage of Saint Thomas Aquinas, which illuminates with great precision the **nature of the Christian act of faith** and thereby demonstrates its inner openness toward theology: that is, *De veritate*, q. 14, a. 1 corp.

First of all, following Augustine, Thomas defines believing as **"thinking with assent"**. This coexistence of thinking and assent is something faith has in common with science. It is characteristic of science for thinking to result in assent.

Anyone following its progression ends by saying: Yes, that is right. Assent is also a part of believing. This is not an act of abstention, but a decision, a certainty. Being eternally open, and keeping oneself open in all directions, is exactly what faith is not. It is "hypostasis", the Letter to the Hebrews says (11:1): taking one's stand, and standing firm, on what is hoped for; being convinced.

Yet the relationship between assent and thought is different in faith from what it is in science, in knowledge in general. In the case of a scientific demonstration, the obviousness of the business forces us, by inner necessity, into assent.[3] The act of perception itself brings about the "Yes, that is right." Thomas says that the certainty attained "determines" our thinking. Thus, in the insight obtained, the movement of thought comes to rest; it finds its conclusion. The structure of the act of faith is quite different. Thomas says about this that here the thought process and the assent balance each other, they are "ex aequo".[4] What does that mean? First, it means that in the act of believing the assent comes about in a different way from the way it does in the act of knowing: not through the degree of evidence bringing the process of thought to its conclusion, but by an act of will, in connection with which the thought process remains open and still under way. Here, the degree of evidence does not turn the thought into assent; rather, the will commands assent, even though the thought process is still

---

[3] See Thomas Aquinas, *Summa contra gentiles* III, 40, no. 3: "In cognitione autem fidei principalitatem habet voluntas: intellectus enim assentit per fidem his quae sibi proponuntur, quia vult, non autem ex ipsa veritatis evidentia necessario tractus" (Thomas Aquinas, *Opera omnia*, vol. 2 [Stuttgart, 1980], p. 71).

[4] Thomas Aquinas, *De veritate*, q. 14, art. 1, contra: "In scientia enim motus rationis incipit ab intellectu principiorum, et ad eumdem terminatur per viam resolutionis; et sic non habet assensum et cogitationem quasi ex aequo: sed cogitatio inducit ad assensum, et assensus cogitationem quietat. *Sed in fide est assensus et cogitatio quasi ex aequo*" (ibid., 3:91).

under way. How can it do that without doing violence to the thinking? To answer this question, we must first be aware that in Thomas Aquinas' terminology the concept of will is more far-reaching than we understand it to be today. What Thomas calls the will corresponds roughly to what in biblical language is called "the heart". Thus, Pascal's well-known saying comes to mind: "Le coeur a ses raisons, que la raison ne connaît point." [5] The heart has its reasons; it has its own rationality, which reaches beyond "mere" reason. On the basis of the logic of this sentence we can get to the meaning: Any perception presupposes a certain sym-pathy with what is perceived. Without a certain inner closeness, a kind of love, we cannot perceive the other thing or person. In this sense the "will" always somehow precedes the perception and is its precondition; and the more so, the greater and more inclusive is the reality to be perceived. We are able to give the assent of faith because the will—the heart—has been touched by God, "affected" by him. Through being touched in this way, the will knows that even what is still not "clear" to the reason is true.

Assent is produced by the will, not by the understanding's own direct insight: the particular kind of freedom of choice involved in the decision of faith rests upon this. "Cetera potest homo nolens, credere non nisi volens", says Thomas on this point, quoting Saint Augustine: Man can do everything else against his will, but he can believe only of his free will.[6]

---

[5] *Pensées sur la religion* (1669), no. *277, as edited by C.-M. des Granges (Paris: Garnier, 1964), p. 146.

[6] Thomas Aquinas, *De veritate*, q. 14, art. 1, contra: "Et ideo dicit Augustinus, quod *cetera potest homo nolens, credere nisi volens*" (*Opera omnia*, 3:91); Peter Lombard, *Sententiae* l. 2, dist. 26, c. 4, p. 2: "Non est tamen ignorandum quod alibi augustinus significare uidetur quod ex uoluntate sit fides, de illo uerbo apostoli scilicet, corde creditur ad iustitiam, ita super ioannem tractans: ideo non simpliciter apostolus ait creditur, sed corde creditur, quia cetera potest homo nolens, credere non nisi uolens; intrare ecclesiam et accedere ad altare potest nolens, sed non credere"; Augustine, *In Iohannis euangelium tractatus* 26, 2:

When we realize this, the peculiar spiritual structure of believing becomes clear. Believing is not an act of the understanding alone, not simply an act of the will, not just an act of feeling, but an act in which all the spiritual powers of man are at work together. Still more: man in his own self, and of himself, cannot bring about this believing at all; it has of its nature the character of a dialogue. It is only because the depth of the soul—the heart—has been touched by God's Word that the whole structure of spiritual powers is set in motion and unites in the Yes of believing. It is through all this that we also begin to see the particular kind of truth with which believing is concerned; theology talks about "saving truth". For how is it that God actually touches our heart? What gives the "will" the illumination and the confidence that can then also be shared with the understanding? Augustine says, reflecting on his own experience of life: The inmost heart of the human will is the will for happiness. Everything a man does or allows to happen to him can, ultimately, be derived from his will to be happy. When the heart comes into contact with God's Logos, with the Word who became man, this inmost point of his existence is being touched. Then, he does not merely feel, he knows from within himself: That is it; that is HE, that is what I was waiting for. It is a kind of recognition. For we have been created in relation to God, in relation to the Logos, and our heart remains restless until it has found what the songwriter Paul Gerhardt (d. 1676) was talking about in the marvelous Christmas carol "Ich steh an deiner Krippen hier" [Here I stand beside your crib]: "Before your hand had made me, you had already thought of how you wanted to be mine."

"Intrare quisquam ecclesiam potest nolens, accedere ad altare potest nolens, accipere sacramentum potest nolens; credere non potest nisi uolens. si corpore crederetur, fieret in nolentibus; sed non corpore creditur. apostolum audi: corde creditur ad iustitiam (Rom 10:5)" (PL 35, 1607; CChr. Ser. Lat. 36, 260).

The "will" (the heart), therefore, lights the way for the understanding and draws it with it into assent. That is indeed how thought begins to see, yet believing does not come from seeing, from perceiving, but from hearing. The process of thought is not completed; it has not yet come to rest. Here it becomes particularly clear that believing is a pilgrimage, and also a pilgrimage of thought, which is still following the way. Thomas described this continuing restlessness of thought in the midst of the established certainty of faith in quite drastic fashion on the basis of 2 Corinthians 10:5, where the Apostle says: "We . . . take every thought captive to obey Christ." The Doctor Communis comments: Because the process of thought has not attained to assent in its own way, but on the basis of the will, it has not yet found its rest; it is still reflecting and is still in a state of seeking (*inquisitio*). It has not yet reached satisfaction. It has been brought to an end only "from outside". That is why the Apostle says that it has been taken captive. That is also why it is, says Thomas, that within faith, however firm the assent, a contrary motion (*motus de contrario*) can arise: Struggling and questioning thought remains present, which ever and again has to seek its light from that essential light which shines into the heart from the Word of God.

Assent and the process of thought "in some sense" (*quasi*) balance each other—they are "ex aequo". In this little sentence, which looks at first just like a textbook formula from the past, is contained the whole drama of faith in history; and in it the nature of theology, with its greatness and its limitations, also becomes apparent. It demonstrates the connection between faith and theology. Thinking the whole thing over again, we could say: Faith is an anticipation that is made possible by the will through the heart being touched by God. It grasps in advance what we cannot yet see and cannot yet have. This anticipation sets us in motion. We have to follow that motion. Because assent has been anticipated, thought has to try to catch up with that and is also constantly having to overcome the contrary movement, the *motus de contrario*. This is the situation of believing so long as man stands within this history. That is why there must always be theology, right throughout history; that is why the task of theology within history remains unfinished. Thought is still on its pilgrim's journey, as we ourselves are. And we are not making our pilgrimage aright unless our thought is on pilgrimage, too.

Anyone who immerses himself, even for a little while, in the history of theology can see the drama of this tension, this never-finished pilgrimage of thought toward Christ, in the attempts it makes again and again; thus he can come to know the beauty and the fascination of the adventure we call theology. Above all, he will see how the Word of God is always in advance of us and of our thinking. Not only is it never out of date; everything that claims to be making it outdated quickly becomes dated itself and becomes part of the past, if not altogether forgotten. We can never overtake it; we do not even catch up with it. The *motus de contrario*, which often seems all but invincible, turns out when viewed from a distance to be always motion in reverse after all. Thus history, with its ups and downs, has an encouraging side: it lets us have confidence that anyone who is following the Word of God, anyone who follows the heart's command to assent, and takes this a signpost for the onward journey of thinking and living, is on the right track. History shows us that thinking along with the Word of God has always something new in store and never becomes boring, never pointless. Anyone who looks into history is not just looking backward. He is also getting a better idea of which way to go forward. Without the anticipation of faith, thought would be groping around in emptiness; it would be able to say nothing further about the things that are really essential to man. It would have to conclude, with Wittgenstein, that we must be silent about what is ineffable. It is not doubt but affirmation that opens up the wide horizons to thought. Anyone who encounters the history of theology sees that the suspicions of Heidegger and Jaspers are unfounded. The preknowledge of believing does not oppress thought; it remains "ex aequo"—that is, it is that which really challenges thought and sets it in a restless motion that produces results.

What I am expounding here is not just a theory, even if I did first learn all this from the great masters like Augustine, Bonaventure, and Thomas Aquinas; and even though, first of all, I was guided to these masters by my teacher, Gottlieb Söhngen. I have now been traveling with theology for more than half a century. And so the way that God's Word goes before us, which we follow in our thinking, has increasingly become a quite personal experience. When I was a student, the historico-critical method of exegesis seemed to have said the last word on many subjects. One of my friends, who at that time—in the late forties—was studying in Tübingen, was told by the very learned professor for New Testament exegesis there, Stephan Lösch, that he could no longer offer dissertation subjects on the New Testament, since everything in the New Testament had already been researched. Bernhard Bartmann, the important teacher of dogmatics at Paderborn, who was deservedly revered, said at that time that in dogmatics as such there were no longer any open questions and that one could only further develop knowledge of the history of theology and dogmatics. Theology was then in the process of withdrawing into the past. But how far the Word of God, and the faith of the Church that is based upon it, has left us behind meanwhile! All at once we can see once more what a long journey through a landscape of mysteries and promises is opening up before us, how immeasurably great the country of faith is, which no human travels can ever quite cross. It is becoming apparent that that very *motus de contrario* which we feel so strongly today can be the challenge summoning forth a deeper knowledge. Certainly, that restlessness of thought which can never quite catch up with what is already given by God's Word can lead us away from faith—we can see that. Yet it can, above all, be productive, guiding us into walking on the way of thought toward God. That is the fine task of a theological faculty.

My thanks for the honorary doctorate are thus at the same time heartfelt wishes for blessings upon the future work of this venerable theological faculty.

What in Fact Is Theology?

Expression of thanks for the conferring of the degree of
Doctor honoris causa at the Faculty of Theology of
the University of Navarre in Pamplona

Excellentissimo y Reverendissimo Señor Gran Canciller!
Dear Professors!
Ladies and Gentlemen!

I should first of all like to express to you, my dear Chancellor, and likewise to the most honorable Theological Faculty, my profound thanks for the great honor you have shown me in conferring on me the title of Doctor honoris causa. Most especially I should like to thank you, my very dear colleague, Señor Rodriguez, for the sensitive and very thorough way you have praised my theological work far beyond my just deserts. Through discovering and furnishing the critical edition of the original manuscript of the *Catechismus Romanus*, you have rendered a service to theology that goes beyond the present moment and that was of great significance for my own task in the preparation of the *Catechism of the Catholic Church*. You are a member of a faculty that, in the relatively short period of its existence, has won a significant place in the worldwide discussions of theology. Thus it is a great honor and a joy to me, through this doctorate, to belong to this faculty, to which I have already long been bound by personal friendships as also by academic discussion.

On such an occasion, the question inevitably arises: What in fact is a doctor of theology? And besides that, in my case, the quite personal question: Am I justified in regarding myself as one? Do I come up to the standard implied by this dignity? As far as I personally am concerned, for many people a serious objection will arise: Is not the office of Prefect of the Congregation of the Doctrine of the Faith, which people nowadays like to characterize and also thereby criticize with the title "inquisitor"—is this not in contradiction to the very nature of academic study and, thereby, with the nature of theology? Are not scholarly study and external authority mutually exclusive? Can scholarship recognize any authority other than its own insights and perceptions, other than that of argument? Is not a teaching office that tries to set limits for thought in academic study a contradiction in itself?

Such questions, which touch on the very nature of Catholic theology, no doubt demand a constantly renewed examination of conscience by theologians, as also by those in official positions, who of course also have to be theologians in order properly to fulfill their office. They bring before us the basic problem: **What in fact is theology?** Has it been adequately described when we say that it is a methodically ordered reflection on the questions of religion, of men's relationship with God? I would answer: No. For that takes us only as far as what is called "religious studies". The philosophy of religion and religious studies in general are no doubt very significant disciplines, but their limitations can least of all be overlooked at the point at which they try to move beyond the academic world. For they can offer man no counsel. Either they are talking about what is past or they describe what exists in contradictory fashion, side-by-side and linked together, or else they become a fumbling after what has to do with man's ultimate questions, a fumbling that must always in the end remain a question without being able to overcome the darkness that surrounds man most of all when he is asking where he comes from and where he is going, asking about himself.

If theology wishes and should be something other than religious studies, other than occupying ourselves with ever unsolved questions concerning what is greater than ourselves and nonetheless makes us what we are, then it can only be based on starting from an answer that we ourselves have not devised; yet in order for this to become a real answer for us, we have to try to understand it, not to resolve it. That is what is **peculiar to theology**, that it **turns to something we ourselves have not devised** and that is able to be the foundation of our life, in that it **goes before us and supports us**; that is to say, it is greater than our own thought. The path of theology is indicated by the saying, "Credo ut intelligam": I accept **what is given in advance**, in order to find, starting from this and in this, the path to the right way of living, to the right way of understanding myself. Yet that means that theology, of its nature, presupposes *auctoritas*. It exists only through awareness that the circle of our own thinking has been broken, that our thinking has, so to say, been given a hand and helped upward, beyond what it could achieve for itself. Without what was given in advance, which is always greater than we can devise ourselves and never becomes part of what is just our own, there is no theology.

But now the next question arises: **What does this advantage**, which was given in advance, **look like**—this answer that alone can get our thinking under way and that shows it the way? **This authority is a word**, we can say to start with. Given the subject we are dealing with, that is quite logical: the Word comes from understanding and is intended to lead to understanding. The advantage given to the seeking human spirit is the Word, which is quite reasonable. In the procedure of science, the idea comes before the word. It is translated into the word. But here, where our own thinking fails, down to us from the eternal reason is thrown the Word, in which is hidden a splinter of its splendor—as much as we can bear, as much as we need, as much as human speech can encompass. **To perceive the meaning in this Word, to understand this Word—that is the ultimate basis of theology, something that can never be entirely absent from the path of faith, not even from that of the most humble believer.**

The advantage, what is given in advance, is the Word— thus, it is **Scripture**, we might say, and we might at once ask: Beside this essential authority of theology, can there be any other? The answer would seem to have to be No: this is the critical point in the dispute between Reformed and Catholic theology. Nowadays, even the greater part of evangelical theologians recognize, in varying forms, that *sola Scriptura*, that is, the restriction of the Word to the book, cannot be maintained. On the basis of its inner structure, the Word always comprises a surplus beyond what could go into the book. This relativizing of the scriptural principle, from which Catholic theology also has something to learn and on account of which both sides can make a new approach to each other, is in part the result of ecumenical dialogue but, to a greater degree, has been determined by the progress of historico-critical interpretation of the Bible, which has in any case learned thereby to recognize its own limits. Two things have above all become clear about the nature of the biblical word in the process of critical exegesis. First of all, that the word of the Bible, at the moment it was set down in writing, already had behind it a more or less long process of shaping by oral tradition and that it was not frozen at the moment it was written down, but entered into new processes of interpretation—"relectures"—that further develop its hidden potential. Thus, the extent of the Word's meaning cannot be reduced to the thoughts of a single author in a specific historical moment; it is not the property of a single author at all; rather, it lives in a history that is ever moving onward and, thus, has dimensions and depths of meaning in past and future that ultimately pass into the realm of the unforeseen.

It is only at this point that we can begin to understand the nature of inspiration; we can see where God mysteriously enters into what is human and purely human authorship is transcended. Yet that also means that Scripture is not a meteorite fallen from the sky, so that it would, with the strict otherness of a stone that comes from the sky and not from the earth, stand in contrast to all human words. Certainly, Scripture carries **God's thoughts** within it: that makes it unique and constitutes it an "authority". Yet it is **transmitted by a human history**. It carries within it the life and thought of a historical society that we call the "People of God", because they are brought together, and held together, by the coming of the divine Word. There is a reciprocal relationship: This society is the essential condition for the origin and the growth of the biblical Word; and, conversely, this Word gives the society its identity and its continuity. Thus, the analysis of the structure of the biblical Word has brought to light **an interwoven relationship between Church and Bible, between the People of God and the Word of God**, which we had actually always known, somehow, in a theoretical way but had never before had so vividly set before us.

The second element that relativizes the scriptural principle follows from what we have just said. Luther was persuaded of the "perspicuitas" of Scripture—of its being unequivocal, a quality that rendered superfluous any official institution for determining its interpretation. The idea of an unequivocal meaning is constitutive for the scriptural principle. For if the Bible is not, as a book, unequivocal in itself, then in itself alone, as a book, it cannot be what was given in advance, which guides us. It would then still be leaving us again to our own devices. Then, we should still be left alone again with our thinking, which is helpless in the face of what is essential in existence. Yet this fundamental postulate of Scripture's unambiguousness has had to be dropped, on account of both the structure of the Word and the concrete experiences of scriptural interpretation. It is untenable on the basis of the objective structure of the Word, on account of its own dynamic, which points beyond what is written. It is above all **the most profound meaning of the Word that is grasped only when we move beyond what is merely written.** Yet the postulate is also untenable from its subjective side, that is to say, on the basis of the essential laws of the rationality of history. The history of exegesis is a history of contradictions; the daring constructions of many modern exegetes, right up to the materialistic interpretation of the Bible, show that the Word, if left alone as a book, is a helpless prey to manipulation through preexisting desires and opinions.

Scripture, the Word we have been given, with which theology concerns itself, does not, on the basis of its own nature, exist as a book alone. Its human author, the People of God, is alive and through all the ages has its own consistent identity. **The home it has made for itself and that supports it is its own interpretation, which is inseparable from itself.** Without this surviving and living agent, the Church, Scripture would not be contemporary with us; it could then no longer combine, as is its true nature, synchronic and diachronic existence, history and the present day, but would fall back into a past that cannot be recalled; it would become literature that one interpreted in the way one can interpret literature. And with that, theology itself would decline into literary history and the history of past times, on one hand, and into the philosophy of religion and religious studies in general, on the other.

It is perhaps helpful to express this interrelationship in a more concrete way for the New Testament. Along the whole path of faith, from Abraham up to the completion of the biblical canon, a confession of faith was built up that was given its real center and shape by Christ himself. The original sphere of existence of the Christian profession of faith, however, was the sacramental life of the Church. It is by this criterion that the canon was shaped, and that is why the Creed is the primary authority for the interpretation of the Bible. Yet the Creed is not a piece of literature: for a long time, people quite consciously avoided writing down the rule of faith that produced the Creed, just because it is the concrete life of the believing community. **Thus, the authority of the Church that speaks out, the authority of the apostolic succession, is written into Scripture through the Creed and is indivisible from it.** The teaching office of the apostles' successors does not represent a second authority alongside Scripture but is inwardly a part of it. This *viva vox* is not there to restrict the authority of Scripture or to limit it or even replace it by the existence of another—on the contrary, it is its **task to ensure that Scripture is not disposable, cannot be manipulated, to preserve its proper *perspicuitas*, its clear meaning, from the conflict of hypotheses.** Thus, there is a secret relationship of reciprocity. Scripture sets limits and a standard for the *viva vox*; the living voice guarantees that it cannot be manipulated.

I can certainly understand the anxiety of Protestant theologians, and nowadays of many Catholic theologians, especially of exegetes, that the principle of a teaching office might impinge upon the freedom and the authority of the Bible and, thus, upon those of theology as a whole. There is a passage from the famous exchange of letters between Harnack and Peterson in 1928 that comes to mind. Peterson, the younger of the two, who was a seeker after truth, had pointed out in a letter to Harnack that he himself, in a scholarly article entitled "The Old Testament in the Pauline Letters and the Pauline Congregations", had for practical purposes expressed the Catholic teaching about Scripture, tradition, and the teaching office. To be precise, Harnack had explained that in the New Testament the "authority of the apostolic teaching is found side by side with . . . the authority of 'Scripture', organizing it and setting limits to it", and that thus "biblicism received a healthy correction". In response to Peterson's pointing this out, Harnack replied to his younger colleague, with his usual nonchalance: "That the so-called 'formal principle' of early Protestantism is impossible from a critical point of view and that the Catholic principle is in contrast *formally* better is a truism; but *materially* the Catholic principle of tradition wreaks far more havoc in history." [1] What is obvious, and even indisputable, in principle arouses fear in reality.

Much could be said about Harnack's diagnosis of where more havoc has been wreaked in history, that is, where the advance gift of the Word has been more seriously threatened. This is not the time to do so. Over and beyond any disputes, it is clear that neither side can dispense with relying on the power of the Holy Spirit for protection and guidance. An ecclesiastical authority can become arbitrary if the Spirit does not guard it. But the arbitrary whims of interpretation left to itself, with all its variations, certainly offers no less danger, as history shows. Indeed, the miracle that would have to be worked there in order to preserve unity and to render the challenge and stature of the Word effective is far more improbable than the one needed to keep the service of the apostolic succession within its proper bounds.

Let us leave such speculation aside. The structure of the Word is sufficiently unequivocal, but the demands it makes on those called to responsibility in succession to the apostles are

---

[1] E. Peterson, *Theologische Traktate* [Theological tracts] (Munich, 1951), p. 295.

indeed weighty. The task of the teaching office is, not to oppose thinking, but to ensure that the authority of the answer that was bestowed on us has its say and, thus, to make room for the truth itself to enter. To be given such a task is exciting and dangerous. It requires the humility of submission, of listening and obeying. It is a matter, not of putting your own ideas into effect, but of keeping a place for what the Other has to say, that Other without whose ever-present Word all else drops into the void. The teaching office, properly understood, must be a humble service undertaken to ensure that true theology remains possible and that the answers may thus be heard without which we cannot live aright.

The Holy Spirit as Communion

On the relationship between pneumatology and spirituality in the writings of Augustine

The words "pneumatology" and "spirituality", which together form my subject here, are, simply from the linguistic point of view, very closely related: one word is a translation of the other. A connection of fundamental importance thereby finds expression: the Holy Spirit may be recognized in the way in which he shapes human life; and, vice versa, life shaped by faith points us toward the Holy Spirit. Reflecting on "Christian spirituality" means talking about the Holy Spirit, who is making himself known when human life receives a new center; talking about the Holy Spirit includes looking at him in people to whom he has given himself.

Nonetheless, in all our talking about the Holy Spirit there remains a certain embarrassment and also a certain danger: even more than Christ, he is withdrawn from us into mystery. The suspicion that only our own speculations are being displayed here and that human life is thus being based upon intellectual fantasies and not on reality is frequently all too well founded. That is why, in the end, I could not bring myself to offer you some reflections on my own account, so to speak. In order to talk about the Holy Spirit in a meaningful, trustworthy, and responsible way, it seems to me three conditions must be fulfilled: What is said cannot be on the basis of sheer theory; rather, it has to rest on reality that has been experienced, that is being interpreted in thought and, thus, is being shared. Yet experience is not enough; it must be tried and tested experience, so that "one's own spirit" is not parading as the "Holy Spirit". That means, thirdly, that suspicion is always appropriate whenever someone speaks on his own account and "of himself"; that contradicts the characteristic action of the Holy Spirit, which is typified by "not speaking on his own authority" (Jn 16:13)—in this area, originality and truth can easily enter into opposition.[1] That, however, means that trust is appropriate only where what is being said is not on anyone's purely private account but when the spiritual experience that has been tried and approved before everyone and stands in the midst of all is being expressed— where experience of the Spirit has been tested before the whole of the Church as such. In all this the basic assumption of Christian faith, which is, as it were, presupposed as both the fourth and the first condition, is that the Church herself, in her essence as the Church, is a creation of the Spirit.

Starting from that point, dealing with my subject correctly would consist of summarizing the great witnesses to the Spirit in the Church's history for an instruction book for living from the Spirit. Since I have not done the necessary preparation, I have decided on an excerpt, namely, some pointers from Augustine's teaching on the Spirit.[2] That has the disadvantage

---

[1] See E. M. Heufelder, *Neues Pfingsten* [New Pentecost], 2nd ed. (Meitingen and Freising, 1970), esp. p. 51; J. Pieper, *Überlieferung* [Tradition] (Munich, 1970), pp. 38ff.; 97–108. The subject set for me at first was simply: "Pneumatology and Spirituality"; the reason for my having thus restricted it is given in the introduction.

[2] This restriction is made here, not with reference to history, but simply in view of the practical question of what we can learn from Augustine today. I deliberately do not enter into the historians' discussion of Augustine's doctrine of the Trinity; on that subject, see the literature in C. Andresen, *Bibliographia Augustiniana* (Darmstadt, 1962), pp. 78–80, and the ongoing bibliographies of the *Revue des Études Augustiniennes*. I will just mention here M. Schmaus, *Die psychologische Trinitätslehre des heiligen Augustinus* [Saint Augustine's psychological

of being less timely and the advantage of having a great witness to the tradition speak to us here, likewise the advantage of being more objective—what has survived the sieve of one and a half thousand years of history as the expression of a shared faith, what has become the starting point for living from the Spirit, can show a certain degree of approval.

Augustine himself is most conscious of the difficulty of the matter; he too struggles for objectivity: for him, originality is precisely what is questionable here, and what is objective, what may be found in the shared faith of the Church, is what can be trusted. He proceeds by trying to identify the nature of the Holy Spirit through expounding the meaning of his traditional names. In doing this, he is not looking for the theme of "Pneumatology and Spirituality"—for him, asking about pneumatology is of itself asking about spirituality, asking not about a subject matter but about him who has been defined as Light and Love and who can thus be seen only by entering into his luminosity, into his warmth.

1. The Name "Holy Spirit" as Indicating the Particular
    Nature of the Third Person of the Trinity

As we have said, Augustine tries to identify the particular physiognomy of the Holy Spirit by investigating his traditional names and first, therefore, the term "Holy Spirit".[3] Yet precisely this confronts him with a difficulty. While in the

---

doctrine of the Trinity], 2nd ed. (Münster, 1967); A. Dahl, *Augustin und Plotin* [Augustine and Plotinus] (Lund, 1945); O. du Roy, *L'Intelligence de la foi en la trinité selon St. Augustin: Genèse de sa théologie trinitaire jusqu'en 391* [Understanding belief in the Trinity according to Saint Augustine: The origins of his teaching, up to 391] (Paris, 1966); and also the edition of *De Trinitate* with commentary in the *Bibliothèque Augustinienne: Oeuvres de St. Augustin*, vol. 15, ed. M. Mellet, T. Camelot, and E. Hendrikx, and vol. 16, ed. P. Agaesse and J. Moingt, referred to as *Oeuvres* 15 and 16.

[3] *De Trinitate* V, 11, 12—12, 13. See on this, J. Moingt's excursus, "Les Noms du Saint-Esprit" [The names of the Holy Spirit], in *Oeuvres* 16, pp. 651–54.

names "Father" and "Son" what is particular to the first and the second Persons of the Trinity is really made clear, the giving and receiving, being as giving and being as receiving, as word and answer, yet so fully one that this results, not in subordination, but in unity, the denomination "Holy Spirit" certainly does not achieve the presentation of what is particular about the third Person. On the contrary, each of the other two Persons of the Trinity could also be called that; above all, God himself, as such, could be called that, as we find in John 4:24: "God is Spirit." Being a spirit and being holy is how the nature of God himself is described, what is characteristic about God.

Thus, the attempt to gain some kind of concrete understanding of the Holy Spirit from this seems to have the reverse effect and really to make him wholly unknowable. And yet Augustine sees in this very thing an expression of **what is particular about the Holy Spirit**: If he is called by what is divine about God, what is shared by Father and Son, then **his nature** is in fact this, **being the *communion* of the Father and the Son**. The particular characteristic of the Holy Spirit is obviously being what is shared by the Father and the Son. His particular quality is to be unity. And in that sense, precisely the general name of "Holy Spirit" is, in its very generality, the most appropriate way to describe him in the paradox of his particular quality, which is in fact that of being shared in common.

I believe that in this analysis something very important is happening: The mediation of Father and Son to complete unity is being seen, not in a general ontic consubstantiality, but as communion, that is to say, not on the basis of a general metaphysical substance of being, but on the basis of the Persons—it is, in keeping with the nature of God himself, **personal**. In the Trinity the *Duas* turns back into unity without closing or resolving the dialogue and is, indeed, affirmed thereby. A medium for attaining unity who was not in turn a Person would close or resolve the dialogue as such. The Spirit is Person as unity, unity as Person.

The definition of the Spirit as "communion", which Augustine thus derives from the expression "Holy Spirit", has for him, as will be reaffirmed in the case of the other names of the Holy Spirit, clearly a fundamentally **ecclesiological** sense, which opens up pneumatology in the direction of ecclesiology, or we might say, vice versa, that it opens up a connection from ecclesiology back into theo-logy: becoming a Christian means becoming "communion" and, thus, entering into the mode of existence of the Holy Spirit. That can, however, in turn take place only through the Holy Spirit, who is the power of communication, its element of mediation, of enabling, and who is as such himself a Person.

Spirit is the unity God gives to himself, in which he gives himself to himself, in which Father and Son give themselves back to each other. His paradoxical peculiarity, his *proprium*, is to be communion, to find the highest degree of personal identity in being fully the movement toward unity. "Spiritual" would on that basis always have an essential connotation of reuniting, communicating.

That means that Augustine has thereby silently achieved an important reappraisal of the concept of the Spirit as such; a bit of metaphysics of the Spirit has come about incidentally. At first he allows the Johannine phrase "God is Spirit" to stand in a purely ontological sense—Spirit: not matter, is what it first means for him. We could immediately object that that is not at all what John is talking about, that the word "Spirit" expresses the otherness of God as against what is of the world; the opposite of "Spirit", here, is therefore not "matter", but rather "this world".[4] It is meant, not to be ontological in the

---

[4] See, for instance, R. Schnackenburg, *Das Johannesevangelium*, vol. 1 (Freiburg, 1965), pp. 474, 226.

Greek sense, but rather axiological, we might say, pointing to the specifically religious quality of being "wholly other" and, in that sense, referring to the Holy Spirit as the expression of this quality of God's of being reserved: pointing to the "holiness" that this "otherness" means. This is in many respects an incomparably more radical opposition than the contrasting of spirit and matter, since spirit in that sense can after all also be mundane and does not necessarily imply any transcendence of inner-worldly reality as a whole. If we look at Augustine's reflections as a whole, we can say that he does effectively follow up this insight, leaving the classical metaphysics of the spirit far behind, precisely because he has to explain "spirit", not in a general metaphysical sense, but on the basis of the Father-Son dynamics. Communion thereby becomes the constitutive element of the concept of the Spirit and is thus, after all, given content and thoroughly personalized: only someone who knows what "Holy Spirit" means knows what "spirit" means at all. And only someone who is beginning to know what God is can know what the Holy Spirit is; yet only someone who has begun to have some notion of what the Holy Spirit is can begin to know who God is.

2. The Holy Spirit as Love

Analyzing biblical pneumatology leads Augustine to formulate the thesis that besides the term "Holy Spirit", the terms "love" (*caritas*) and "gift" (*donum*) are also, in strict terms, names for the Holy Spirit. Let us start with the analysis of the word "love", which leads Augustine to this view.[5]

a. The central text from which he develops his thesis is found in the First Letter of Saint John: "God is love" (1 Jn

---

[5] *De Trinitate* XV, 17, 27—18, 32.

4:16). Augustine points out that this assertion refers, first of all and fundamentally, to God as the undivided Trinity; yet it does nonetheless express a particular characteristic of the Holy Spirit. The situation here is similar to the one with the words "wisdom" and "word", which, on one hand, express qualities of God in general but which the Bible refers, each in a quite specific sense, to the Son. Augustine finds evidence for the pneumatological sense of *caritas* in the textual context of 1 John 4:7–16.[6] What is decisive for him in this case is a comparison between verse 12, together with 16b, and verse 13:

Verse 12: "If we love one another, God abides in us."

Verse 16b: "God is love, and he who abides in love . . . God abides in him."

Verse 13: "By this we know that we abide in him and he in us, because he has given us of his own Spirit."

In one case, it is love that grants the abiding; in the other case, the Holy Spirit—in the structure of the sentences quoted, Pneuma can replace love, and vice versa. Or, literally: "The Holy Spirit, of whom he has given us, makes us remain in God and God in us; yet it is love that effects this. He himself, the Spirit, is therefore God as love." To make things clear, Augustine adds that Romans 5:5 says: "God's love has been poured into our hearts through the Holy Spirit who has been given to us." It seems to me that these observations are in principle correct: The gift of God is the Holy Spirit. The gift of God is love—**God shares himself as love in the Holy Spirit**. Yet there are thereby given, for Augustine, a whole series of important perceptions concerning content. First of all, the presence of the Holy Spirit makes itself known in the manner of love. Love is the criterion of the Holy Spirit as against unholy spirits; indeed, it is the presence of the Holy Spirit himself and, in that sense, the presence of God. The

---

[6] Ibid., 17, 31.

essential and central concept summing up what the Holy Spirit is and what he effects is, in the end, not "knowledge" but love. The filling out of the concept of "spirit", the interpretation of what is for Christians the "wholly other" aspect of God, is thereby made concrete from that point onward by contrast. The complete clarity of this statement, of course, emerges, on the other hand, only in the ecclesiological sphere, where Augustine is practically obliged to ask: What does "love" mean here, as the criterion of the presence of the Holy Spirit and, thereby, also the criterion of being Christian and of the Church?

One further important detail emerges directly from the analysis of the text from 1 John itself: the basic criterion of love, its "proper work", so to speak—and, thereby, the "proper work" of the Holy Spirit—is this, that it achieves **abiding**. Love shows itself by being enduring. It can by no means be recognized at a given moment and in the moment alone; but in abiding, it does away with uncertainty and carries eternity within it. And thus in my view the relationship between love and truth is also thereby given: love, in the full sense, can be present only where something is enduring, where something abides. Because it has to do with abiding, it can occur, not just anywhere, but only there where eternity is.

And with this, an outline of the basic structure of a doctrine of the discernment of spirits and of counsel for the spiritual life has emerged. For it is now clear that anyone who looks for "Pneuma" only as something "exterior", in what is always unpredictable, is on the wrong track. Anyone who does so is failing to recognize **the fundamental activity of the Holy Spirit: the love that unites and draws into abiding unity.** A distinction of great importance appears at this point: Is the Pneuma to be sought only in what is discontinuous, or is it in "abiding" itself that he dwells, in enduring and creative faithfulness? If the latter is the case, that also means that the Pneuma is not to be found where people speak "in their own name", "seeking their own honor", and parties arise on their account. The Pneuma shows his credentials, indeed, in "bringing to remembrance" (Jn 14:26) and in unifying. We will have to come back to these statements, in which pneumatology developed for Augustine into indicators for practical action. Let us first pursue our analysis.

b. I should like just briefly to refer to a second context in which Augustine saw confirmation of his idea that by the word "love" Holy Scripture specifically intends to refer to the Holy Spirit.[7] Augustine now compares verses 7 and 16 of the fourth chapter of the First Letter of John and finds in the complementary interpretation of these two texts renewed confirmation of what he had concluded by comparing verses 12 and 16 with verse 13. Verse 16 says, "God is love." In verse 7 we read, "love is of God." Love is therefore, on one hand, "God" and, on the other, "of" or "from God"; that is, taking the two together, it is just as much "God" as "from God": it is "God from God". Together with the previous textual comparison, that seems to make clear yet again that this "God from God", God as the power of going forth and going toward, as the power of new birth, of the new "whence" for man, is the Holy Spirit and that in what is being said about *agape* we may receive enlightenment about what the Holy Spirit is.

3. The Holy Spirit as Gift

The central text from which Augustine derives the understanding that the word "gift" (*donum*) represents a way of talking about the Holy Spirit is John 4:7–14: Jesus in conver-

---

[7] Ibid.

sation with the Samaritan woman, whom he asks for the "gift" of water so as thereby to reveal himself as the giver of better water.[8] "If you knew the gift of God, and who it is who is saying to you, 'Give me a drink,' you would have asked him and he would have *given* you living water." This text, for Augustine, is brought to completion, according to an inner logic, by Jesus' promise of water at the Feast of Tabernacles: "If any one thirst, let him come to me and drink. He who believes in me, as the scripture has said, 'Out of his heart shall flow rivers of living water' " (Jn 7:37–38). At this point, the Evangelist himself adds: "Now this he said about the Spirit, which those who believed in him were to receive" (Jn 7:39). Augustine finds the same pneumatological exegesis of living water in 1 Corinthians 12:13: "We . . . all were made to drink of one Spirit." The significance of this promise of the Spirit in the image of water, as formulated in John 4 and John 7, furnishes for Augustine, in the first place, the **connection between Christology and pneumatology**: Christ is the spring of living water—**the crucified Lord is the spring that makes the world fruitful.** The source of the Spirit is the crucified Christ. Yet from him every Christian also becomes a spring of water.

It is also important that the whole power of the image is here involved in pneumatology: the ultimate thirst of men cries out for the Holy Spirit. He, and he alone, is, at a profound level, the fresh water without which there is no life. In the image of a spring, of the water that irrigates and transforms a desert, that man meets like a secret promise, the mystery of the Spirit becomes visible in an ineffable fashion that no rational meditation can encompass. In man's thirst, and in his being refreshed by water, is portrayed that infinite, far more radical thirst that can be quenched by no other water.

---

[8] Ibid., 19, 33; see V, 14, 15—15, 16.

We should add that Augustine did not, of course, in this context, give any further exposition of the connection between the theology of the Cross and that of the Spirit, as suggested especially by John 19—Hugo Rahner has effectively depicted the large place it occupies in patristic theology.[9]

The second important point derived from combining John 4 with John 7 is for Augustine the certainty that the word **"gift" is a name for the Holy Spirit**, so that a theology (or, more accurately, a pneumatology) of giving and of the gift becomes possible, while conversely the nature of God as Holy Spirit is also illuminated by the idea of the gift. On that basis, Augustine can first of all clarify the distinction between Son and Pneuma, thus answering the question: "How is it that the Spirit, who is, after all, likewise 'God from God', is not also 'Son'? What is different here?" Augustine replies, "He comes from God, not as begotten, but as given (*non quomodo natus, sed quomodo datus*). That is why he is not called 'Son', because he is neither 'begotten' like the only begotten Son nor 'created' . . . like us (*neque natus . . . neque factus*)." [10] Three ways of coming from God are thus distinguished: begotten—given—created (*natus—datus—factus*). If one can best describe the nature of the Son, his particular relationship to his Father, with the concept of "begetting", then that of the Spirit is described with that of "giving". The motion of giving is the motion specific to the Holy Spirit.

Although this term "given" (*datus*) is not intended as an intermediate stage between "begotten" and "created" (*natus* and *factus*) and by no means blurs the distinction between creature and God, but rather remains limited to the inner reality of divinity, it does represent an opening onto history and toward man. Augustine asks, in fact, whether the Holy

---

[9] H. Rahner, *Symbole der Kirche* [Symbols of the Church] (Salzburg, 1964), pp. 175–235.

[10] *De Trinitate* V, 14, 15.

Spirit derives from the fact of being given only his nature of being given or his being as such. Has he any existence independent of his being given and before he is given; or is his essence precisely this: being God's gift? The Church doctor from Hippo answers Yes to this—the Holy Spirit is eternally, of his very nature, God's gift, God as wholly self-giving, God as sharing himself, as gift.[11] In that sense, the inner reason and basis for creation and salvation history do after all lie in this quality of being of the Holy Spirit, as *donum* and *datum*—and, indeed, the basis in advance for salvation history, for the complete self-giving of God, which for its part appears as the inner reason and basis for creation. Thus, on one hand, the "immanent" doctrine of the Trinity is wholly opened up to the "economic", yet conversely salvation history is also related back to theology: the gift of God is God himself. He is the content of Christian prayer. He is the only gift worthy of God: as God, God gives nothing other than God; he gives himself and thereby everything.

That is why properly Christian prayer, again, does not beg for just anything; rather, it begs for the gift of God that is God himself, begs for him. This connection is beautifully expressed in Augustine's writings in that at this point he interprets the petition "Give us this day our daily bread" in the Our Father as quite self-evidently referring to the Holy Spirit: He is "our bread"—ours as what is not ours, as what is entirely and wholly given. "Our" Spirit is not our spirit.[12]

Thus it is in fact entirely a question of whether God as gift is truly God—that is, a question of the divinity of the Holy

---

[11] Ibid., 15, 16.

[12] Ibid., 14, 15: "Spiritus ergo et Dei est qui dedit, et noster qui accepimus. Non ille Spiritus noster quo sumus, quia ipse Spiritus est hominis qui in ipso est: sed alio modo iste noster est, quo dicimus et: Panem nostrum da nobis (Mt 6:11). Quamquam et illum spiritum qui hominis dicitur, utique accepimus. Quid enim habes, inquit, quod non accepisti (1 Cor 4:7)? Sed aliud est quod accepimus et essemus, aliud quod accepimus ut sancti essemus."

Spirit. The classical precision of Augustine's formulation here can hardly be translated, either verbally or materially. "There is there [= in God], not a subordination of the given and a domination of the giver, but a being one at heart (*concordia*) between given and giver." Beyond that the point is confirmed yet again for Augustine that he had earlier deduced from the name "Holy Spirit": "Because he is the one who is in common between both, his own name is what they have in common." This statement restores the inner unity of the designations "love" and "gift" with the principal title of "Holy Spirit"; thus it is once more shown that they are correct, and at the same time the whole is combined into a mutually interpretative unity.

4. Opening Up to Salvation History

Opening up to salvation history comes about, as we have seen, to an equal extent from the concepts of "love" and "gift". I will try to show the importance of this connection from two texts in rather more detail.

a. Let us start from *De Trinitate* XV, 18, 32, where Augustine develops the eschatological significance of the Pneuma on the basis of love's eschatological function as judge. *Caritas* does not stand opposed to the law; it is itself the law court; it alone and in particular is the divine court of law: it discriminates between left and right (Mt 25!). Whoever loves stands "on the right", and whoever does not love is turned to the left. Without it, nothing "good" is good. In witness thereof, Augustine brings forward together the apparently opposing proclamations of the gospel by Paul and James, the Letter to the Galatians and the Letter of James. According to Galatians 5:6, in the end neither being circumcised nor being uncircumcised will help, but only faith at work in love; here Paul is only briefly repeating what he said in dramatic fashion in 1 Corinthians 13:1–3: Without love, everything else, faith and works, is nothing, simply of no account. And thus Paul and James meet at this point, for with his reference to the faith at work in love, the Apostle draws a line between saving faith, the faith inspired by the Pneuma, and the belief that demons also have but that cannot save (Jas 2:19). Without love, says Augustine, faith can indeed "exist, but not save"— "esse, non prodesse" is what the inimitable Latin of the Bishop of Hippo says.

Upon these statements, which interpret *caritas*, that is, Pneuma, as the eschatological court of judgment and, thus, as the **distinguishing mark of what is Christian,** is founded Augustine's entire teaching about the sacraments and about ecclesiology, and on this basis it is tied in with pneumatology. It is upon this basis that Augustine engaged in the argument with the Donatists. The Donatists had the same sacraments as the Catholic Church—where, then, was the real difference? How did they fall short? Augustine's answer (with a view to the previous history of this division as well as to its enduring form) runs thus: They have broken the bond of love. They went off because they set their idea of perfection above unity. They have retained everything that makes up the Catholic Church—it was only love they gave up together with unity. And that is why everything else is empty. Here the word *caritas* is being given a quite concrete, ecclesial meaning—indeed, a complete interpenetration of concepts makes its appearance in Augustine's language, in that he can say: **The Church is** *caritas*. In one respect that is a dogmatic thesis for him. As the creation of the Spirit, as the body of the Lord built up by the Pneuma—which, indeed, becomes the body of Christ through the Pneuma making men into "communion"—as the creation of the Spirit, then, the Church is the "gift" of God in this world, and this "gift" is love.

Yet this dogmatic thesis has for him at the same time a quite concrete character: one cannot develop one's Christian "being" in a sect, in isolating oneself from others. For what is then missing is the very life of the whole thing, even if one has all the separate parts. Accepting the whole community of believers is, indeed, part of being a Christian, the humility (*humilitas*) of love (*caritas*), the "bearing with one another"— for otherwise the Holy Spirit himself is missing, the One who unites. Thus, the dogmatic statement "Church is *caritas*" does not simply remain in the dogmatic-Scholastic realm but refers to the dynamic impulse that brings unity and is shown in the way the Church holds together. In that sense, schism is for Augustine a pneumatological heresy, located in the practical business of living: departing from the abiding that is of the Spirit, from the patience of *caritas*—a revocation of love in the revocation of abiding and, thereby, a renunciation of the Holy Spirit, who is the patience of abiding and being reconciled. It is for Augustine by no means automatically the case that anyone who remains in the Church thereby has *caritas*, but there is indeed certainty about the contrary: anyone who deliberately does not remain is departing from *caritas*. Hence his formula: However much anyone loves the Church, that is how much he has of the Holy Spirit. The theology of the Trinity becomes a direct standard for ecclesiology; the designation of the Spirit as love becomes the key to Christian living, and at the same time love is interpreted in practical terms, as patience in the Church.[13]

In order to understand Augustine's concentration of an ecclesiological dispute with his pneumatological ecclesiology, we should perhaps add here that it was not at all just that at the beginning pride in greater perfection existed; rather, the phe-

---

[13] See the way these connections are presented in my book *Volk und Haus Gottes in Augustins Lehre von der Kirche* [People of God and house of God in Augustine's doctrine of the Church] (Munich, 1954), pp. 136–58.

nomenon of this schism in particular was marked by hatred to such a degree that the diagnosis really forced itself upon him that the heart of this division was a withdrawal from the fellowship of love. To illustrate this, I quote a few sentences in which F. van der Meer vividly captures the experience of Donatism, as presented to Augustine:

> People said that they [= the Donatists] washed clean the ground on which a Catholic had been standing. And what was worse, they controlled gangs, bands of embittered proletarians, who were perhaps dreaming of an earthly kingdom of God and who repeatedly attacked the *cellae*, or isolated farmhouses, the country houses, churches, and castles of the Catholics . . . ; who, wherever people were not compliant, plundered tools and utensils, "stole dry goods and poured out liquids", set fire to basilicas, books and all, roughed up the clergy, and later, when their time was running out, among other things, threw lime and vinegar into Catholics' eyes to blind them, "something even barbarians had never done"; they did not forget to demand the return of promissory notes, to cancel contracts, extort from people the emancipation of the most idle good-for-nothings among the slaves, and if necessary to set to the treadmill any master who opposed them.[14]

We would have to admit, even so, that striking an equivalence between Church and love, however well-grounded at a profound level and however superficially understandable, does have its risks. The consequent turning of Spirit and love into something ecclesiastical corresponds to one side of the subject

---

[14] F. van der Meer, *Augustinus der Seelsorger* (Cologne, 1951), p. 113; also the entire section, "Die pars Donati und die Ketzer" [The pars Donati and the heretics], pp. 109–63; Eng. trans.: *Augustine the Bishop* (London and New York: Sheed and Ward, 1961). On the history of the Donatists, see H. I. Marrou, in J. Daniélou and H. I. Marrou, *Geschichte der Kirche* [History of the Church], vol. 1 (Einsiedeln, 1953), pp. 256–60; W. H. C. Frend, "Donatismus", in *Reallexikon für Antike und Christentum*, 4:128–47.

matter, no doubt; yet it can also lead to a dangerous narrowing of ideas as soon as using "love" to designate the Church no longer shows her relation to the Spirit as an objective standard for the Church, as a practical challenge, but appears to be the institution's self-evident content. A rigidity then develops, signs of which can already be seen in Augustine's later writings and which subsequently developed into that dangerous hardening of attitudes that medieval and modern Church history tells us about.

Perhaps connected with this is the fact that in the heretical movements of the Middle Ages, as also of the Reformation, Spirit is declared to be the very opposite of institutional Church. And yet this setting of Pneuma and institution in opposition, which is flourishing again today, is the expression of a romanticism that is not even accurate in the worldly realm (in this very century [twentieth], Germany has had dramatic experience of the power of romantic movements to destroy body and soul)—it is certainly unable to cope with the problem of Church and Spirit. If the "official Church" or "empirical Catholic Church" appears today as the contrary to "Spirit", Augustine would deny the validity of these concepts and repudiate them as misunderstandings of the Church that may be excusable in a pagan but should be impossible for a believer. For the Church, which confers the sacraments and attentively interprets the Word of God, is never merely an "empirical Catholic Church"; she cannot be cut up into "Spirit" and "institution". In the very fact of being visible, "empirical", in the sacraments, in the Word, and in love, she is the home of the Spirit, and the Spirit grants his presence in the concrete community of those who support and bear with one another on Christ's account. For Augustine, the idea that the Spirit manifests himself only in what is discontinuous, only in the chance eruptions of self-taught and self-formed groups, is utterly inconceivable. Anyone looking for the Spirit only in externals—Augustine would say—is failing to recognize the fundamental activity of the Holy Spirit: the love that unites and draws into abiding unity. At this point, a choice of decisive significance opens up: Is Pneuma only in what is discontinuous or precisely in the gift that has been given? . . .

b. In this connection, the interpretation that Augustine has given of Ephesians 4:7–12, within the framework of his pneumatology, seems to me important.[15] Here he comes upon the subject of Spirit as liberation and on the blossoming of the gift in the "gifts", which Paul (among others) calls "charisms"—thus, he meets some questions that play a decisive role in the contemporary option for Pneuma as the opposite pole of "institution". Augustine starts from the words of the Letter to the Ephesians: "Grace was given to each of us according to the measure of Christ's gift. Therefore it is said, 'When he ascended on high he led a host of captives, and he gave gifts to men'" (Eph 4:7f. together with Ps 68[67]:18). The key word "gift" indicates to Augustine that this text is pneumatological. At the same time it offers him some impressive teaching on the connection between Christ and the Spirit: The gifts of the Spirit, in which ultimately the Spirit himself is the gift, are the gifts of the victorious Christ, the fruits of his victory, of his Ascension to the Father. In interpreting this, Augustine also finds important two apparently opposed versions of Psalm 68[67] in the Latin Bible. According to the one, it says: "You receive gifts in men"; according to the other, which the New Testament follows, it says: "He gave gifts to men." For Augustine, the two sides of the christological mystery itself are represented in the opposition of these variants. Christ, as the ascended One, remains the One who descended. He stands at the same time beside God

---

[15] *De Trinitate* XV, 19, 34.

who is giving and man who is receiving. He is head and body, giving from God and receiving in men. And this, again, unites ecclesiology and Christology: in the Church he remains the One who descended; she is Christ as the One who descended, the continuation of the humanity of Jesus Christ.

Augustine's main interest, accordingly, continues to be concentrated on the relations between Christ, Spirit, and Church represented in this text; it is not directed to the individual gifts, as such, referred to in the New Testament text. What is important, rather, is that in all the gifts the Gift—the Holy Spirit—is given. Materially, Augustine certainly is in any case following the main thrust of the text itself, and thus he is right to quote 1 Corinthians 12:11 as a parallel supporting his case: "All these are inspired by one and the same Spirit, who apportions to each one individually as he wills." If, however, the gifts are in the end just one Gift in many forms, that is, the Spirit of God, and if the Spirit is the gift of Jesus Christ, which he gives and which he, in men, receives, then the inmost orientation of all the gifts is: unity. Then it becomes clear that the passage from the Letter to the Ephesians with which he is dealing is directed toward defining a single purpose: all this is "for building up the body of Christ".

Augustine has thereby arrived at his pet ecclesiological and pneumatological idea, the notion of building, again, that of abiding, of unity, of love. Here he finds an opportunity to give it new overtones by casting fresh illumination upon it from Psalm 127[126]:1: "Unless the LORD builds the house. . . ." He locates this psalm in the postexilic prophetic proclamation concerned with the building of the house "after the captivity"; the key word "captivity" establishes the connection with Psalm 68[67] and Ephesians 4: "The Lord has taken captivity captive and has given gifts." His gift is the Spirit, yet the Spirit is the building up that can at last take place after the captivity. And thereby he touches indirectly on the theme of freedom:

that captivity now led captive, which formerly prevented the building, is the devil—or, vice versa, the devil is captivity, the bonds that fetter man, the exile, the way man is led away from himself. The whole anthropological analysis of the *Confessions* has to be heard in the background along with this: man, who has been led away from himself, is wandering in emptiness with no place of his own—it is in this very semblance of freedom that he is exiled, captive, betrayed.[16]

Here again, Augustine is not talking about some dogmatic or philosophical theory but is speaking from the experience of his own life. In the indeterminate and apparent freedom of an existence in which everything was possible but nothing made sense, he was enslaved by an illusory image of freedom: banished from his true self and unfree in an utter lack of relationship that was founded on being distanced from his own self, on separation from the truth of his own self. In contrast with that, the gift of the victorious Christ is that of coming home and the building of a house that that makes possible; but the house is called "Church". Here the theme of the Spirit as freedom, as liberation, is clearly coming into play, but in a way that is paradoxical for thinking nowadays: freedom consists of oneself becoming a part of the house, to be taken and used in the building. This conception is not paradoxical from the point of view of the classical concept of freedom: anyone is free who belongs to the house; freedom is being at home.[17]

---

[16] See esp. *Conf.* VIII, 5, 12—12, 30; esp. also 7, 16: ". . . retorquebas me ad me ipsum, auferens me a dorso meo, ubi me posueram." See on this point the commentary of A. Solignac, in *Oeuvres* 14, p. 543 ("La Psychologie augustinienne de la volonté"), and also vol. 13, pp. 689–93 ("Regio dissimilitudinis").

[17] See on this the thorough investigation of D. Nestle, *Eleutheria: Studien zum Wesen der Freiheit bei den Griechen und im Neuen Testament*. Part 1, *Die Griechen* [Eleutheria: Studies on the nature of freedom in the view of the Greeks and in the New Testament. Part 1, The Greeks] (Tübingen, 1967); E. Coreth, "Zur Problemgeschichte menschlicher Freiheit" [On the history of the problem of

Augustine presupposes this concept of social freedom, from classical thought, and now decisively transcends it, on the basis, of course, of Christian belief: **Freedom is indissolubly related to truth, which is the real home of man.**[18] Accordingly, man is free only when he is at home, that is, when he is dwelling in truth. Any movement that takes man away from the truth of himself, from truth itself, can never be freedom, because it destroys man, alienates him from himself, and thus takes from him the sphere in which he is actually free to move, takes away his ability to become himself. That is why the devil is captivity; that is why the exalted Christ, who brings man into the house and makes him part of it and builds him up, is liberation; and that, finally, is why the individual gifts of the Spirit, the charisms, are able to be included in the concept of building. What Augustine takes from the teaching about charisms at this point is basically just the key word, "building".

Here again, as above with the connection between Church and love, we would have to say that a "narrowing down" of this kind can have its risks. That it can lead to overlooking the multiplicity of ways in which the Spirit works in order to favor faithfulness to established institutions, which may ultimately set themselves up as being identical with the Spirit. To that extent, these passages do not on their own offer a pneumatology that is satisfactory all around or a teaching about Christian spirituality that is balanced in every direction. Yet they do make a contribution to that and, in Augustine's situation, represent an entirely appropriate application of the Bible. For quite apart from the fact that there was hardly a surplus of charisms in Augustine's diocese and that the prob-

---

human freedom], *Zeitschrift für katholische Theologie* 94 (1972): 258–89; on this point, pp. 264f. and 268f.

[18] On the connection between freedom and truth, see Coreth, "Zur Problemgeschichte", p. 289.

lem facing him was thus different from that in Corinth in Saint Paul's time (and in any case Paul had also posited building, love, as being in the end, along with prophecy, comprehensible proclamation, the only important charism and the only one important for everybody)[19]—quite apart from that, Augustine was quite right, in a Church torn apart by hatred and faction, to challenge people to show the one decidedly necessary charism, that of building up the unity of the Church. And he is entirely on the side of the Apostle in seeing the Pneuma conclusively demonstrated in positive things: in the Yes that makes a man into a "house" and ends "captivity". The "house" is freedom, not diversion. The work of the Spirit is "the house", the granting of a homeland, of unity. For the Spirit is love.

---

[19] See H. Schlier, "Über das Hauptanliegen des 1. Briefes an die Korinther" [On the main purpose of the First Letter to the Corinthians], in *Die Zeit der Kirche* [The age of the Church], 2nd ed. (Freiburg, 1958), pp. 147–59; J. Ratzinger, "Bemerkungen zur Frage der Charismen in der Kirche" [Remarks on the question of charisms in the Church], in G. Bornkamm and K. Rahner, *Die Zeit Jesu* [The Age of Jesus]: *Festschrift für Heinrich Schlier zum 70. Geburtstag* (Freiburg, 1970), pp. 257–72.

Communion

Eucharist—Fellowship—Mission[1]

When I was invited to speak about the connection between the Eucharist, Church fellowship, and the mission of the "congregation", the second chapter of the Acts of the Apostles (v. 42) at once came to mind. Luke says there that the

[1] This paper—which has meanwhile also been published in J. Ratzinger, *Schauen auf den Durchbohrten: Versuche zu einer spirituellen Christologie* (1984; 2nd ed., Einsiedeln, 1990), pp. 60–84; Eng. trans.: *Behold the Pierced One: An Approach to a Spiritual Christology* (San Francisco: Ignatius Press, 1986)—was first read in the setting of a meeting for continuation training for priests, in Collevalenza; it was intended to throw light on the relation between the Eucharist and *comunità*. The starting point for my reflections was provided by this word: What is *comunità*?—"Congregation"? Fellowship? Communion? Or do all these belong together? It at once became clear to me that the problem of our sacramental and ecclesiological language was the problem of the matter itself. The senses established by our language do not correspond to the linguistic and conceptual framework of the Bible and of the great tradition: showing that and correcting our way of talking, as of thinking, thus obviously became one of the main purposes of this paper. On the other hand, there arose the difficulty of expressing what was meant with the means available in our language. Since there is no word available that corresponds to the biblical synthesis of the various meanings, I have to a great extent worked with such words as "communion" or "communio" so as to make clear to some extent the connections with which we are concerned. Certainly I was unable to find an entirely satisfactory solution to the linguistic problem, and a certain degree of arbitrariness in my choice of words could not be avoided. I hope that the context nonetheless makes what I meant sufficiently clear.

On this whole subject one should see J. Hainz, *Koinonia: "Kirche" als Gemeinschaft bei Paulus* [Koinonia: "Church" as fellowship in the writings of Paul] (Regensburg, 1982); P. C. Bori, ΚΟΙΝΩΝΙΑ [Koinonia]: *L'idea della*

primitive Church persisted in "the apostles' teaching and fellowship, . . . the breaking of bread and the prayers". This sentence seems to me to offer the real key to the correct understanding of our question.

A glance at the context, and thus at the **basic purpose of the Acts of the Apostles**, is, however, a necessary preliminary. Luke does in fact sketch out in this book something like a first ecclesiology, intended to convey a standard for any future understanding of the Church.[2] Luke does not, of course, offer an ecclesiology in the form of a systematically constructed framework of concepts. Rather, he portrays what the Church is by showing the dynamics of her path in history. This path begins with the sending of the Holy Spirit, who gives himself to a community that is united in prayer and centered on Mary and the apostles (Acts 1:12–14; 2:1).

If we reflect for a moment on what is said here, we may note that three of the **basic characteristics of the Church** to which tradition strongly holds unmistakably make their appearance: the Church is **apostolic**; she is a **praying** Church and, thus, turned toward the Lord—"holy"; and she is **one**. The first sign by which the Holy Spirit manifests himself adds a fourth characteristic to these: the presence of the Spirit is displayed in the **gift of tongues**. In this way it **reverses what happened at the tower of Babel**; the new community, the new People of God, speaks in all languages,

---

communione nell'ecclesiologia recente e nel Nuovo Testamento [Koinonia: The idea of communion in recent ecclesiology and in the New Testament] (Brescia, 1972); E. Kunz, "Eucharistie—Ursprung von Kommunikation und Gemeinschaft" [The Eucharist—The origin of communication and community], *Theol. Phil.* 58 (1983): 321–45.

[2] On the question of the basic line of approach in the Acts of the Apostles, G. Schneider, "Apostelgeschichte und Kirchengeschichte" [The Acts of the Apostles and Church history], *Internationale katholische Zeitschrift "Communio"* 8 (1979): 481–85, is helpful; also Schneider, *Die Apostelgeschichte* [The Acts of the Apostles], vol. 1 (Freiburg, 1980), pp. 134–54, with full bibliography.

and thus from the first moment of its existence it is portrayed as "**catholic**". The realization of the dynamic contained in this sign, which obliges the Church to go to the ends of space and time—this is the underlying theme of all the chapters of the Acts of the Apostles, which describe how the gospel passed over from the Jews to the Gentiles, from Jerusalem to Rome. Within the structure of this book, Rome—at its close—stands, as it were, as an abbreviation for the world of the Gentiles as a whole, for the world of the nations, as opposed to the old People of God. The Acts of the Apostles ends with the arrival of the gospel in Rome—not as if the result of Paul's trial were unimportant, but simply because this book is not a novel and not a biography. With the arrival in Rome, the journey begun in Jerusalem has reached its goal; the universal—the catholic—Church has come into being, continuing the old chosen People of God and taking over its history, its mission. In that sense, Rome, which sums up the world of the nations, has a theological status in the Acts of the Apostles; it cannot be bracketed out from the Lucan idea of catholicity.[3]

If, at the end of this very rough suggestion of the outline of Lucan ecclesiology, we want to specify some of the traits of the concept of the Church expounded there, then we could say: First of all, we are faced here with a pneumatological

---

[3] The idea of a transfer from Jerusalem to Rome is portrayed in K. Hofstetter, "Das Petrusamt in der Kirche des 1.–2. Jahrhunderts: Jerusalem—Rom" [The Petrine office in the Church of the first and second centuries: Jerusalem to Rome], in M. Roesle and O. Cullmann, eds., *Begegnung der Christen* [The meeting of Christians] (Stuttgart, 1960); see J. Ratzinger, *Das neue Volk Gottes* [The new people of God] (Düsseldorf, 1969), pp. 128–31. Also of importance for this question is V. Twomey, *Apostolikos Thronos: The Primacy of Rome as Reflected in the Church History of Eusebius and the Historico-Apologetic Writings of St. Athanasius the Great* (Münster, 1982). Twomey shows how the idea of the transfer from Jerusalem to Rome is fundamental to the construction of Eusebius' *Church History*; this shows itself to be a very old tradition, which was gradually forgotten in the Constantinian era.

ecclesiology—it is the Spirit who makes the Church. We are faced with a dynamic ecclesiology of salvation history, of which the dimension of catholicity is an essential part. Finally, we are faced with a liturgical ecclesiology: the assembly receives the gift of the Holy Spirit in the act of praying.

I. THE KEY TO OUR SUBJECT:
THE WORD κοινωνία (KOINONIA)—COMMUNION

1. The Description of the Church in Acts 2:42

At the start of our reflections we noted that Luke describes for us the essential aspects of the Church by showing her on the path along which the Holy Spirit is taking her. Woven into the Lucan text, however, we can recognize yet another thread by which Luke intends to clarify the nature of the Church; that is, when he sketches out in the picture of the **primitive Church** the **exemplary form of the Church of all ages**. In verse 42, which we discussed at the start, Luke sums up this view. Let us recall its content: the first Christians, according to the description in the Acts of the Apostles, persisted in "the apostles' teaching and fellowship [communion], . . . the breaking of bread and the prayers". We are faced, then, with four concepts in which the nature of the Church is described; if we compare them with the Pentecost story, it becomes clear that they correspond to its basic elements, which they extend and develop.[4]

Here, too, unity is a characteristic element of the Church. Here, too, unity comes from fellowship with the apostles and from turning to the living God in prayer. But what fellowship

---

[4] For the interpretation of these verses, see F. Mußner, "Die UNA SANCTA nach Apg. 2:42" [The Una Sancta according to Acts 2:42], in his *Praesentia Salutis* (Düsseldorf, 1967), pp. 212–22.

with the apostles means is now specified as **"persistent remaining in the teaching of the apostles"**. Unity thus has a content that is expressed in teaching. **The teaching of the apostles is the practical mode of their abiding presence in the Church.** Thanks to this teaching, the future generations after the death of the apostles also remain in unity with them and thus constitute the same one, apostolic Church. To see these relationships more clearly, we have to set them beside the farewell speech of Paul to the presbyters at Ephesus, related in chapter 20 of the Acts of the Apostles (20:18–35). Here the idea of "apostolic teaching" is explained, in the sense that Luke develops the concept of apostolic succession. The teaching of the apostles—it now appears—has a personal and an institutional aspect. The "presbyters" have the responsibility of representing the teaching of the apostles, keeping it present. They are the personal guarantee for "persisting in the teaching" of the origin.[5]

The idea of apostolicity is thus developed and given concrete application in the direction of an enduring structure for the Church. A second idea from the Pentecostal ecclesiology is also extended and clarified: the prayer of the Church centers on the "breaking of bread"—the Eucharist emerges as the heart of the Church's life. Yet we still have to unlock the meaning of one word from this description of the primitive Church and, thus, of the Church as such: the word κοινωνία (*koinonia*)—in the Vulgate, *communicatio*. On account of its semantic breadth, this word has to be the key concept for our reflections, since it means "Eucharist" and can equally well denote "fellowship" or "congregation". The two realities, Eucharist and congregation, Communion as sacrament and communion or community as a social and institutional

---

[5] See ibid., pp. 215f.; H. Schürmann, *Traditionsgeschichtliche Untersuchungen zu den synoptischen Evangelien* [Investigations into the history of traditions in the Synoptic Gospels] (Düsseldorf, 1967), pp. 310–40.

entity, which in our linguistic usage are clearly separated, are united in this term.

The path for our further reflections is at once marked out with this observation. It is first a matter of following the trail of the word κοινωνία (*koinonia*) in its various ramifications so as to cast light on the relationship between Eucharist and congregation—or, better, the eucharistic dynamic of the Church community—as mirrored in this concept. Then in a second stage of reflection we will turn to the figure of Jesus Christ so as to discover, starting from him, the origin and the heart of Christian communion, a spirituality of communicating that would also be open to those who cannot participate in the narrower sense of receiving sacramental Communion. "Communicating" in the Christian sense is not an action specific to a particular group, which marks off a congregation from other people, but is on account of its christological basis always likewise mission, being representative, going to meet other people who are still "outside". It hardly needs to be pointed out that within the limits of a short essay this program can only be roughly outlined, not given in detail. It will just be a matter of emphasizing anew a few essential traits of the Catholic tradition and, thus, giving an impulse to further thought.

2. The Juristic, Sacramental, and Practical Content of Communion in Acts 2:42 and Galatians 2:9–10

Before we take this program any farther, we will just take another look at the results of our analysis of Acts 2:42. Up to now we have merely established in a general way that the word κοινωνία (*koinonia*), with its breadth of meaning, occupies an important place in the description of the nature of the Church there. Yet it still has to be asked what its exact meaning is in that verse. The exegetes reply in varying ways, and the context scarcely permits a definitive judgment. Two things, however, can be noted in any case. The word stands between the two concepts "teaching" and "breaking of bread" (Eucharist); in some respect it seems to link the two together, to be a kind of bridge between the two. We can add to this that Luke sets out the four concepts we have here in two pairs: "teaching and communion", "breaking of bread and prayers". Communion is thus linked with "apostolic teaching", making, as it were, a united whole with this, and is thus also distinguished to a certain extent from the breaking of bread (Eucharist); it is at any rate portrayed as extending beyond the liturgical action and as essentially based on the underlying factor of keeping consistent hold of the tradition and its ecclesiastical form.

We meet this aspect, which at first seems surprising, more strongly and more clearly in Saint Paul's defense of his conduct in the Letter to the Galatians, where in justifying his own mission he develops at the same time his basic understanding of Church fellowship (Gal 1:13—2:14). In the part of this most important passage that interests us, Paul tells how the so-called "pillars of the Church"—James, Peter, and John—gave him and Barnabas "the right hand of fellowship [κοινωνίας / koinonias; in the Vulgate, societatis]".[6] These three "pillars" were apparently the continuation in the primitive Church of that group of three apostles whom Jesus had included, as the inmost circle of the Twelve, in the event of his Transfigu-

---

[6] See H. Schlier, *Der Brief an die Galater* [The Letter to the Galatians] (Göttingen, 1962), pp. 78–81; F. Mußner, *Der Galaterbrief* [Galatians] (Freiburg, 1974), pp. 115–27 and 423; Mußner, "'Das Wesen des Christentums ist συνεσθίειν': Ein authentischer Kommentar" ["συνεσθίειν is the essence of Christianity": An authentic commentary], in H. Roßmann and J. Ratzinger, *Mysterium der Gnade: Festschrift für J. Auer zum 65. Geburtstag* [The mystery of grace: Essays presented to J. Auer on his sixty-fifth birthday] (Regensburg, 1975), pp. 92–102.

ration as well as in the hour of agony in Gethsemane (see Mk 9:2; 14:33; see also Mk 5:37). These "pillars" were obviously responsible for the leadership of the Church as she grew; they decided on membership and **exclusion**.[7] If they accorded Paul and Barnabas the right of communion, this was a fully valid and binding recognition of Church fellowship—an action that was indispensable even for Paul, however much he emphasized his being directly called by the Lord and receiving a direct revelation. For him too, Church unity is unthinkable without "remaining in the teaching of the apostles", that is, in the apostolic structure of the Church. Accordingly, the word "communion" has at this point its full Christian content, which includes the sacramental and spiritual dimension as well as the institutional and personal one. This "handshake" of *communio*—which is to be identified with the so-called "council of the apostles" we are told about in the Acts of the Apostles (Acts 15:1–35)—legitimized the direction in which Paul and Barnabas were taking the Gentile Church, freed from the Jewish law, and thus founded ecclesiastical communion in the proper sense: the new people made up of Jews and Gentiles, both accepted by the open hands of the crucified Christ (see Jn 12:32).

---

[7] The Qumran community also made a distinction between the group of twelve and the group of three, with their respective underlying symbolism. For the relationship with and distinction from the way in which the company of Jesus' disciples was built up, see, for example, A. Vögtle, "Das öffentliche Wirken Jesu auf dem Hintergrund der Qumranbewegung" [The public ministry of Jesus against the background of the Qumran movement], *Freiburger Universitätsreden* (1958), pp. 15f.; F. Nötscher, "Vorchristliche Typen urchristliche Ämter? Episkopos und Mebaqqer" [Pre-Christian models for primitive Christian offices? Episkopos and Mebaqqer], in W. Corsten, A. Frotz, and P. Linden, eds., *Die Kirche und ihre Ämter und Stände: Festgabe für Joseph Kardinal Frings* [The Church and her offices and ranks: Essays presented to Joseph Cardinal Frings] (Cologne, 1960), pp. 315–38, esp. 328f. It seems to me worthy of note that after the death of James the son of Zebedee, the Church continued the group of three created by Jesus by replacing the son of Zebedee with the brother of the Lord.

The following section from Paul's defense of his conduct certainly does show how difficult it was to live up to the demands of this decision and thus shows how profound the question was. For in spite of the clarification that had already taken place, the question of the prescriptions concerning food led once more at Antioch to the edge of a split. The question had made table fellowship between the two groups impossible; the two groups could not eat the same things and, thus, could not eat together, because for those Christians who came from a Jewish background the prescriptions concerning food belonged to the core of their religious observance and thus seemed indispensable, while the Gentile Christians, on the other hand, knew that they did not apply to them. A split in the "profane" table fellowship (which, of course, for the Jewish Christians was never by any means merely "profane", on account of the law) would with inevitable logic also have led to a split in fellowship at the Lord's Supper. Thus once more, and with still greater clarity, the question arose with which the basic understanding about communion reached in Jerusalem had been concerned: either the Church would become a Jewish sect, of which there were many, or she would allow herself to be cut off from her roots in the Old Testament, upon which her legitimacy as a religion of revelation nonetheless depended.

For one cannot have the Son without the Father; one cannot have Jesus without his Bible, which we call the Old Testament. The attempt to do this, which Marcion made in the second century in a radical form of Paulinism and which has repeatedly had successors, even among modern theologians, is self-contradictory and doomed to failure. Turning back to the handshake in Jerusalem, in this situation, meant: We do have the Old Testament in Jesus, in whom the law is fulfilled. It means that faith in Christ is the foundation of communion, and that alone. If Paul holds the "pillars"—or, let us be specific, Peter—to the communion of Jerusalem with such emphasis, then the passion with which he insists on this just shows yet again that **in order to remain in unity with the crucified and risen Lord, the practical sign of juridical unity, "remaining in the teaching of the apostles", is indispensable**.

But we must turn again to the account of the Jerusalem decision to have a look at yet another aspect of communion, which once again affects both the visible, "institutional" life together and, at the same time, the spiritual dimension of Christian life. Paul emphasizes that the complete freedom from the law enjoyed by Gentile Christians (and thus by all Christians) was accepted without qualification. Yet there was a requirement imposed on Gentile Christians, although it was of a quite different kind: that of concerning themselves with the "*poor*" of Jerusalem. What was meant by this?

I believe we must first strongly emphasize the social character of this prescription: **Fellowship in the body of Christ and in receiving the Body of Christ means fellowship with one another. This of its very nature includes mutual acceptance, giving and receiving on both sides, and readiness to share one's goods.** The fact that some people are indulging themselves while others are in want cannot be reconciled with Church fellowship. This is always "table fellowship" in the most demanding sense of the word, and its members always have to give each other "life"—physical and spiritual, but especially physical, too. In this sense, the social question is given a quite central place in the theological heart of the Christian concept of communion.

Yet there is another aspect. If the "poor" are being spoken of here, then this is not simply (and probably not primarily) a social category; rather, it is a title of messianic dignity accorded to the Jerusalem congregation, similar to being called "holy". The collection for the poor is thus at the same time a recognition of the place occupied in the history of salvation by **Jerusalem as the effective site of unity**, as the point of concentration of salvation history.[8] It is an expression of the primacy of Jerusalem, and in saying that we must bear in mind that this was formulated at a time when Jerusalem was still the center of things for Christians and the transfer to Rome was not yet complete. The Jerusalem theme and the idea of primacy comprised within it is also part of the essential structure of communion and is a concrete measure of "remaining in the teaching of the apostles". Thus the many levels of the *communio christiana* are marked out in this text, though they all ultimately refer to one and the same thing: to **fellowship with the Word of God who became flesh, who through his death lets us share in his life and intends thereby to lead us also toward service to one another, to a visible fellowship in living our lives.**

3. The Profane Roots of the Concept of κοινωνία (*koinonia*) and Their Significance for the New Christian Reality

a. The reshaping of the profane meaning in the Gospel of Luke

Human words, at any rate the great fundamental words, always carry within them a whole history of human experi-

---

[8] Thus, for example, H. O. Wendland, "Geist, Recht und Amt in der Urkirche" [Spirit, law, and office in the primitive Church], *AEvKR*, new series, 2 (1938), p. 299. Schlier, *Brief an die Galater*, pp. 80f. (see n. 5), also shows that the collection for the "poor" of Jerusalem had less of the sense of help for those in need than that of recognition of the primacy of Jerusalem and of the unity of the Church. Schlier does in any case emphasize that this was a matter of religious and moral primacy, not a juridical one. This distinction is, however, relevant only if we are assuming the narrower modern sense both of "moral" and of "juridical", which corresponds to our habits of thought and speech but is not in accord with the views of that period.

ences, of human questioning, understanding, and suffering of reality. The great theme words of the Bible bring with them into the process of revelation also, in acceptance and contradiction, the fundamental experiences of mankind. So in order to understand the Bible aright, one must always also turn to question the history preserved in its words. Let us try in this way to discover something of the historical load carried by the concept κοινωνία (*koinonia*).

A first clue to its previous profane meaning may be seen in a passage from the Gospel of Luke that throws light on the beginnings of the Church's growth. I am talking about the first eleven verses of chapter 5, where, in a scene of incomparable beauty, the Evangelist recounts the calling of the first disciples. After a night in which the fishermen had spent their efforts in vain on the Lake of Gennesaret, with the new morning of the dawning Gospel the Lord grants them a marvelous catch and calls Peter and his associates to become fishers of men. According to the Fourth Gospel, this scene would be repeated after the Resurrection (Jn 21:1–14)—after the denial of Peter, it now includes a definitive mission for the wide ocean of the whole world.

It seems to me most important that in this scene as portrayed by Luke, which stands as a vision of what is to come, our word is to be found: James and John are described as κοινωνοί (*koinonoi*) of Simon (v. 10), a term we translate somewhat unsatisfactorily in English with "partners"—the special quality of this word, which we are trying to track down, is in fact blurred with this translation. The three men, whose community (as we saw) will be continued in the "pillars" of the Letter to the Galatians, are here at the start of Jesus' public ministry and make up a "commune" together. It is clear that the word has not yet any theological meaning here; it is rather being used in a generally current technical sense. James and John are "partners", "associates" of Simon in the fishing trade; the three make up a "business partnership". They are joint owners of a little business, the head of which is Simon.[9] We thus find here the original profane sense of the word, which remains important for the understanding of its new religious meaning: κοινωνία (koinonia) refers to shared property, shared work, shared values. In Jesus' saying, "You will be catching men", Simon's previous occupation becomes an allegory for his future one; yet in the same way, in this fishing partnership too, **the new partnership, the new communion,** is outlined; the Christians will be the "partnership in the little ship of the Church": one through the call that comes from Jesus, one through the miracle of grace, which grants all the wealth of the ocean after the nights without hope. One in the gift, they will likewise be one in the mission, which is what grace is.

Looking back and meditating on this passage, the early Church also recognized the most profound basis for the unity of this "partnership": it is ultimately one through the mysterious fish, the risen Lord, who has gone down into the depths of the sea—into the night of death—and allowed himself to be caught by us and for us, so as to become our nourishment for eternal life. We are Peter's little ship, and in it we are those called by the Lord; we are the companions of Peter, yet we are not the partnership of Peter; rather, we are the communion of the Lord himself, who grants what we could never have achieved by our own resources. Receiving comes before acting, or, as J. Hamer expresses it: In communion (κοινωνία) the horizontal dimension is the result of the vertical and can be understood at all only on that basis.[10]

---

[9] See J. Hamer, *L'Église est une communion* [The Church is a communion] (Paris, 1962), p. 176; F. Hauck, κοινωνία in ThWNT 4:804 [reference to German version]; H. Schürmann, *Das Lukasevangelium* [The Gospel of Luke], vol. 1 (Freiburg, 1969), pp. 270f.

[10] Hamer, *L'Église*, p. 176.

b. The Jewish root

As could only be expected, the Greek New Testament word
we are trying to understand has also, and above all, a Hebrew
root. The Hebrew word *chaburah* corresponds to the Greek
κοινωνία (*koinonia*) and, like that word, denotes a business
partnership, a "cooperative". Yet the specific situations of
Hebrew society are obviously reflected in this term and lend
particular shades to its application.

There are above all three aspects to this. As early as the first
century before Christ, the group of Pharisees is describing
itself as a *chaburah*. From the second century A.D. this designation is also being used for the rabbis. And finally, the group of
people assembled for the Passover meal (at least ten persons)
was **characterized** with this word.[11] In this last usage of the
word it is quite directly clear how it applied to the mystery of
the Church: she is the *chaburah* of Jesus in a most profound
sense—the **company of his Pascha**, the family in which his
eternal longing to eat the Pascha with us (see Lk 24:15) is
fulfilled. This, his Pascha, is, however, **far more than a meal:
it is loving unto death. It is consequently sharing out
[*Teilgabe*] and sharing in [*Teilhabe*] his own life, which is
torn open for everyone in death.** It is shared in a free
anticipation of death that is effected when he says: Take this,
all of you, and eat it: This is my body which will be given up
for you. Take this, all of you, and drink from it: This is the
cup of my blood; it will be shed for many.

Here, with unique clarity, we encounter **what is specific
to the New Testament**, what makes it new in comparison
with the previous covenant history, which thus becomes the
Old Testament. In the Old Testament, too, the purpose of the

---

[11] Hauck, κοινωνία, pp. 802f. See Ratzinger, "Das Pascha Jesu und die
Kirche", in *Schauen auf den Durchbohrten*, pp. 87–92; Eng. trans.: "The Passover
of Jesus and the Church", in *Behold the Pierced One*, pp. 103–10.

sacrifice and the sacrificial meal is to establish community between God and his people. Yet the word *chaburah—communion*—is never used to designate the relationship between God and man; it is exclusively used to express relationships between men. There is no "communion" between God and man; the Creator's transcendence remains insuperable. That is why the concrete relationship that is essential for the Old Testament is described, not by the word "communion", but by the word "covenant" (*berith*).[12] This terminology guarantees that God, who alone can establish the relation of his creature to himself, remains exalted; this term thus includes the distance that is maintained in the relationship. Some exegetes, on account of this, hold it to be wrong to translate *berith* with "covenant", because this word presupposes a certain equality between the partners in the "covenant" that can never be, according to the Old Testament view, in the relationship between God and man. We need not go any farther into this question here; for us, it is important to note that **the Old Testament knows nothing of any "communion" (*chaburah*, κοινωνία) between God and man; the New Testament is this communion, in and through the person of Jesus Christ.**

c.   The Greek root and the problem of the
     Hellenization of Christianity

We find a third root of the Christian word in Greek philosophy, the views of which—as will immediately become apparent—are in opposition to the thought of the Hebrew Bible. Thus, from the particular point of view of the questions we are pursuing, we will at the same time be able to look at the much-discussed problem of a "Hellenization" of Christianity.

---

[12] Hauck, κοινωνία, pp. 801f.

The Old Testament sets the transcendence and the unity of God in opposition to pagan polytheism; from that follows—as we have just seen—the repudiation of the idea of actual "communion" between God and man. For the pagan world, on the other hand, this very idea occupies the center of their religious seeking. Thus, in the *Symposium*, Plato talks about the reciprocal communion between gods and men (ἡ περὶ θεοὺς καὶ ἀνθρώπους κοινωνία). According to him, communion with the gods also brings about fellowship among men. He notes that this communion is the ultimate intention and the most profound content of all sacrifices, of worship as such. In this connection he coins a marvelous phrase that we might refer to as a presentiment of the eucharistic mystery when he says that **worship** is entirely concerned with the **wholeness and the healing of love**.[13] Let us add that for Hellenistic mysticism too, the communion between divinity, men, and all rational beings is a central concept. Yet the real object of longing for this mysticism is, not communion, but union; the end, here, is, not relationship, but identity.[14] If Philo, for his part, diverges from traditional Hebrew terminology and, within the context of concepts from Hellenistic mysticism, talks about "communion" between God and the pious man in worship, then we may well speak with some justification of a "Hellenizing" of Hebrew thought.

Something quite different confronts us, however, if in the New Testament the Church is communion—not merely communion of men with one another, but, by the medium of the death and Resurrection of Jesus, communion with Christ, the Son who became man, and thus communion with the eternal triune love of God. For this is not the product of a new synthesis of thought; rather, it is the fruit of

---

[13] *Symposium* 188 b–c: . . . οὐ περὶ ἄλλο τι ἐστὶν ἢ περὶ Ἔρωτος φυλακήν τε καὶ ἴασιν. See Hauck, κοινωνία, p. 800.

[14] Ibid.

a new reality that was not previously there. The one transcendent God of the Old Testament uncovers his inmost life; he shows that he is in himself a dialogue of eternal love. Because he is in himself relationship—word and love—that is why he can speak, feel, respond, and love. Because he is relationship, he is able to open himself up and establish a relationship of his creature to himself. In the Incarnation of the eternal Word, there comes about that communion between God and the being of man, his creature, which had hitherto seemed impossible to reconcile with the transcendence of the one God.

Plato's assertion that everything concerned in worship is related to the communion between the gods and the being of man and that all this is directed toward **wholeness and the healing of love**—this assertion now acquires a **new meaning**. Let us note that Plato is talking, not about God, but about the gods and that Hellenistic mysticism, too, prefers to talk about the divinity rather than about God. Yet in Jesus occurs the new event, the one God entering into concrete communion with men by incarnating himself in human nature. Divine and human nature intermingle—"without mixing and undivided"—in the Person of Jesus Christ. It would be quite obviously absurd to talk about a "Hellenizing" of Christianity here and to demand that we get back to the Hebrew original. Such a procedure would quite simply mean dispensing with what is actually Christian, with the Christian innovation. The Incarnation is in fact the new synthesis that has been brought about by God himself: it transcends the limits of the Old Testament—necessarily so—while taking up and preserving the whole of its legacy so as to open it up and to fill it with the wealth of the other cultures: the Incarnation is at the same time the reconciliation, atonement, and fellowship (communion) of those who hitherto were set in opposition to one another—Jews and Gentiles (see Eph 2:11–22);

this is also true in the realm of thought. The reproach of Hellenization and the purist attitude that demands a return to unchanged Hebraic categories are in reality evidence of blindness to the essence of Christianity.

II. EUCHARIST—CHRISTOLOGY—ECCLESIOLOGY: THE CHRISTOLOGICAL CENTER OF OUR THEME

1. Eucharist and Christology

The analysis of the inner development of the Christian concept of communion in the reception and reshaping of the pre-Christian inheritance has now of its own accord led us to the heart of Christian communion. We can now see that its origin is to be sought in Christology: the incarnated Son is the "communion" between God and men. Being a Christian is in reality nothing other than partaking in the mystery of the Incarnation, or, to use Saint Paul's expression: the Church, insofar as she is the Church, is the "body of Christ" (that is, in fact, men's partaking of the communion between man and God, which is what the Incarnation of the Word is). Once this has been grasped, then the indivisibility of Church and Eucharist, of sacramental Communion and congregational communion, is obvious.

In the light of these insights the meaning of Saint Paul's fundamental remarks about our question becomes clear, as we read them in the First Letter to the Corinthians:

> The cup of blessing which we bless, is it not a participation [κοινωνια; Vulgate, *communicatio*] in the blood of Christ? The bread which we break, is it not a participation [κοινωνια; Vulgate, *participatio*; Neo-Vulgate, *communicatio*] in the body of Christ? Because there is one bread, we who are many are one body, for we all partake of the one bread. (1 Cor 10:16–17)

For Augustine, these verses became the center of his theological thinking; his homilies for Easter Night, which represent his catechesis on the Eucharist for the newly baptized
Christians, circle around these words. By eating the one
bread, he comments, we ourselves become what we are eating.[15] This bread (he explains in the *Confessions*) is the food of
the strong.[16] Normal foodstuffs are less strong than man, they
serve him: they are taken in so that they may be assimilated
into man's body and build him up. This special food, however—the Eucharist—is, on the contrary, superior to man, is
stronger than he is, and thus the process toward which the
whole thing is directed is reversed: the man who takes this
bread is assimilated to *it*, is taken into it, is fused into this bread
and becomes bread like Christ himself. "Because the bread is
one, we, the many, are one body." The conclusion to be
drawn from such an insight is clear: The Eucharist is never an
event involving just two, a dialogue between Christ and me.
Eucharistic Communion is aimed at a complete reshaping of
my own life. It **breaks up man's entire self and creates a
new "we". Communion with Christ is necessarily also
communication with all who belong to him: therein I
myself become a part of the new bread that he is creating
by the resubstantiation of the whole of earthly reality.**

At this point the close connection between the concept of
communion and the understanding of the Church as "the
body of Christ" becomes evident; related images, such as that
of Christ as the true vine, also have their place in the same
connection. All these biblical ideas throw light on the Christian community as originating from Christ. The Christian
"community" cannot be explained in a "horizontal", essen-

---

[15] See J. Ratzinger, *Volk und Haus Gottes in Augustins Lehre von der Kirche* [The
people and the house of God in Augustine's doctrine of the Church], 2nd ed.
(St. Ottilien, 1992).

[16] *Confessions* VII, 10, 16.

tially sociological way. Its relation to the Lord, its origin from him, and its dependence on him constitute the condition for its existence; indeed, we might go so far as to say: **The Church is of her nature a relationship, a relationship set up by the love of Christ, which in its turn likewise founds a new relationship of men with one another.** We may say, using those fine words of Plato we encountered earlier, that the Eucharist is indeed the "healing of our love".

2. The Communion in Christ of Being God and Being Man

In a second stage, we now have to specify more precisely the christological basis of Christian life, so as to feel our way toward the heart of eucharistic spirituality as also that of a spirituality of the Church. Jesus Christ, as we have acknowledged in our reflections thus far, opens the way to what is supposedly impossible, to the communion between God and man, because, as the incarnate Word, he is that communion. In him we find the realization of that "alchemy" which transforms human existence and blends it into the being of God. Receiving the Lord in the Eucharist, accordingly, means entering into a community of existence with Christ, entering into that state in which human existence is opened up to God and which is at the same time the necessary condition for the opening up of the inner being of men for one another. The path toward the communion of men with one another goes by way of communion with God. In order to grasp the spiritual content of the Eucharist, we therefore have to understand the spiritual tension of the divine man: only in a spiritual Christology will the spirituality of the Sacrament also open up.

On account of its overwhelming interest in metaphysics

and history, Western theology has somewhat neglected this point of view, even though in reality it represents precisely the link between the various parts of theology as likewise between theological reflection and the concrete spiritual realization of Christianity. The Third Council of Constantinople—the thirteen-hundredth anniversary of which in 1981 was, quite typically, almost overlooked along with the commemoration of the First Council of Constantinople and that of Ephesus—offers the decisive starting points for this, which are also in my opinion indispensable for the correct interpretation of the Council of Chalcedon. A detailed exposition of the difficulties is not possible here, of course; let us just try to summarize here what is relevant for us.[17] Chalcedon had defined the ontological content of the Incarnation with its well-known formula of two natures in one Person. The Third Council of Constantinople, however, was faced—after all the conflict that had been unleashed by that ontology—with the question: What is the spiritual content of such an ontology? Or, in more concrete terms: What does "one Person in two natures" mean, for practical purposes, in real life? How can a person live with two wills and a dual intellect? And this is by no means just a matter of mere theoretical curiosity; this certainly also concerns us ourselves in the form of the question: How can we live as baptized Christians, as people of whom, according to Paul, it should be true that: "It is no longer I who live, but Christ who lives in me" (Gal 2:20)?

It is well known that at that time—in the seventh century—just as today, there were two solutions available, which were both equally unacceptable. Some people said: There just

---

[17] Text in *Conciliorum oecumenorum decreta*, ed. Alberigo et al., 3rd ed. (Bologna, 1973), pp. 124–30. See thesis no. 6 of the article "Christologische Orientierungs punkte" in Ratzinger, *Schauen auf den Durchbohrten*, pp. 33–37; Eng. trans.: "Taking Bearings in Christology", in Ratzinger, *Behold the Pierced One*, pp. 13–46.

was no individual human will in Christ. The Third Council of Constantinople rejected this picture of Christ as the portrait of a "Christ with neither will nor strength". The other solution proposed, in exactly the contrary sense, two entirely separate spheres of willing. Yet in this way we end up with a kind of schizophrenia, with a conception that is as monstrous as it is unacceptable. The Council's response ran as follows: The ontological *union* of two wills that remain independent within the unity of the person means, on the level of daily life, *communion* (κοινωνία) of the two wills. With this interpretation of the union as communion, the Council was devising an ontology of freedom. The two "wills" are united in that way in which one will and another can unite: in a common assent to a shared value. To put it another way: Both of these wills are united in the assent of the human will of Christ to the divine will of the Logos. Thus on a practical level— "existentially"—the two wills become one single will, and yet ontologically they remain two independent entities. The Council comments: Just as the flesh of the Lord may be called the flesh of the Word, so also we may refer to his human will as the Logos' own will.

In point of fact the Council is here applying the trinitarian model (with the appropriate analogical distinction) to Christology: the highest unity there is—the unity of God—is not a unity of something inseparable and indistinguishable; rather, it is a unity in the mode of communion—the unity that love creates and love is. In this fashion, the Logos takes the being of the man Jesus into his own being and talks about it with his own "I": "I have come down from heaven, not to do my own will, but the will of him who sent me" (Jn 6:38).[18] It is in the obedience of the Son, in the uniting of both these wills in one assent to the will of the Father, that the communion

---

[18] Alberigo, *Conciliorum,* p. 128, ll. 30ff.

between human and divine being is consummated. The "marvelous exchange", the "alchemy of being": this is here becoming a reality as a liberating and reconciling communication that develops into a communion between Creator and creature. It is in the pain of this exchange, and only here, that the fundamental change in man that can alone redeem him, and that changes the conditioning factors of the world, is achieved; here it is that community is born; here Church comes into being. The act of participation in this filial obedience, as truly effecting a change in man, is at the same time the only effective action that truly has power to change and renew society and the world as such: only when this act takes place is there any change for the better—in the direction of the Kingdom of God.[19]

One further observation seems to me necessary to complete our reflections. We had already noted that the Incarnation of the Son creates communion between God and man and thus opens up the possibility of a new communion of men with one another. This communion between God and man that is realized in the person of Jesus Christ for its own part becomes communicable to others in the Paschal Mystery, that is, in the death and Resurrection of the Lord. The Eucharist effects our participation in the Paschal Mystery and

---

[19] It is Maximus the Confessor who worked out the theological implications of the Third Council of Constantinople; see F.-M. Lethel, *Théologie de l'agonie du Christ* [The theology of Christ's agony] (Paris, 1979); F. Heinzer, *Gottes Sohn als Mensch: Die Struktur des Menschseins Christi bei Maximus Confessor* [God's Son as a man: The structure of the human existence of Christ according to Maximus the Confessor] (Fribourg, 1980); K. H. Uthemann, "Das anthropologische Modell der hypostatischen Union bei Maximus Confessor: Zur innerchalkedonischen Transformation eines Paradigmas" [The anthropological model of the hypostatic union in the writings of Maximus the Confessor: On the transformation of a paradigm within the Chalcedonian tradition], in F. Heinzer and C. Schönborn, eds.: *Maximus Confessor* (Fribourg, 1982), pp. 223–33; L. Weimer, *Die Lust an Gott und seiner Sache* [Joy in God and in God's work] (Freiburg, 1981), pp. 101–6.

thus constitutes the Church, the body of Christ. Hence the necessity of the Eucharist for salvation. The Eucharist is necessary in exactly the sense that the Church is necessary, and vice versa. It is in this sense that the saying of the Lord is to be understood: "Unless you eat the flesh of the Son of man and drink his blood, you have no life in you" (Jn 6:53). Yet thereby appears the necessity of a visible Church and of visible, concrete (one might say, "institutional") unity. The inmost mystery of communion between God and man is accessible in the sacrament of the Body of the Risen One; and the mystery, on the other hand, thereby demands our body and draws it in and makes itself a reality in one *Body*. The Church, which is built up on the basis of the Sacrament of the Body of Christ, must for her part likewise be one body and, in fact, be a single body so as to correspond to the uniqueness of Jesus Christ, and the way she corresponds to this is seen, again, in her unity and in remaining in the teaching of the apostles.

3. The Problem of the Excommunicated

Yet if this is how things are, then what should we say about those many Christians who believe and hope in the Lord, who long for the gift of his Body, but who cannot receive the Sacrament? I am thinking now about quite varied forms of being excluded from sacramental Communion. There is first of all the quite simple practical impossibility of receiving the Sacrament in times of persecution or when there are not enough priests. And, on the other hand, there are the forms of excommunication founded on canon law, as for example in the case of those people who have been divorced and who have remarried. In a certain sense, the ecumenical problem, the lack of communion between Christians who are divided, is touched upon here. It is of course impossible to elucidate such varied and far-reaching questions as these within the framework of this discussion. Yet simply to leave them aside would show a lack of honesty. If it is impossible to provide a response here, I would nonetheless like to touch on one important consideration.

In his book *L'Église est une communion* [The Church is a communion], J. Hamer shows that medieval theology, which was likewise unable simply to pass over the problem of excommunication, discussed it in the most careful manner. For the thinkers of the Middle Ages, it was no longer possible—as it had been in the patristic era—simply to identify membership in the visible communion of the Church with someone's relation to the Lord. Even Gratian had still written: "Beloved, a Christian who has been excommunicated by the priest is handed over to the devil. Why? Because outside the Church there is the devil, just as in the Church there is Christ." [20] The theologians of the thirteenth century, in contrast to this, were faced with the task of preserving, on the one hand, the indispensable connection between interior and exterior, between sign and reality, between body and spirit; yet at the same time they also had to do justice to the distinction between the two. Thus, for example, in the writings of William of Auvergne we find him making the distinction by which outward and inward communion are connected as are sign and reality. He then explains that the Church would never wish to deprive anyone of that inner communion. When she wields the sword of excommunication, then, according to him, this happens only in order to heal the spiritual communion with this medicine. He then adds a thought that is at the same time consoling and stimulating. He knows, he tells us, that for not a few people the burden of excommunication

---

[20] Hamer, *L'Église*, p. 184; Decret. Gratian, C XI, q. 3, c. 32.

is as hard to bear as martyrdom. But, he says, very often a person makes more progress in patience and humility as an excommunicate than in the situation when he is outwardly in communion.[21]

Bonaventure developed this idea more profoundly. He found an altogether modern objection being advanced against the Church's right of exclusion, which ran as follows: Excommunication is being shut off from communion. Yet Christian communion, of its very nature, exists through love; it is a fellowship of love. But no one has the right to shut anyone out from love; therefore there is no such thing as the right to excommunicate anyone.[22]

Bonaventure responds to this by distinguishing three levels of communion; in this way he can keep hold of Church discipline and the Church's canon law and, at the same time, say, taking full responsibility as a theologian, "I take note that no one can be excluded from the communion of love, nor should they be, as long as they are alive upon earth. Excommunication is not exclusion from this communion."[23]

Quite obviously, we cannot conclude from such reflections, which would need to be taken up anew and further developed today, that a concrete sacramental communion fellowship is superfluous or that it is any less important. The "excommunicated" person is in fact being supported by the love of the living body of Christ, by the suffering of the saints, who join themselves to *his* suffering as they do to his spiritual hunger, while both of them are surrounded by the suffering, by the hunger and the thirst of Jesus Christ, who bears with us all and supports us. On the other hand, the suffering of the person who is excluded, his yearning for communion (both

---

[21] *De sacramento Ordinis*, cap. 12 (Venice, 1591), 519 A–C; see Hamer, *L'Église*, p. 187.

[22] IV Sent., d. 18, p. 2, a. un q. 1, contr. 1; Hamer, *L'Église*, pp. 187f.

[23] Ibid., ad 1; Hamer, *L'Église*, p. 188.

that of the Sacrament and that of the living limbs of Christ), is the link that holds him to the saving love of Christ. From both points of view, then, the Sacrament and the visible fellowship of communion that it builds up are present and are indispensable. Thus here too, the "healing of love", the ultimate purpose of the Cross of Christ, of the sacraments, of the Church, is being effected. Hence we can understand how, through the affliction of being distanced, in the pain of longing and the growth of love that results, the impossibility of sacramental Communion can lead to spiritual progress, while rebellion against it—as William of Auvergne rightly observes—necessarily undermines the positive and constructive point of the excommunication. Rebellion is not healing but is destructive of love.

In this connection I am strongly reminded of a reflection of a more general pastoral kind. When Augustine felt his death approaching, he "excommunicated" himself and took upon himself ecclesiastical penitence. In his last days, he set himself alongside, in solidarity, with the public sinners who seek forgiveness and grace through the pain of not receiving Communion.[24] He wanted to meet his Lord in the humility of those who hunger and thirst for righteousness, for Him, the righteous and gracious One. Against the background of his sermons and writings, which describe the mystery of the Church as a communion with the body of Christ and as the body of Christ, on the basis of the Eucharist, in a really marvelous way, this gesture is quite shocking. It seems to me more profound and fitting, the more often I ponder it. Do we not often take things too lightly today when we receive the most Holy Sacrament? Could such a spiritual fasting not sometimes be useful, or even necessary, to renew and establish more deeply our relation to the Body of Christ?

---

[24] See F. van der Meer, *Augustinus der Seelsorger* (Cologne, 1951), p. 324; Eng. trans.: *Augustine the Bishop* (London and New York: Sheed and Ward, 1961).

In the early Church there was a most expressive exercise of this kind: probably since the time of the apostles, eucharistic fasting on Good Friday was a part of the Church's spirituality of Communion. Not receiving Communion on one of the most holy days of the Church's year, which was celebrated with no Mass and without any Communion of the faithful, was a particularly profound way of sharing in the Passion of the Lord: the sorrowing of the bride from whom the bridegroom has been taken away (see Mk 2:20).[25] I think that a eucharistic fast of this kind, if it were deliberate and experienced as deprivation, could even today be properly significant, on certain occasions that would have to be carefully considered—such as days of penitence (and why not, for instance, on Good Friday once more?), or also perhaps especially at great public Masses when there are so many people that a dignified distribution of the Sacrament is often just not possible, so that by not receiving the Sacrament people could truly show more reverence and love than by doing so in a way that contradicts the sublime nature of this event.

Such fasting—which could not be allowed to become arbitrary, of course, but would have to be consonant with the spiritual guidance of the Church—could help people toward a deepening of their personal relation to the Lord in the Sacrament; it could be an act of solidarity with all those who have a yearning for the Sacrament but cannot receive it. It seems to me that the problem of people who have been divorced and remarried, yet equally the problem of intercommunion (in mixed marriages, for example), would be less

---

[25] On the question of Christian fasting, in connection with Mark 2:20, see R. Pesch, *Das Markusevangelium* [The Gospel of Mark], vol. 1 (Freiburg, 1976), pp. 175f.; and on the problem of eucharistic fasting, eschatologically motivated, see J. Blank, *Meliton von Sardes: Vom Passa: Die älteste christliche Osterpredigt* [Melito of Sardis: "On the Pascha": The oldest Christian sermon for Easter] (Freiburg, 1963), pp. 26–41.

of a burden if voluntary spiritual fasting was at the same time undertaken in visible recognition and expression of the fact that we are all dependent upon that "healing of love" which the Lord effected in the ultimate solitude of the Cross. I would not of course wish to suggest by this a return to some kind of Jansenism: in biological life, as in spiritual life, fasting presumes that eating is the normal thing to do. Yet from time to time we need a cure for falling into mere habit and its dullness. Sometimes we need to be hungry—need bodily and spiritual hunger—so as once more to comprehend the Lord's gifts and to understand the suffering of our brethren who are hungry. Spiritual hunger, like bodily hunger, can be a vehicle of love.

CONCLUDING REMARKS

Let us attempt a summary, which will also lead into our final observations. The biblical and patristic word κοινωνία (*koinonia*) unites the two meanings of "Eucharist" and "congregation" (community). With this semantic synthesis, the term is not merely a pointer toward the heart of any ecclesiology that is rightly understood; at the same time, it makes clear the **synthesis of the particular Church and the universal Church** that is needed. For the celebration of the Eucharist does indeed take place at a certain place, and that is where it builds up a cell of Christian brotherhood. The local "congregation" grows on the basis of the living and effective presence of the Lord in the Eucharist. Yet at the same time it is true that the Lord is one, in all places and in every Eucharist. The indivisible presence of one and the same Lord, who is also the Word of the Father, therefore presumes that each individual congregation stands within the *one* and *whole* body of Christ; that is the only way they can celebrate the Eucharist. Within this concept, as we have seen, is included standing in the "teaching of the apostles", and the presence of the apostles has its indicator and its guarantee in the institution of the "apostolic succession". Outside of this great network the term "congregation" becomes empty, a romantic gesture, a demand for security within a small group that nonetheless lacks any real content.[26] **Only a power and a love that are stronger than all our own initiatives can build up a fruitful and reliable community and impart to it the impetus of a fruitful mission. The unity of the Church, which is founded upon the love of the one Lord, does not destroy what is particular in the individual communities; rather, it builds them up and holds them together as a real communion with the Lord and with each other. The love of Christ, which is present for all ages in the Sacrament of his Body, awakens our love and heals our love: the Eucharist is the foundation of community as it is of mission, day by day.**

---

[26] On the questions raised here, see J. Ratzinger, *Theologische Prinzipienlehre* (Munich, 1982), pp. 300–314; Eng. trans.: *Principles of Catholic Theology* (San Francisco: Ignatius Press, 1987).

Eucharist and Mission[1]

PRELIMINARY THOUGHTS ABOUT
EUCHARIST AND MISSION

An old legend about the origin of Christianity in Russia tells how a series of people presented themselves before Prince Vladimir of Kiev, who was seeking to find the right religion for his people: each in turn, representatives of Islam from Bulgaria, representatives of Judaism, and then emissaries of the pope from Germany, offered him their faith as being the right one and the best. Yet the prince remained unsatisfied by any of these things being offered. The decision was made, it is said, when his ambassadors returned from a solemn liturgical celebration in which they had taken part in the Church of Hagia Sophia in Constantinople. Filled with enthusiasm, they told the prince: "Then we came to the Greeks, and we were taken to the place where they worship their God. . . . We do not know whether we have been in heaven or on earth. . . . We have experienced how God dwells there among men."[2]

This story, as such, is certainly not historical. The way the "Rus" turned to Christianity and the final decision in favor

---

[1] The subject "Eucaristia come genesi della missione" [Eucharist as the birthplace of mission] was the general theme of the Eucharistic Congress of the diocese of Como, within which setting this paper was delivered on September 10, 1997. I repeated the lecture, with minor alterations, on September 25, 1997, at the National Eucharistic Congress in Bologna.

[2] See P. B. I. Bilaniuk, *The Apostolic Origin of the Ukrainian Church* (Toronto, 1988).

of the link with Byzantium constitute a long and complicated process, and historians now believe they can trace its
main outlines.[3] Yet as is always the case, there is also a kernel
of profound truth within this legend. For the inner power of
the liturgy has without doubt played an essential role in the
spread of Christianity. The legend of the liturgical origin of
Russian Christianity, however, above and beyond this general
connection between worship and mission, tells us something
particular about their inner relationship. For the Byzantine
liturgy, which transported to heaven the foreign visitors in
search of God, was not of itself missionary in character. It did
not advertise the faith with an interpretation for outsiders,
for nonbelievers, but dwelt entirely within the inner home of
faith. The report in Acts 20:7 of how Paul celebrated the
Eucharist with the Christians of Troas "in the upper room"
was, in the early Church, as a matter of course, connected
with the story according to which, after the Lord's Ascension
into heaven, the disciples together with Mary waited in
prayer for the Holy Spirit in the upper room and received
him there (Acts 1:3). This upper room, in turn, was identified—historically, this was probably correct—with the
room in which the Last Supper was held, where Jesus had
celebrated the first Eucharist with the Twelve. The upper
room became a symbol of the inner recollection of the
faithful, for the way the Eucharist is removed from ordinary
everyday life. It became an expression for the "mystery of
faith" (1 Tim 3:9; cf. 3:16), in the inmost heart of which
stands the Eucharist. If the Roman liturgy has inserted this
acclamation, **"The mystery of faith"**, into the institution
narrative and has thus made it a part of the central action of

[3] See H. Jedin, ed., *Handbuch der Kirchengeschichte*, vol. 3, pt. 1, *Die mittel-
alterliche Kirche* [Handbook of church history, vol. 3, pt. 1, The medieval
Church], by Friedrich Kempf (Freiburg, 1966), pp. 275–78, and the detailed
bibliography given there, pp. 268f.

the Eucharist, then its interpretation here of the heritage from primitive Christianity is entirely correct—the eucharistic liturgy is not, as such, directed toward nonbelievers; rather, it presupposes, as a mystery, that worshippers are "initiated": only those who have entered into the mystery with their whole life, who know Christ no longer just from the outside—like "the people" whose opinions Peter recounts to the Lord before his confession of faith at Caesarea Philippi (Mk 8:28)—only these can come to the Eucharist. Only someone who, in the communion of faith, has arrived at the point of an inner agreement and an understanding with him can communicate with Christ in the Sacrament.

Let us turn back to our legend: What persuaded the emissaries of the Russian prince of the truth of the faith celebrated in the Orthodox liturgy was not a kind of missionary persuasiveness, with arguments that seemed to them clearer than those of the other religions. What moved them was in fact the mystery as such, which demonstrated the power of the truth actually in transcending the arguments of reason. To put it again another way: The Byzantine liturgy was not, and is not, concerned to indoctrinate other people or to show them how pleasing and entertaining it might be. What was impressive about it was particularly its sheer lack of a practical purpose, the fact that it was being done for God and not for spectators; it was simply striving to be εὐάρεστος—εὐπρόσδεκτος (Rom 12:1; 15:16) before God and for God: to be pleasing to God, as the sacrifice of Abel had been pleasing to God. The very selflessness of this standing before God and turning the gaze toward God was what allowed God's light to stream down into what was happening and for it to be detected even by outsiders.

With this we have established in advance one first important result for our investigation. The way of talking about "missionary liturgy" that became widespread in the fifties is, at the least, ambiguous and problematical.[4] In many circles, among people concerned with liturgy, it led, in a quite inappropriate fashion, to turning a didactic element in the liturgy, and its comprehensibility even for outsiders, into the primary standard for shaping liturgical celebrations. Likewise, the saying that the choice of liturgical forms must be made with respect to "pastoral" points of view betrays the same anthropocentric error. The liturgy is then being constructed entirely for men; it is either serving to convey certain contents or—after people are tired of the rationalism that arises that way and of its banality—to build up community in a way that is related, no longer necessarily to any comprehensible content, but to processes in which people draw close to one another and experience community. Thus, suggestions for styling the liturgy became—and are still becoming—more one-sided and more dependent upon profane models, drawn, for instance, from the way meetings are held or from ancient or even modern socialization rituals. God does not actually play any role there; it is all concerned with winning people over, or keeping them happy and satisfying their demands.

No faith is aroused that way, of course, since faith has to do with God, and it is only where his closeness is felt, where human intentions take second place to reverence before him, that the credibility comes about that creates belief. We have no need to discuss here the various paths to be pursued and opportunities that open up in mission, which no doubt often have to begin with very simple human contacts, yet contacts that are illuminated by love for God. For us it is sufficient to

---

[4] The main representative of the idea of "missionary liturgy" in German-speaking countries in the fifties was J. Hofinger; see J. Hofinger, ed., *Mission und Liturgie: Der Kongreß von Nimwegen 1959* [Mission and liturgy: The Nijmegen Congress of 1959] (Mainz, 1960); J. Hofinger and J. Kellner, *Liturgische Erneuerung in der Weltmission* [Liturgical renewal in the worldwide mission] (Innsbruck, 1957).

note that the Eucharist, as such, is not directly oriented toward the awakening of people's faith in a missionary sense. It stands, rather, at the heart of faith and nourishes it; its gaze is primarily directed toward God, and it draws men into this point of view, draws them into the descent of God to us, which becomes their ascent into fellowship with God. It aims at being pleasing to God and at leading men to see this as being likewise the measure of their lives. And to that extent it is, of course, in a more profound sense, the origin of mission.

I. THE THEOLOGY OF THE CROSS AS THE PRESUPPOSITION AND BASIS OF EUCHARISTIC THEOLOGY

Following this anticipation of the answer to our question, which has been provided by the old legend of the conversion of Russia, we now have to try to work our way farther into the network of relationships we have thus far glimpsed in a few suggestions. In doing this, I would like to concentrate on the witness of Holy Scripture and, in it, on some central passages from Saint Paul, so as to put some boundaries to the subject. If, accordingly, we try to grasp what Paul says about the connection between the Eucharist and faith, then the first thing we see is that there are three very different levels at which this subject is presented—which are, of course, nonetheless closely interlinked, both in their roots and in their intentions. The first thing is **the interpretation of Christ's death on the Cross in terms of the cult**, which represents **the inner presupposition of all eucharistic theology**. We are still hardly able to grasp the enormous importance of this step. An event that was in itself profane, the execution of a man by the most cruel and horrible method available, is described as a cosmic liturgy, as tearing open the closed-up heavens—as the act by which everything that had hitherto been ultimately intended, which had been sought in vain, by all forms of worship, now in the end actually comes about.

In Romans 3:24–26, making use of older, pre-Pauline formulas, Paul has put together the fundamental text for this interpretation.[5] Yet, possibly, this was only because Jesus himself, at the Last Supper, had anticipated his own death, had gone through it in advance and transformed it from within into an event of self-sacrifice and love. On that basis, Paul could describe Christ as *hilasterion*, which in the cultic terminology of the Old Testament meant the center of the temple, the cover that lay upon the ark. It was called *kapporeth*, which was translated into Greek with *hilasterion*, and was seen as the place above which Yahweh appeared in a cloud. This *kapporeth* used to be sprinkled with the blood from expiatory sacrifices, in order that God might thus come as close as possible.[6] If, then, Paul says that Christ is the heart of the temple, which has been lost ever since the Exile, the real place of atonement, the true *kapporeth*, then modern exegesis has represented this as a spiritualizing reinterpretation of the old cult and, thus, in fact as the abolition of the cult, as its replacement by spiritual and ethical elements. Yet the contrary is the truth: For Paul, it is not the temple that is the true reality of worship, and the other thing a kind of allegory, but vice versa. Human cults, including that of the Old Testament, are mere "images", foreshadowing the real worship of God, which is what does not happen in the animal sacrifices. When the tabernacle of the covenant, which is the model for the

---

[5] See H. Schlier, *Der Römerbrief* [The Letter to the Romans] (Freiburg, 1977), pp. 106–16.

[6] See H. Gese, *Zur biblischen Theologie: Alttestamentliche Vorträge* [On biblical theology: Lectures on the Old Testament] (Munich, 1977), pp. 85–106, esp. pp. 105f.; B. Lang, *"kippaer-kapporaet"*, etc., in Botterweck, Ringgren, and Fabry, *Theologisches Wörterbuch zum Alten Testament* [Theological wordbook to the Old Testament], vol. 4 (Stuttgart, 1984), pp. 303–18.

temple, is portrayed in the Book of Exodus, and it is said that Moses arranged everything in accordance with the image he saw when he was with God, then the Fathers saw in this an expression of the fact that the worship of the temple was a mere copy.[7] And indeed, the sacrifices of animals and other things are only ever helpless attempts to substitute for man, who ought to be giving himself—not in the horrible form of human sacrifices, but in the entire wholeness of his being. Yet this is precisely what he is incapable of.

Thus for Paul, as for the whole Christian tradition, it is clear that the **voluntary self-sacrifice of Jesus** is **not an allegorical abolition of the concept of worship**; rather, here the **intent and purpose of the Feast of Atonement** become **reality**, just as the Letter to the Hebrews has portrayed in detail. It is not the killers of Christ who are offering a sacrifice—it would be a perversion to think that. Christ gives glory to God by sacrificing himself and thus bringing human existence within God's own being. H. Gese has interpreted the meaning of Romans 3:25 like this:

> He who is crucified represents God on his throne and unites us with him through the sacrifice of the human blood that is his life. God becomes accessible to us and appears to us in him who is crucified. The reconciliation is effected, not from man's side in a rite of substitutionary shedding of blood or giving of life, but from God's. God sets up the link between us. . . . The curtain in front of the Holy of Holies is torn asunder; God is very close to us; he is present for us in death, in suffering, in dying.[8]

Yet the question then arises: How could it ever occur to anyone to interpret the Cross of Jesus in such a way as to see

---

[7] See Ex 25:8, 40; 26:30; 27:8; see also Ex 39:43; 40:23, 29; further, Heb 8:5. See Irenaeus, *Adversus haer.* IV, 14, 3 (SC 100, p. 548; Fontes Christiani 8/4, pp. 109–11).

[8] Gese, *Zur biblischen Theologie*, p. 105.

it as actually effecting what had been intended by the cults of the world, especially by that of the Old Testament, by what had often been dreadfully distorted in them and had never truly been achieved? What opened up the possibility at all of such a tremendous reworking of this event, of transferring the whole of the Old Testament's theology of worship and the cult to this apparently most profane occurrence? I have already hinted at the answer: Jesus himself had told the disciples about his death and had interpreted it in terms of prophetic categories, which were available to him above all in the Servant Songs of Deutero-Isaiah. Thus the theme of atonement and of substitution, which belongs to the broad sphere of cultic thought, had already been introduced. At the Last Supper, he developed this more profoundly by welding together Sinaitic covenant theology and prophetic theology, which go to shape the sacrament in which he accepts and anticipates his death and, at the same time, makes it capable of becoming present as the holy cult for all ages.[9] Without this kind of essential foundation in the life and activity of Jesus himself, the new understanding of the Cross is unthinkable—no one would have been able, as it were, to overlay the Cross with this understanding at a later stage. Thus the **Cross** also becomes the **synthesis of the Old Testament festivals, the Day of Atonement and the Pascha in one, the point of passage into a New Covenant.**[10]

---

[9] I have described the interrelationship of all this somewhat more fully in my little book *Die Vielfalt der Religionen und der eine Bund* (Hagen, 1998), pp. 47–49; Eng. trans.: *Many Religions—One Covenant: Israel, the Church, and the World* (San Francisco: Ignatius Press, 1999), pp. 57–60.

[10] In his important book *Le Sacerdoce du Christ et ses ministres* [The priesthood of Christ and his ministers] (Paris, 1972), A. Feuillet has shown that John 17 is rooted in the Jewish liturgy of the Day of Atonement; see esp. pp. 39–63. From this point of view, the Gospel of John is close to the Epistle to the Hebrews, which also understands the Cross of Christ entirely on the basis of the liturgy of Yom Kippur. On the other hand, John—like the Synoptic Gospels—links the Cross with the Jewish liturgy and theology of the Pascha. T. Maertens, in

Because this is the state of affairs, we can say that the theology of the Cross is eucharistic theology, and vice versa. Without the Cross, the Eucharist would remain mere ritual; without the Eucharist, the Cross would be merely a horrible profane event.[11] Thus something else becomes clear: **the close connection between life as it is lived and experienced and sacral actions in worship**. From that then develops the third level of eucharistic theology we have to discuss: Just as the Cross of Christ provides the eucharistic liturgy with its reality and content and lifts it above what is merely ritual and symbolic, making it into the real worship for all the world, so the Eucharist must ever and again press out beyond the sphere of mere cult, must become reality over and beyond that sphere, precisely in order that it may wholly become what it is and remain what it is. We shall have to consider a series of Pauline texts in which martyrdom, the Christian life, and finally the special apostolic service of preaching the faith are described in terms of strictly cultic concepts, so that they

---

Heidnisch-jüdische Wurzeln der christlichen Feste [Pagan and Jewish roots of the Christian festivals, trans. from French] (Mainz, 1965), shows on pp. 59–72 that elements from the theology and the liturgy of the Feast of Booths have also found their way into the Christian theology of Easter.

[11] That is why we must inevitably level criticism at any accounts by liturgical specialists of the development of the liturgy that—quite rightly—do make use of preliminary reflections from the history of religions and in which the roots of the Eucharist in the Old Testament and in Judaism are investigated but in which the *Cross*—because it cannot be classed as a liturgical action—is left to one side. Thereby we fail from the start to do justice to the realism proper to the Christian liturgy, to what is new in Christian liturgy, although this is what links it, in a quite unexpected way, with the worship of the other world religions. Would it ever occur to anyone to describe the Jewish Passover liturgy without starting from the fundamental event described in Exodus 12, which the liturgy is meant to make present? This objection unfortunately has to be raised even against the account given by H. B. Meyer—which is in many respects a model one—in *Eucharistie* [Eucharist], Gottesdienst der Kirche: Handbuch der Liturgiewissenschaft [The worship of the Church: A guide to liturgical studies], vol. 4 (Regensburg, 1989), where even in the little section "Sign of Giving His Life" the word "Cross" does not occur (pp. 70f.).

are thus brought into line with the Cross of Christ himself, so that they appear as the continuing realization of what is portrayed in the Eucharist, and thus hold fast, throughout the epoch of the Church, that close connection between sacrament and life which stands at the origin of the Sacrament and is what alone constitutes the Sacrament as such. **Thus the three dimensions, of theology of the Cross, theology of the Eucharist as a sacrament, and also theology of martyrdom and of preaching, belong together inseparably. Only in their interplay and interconnection can we learn to understand what the Eucharist means.**

II. EUCHARISTIC THEOLOGY IN THE FIRST LETTER TO THE CORINTHIANS

With respect to the theology of the Cross, I should be happy to make do with those references we have already made; let us now look at the other two dimensions. Again, we shall have to stay with a selection of passages; for eucharistic theology in the narrower sense—the second dimension—I should like to restrict my attention to the First Letter to the Corinthians, which is of course particularly productive for this theme. There are four passages here that have something more or less detailed and explicit to say about the Sacrament of the Body and Blood of the Lord, and we shall look at them each in turn.

1. 1 Corinthians 5:6: The Christian Pascha

First there is 1 Corinthians 5:6–8:

> Do you not know that a little leaven leavens all the dough? Cleanse out the old leaven that you may be new dough, as you really are unleavened. For Christ, our Paschal Lamb, has

been sacrificed. Let us, therefore, celebrate the festival, not
with the old leaven, the leaven of malice and evil, but with
the unleavened bread of sincerity and truth.

Here are seen the two essential elements of the Old Testament
Pascha: the **lamb that is sacrificed** and the **unleavened
bread**; thus the **christological basis** and the **anthropological
consequence,** the **application in life** of the sacrifice of
Christ, are apparent. If the lamb represents Christ in anticipation, then the bread becomes the symbol of the Christian life.
The absence of leaven becomes a sign of the new start: being
a Christian is portrayed as a continuing celebration on the
basis of the new life. We might talk about an interpretation of
the Old Testament Pascha that is at the same time christological and existential and in which the themes associated
with the Exodus are probably to be heard in the background:
The sacrifice of Christ becomes a breakthrough, a setting out
into a new life, a life whose simplicity and sincerity are represented in the symbol of the unleavened bread. In any case, the
German ecumenical translation unfortunately obscures one
aspect of the whole thing: where it gives "Get rid of the old
leaven", the Greek has "Purify the old leaven away." The old
cultic concept of purity is now becoming a category of everyday life: this does not refer to ritual purifications but to the
breakthrough to a new way of life.

The Eucharist itself is not mentioned in the text, but we
are still aware of it as the constant basis of life for Christians, as
the motive force that shapes their existence. The whole passage makes it impressively clear that the Eucharist is much
more than a liturgy and a rite, yet it also makes clear, on the
other hand, that Christian life is more than just moral striving—that at a profound level it draws life from him who, for
our sake, became a lamb and sacrificed himself.

2. 1 Corinthians 6:12–19: Uniting Oneself to the Lord

The second text, 1 Corinthians 6:12–19, is of some importance for our question, and I would like just to concentrate on
verses 15–17:

> Do you not know that your bodies are members of Christ?
> Shall I therefore take the members of Christ and make them
> members of a prostitute? Never! Do you not know that he
> who joins himself to a prostitute becomes one body with
> her? For, as it is written, "The two shall become one." But he
> who is united to the Lord becomes one spirit with him.

Here, the most profound content of Christian eucharistic
piety is formulated as a standard of conduct, and at the
same time the heart of Christian mysticism is presented: this
does not rely on human techniques of self-elevation or self-
emptying, useful though these well may be; it is based on the
mysterion, that is, on the descent and self-giving of God,
received by us in the Sacrament. We should bear in mind here
that "sacrament" is the translation of *mysterion* and that the
word "mysticism" is linguistically connected to this. According to this text, receiving the Eucharist means **blending one's
existence**, closely analogical, spiritually, to what happens
when man and wife become one on the physical-mental-
spiritual plane. The dream of blending divinity with humanity, of breaking out of the limitations of a creature—this
dream, which persists through all the history of mankind and
in hidden ways, in profane versions, is dreamed anew even
within the atheistic ideologies of our time, just as it is in the
drunken excesses of a world without God—this dream is here
fulfilled. Man's promethean attempts to break out of his
limitations himself, to build with his own capacities the
tower by which he may mount up to divinity, always necessarily end in collapse and disappointment—indeed, in despair.

This blending, this union, has become possible because God came down in Christ, took upon himself the limitations of human existence, suffering them to the end, and in the infinite love of the Crucified One opened up the door to infinity. The real end of creation, its underlying purpose—and conversely that of human existence as willed by the Creator—is this very union, "that God may be all in all". The eros-love of the created being is taken up into the agape-love of the Creator and, thus, into that fulfilling and holy embrace of which Augustine speaks. The Letter to the Ephesians took up the theme of this passage in 1 Corinthians and developed it; it quotes in full the prophecy connected with Adam, about husband and wife "becoming one", and quotes it as the vision, at the very beginning of mankind, of the mystery of which the eros-love of man and woman constitutes the fundamental analogy in concrete reality, a vision that is, as it were, ever driving mankind onward.[12]

There is something else in this passage from 1 Corinthians that is important for the question we are raising: here we have also come upon the starting point for referring to the **Church as the body of Christ**, upon the inner interlacing of the Eucharist and ecclesiology. This way of talking of the Church as the body of Christ is more than just some term that might be taken from the social pattern of the ancient world to compare a concrete body with a body consisting of many people. This expression takes as its starting point the Sacrament of the Body and Blood of Christ and is therefore more than just an image: it is the expression of the true nature of the Church. **In the Eucharist we receive the Body of the Lord and, thus, become one body with him**; we all receive the same Body and, thus, ourselves become "all one in Christ Jesus" (Gal 3:28). The Eucharist takes us out of ourselves and

---

[12] See H. Schlier, *Der Brief an die Epheser*, 2nd ed. (Düsseldorf, 1958), pp. 252–80; esp. the considerable excursus "Hieros Gamos", pp. 264–76.

into him, so that we can say, with Paul, "It is no longer I who live, but Christ who lives in me" (Gal 2:20). I, yet no longer I—a new and greater self is growing, which is called the one body of the Lord, the Church. **The Church is built up in the Eucharist; indeed, the Church *is* the Eucharist. To receive Communion means becoming the Church, because it means becoming one body with him.** Of course, this "being one body" has to be thought of along the lines of husband and wife being one: one flesh, and yet two; two, and yet one. The difference is not abolished but is swallowed up in a greater unity.

3. 1 Corinthians 10:1–22: One Body with Christ, but without Any Magical Guarantee of Salvation

The same ideas recur in the third eucharistic text in the First Letter to the Corinthians, in 10:1–22, and here they are further developed and added to. In the second part of this passage, the Eucharist is contrasted to sacrificing to idols: anyone who makes sacrifices to idols makes common cause with them, gives himself up to them, and ultimately belongs in their sphere and is under their power. There are of course no gods as such, but there are forces that we make into gods this way and to which, in doing so, we give power over us, allowing ourselves to be guided and shaped by these forces. Just as idolatry draws us into the sphere of power of these false idols and shapes us in their image, something analogous to this—and yet quite different—happens in connection with the sacrifice of Christ: "The bread which we break, is it not a participation in the body of Christ? Because there is one bread, we who are many are one body, for we all partake of the one bread" (10:16–17).

Once more, the religious attitude toward Communion and

that toward the Church blend into one another: **the one bread makes us into one body; the Church is simply that unity created by eucharistic Communion, the unity of the many in and through the one Christ.**

This section of Paul's letter, which shows the hope and the magnitude of the Christian life, is preceded by a little catechism, which emphasizes the **risks run by the person in Christ.** We can deal with this briefly, because the essential point of this passage can be seen as part of the interpretation of the fourth passage about the Eucharist in this letter. Paul compares the Christians with the generation of Israel wandering in the wilderness and says about these latter that they all enjoyed the same spiritual food and drank the same spiritual drink, which came from the spiritual Rock that was following them. "And the Rock was Christ" (10:4). Nevertheless (Paul continues), with most of them God was not pleased, and in fact they came to grief in the wilderness. Paul applies this to Christians: If they, like the generation of Israel in the wilderness, tempt God or murmur against him, then they run the same risk. Three things are important here. First, Paul talks about the universal presence of Christ: he, too, was wandering in the wilderness, along with Israel, and in mysterious fashion he was feeding them and giving them to drink with the Holy Spirit; he gave himself to them sacramentally, that is, in a secret fashion, through external food and drink. The second important point is that the life of the Christian, and that of the Church, is interpreted as a wandering. The theology of the wandering people of God, who have "no lasting city" here but are simply on their way to the Promised Land, to their inheritance, has here one of its basic starting points. The Eucharist is nourishment for pilgrims; Christ is the spiritual Rock, who is wandering along with us. And finally a third point follows: The Eucharist does not grant us any quasi-magical assurance of salvation. It always demands and involves our freedom. And therefore the risk of losing our salvation always remains; our gaze remains fixed on the judgment to come.

4. 1 Corinthians 11:17–33: The Institution of the Eucharist and the Right Way to Celebrate It

And that brings us to the final and most important passage about the Eucharist in the First Letter to the Corinthians, which also includes Paul's version of the institution narrative: 11:17–33. First of all, the **connection between the Eucharist and the congregation** is important here, and we may recall that the word *Ecclesia*, "Church", comes from the Old Testament, where it is the classic expression for the assembly of the People of God, the prototype and pattern for which was the assembly at Sinai, the people congregating at the feet of the God who spoke, whose word called people together and united them. Yet the assembly at Sinai goes beyond the word: in the covenant, it unites God and man in a kind of community of blood, as blood relations, symbolically represented there, which is the heart of the "covenant". Because the Eucharist is the New Covenant, it is the renewal of the assembly at Sinai, and that is why, on the basis of the word and the Body and the Blood of Christ, it brings into being the People of God.

But let us take things in order. The Eucharist gathers people together; it creates for human beings a blood relationship, a sharing of blood, with Jesus Christ and, thus, with God, and of people with one another. Yet in order for this, the coming together on the highest level, to come about, there must first be a simpler level of getting together, so to speak, and people have to step outside their own private worlds and meet together. People's coming together in response to the

Lord's call is the necessary condition for the Lord's being able to make them into an assembly in a new way. Respecting all this, the Apostle's gaze is directed in the first place at the local congregation of Corinth, who lack any true sense of coming together, in that when they meet the various groups still remain apart. But the horizon of this perspective lies far beyond the particular place and includes the Church as a whole: **All eucharistic assemblies taken together are still just *one* assembly, because the body of Christ is just *one*, and hence the People of God can only be *one*.** Thus, an exhortation directed to one local congregation is relevant to all congregations in the Church as a whole: they must celebrate the Eucharist in such a way that they all come together, on the basis of Christ and through him. Anyone who does not celebrate the Eucharist with everyone is merely creating a caricature of it. **The Eucharist is celebrated with the one Christ, and thus with the whole Church, or it is not being celebrated at all.** Anyone who is only looking for his own group or clique in the Eucharist, who is not, in the Eucharist—and through it—plunging himself into the whole Church, moving beyond his own realm, is doing exactly what is being criticized in the Corinthians' behavior. He is, so to say, sitting down with his back to the others and is thus annihilating the Eucharist for himself and spoiling it for the others. He is then just holding his own meal and is despising the Churches of God (1 Cor 11:21f.). If the eucharistic assembly first brings us out of the world and into the "upper room", into the inner chamber of faith (as we have seen), this very upper room is yet the place of meeting, a universal meeting of everyone who believes in Christ, beyond all boundaries and divisions; and it thus becomes the point from which a universal love is bound to shine forth, overcoming all boundaries and divisions: if others are going hungry, we cannot live in opulence. On the one hand, the Eucharist is a turning inward and upward; yet only from the depths within, and from the heights of what is truly above, can come the power that overcomes boundaries and divisions and changes the world.

We shall have to come back to that point. Let us first take another look at the implications of the congregational assembly. Coming together in the fellowship of Christian worship does not yet, in Paul's writings, presume the existence of any sacred place in an external sense; in the situation in which the Christians found themselves as the Church came into being, that would have been impossible. Yet it nonetheless involves making a distinction between the sacred and the profane. The Eucharist and the profane meal are sharply separated. "Do you not have houses to eat and drink in?" (v. 22). "If anyone is hungry, let him eat at home—lest you come together to be condemned" (v. 34). **In the Eucharist, God's holiness enters in among us.** Thus it creates a sacred sphere of itself and demands of us reverence before the Lord's mystery. At the beginning of the second century, in the *Didachē*, the sharing out of the sacred gifts is preceded by the cry: "Let anyone who is holy draw near! Let anyone who is not holy do penance" (10:6).[13] Taking as its starting point Jesus' command to be reconciled before bringing a gift to the altar [Mt 5:23–24], the text expresses it thus:

> On the Lord's Day come together [συναχθέντες], break bread, and hold Eucharist, after confessing your transgressions, that *your offering may be pure*; but let none who has a quarrel with his fellow join in your meeting until he be reconciled, *that your sacrifice be not defiled*. For this is that which was spoken by the Lord, "*in every place and time offer me a pure sacrifice, for I*

---

[13] *Didache-Zwölf-Apostel-Lehre*, Fontes Christiani, vol. 1 (Freiburg im Breisgau; New York, 1991), pp. 124–27; Eng. trans.: *The Didache, or Teaching of the Twelve Apostles*, Apostolic Fathers, vol. 1, Loeb Classical Library (1912; Cambridge, Mass., and London, 1977), pp. 303–33.

am a great king," says the Lord, *"and my name is wonderful among the heathen."* (14:1–3)[14]

These directions for worship breathe the spirit of Paul himself. **Coming together for worship means being reconciled with men and with God.**

The consciousness that this is a holy place, because the Lord is coming in among us, should come over us ever anew—that consciousness by which Jacob was so shaken when he awoke from his vision, which had shown him that from the stone on which he had been sleeping, a ladder was set up on which the angels of God were passing up and down: "And he was afraid, and said, 'How **awesome** is this place! This is none other than the house of God, and this is the gate of heaven'" (Gen 28:17). Awe is a fundamental condition for celebrating the Eucharist correctly, and the very fact that God becomes so small, so humble, puts himself at our mercy, and puts himself into our hands should magnify our awe and ought not to tempt us to thoughtlessness and vainglory. If we recognize that God is there and we behave accordingly, then other people will be able to see this in us, as did the ambassadors of the Prince of Kiev, who experienced heaven in the midst of the earth.

The actual account of the Lord's Supper is introduced by Paul with almost exactly the same words as he uses to present the message of the Resurrection (15:1ff.): "For I received from the Lord what I also delivered to you." The structure and process of receiving, handing over, and passing on are very strictly formulated in this area at the heart of Paul's faith. Where the teaching about the Eucharist is concerned, and the message about the Resurrection, he sets himself most decidedly in **obedience to the tradition**, which is binding to the very last word, because in this tradition what is most holy, and

---

[14] Ibid., pp. 132–35; Eng. trans., pp. 330–31 (Greek-Eng.).

thus most fundamental, comes down to us. Paul, that impetuous creative spirit who opened up new horizons for Christianity, starting from his meeting with the Risen One and from his experience of faith and service, is nonetheless, in the central area of Christian faith, the faithful steward who does not "peddle" God's word (2 Cor 2:17) but hands it on as the precious gift of God, which is beyond **our arbitrary will** and thereby enriches us all. The Eucharist unites us with the Lord and does it in fact by limiting us, binding us to him. Only thus are we freed from ourselves. If nowadays people say to us that the gifts of the Mediterranean world were wheaten bread and wine, and in other spheres of culture we have to use as materials for the sacrament whatever is characteristic for that given culture, those speculations are therefore wrong and in profound opposition to the biblical message. For the Incarnation, which is claimed as a basis for this, is not just some general philosophical principle, in accordance with which we should always have to embody what is spiritual and express it in a way corresponding to the situation at the time. The Incarnation is not a philosophical idea but a historical event, which in its very uniqueness and truth is the point at which God breaks into history and the place at which we come into contact with him. If we deal with it, as is appropriate on the basis of the Bible, not as a principle but as an event, then our conclusion is necessarily the opposite one: God has associated himself with a quite specific point in history, with all its limitations, and wishes us to share in his humility. Allowing oneself to be associated with the Incarnation means accepting this self-limitation of God: these very gifts, which for other spheres of culture—including German culture—are strange and foreign, become for us the sign of his unparalleled and unique action, of his unique historical figure. They are the symbols of God's coming to us, he who is a stranger to us and who makes us his neighbors through his gifts. The response to

God's descent can only be one of humble obedience, an obedience that in receiving the tradition and remaining faithful to it is granted as a gift the certainty of his close presence.

I have no wish to embark upon an exegesis of the institution narrative at this point; that would go beyond the limits of this lecture. We have already seen how the words of institution are a theology of the Cross and a theology of the Resurrection—they reach right down into the heart of the historical event, and in the inwardness of Jesus that transcends time they rise up so that this essential core of the event now reaches into every age: this inner core now becomes the point at which time opens up to God's eternity. That is why the **"memorial"** constituted by the Eucharist is more than a remembrance of something in the past: it is the act of **entering into that inner core which can no longer pass away**. And that is why the **"preaching"** of Christ's death is more than mere words: it is a **proclamation that bears the truth within it**. In the words of Jesus, as we have seen, all the streams of the Old Testament—law and prophets—flow together into a new unity that could not have been foreseen. Those words that had simply been waiting for their real speaker, such as the song of the Suffering Servant, now become reality. We could even go farther and say that ultimately this is where all the great streams of the history of religions meet together, for the most profound knowledge of the myths had been that of the world's being built up on sacrifice, and in some sense, beneath shadowy forms that were often dark, it was being taught that, in the end, God himself must become a sacrifice so that love might prevail over hatred and lies.[15] With its vision of the cosmic liturgy, in the midst of

---

[15] See in this context the Vedic Purusa myth: the creation arises from the sacrifice of the primeval giant Purusa: the world is based on sacrifice. See J. Gonda, *Die Religionen Indiens*, vol. 1, *Veda und älterer Hinduismus* [The religions of India, vol. 1, The Vedas and ancient Hinduism] (Stuttgart, 1960), p. 187, etc.

which stands the Lamb who was sacrificed, the Apocalypse has presented the essential contents of the eucharistic sacrament in an impressive form that sets a standard for every local liturgy. From the point of view of the Apocalypse, the essential matter of all eucharistic liturgy is its participation in the heavenly liturgy; it is from thence that it necessarily derives its unity, its catholicity, and its universality.[16]

Paul returns once more to the theme of Christian worship not being profane, being sacred, after the institution narrative, when he emphatically demands that each of the communicants should examine himself: "Any one who eats and drinks without discerning the body eats and drinks judgment upon himself" (v. 29). Anyone who wants Christianity to be just a joyful message in which there can be no threat of the judgment is distorting it. Faith does not reinforce the pride of a sleeping conscience, the vainglory of people who make their own wishes the norm for their life, and who thus refashion grace so as to devalue both God and man, because God can then in any case only approve, and is only allowed to approve, everything. Yet any one of us who is suffering and struggling can be certain that "God is greater than our hearts" (1 Jn 3:20) and that whatever my failures, I may be full of confident trust, because Christ suffered for me, too, and has already paid the price for me.

III. MARTYRDOM, CHRISTIAN LIFE, AND APOSTOLIC SERVICE AS WAYS OF LIVING OUT THE EUCHARIST

Following this attempt to look at the broad outlines of eucharistic theology in the New Testament at a genuinely

---

[16] See J. Ratzinger, *Ein neues Lied für den Herrn: Christusglaube und Liturgie in der Gegenwart* (Freiburg, 1995), pp. 165ff.; Eng. trans.: *A New Song for the Lord: Faith in Christ and Liturgy Today* (New York, 1997), pp. 174–76.

sacramental level, as we find it in the First Letter to the Corinthians, we will have at least to look briefly at the third level, which I should like to call "existential", before we then try to draw some conclusions about the theme of Eucharist and mission. I should like to present for your consideration three texts: Philippians 2:17, to which 2 Timothy 4:6 again makes brief reference; Romans 12:1; and Romans 15:16.

1. Martyrdom as a Way in Which the Christian Can Become a Eucharist

In the Letter to the Philippians, Paul, who is sitting in prison awaiting trial, talks about the possibility of becoming a martyr, and he does so, surprisingly, in liturgical terminology: "Even if I am to be poured as a libation upon the sacrificial offering of your faith, I am glad. . . ." The witness of the Apostle's death is **liturgical in character**; it is a matter of his life being spilled out as a sacrificial gift, of his letting himself be spilled out for men.[17] What happens in this is a **becoming one with the self-giving of Jesus Christ, with his great act of love, which is as such the true worship of God**. The Apostle's martyrdom shares in the mystery of the Cross of Christ and in its theological status. It is worship being lived out in life, which is recognized as such by faith, and thus it is serving faith. Because this is true liturgy, it achieves the end toward which all liturgy is directed: joy—that joy which can arise only from the encounter between man and God, from the removal of the barriers and limitations of earthly existence.

What Paul briefly hints at here in a single short sentence has been fully thought out in the account of the **martyrdom of Saint Polycarp**. The entire martyrdom is depicted as lit-

---

[17] See P. Bonnard, "Mourir et vivre avec Jésus-Christ selon Saint Paul", *Rev. d'histoire et de philosophie religieuse* 36 (1956): 101–12.

urgy—indeed, as the process of the martyr's becoming a Eucharist, as he enters into full fellowship with the Pascha of Jesus Christ and thus becomes a Eucharist with him. First we are told how the great bishop is fettered and his hands are tied behind his back. Thus he appeared "as a noble *ram (lamb!)* out of a great flock, for an oblation, *a whole burnt offering made ready and acceptable to God*". The martyr, who has meanwhile been brought to the ready-laid fire and bound there, now utters a kind of eucharistic prayer: he gives thanks for the knowledge of God that has been imparted to him through his beloved Son Jesus Christ. He praises God that he has been found worthy to come to share in the cup of Jesus Christ in the prospect of resurrection. Finally, using words from the Book of Daniel that were probably included in the Christian liturgy at an early stage, he asks "may I, today, be received . . . before thee as *a rich and acceptable sacrifice*." This passage ends with a great doxology, just like Eucharistic Prayers in the liturgy. After Polycarp has said "Amen", the servants set fire to the woodpile, and now we are told of a triple miracle in which the liturgical character of the event is manifested in all its diversity. First, the fire swells out in the shape of a sail, which enfolds the saint all around. The blazing pile of wood appears like a ship with billowing sails, carrying the martyr beyond the bounds of earth and into the hands of God. But his burned-up body, so it is said, looked, not like burned flesh, but like *baked bread*. And then finally there is no smell of burned flesh arising, but those who were present became aware of a sweet odor "like that of incense or of costly spices". The *sweet smell*, in the Old Testament just as in the New, is an essential element in the theology of sacrifice. In the writings of Paul it is an expression for a life that has been made pure, giving forth, no longer the stench of lies and corruption or death's smell of decay, but the refreshing air of life and love, the atmosphere appropriate for God and one that heals people. Thus, the image of the sweet odor goes along with that of being changed into bread: the martyr has become like Christ; his life has become a gift. From him comes, not that poison of the power of death which undermines living things, but the dynamic force of life; he builds life up, just as good bread helps us live. The self-giving into the body of Christ has overcome the power of death: the martyr lives, and gives life, above all through his death, and thus he has himself entered into the eucharistic mystery. Martyrdom is the source of faith.[18]

This theology of martyrdom is found in its most popularized version in the story of Saint Lawrence being roasted on the grill, which was seen at a very early stage as an image of Christian life as such: the troubles of life may turn into that purifying fire which gradually remolds us so that our life becomes a gift for God and for other people. In our own time, the martyrdom of Saint Maximilian Kolbe is perhaps the most impressive demonstration of all this. He dies for someone else; he dies amid songs of praise; he is burned, and his ashes are scattered—his whole life is destroyed, and in that very way the radical self-giving, the giving away of himself, is consummated: whoever would save his life will lose it; and whoever loses his life will save it.

2. Worship Consistent with the Logos—Christian Living as a Eucharist

Let us end by listening to those two marvelous passages from the Letter to the Romans that I mentioned earlier. In 12:1 the

---

[18] The text in Greek and German is found in A. Lindemann and H. Paulsen, *Die Apostolischen Väter* (Tübingen, 1992), pp. 258–85; Greek and English text in *The Apostolic Fathers*, vol. 2, Loeb Classical Library (1913; Cambridge, Mass., and London, 1976), pp. 307–45. See also G. Buschmann, *Das Martyrium des Polykarp*, Kommentar zu den Apostolischen Vätern [Commentary on the Apostolic Fathers], vol. 6 (Göttingen, 1998).

Apostle exhorts the Romans to "present" their bodies—that is, themselves—"as a living sacrifice, holy and acceptable to God, which is your spiritual worship [is for you the true and appropriate worship / the rational worship]". Let us first look a little more closely at that last phrase, which is really impossible to translate. In the Greek it is λογικὴ λατρεία—worship characterized by logos. That is an expression that had developed in the sphere of the encounter of Jewish with Greek religion at around the time of Christ.[19] In contrast to the worship involving external sacrifices such as animals and things—and building on perceptions from Israel's time in exile—it is now being said that the true sacrifice to God is that of man's inmost being, which is itself transformed into worship. The word is the sacrifice; the sacrifice must be wordlike (*logikon*), but the word meant here is of course the "word" in which the whole of man's spirit sums itself up and expresses itself.

---

[19] The classic article by O. Casel, "Die λογικὴ λατρεία der antiken Mystik in der christlichen Umdeutung" [The Christian reinterpretation of the λογικὴ λατρεία of ancient mysticism], in *Jahrbuch für Liturgiewissenschaft* 4 (1924): 37–47, takes into account—as is consistent with the basic orientation of Casel's thought, with its somewhat negative stance toward the Old Testament—merely the Hellenistic Greek roots of this concept. It is certainly no accident that the idea and the term make their first appearance in the realm in which Judaism, Hellenism, and Christianity are in contact, such as in Philo, in the Odes of Solomon, and in the Jewish prayers of the seventh and eighth books of the Apostolic Constitutions. The idea, as such, had in fact fully developed within the Old Testament; we need only think of Hosea 14:3; Psalm 50 (49):8–14, "I will accept no bull from your house. . . . If I were hungry, I would not tell you. . . . Do I eat the flesh of bulls, or drink the blood of goats? Offer to God a sacrifice of thanksgiving"; Psalm 51 (50):16–17, "Were I to give a burnt offering, you would not be pleased. The sacrifice acceptable to God is a broken spirit"; Psalm 68 (67):31f.; Psalm 119 (118):108, "Accept my offerings of praise [lit., the offerings of my mouth], O LORD." We are justified in saying that the concept of the sacrifice of words derives from the Old Testament and that the door had thus been opened for the Christian concept of sacrifice and also for new developments arising from the encounter with Greek thought.

In Greek mysticism of the first centuries A.D., that was then developed into the notion that **the divine logos itself is praying within man** and is thus drawing man into its own participation in the divine being.[20] We find the same word, too, in the Roman Canon, where we ask, immediately before the Consecration, that our sacrifice may be made *rationabilis*. It is not enough—indeed, it is quite wrong—to translate this as saying that it should become rational. We are asking rather that it may become a logos-sacrifice. In this sense we are asking for the gifts to be transformed—and then, again, not just for that; rather, this petition is going in the same direction as suggested by the Letter to the Romans: We ask that the Logos, Christ, who *is* the true sacrifice, may himself draw us into his act of sacrifice, may "logify" us, make us "more consistent with the word", "more truly rational", so that his sacrifice may become ours and may be accepted by God as ours, may be able to be accounted as ours. We pray that his presence might pick us up, so that we become "one body and one spirit" with him.[21] We ask that his sacrifice might become present not just in an exterior sense, standing over against us and appearing, so to speak, like a material sacrifice, that we might then gaze upon and regard as men once did the physical sacrifices of old. We would not in that case have entered into the New Covenant at all. We are asking rather that we ourselves might become a Eucharist with Christ and, thus, become acceptable and pleasing to God. What Paul is saying in the First Letter to the Corinthians about cleaving to the Lord, that we might become one with him in a single spiritual life—that is exactly what is meant.

I am persuaded that the Roman Canon has in its petition hit upon the real intention of Paul in his exhortation in

---

[20] See the relevant passages and their interpretation in Schlier, *Römerbrief*, pp. 356ff.

[21] See J. A. Jungmann, *Missarum Sollemnia,* vol. 2 (Freiburg, 1952), pp. 236f.

Romans 12. The application of liturgical language to Christian life is not a moralizing allegory; it does not bypass the Cross and the Eucharist; on the contrary, it is correctly understood only when it is read in the context of the Eucharist and of the theology of the Cross. The corrections that are being made here to the ideas of Hellenistic mysticism are important ones, and they help us to see the true nature of Christian mysticism. The mysticism of identity, in which the Logos and the inner dimension of man blend together, is transcended by a christological mysticism: **the Logos, who is the Son, makes us sons in the sacramental fellowship in which we are living**. And if we become sacrifices, if we ourselves become conformed to the Logos, then this is not a process confined to the spirit, which leaves the body behind it as something distanced from God. The Logos himself has become a body and gives himself to us in his Body. That is why we are being urged **to present our bodies as a form of worship consistent with the Logos, that is to say, to be drawn into the fellowship of love with God in our entire bodily existence, in bodily fellowship with Christ.**[22]

Paul tells us in the following verses what that looks like: it signifies our "metamorphosis", our being reshaped in a way that takes us beyond this world's scheme of things, beyond sharing in what "people" think and say and do, and into the

---

[22] See Schlier, *Römerbrief*, pp. 355f. The interpretation of Romans 12:1–2 in the commentary by E. Peterson, which has now finally been edited from his posthumous papers by B. Nichtweiß and F. Hahn: *Der Brief an die Römer*, in *Schriften*, vol. 6 (Würzburg, 1997), pp. 331f., is most profound. Peterson shows with great emphasis the connection with Christ's death on the Cross, understood as a cultic action, as likewise the cultic significance of these verses as a whole. He also underlines the silent polemic directed against animal sacrifice: "Anyone who sacrifices his body is making sacrifice more in conformity with the λογος than anyone who presents animals to God" (p. 332). On that basis, finally, he emphasizes the Logos nature of Christian worship: "The Logos nature of Christian faith, in contrast to all irrational beliefs and attitudes, can be recognized in it."

will of God—thus we enter into what is good and pleasing to God and perfect. The transformation of the gifts, which is to be extended to us—thus the Roman Canon, following the Letter to the Romans—has to become, for us ourselves, a process of remolding: bringing us out of our restricted self-will, out into union with the will of God. Self-will, however, is in reality a subordination to the schemes and systems of a given time, and, despite appearances, it is slavery; the will of God is truth, and entering into it is thus breaking out into freedom. It seems to me no accident that the following verses, 4 and 5, talk about the way we should become **all of us one body** in Christ. **The bodies—that is, the bodily persons— that become a Eucharist no longer stand alongside each other but become one with and one in the one Body and in the one living Christ.** Thus, the ecclesiological and eucharistic background of the whole train of thought clearly comes to light here.

3. Mission as Service in the Cosmic Liturgy

Still more important for our question about Eucharist and mission is the final passage we have to look at, Romans 15:16. Paul is here justifying his boldness in writing a letter to the Romans, whose congregation he neither founded nor knows at all well. The reason for the Letter to the Romans that Paul offers here is quite profound: his understanding of the office of apostle, of the task he has been charged with, is manifested here in a depth that, despite all the great declarations about the apostolate, appears nowhere else with such clarity. Paul says that he has written the letter "to be a minister of Jesus Christ to the Gentiles in the priestly service of the gospel of God, so that the offering of the Gentiles may be acceptable, sanctified by the Holy Spirit" (15:16). The Letter to the

Romans, this word that has been written that it may then be proclaimed, is an apostolic action; more, it is a liturgical—even a cultic—event. This it is because it helps the world of the pagans to change so as to be a renewal of mankind and, as such, a cosmic liturgy in which mankind shall become adoration, become the radiance of the glory of God. If the Apostle is handing on the gospel by means of this letter, this is not a matter of religious or philosophical propaganda, nor is it a social mission or even a personal and charismatic enterprise, but (as Heinrich Schlier puts it) "the accomplishing of a mandate authorized by God, legitimized by him, and delegated by him to the Apostle". This is a priestly sacrificial action, an eschatological service of ministry: the fulfillment and the perfecting of the Old Testament sacrificial services. In this verse Paul presents himself—again, it is Schlier who says it—"as sacrificial priest of the eschatological cosmos".[23]

If, in the Letter to the Philippians, we found martyrdom being presented as a liturgical event, associated with the theology of the Cross and with eucharistic theology; if, in Romans 12, the same was being said to us about the Christian life as such; now it is the specifically apostolic service of preaching the faith that appears as a priestly activity, as actually performing the new liturgy, open to all the world and likewise worldwide, which has been founded by Christ. The connection with the Pascha of Jesus Christ and with his presence in the Church through the Eucharist is not immediately evident here. And yet we cannot disregard it. Here, too, the "cleaving

---

[23] Schlier, *Römerbrief*, pp. 430f. Peterson, *Brief an die Römer*, p. 367, points out the connection between this passage and Isaiah 66:20: "And they shall bring all your brethren from all the nations as an offering [*minchah*] to the LORD." Peterson comments, "Paul feels himself to be the one who is carrying out this promise that had been envisaged as being part of the end." There is also a reference to Isaiah 66:20 in J. A. Fitzmyer, *Romans*, Anchor Bible (Doubleday, 1993), p. 712. Fitzmyer likewise emphasizes the connection with Philippians 2:17 and Romans 12:1.

to the Lord" that unites us with him in a life of body and soul
is ultimately indispensable as a spiritual foundation. For without this concrete christological cohesion, the whole thing
would just simply decline into a mere fellowship in thought,
will, and activity—that is, it would be reduced to what relates
to morality and rational considerations. That, however, is
exactly what Paul is trying to counter by talking about liturgy,
which he uses to show that mission is more than that: that it
has a sacramental basis, that it involves being united in a
concrete sense with the Body of Christ, which was sacrificed
and is living eternally in the Resurrection. So the ideas that
came to us in considering Romans 12 are after all being taken
up and further developed. The Eucharist, if it continued to
exist over against us, would be relegated to the status of a
thing, and the true Christian plane of existence would not be
attained at all. Conversely, a Christian life that did not involve
being drawn into the Pascha of the Lord, that was not itself
becoming a Eucharist, would remain locked in the moralism
of our activity and would thus again fail to live up to the new
liturgy that has been founded by the Cross. Thus, the missionary work of the Apostle does not exist alongside the
liturgy; rather, both constitute a living whole with several
dimensions.

CONCLUDING REFLECTIONS:
THE EUCHARIST AS THE SOURCE OF MISSION

What does that ultimately mean for the connection between
the Eucharist and mission? In what sense can we say that the
Eucharist is the source of mission? We cannot, as we have
seen, talk as if the Eucharist were some kind of publicity
project through which we try to win over people for Christianity. If we do so, then we are damaging both the Eucharist

and mission. We might rather understand the Eucharist as being (if the term is correctly understood) the mystical heart of Christianity, in which God mysteriously comes forth, time and again, from within himself and draws us into his embrace. The Eucharist is the fulfillment of the promise made on the first day of Jesus' great week of climax: "I, when I am lifted up from the earth, will draw all men to myself" (Jn 12:32). In order for mission to be more than propaganda for certain ideas or trying to win people over for a given community—in order for it to come from God and lead to God, it must spring from a more profound source than that which gives rise to resource planning and the operational strategies that are shaped in that way. It must spring from a source both deeper and higher than advertising and persuasion. "Christianity is not the result of persuading people; rather, it is something truly great", as Ignatius of Antioch so beautifully puts it in one place (*Epistle to the Romans* 3:3).

The sense in which Thérèse of Lisieux is patroness of missions may help us to understand in what way that is meant. Thérèse never set foot in a missionary territory and was never able to practice any missionary activity directly. Yet she did grasp that the Church has a heart, and she grasped that love is this heart. She understood that the apostles can no longer preach and the martyrs no longer shed their blood if this heart is no longer burning. She grasped that love is all, that it reaches beyond times and places. And she understood that she herself, the little nun hidden behind the grille of a Carmel in a provincial town in France, could be present everywhere, because as a loving person she was there with Christ in the heart of the Church.[24] Is not the exhaustion of the missionary

---

[24] Thérèse of Lisieux, "Manuscrit B (Lettre à soeur Marie du Sacré-Coeur)", in *Oeuvres complètes* (Cerf and Desclée, 1992), pp. 225f. A profound interpretation of this text is to be found in U. Wickert, *Leben aus Liebe: Thérèse von Lisieux* [Living on love: Thérèse of Lisieux] (Vallendar-Schönstatt, 1997), pp. 15–40.

impulse in the last thirty years the result of our thinking only of external activities while having almost forgotten that all this activity must constantly be nourished from a **deeper** center? This center, which Thérèse calls simply **"heart"** and **"love"**, is the **Eucharist**. For the Eucharist is not only the enduring presence of the divine and human love of Jesus Christ, which is always the source and origin of the Church and without which she would founder, would be overcome by the gates of hell. As the presence of the divine and human love of Christ, it is also always the channel open from the man Jesus to the people who are his "members", themselves becoming a Eucharist and thereby themselves a "heart" and a "love" for the Church. As Thérèse says, if this heart is not beating, then the apostles can no longer preach, the sisters can no longer console and heal, the laymen no longer lead the world toward the Kingdom of God. The heart must remain the heart, that through the heart the other organs may serve aright. It is at that point, when the Eucharist is being celebrated aright "in the upper room", in the inner sphere of reverent faith, and without any aim or purpose beyond that of pleasing God, that faith springs forth from it: that faith which is the dynamic origin of mission, in which the world becomes a living sacrificial gift, a holy city in which there is no longer any temple, because God the ruler of all is himself her temple, as is the Lamb. "And the city has no need of sun or moon to shine upon it, for the glory of God is its light, and its lamp is the Lamb" (Rev 21:22f.).

The Ecclesiology of the Constitution
Lumen Gentium

In the period when people were preparing for the Second
Vatican Council, and also during the Council itself, Cardinal
Frings often recounted to me a little incident that had obviously deeply moved him. Pope John XXIII had not for his
own part announced any set theme for the Council but had
just invited the bishops of the world to explain their own
priorities, so that the theme of the Council's task should be
knit together from the living experiences of the worldwide
Church. Accordingly, in the German Bishops' Conference
they likewise took counsel as to what tasks they might suggest
for the bishops when they met. Not just in Germany, but to
a considerable extent in the Catholic Church as a whole,
people were of the opinion that the theme must be the
Church: the First Vatican Council, which broke up prema-
turely on account of the Franco-Prussian War, had not been
able to complete its synthesis of ecclesiological teaching but
had simply left a fragment of ecclesiology. The most pressing
task of the coming Second Vatican Council seemed to be that
of picking up the threads from that time and thus of looking
for a single overall view of the Church.

This also seemed obvious in view of the spiritual climate
of the time: the end of the First World War had brought a
profound change in theology. The wholly individualistic
tone of liberal theology had given way, as if of its own
accord, to a newly awakened sense of the Church. It was not

only Romano Guardini who was talking about the awakening of the Church in people's souls; the evangelical Bishop Otto Dibelius coined the expression "the century of the Church", and Karl Barth gave his exposition of dogmatic theology, which was based on the Reformed traditions, the programmatic title of *Church Dogmatics*: dogmatics presupposes the Church, he explained; without the Church, there is no dogmatic theology. Among the members of the German Bishops' Conference, there was thus widespread unanimity that the theme would have to be that of the Church. The elderly Bishop of Regensburg, who as the creator of the ten-volume *Lexikon für Theologie und Kirche*, the third edition of which was then making its appearance, was known and respected far beyond the borders of his diocese, asked to speak (so the Archbishop of Cologne told me) and said: "My dear Brothers, at the Council you must above all talk about God. That is what is most important." The bishops were most struck by this; they could not escape the seriousness of what the bishop said. They could not, of course, make up their minds to suggest simply "God" as the theme. But at least in Cardinal Frings' case an inner unease remained, as he continually asked himself how we might live up to this imperative.

This story came to my mind again when I read the text of the farewell lecture given by Johann Baptist Metz on his retirement from his professorial chair at Münster in 1993. Metz says: "The crisis that has come upon European Christianity is no longer primarily—still less entirely—a crisis of the Church. . . . This crisis runs deeper: it by no means derives from the state in which the Churches find themselves: the crisis has become a crisis concerning God." "The slogan is, 'Religion: yes; God: no'—and again, the 'no' here is not meant to be categorical, as it was in the great atheistic systems. There is no longer any great atheistic system. For the atheism of today can once more take the word 'God' on its lips, in a spirit of distraction or of resignation, without really meaning to talk about him." "The Church has likewise her own notion of immunization against crises concerning God. She no longer talks today—as she still did for instance at the First Vatican Council—about God, but only—as for instance at the last Council—about the God who is preached by the Church. The crisis concerning God is ecclesiologically locked out." [1] Words like this, in the mouth of the man who created "political theology", have to make us sit up and listen. They first remind us, quite rightly, that the First Vatican Council was not just an ecclesiological Council but that, first and foremost, it talked about God—and that, not merely as concerning relations between Christians, but as turning outward to the world—about the God who is the God of everyone, who saves everyone and who is accessible to everyone. Did Vatican II perhaps—as Metz seems to be suggesting—take up only half of the heritage of the previous Council? This is a question that a lecture devoted to the ecclesiology of the Council has to ask for itself.

I should like to make clear at once the basic view I shall expound: The Second Vatican Council certainly did intend to subordinate what it said about the Church to what it said about God and to set it in that context; it intended to propound an ecclesiology that was theo-logical in the proper sense. The way in which the Council's teaching has been received, however, has hitherto overlooked this determinative prefix to all the various individual ecclesiological statements; people have pounced upon individual phrases and slogans and have thus fallen short of the great overall perspectives of the

---

[1] J. B. Metz, "Gotteskrise: Versuche zur 'geistigen Situation der Zeit'" [The Crisis of God: Essays on the "spiritual situation in our time"], in *Diagnosen zur Zeit* [Diagnoses of the age] (Düsseldorf, 1994), pp. 76–92; quotations from pp. 77f.

Council Fathers. Something of the sort can in any case be seen to have happened with the first text issued by Vatican II—with regard to the Constitution on the Sacred Liturgy. There were practical reasons for the fact that this was the first. Yet looking back, we have to say that this made good sense in terms of the structure of the Council as a whole: worship, adoration, comes first. And thus God does. This beginning is in accordance with the rule of Saint Benedict (XLIII): "Operi Dei nihil praeponatur." The Constitution on the Church, which then followed as the Council's second text, should be seen as being inwardly bracketed together with it. The Church derives from adoration, from the task of glorifying God. Ecclesiology, of its nature, has to do with liturgy. And so it is logical, too, that the third Constitution talks about the Word of God, which calls the Church together and is at all times renewing her. The fourth Constitution shows how the glory of God presents itself in an ethos, how the light we have received from God is carried out into the world, how only thus can God be fully glorified. In the period following the Council, of course, the Constitution on the Liturgy was understood, no longer on the basis of this fundamental primacy of adoration, but quite simply as a recipe book concerned with what we can do with the liturgy. In the meantime many liturgical experts, rushing into considerations about how we can shape the liturgy in a more attractive way, to communicate better, so as to get more and more people actively involved, have apparently quite lost sight of the fact that the liturgy is actually "done" for God and not for ourselves. The more we do it for ourselves, however, the less it attracts people, because everyone can clearly sense that what is essential is increasingly eluding us.

As far as the ecclesiology of *Lumen gentium* is concerned, there are, first of all, a few slogans that have stuck in our minds: the concept of the People of God; the collegiality of bishops as a revaluation of the office of bishop over against the primacy of the pope; the new importance attributed to local Churches as against the Church as a whole; the opening up in an ecumenical sense of the concept of the Church and being open to the religions of the world; finally, the question of the specific status of the Catholic Church, which finds definitive expression in the formula that says that the one, holy, Catholic, and apostolic Church of which the Creed speaks "subsistit in Ecclesia catholica". I am leaving this famous formula untranslated here for the moment, because—as could be foreseen—it has received the most contradictory interpretations: from the view that the unique theological character of the Catholic Church in unity with the pope is here expressed to the view that this succeeds in setting the Catholic Church on the same level as all the other Christian churches and that she has now abandoned her specific claims.

In a first stage of the reception, the **concept of the People of God**, together with the theme of collegiality, dominated discussion. This was very soon being understood on the basis of the way "people" is used in political language generally; in the realm of liberation theology it was according to the Marxist usage of "people" as opposed to the ruling classes; and in general it was widely understood in the sense of the rule of the people, which was supposedly at last going to be applied to the Church. This in turn gave rise to extensive debates over structures, in which—depending on the situation—"democratization" was interpreted more in the Western sense or more in the sense of the Eastern "people's democracies". Gradually the "verbal fireworks" (N. Lohfink) surrounding the concept of "People of God" burned away, in the first place (and mainly) because each of these power games unmasked the others and had to give way to down-to-earth work in the everyday Church, yet also, on the other hand, because solid theological work made quite manifest, in a way that was beyond contradiction, how such politicizing of a concept that was in itself entirely different was untenable.

As a result of careful exegetical analyses, for instance, the Bochum exegete Werner Berg states:

> Despite the paucity of passages in which the turn of phrase "People of God" is to be found—and to that extent, "People of God" is a fairly rare biblical concept—we can nonetheless hold fast to some elements in common: the phrase "People of God" expresses the "being related to God", the "relationship established by God", the close connection between God and those people referred to as the "People of God", that is to say, in a "vertical direction". This turn of phrase is less suitable for describing the hierarchical structure of this community, above all if the "People of God" is described "as opposed to" the officeholders. . . . Nor, on the basis of the biblical understanding of it, is this turn of phrase appropriate as a cry of protest against those in office: "We are the People of God." [2]

The Paderborn teacher of fundamental theology Josef Meyer zu Schlochtern closes a tour through the dispute about the concept "People of God" by pointing out that Vatican II's Constitution on the Church ends the chapter devoted to this term, by "specifying the trinitarian structure as being the basis for the ultimate definition of the Church." [3] Thus the debate is brought back again to the essential point: **The Church is**

---

[2] W. Berg, "'Volk Gottes'—Ein biblischer Begriff?" ["People of God"—A Biblical concept?], in W. Geerlings and M. Seckler, eds., *Kirche sein: Nachkonziliare Theologie im Dienst der Kirchenreform* [Being the Church: Postconciliar theology at the service of reforming the Church]: *Festschrift für H. J. Pottmeyer* (Herder, 1994), pp. 13–20; quotation, p. 20. It is from Berg's article that I have taken N. Lohfink's expression "verbal fireworks" (p. 19).

[3] J. Meyer zu Schlochtern, "'Das neue Volk Gottes'—Rückfrage nach einer umstrittenen Bestimmung der Kirche" ["The new people of God"—Retrospective investigation of a disputed term for the Church], in J. Ernst and S. Leimgruber, eds., *Surrexit Dominus vere: Die Gegenwart des Auferstandenen in seiner Kirche* [Surrexit Dominus vere: The presence of the Risen One in his Church]: *Festschrift für Erzbischof J. J. Degenhardt* (Paderborn, 1995); quotation, pp. 224f.

not there for her own sake but should be the instrument of God for gathering men to him, so as to prepare for the moment when God shall be "everything to every one" (1 Cor 15:28). The idea of God is the very thing that had been left aside in the "fireworks" surrounding this term, and it had thereby been deprived of its entire meaning. For a Church that is there only for her own sake is superfluous. And people notice that straightaway. The crisis concerning the Church, as it is reflected in the crisis concerning the concept "People of God", is a "crisis about God": it is the result of leaving out what is most essential. What then remains is merely a dispute about power. There is already enough of that elsewhere in the world—we do not need the Church for that.

We can probably say that perhaps since the extraordinary synod of 1985, which was supposed to draw up a kind of balance sheet for the twenty years since the Council, there has been a new attempt to sum up the whole of the Council's ecclesiology in one basic concept, which dominates discussion, under the term **communio-ecclesiology**.[4] I welcomed this new focus for ecclesiology, and within my limits I also tried to do some preparatory work. We have to admit at the outset, of course, that the term "communion" does not occupy a central place in the Council. It can nonetheless, if

---

[4] On the meaning of "communion" and on communio-ecclesiology, I should like to mention, from among the abundant literature, only the following: P. J. Cordes, *Communio: Utopie oder Programm?* [Communion: A utopia or a program?], QD 148 (Herder, 1993); W. Kasper, "Kirche als Communio: Überlegungen zur ekklesiologischen Leitidee des II. Vatikanischen Konzils [The Church as communion: Reflections on the main ecclesiological theme of the Second Vatican Council], in *Theologie und Kirche* [Theology and the Church] (Mainz, 1987), pp. 272–89. On the process of development of the Constitution on the Church within the Council: G. Alberigo, ed., *Storia del Concilio Vaticano II* [History of the Second Vatican Council], vol. 4: *La chiesa come comunione* [The Church as communion] (Bologna [il Mulino], 1999), esp. pp. 19–118 (J. A. Komonchak, "L'ecclesiologia di communione" [The ecclesiology of communion]).

correctly understood, serve as a synthesis for the essential elements of the conciliar ecclesiology. All the essential elements of the Christian concept of "communion" are to be found together in that significant sentence from 1 John 1:3 that we may see as the standard for any correct Christian understanding of "communion": "That which we have seen and heard we proclaim also to you, so that you may have fellowship with us; and our fellowship is with the Father and with his Son Jesus Christ. And we are writing this that our joy may be complete." The starting point of "communion" is here apparent: the encounter with the incarnate Son of God, Jesus Christ, who comes to men in the preaching of the Church. That is how the fellowship of men with one another arises, which in turn is dependent upon fellowship with God the Trinity.

Fellowship with God is mediated by the fellowship of God with man, which is Christ in person; the encounter with Christ brings about fellowship with him and, thus, with the Father in the Holy Spirit; on this basis it unites men with one another. All this is directed toward perfect joy: the Church bears within herself an eschatological impulse. In that saying about perfect joy there is a connection with the farewell discourses of Jesus and, thus, with the Paschal Mystery and with the coming again of the Lord in paschal contemplation, which is directed toward his perfect coming again in the new world: "You will be sorrowful, but your sorrow will turn into joy. . . . I will see you again and your hearts will rejoice. . . . Ask, and you will receive, that your joy may be full" (Jn 16:20, 22, 24). If we compare the last sentence quoted with Luke 11:13—Luke's version of the exhortation to ask—it becomes clear that "joy" and "Holy Spirit" mean the same thing and that behind the saying about "joy" in 1 John 1:3 lies hidden the Holy Spirit, who is not apparently mentioned. The term "communion" thus has, on the basis of this central biblical meaning, a theological and christological character, one associated with the history of salvation and also ecclesiology. Thereby it also carries within it the sacramental dimension, which appears quite explicitly in the writings of Paul: "The cup of blessing which we bless, is it not a participation [communion] in the blood of Christ? The bread which we break, is it not a participation [communion] in the body of Christ? Because there is *one* bread, we who are many are *one* body" (1 Cor 10:16–17). "Communion" ecclesiology is in its inmost nature a **eucharistic ecclesiology**.

It is thus quite close to the eucharistic ecclesiology that Orthodox theologians have so impressively developed in the twentieth century.[5] There ecclesiology becomes quite concrete in type and yet at the same time remains entirely spiritual, transcendent, and eschatological. In the Eucharist, Christ, who is present in bread and wine and is ever anew giving himself in them, builds up the Church as his body, and through his body that rises again he unites us with God the Trinity and with each other. The Eucharist takes place at whatever place is in question and yet is at the same time

---

[5] N. Afanasieff, A. Schmemann, et al., *La Primauté de Pierre dans l'église orthodoxe* [The primacy of Peter in the Orthodox Church] (Neuchâtel, 1960); J. Freitag and P. Plank, "Eucharistische Ekklesiologie", in LThK, 3rd ed., vol. 3, cols. 969–72. While Afanasieff writes about a eucharistic ecclesiology strictly conceived as located in the local Church, as long ago as 1943 L. Hertling opened the door to a "communion" ecclesiology conceived in a wholly Catholic sense with his article first printed in the *Miscellanea Historiae Pontificiae* (Rome, 1943): "Communio und Primat—Kirche und Papsttum in der christlichen Antike" [Communion and primacy—Church and papacy in Christian antiquity]; on the eve of the Council this was then reprinted in *Una Sancta* 17 (1962): pp. 91–125, and became for me a key text. See J. Ratzinger, *Das neue Volk Gottes* (Düsseldorf, 1969), pp. 75–89. It was from this perspective that we—H. de Lubac, H. U. von Balthasar, and the other founders—gave the title *Communio* to the international journal we were finally able to start up in 1972.

universal, because there is only one Christ and only one body of Christ. The Eucharist includes the priestly ministry of *repraesentatio Christi* and, thereby, also the network of service and ministry, the coexistence of unity and multiplicity, which is already suggested in the term "communion". There is thus no doubt we can say that this concept carries in it an ecclesiological synthesis that links talk about the Church with talk about God and with living with God's help and living with God; a synthesis that comprehends all the essential points that the ecclesiology of Vatican II intended to express and correctly relates them to each other.

For all these reasons I was thankful and rejoiced when the 1985 synod moved the concept of "communion" to center stage. Yet the years that followed showed how no term is completely safe from misunderstanding, not even the best and the most profound. In the same measure as "communion" became the current buzzword, its meaning was distorted and rendered superficial. Just as in the case of the term "People of God", one could not help but notice here an increasing emphasis on the horizontal dimension, the omission of the idea of God. "Communion" ecclesiology began to be reduced to the theme of the relationship between the local Church and the Church as a whole, and that in turn, more and more, declined into the question of the assignment of competent authority as between the one and the other. The theme of egalitarianism of course also once more took a large place, and according to that there could only be perfect equality in "communion". With that we came back again to the disciples' quarrel over precedence, which obviously will not be silent in any generation. It is Mark who relates this most impressively. On the way up to Jerusalem, Jesus had been speaking to the disciples, for the second time, about his coming Passion. When they came to Capernaum, he asked them what they had been talking about among themselves on the way. "But they were silent", because they had been talking about who among them was the greatest—a kind of discussion about primacy (Mk 9:33–37). Is it not also the same today? While the Lord moves toward his Passion, while the Church is suffering, and he suffering in her, we are back on our favorite topic, on the question of our privileges. And if he were to enter into our midst and to ask us what we were talking about, then how we should have to blush and be silent!

That does not mean that the argument about the right ordering of things and the assignment of responsibility should not also be carried on in the Church. And no doubt there will always be things that upset the balance and that have to be put right. There may of course be an extravagant and excessive Roman centralization, which then has to be identified as such and corrected. Yet such questions should not divert us from the real task of the Church: primarily, the Church is not there to talk about herself but about God, and it is only in order that this may be done aright that rebukes are also delivered within the Church, in order to give direction and order to talking about God and about the ministry we all share. Ultimately, it is not for nothing that Jesus' saying about how the last shall be first and the first last crops up again in several different places in the gospel tradition—like a mirror that is always appropriate for everyone.

In view of the narrowing down that quite perceptibly affected the concept of "communion" in the years from 1985 onward, the Congregation for the Doctrine of the Faith deemed it appropriate to put together a "Letter to the Bishops of the Catholic Church on Certain Aspects of the Church as Communion", which was published with the date of June 28, 1992. Since it seems nowadays to have become a veritable duty, for theologians who have any self-confidence, to deliver a negative judgment upon documents issued by the Congregation for the Doctrine of the Faith, such a storm of criticism was unleashed upon it that one could scarcely admit there being anything good in it. Probably the most heavily criticized was the sentence that said that the Church as a whole, in her essential mystery, was a reality that ontologically and temporally preceded the individual particular Churches. In the text this was briefly justified by reference to the fact that, in the writings of the Fathers, the one and only Church precedes creation, and it is she who gives birth to the particular Churches.[6] Here the Fathers are continuing a theme of rabbinic theology by which the Torah and Israel had been conceived of as being preexistent: creation was then conceived as a sphere for the exercise of God's will; this will, however, was held to need a people who might live for God's will and make it into the light of the world. Since the Fathers were fully persuaded that Israel and the Church were ultimately identical, they could not regard the Church as something that came into being at a late hour, by chance, but recognized in this gathering of the nations under the will of God the inner goal of creation.

On the basis of Christology the picture can be extended and developed: history is interpreted—again, following the example of the Old Testament—as a love story involving God and man. God finds for himself a bride for the Son, the one bride who is the one Church. On the basis of the saying in Genesis, that man and wife shall "become one flesh" (Gen 2:24), the image of the bride blends in with the idea of the Church as the body of Christ, which is in turn anchored sacramentally in eucharistic piety. The one body of Christ is prepared for him; Christ and the Church will "become one flesh", will be *one* body, and thus God will become "everything to every one". This ontological precedence of the Church as a whole, of the one Church and the one body, of

---

[6] Congregazione per la dottrina della fede, *Communionis notio: Lettera e commenti* (Libreria Editrice Vaticana, 1994), no. 9, p. 28.

the one bride, over the empirical and concrete realizations in the various individual parts of the Church seems to me so obvious that I find it difficult to understand the objections raised against it.[7] They seem to me to be possible at all only if one refuses to see God's great idea, the Church—perhaps through despair at her inadequacy here on earth—if one will no longer and can no longer see it at all; it then appears as the product of a fit of theological enthusiasm, and all that remains is the empirical structure of the Church, her elements side-by-side in all their confusion and contradiction. Yet that means that the Church is ruled out as a theme of theology at all. If you can no longer see the Church except as existing in human organizations, then hopelessness is in fact all there is left. But in that case you can abandon not only the ecclesiology of the Fathers, but also that of the New Testament and of the Old Testament idea of Israel. Within the New Testament, in any case, there is no need to wait for the Deutero-Pauline letters and the Apocalypse in order to meet with the ontological priority of the Church as a whole, over the parts of the Church, as maintained by the Congregation for the Doctrine of the Faith. In the heart of the great Pauline letters, in the Letter to the Galatians, the Apostle talks to us about the heavenly Jerusalem, and indeed not as an eschatological entity, but as one that comes before us: "the Jerusalem

---

[7] In this connection it may be helpful to refer to Rudolf Bultmann, whom, quite certainly, no one would accuse of a partisan attitude in favor of Roman centralization or of Platonism, as people have done in regard to the text from the Congregation for the Doctrine of the Faith. According to Bultmann, "The organization of the Church developed out of the consciousness that the community as a whole exists before the individual congregations; the outward indication of this is the linguistic usage: ἐκκλησία denotes first, not the individual congregation at all, but the 'People of God'. . . . The notion of the Church as a whole being prior to the individual congregations is further shown in the equivalence of the ἐκκλησία with the σῶμα Χριστοῦ, which includes all believers" [*Theologie des Neuen Testamentes*, 3rd ed. (Tübingen, 1958), p. 96].

above . . . is our mother" (Gal 4:26). H. Schlier observes in this connection that, for Paul as for the related Jewish tradition, the Jerusalem above is the new age. But for the Apostle, the new age is already present "in the Christian Church. This is for him the heavenly Jerusalem in its children." [8]

If the ontological priority of the one Church simply cannot be seriously denied, the question of which came first in time certainly is somewhat more difficult. At this point the letter of the Congregation for the Doctrine of the Faith refers us to the Lucan picture of the birth of the Church from the Holy Spirit at Pentecost. We are not going to discuss here the question of the historicity of this account. It is a matter of the theological message that Luke is concerned to convey. The Doctrine Congregation points out in this connection that the Church begins with the community of 120 gathered around Mary, and especially with the renewed community of the Twelve, who are not members of any local Church but are the apostles who are going to carry the gospel to the ends of the earth. To make things clear, we may add that, since there are twelve of them, they are at one and the same time the old Israel and the new, which—as was fundamentally implicit from the beginning in the concept of the People of God—is now extending itself to all peoples, so as to found in all the nations the one People of God. This indication is reinforced by two further aspects: in this, the hour of her birth, the Church is already speaking in every language. The Church Fathers quite rightly interpreted this story of the wonderful gift of languages as a foreshadowing of the *Catholica*—the Church is *kat'holon* from the very first moment—comprehending the whole universe. Corresponding to this, Luke describes the great crowd of onlookers as

---

[8] H. Schlier, *Der Brief an die Galater* [The Letter to the Galatians], 12th ed. (Göttingen, 1962), pp. 219–26; quotation, p. 223. See F. Mußner, *Der Galaterbrief* [The Letter to the Galatians] (Herder, 1974), pp. 325ff.

being pilgrims from all over the world, using for his description a list of twelve peoples, the point of which is to suggest that this audience is all-inclusive. Luke has added to this list of twelve peoples a thirteenth: the Romans; and no doubt he was trying to emphasize further the idea of the whole globe.[9]

The meaning of the text issued by the Congregation for the Doctrine of the Faith is not quite accurately reproduced by Walter Kasper when he says that the Jerusalem community was in fact both the universal Church and local Church in one and then continues: "This of course represents a Lucan construction, inasmuch as from a historical point of view there were probably several congregations from the start, with several congregations in Galilee besides the Jerusalem congregation."[10] We are here concerned, not with the question—which we are ultimately unable to answer—of exactly when and where Christian congregations first came into existence, but with that of the inner beginning of the Church in temporal existence, which is what Luke is trying to describe and which he ascribes, beyond all empirical factors, to the power of the Holy Spirit. Above all, however, it is not being fair to Luke's account if we say that the "original community at Jerusalem" was at one and the same time the universal Church and local Church. What comes first in Saint Luke's account is not any original community at Jerusalem; what comes first is that, in the Twelve, the old Israel, which is one, becomes the new and that through the wonderful gift of

---

[9] See the various commentaries on Acts, e.g., G. Schneider, *Die Apostelgeschichte* [The Acts of the Apostles], vol. 1 (Herder, 1980), pp. 252–55; R. Pesch, *Die Apostelgeschichte*, Exegetischer-Kritischer Kommentar V/1 (Benziger/Neukirchener Verlag, 1986), pp. 105f.; J. Zmijewski, *Die Apostelgeschichte* (Regensburg, 1994), pp. 110–13.

[10] W. Kasper, "Zur Theologie und Praxis des bischöflichen Amtes" [On the theology and the practice of the office of bishop], in W. Schreer and G. Steins, eds., *Auf neue Art Kirche sein* [Being the Church in a new way]: *Festschrift für Bischof Homeyer* (Munich, 1999), pp. 32–48; quotation, p. 44.

tongues this new Israel of God is then shown, before there is any question of constituting a local community in Jerusalem, to be a unity encompassing every time and place. In the persons of those pilgrims present, who come from all different peoples, it is at once related to all the peoples of the world. We need not, perhaps, overemphasize the importance of the question of the temporal priority of the universal Church, which is clearly portrayed by Luke in his account. Yet it remains important that the Church was born in the Twelve of the Holy Spirit, from the beginning, for all peoples, and hence was from the beginning also oriented toward express-ing herself in all cultures and being thereby the one People of God: here is no local congregation slowly spreading, but the yeast is always related to the whole and, hence, from the very first moment bears universality within itself.

The resistance to the expression of the priority of the uni-versal Church before the individual parts of the Church is difficult to understand in theological terms, perhaps indeed incomprehensible. It becomes comprehensible only out of a suspicion that is thus briefly formulated: "This formula be-comes truly problematical if the one universal Church is co-vertly identified with the Roman Church and, de facto, with the pope and the curia. If that is happening, then the text issued by the Congregation for the Doctrine of the Faith cannot be understood as an aid to clarifying communio-ecclesiology; rather, it has to be understood as dismissing it and attempting to restore Roman centralism." [11] In this pas-sage, the identification of the universal Church with the pope and curia is at first introduced just as a hypothesis, as a danger,

---

[11] Ibid., p. 44. Before that, on p. 43: "This general direction laid down by the Council has been further developed by the Congregation for the Doctrine of the Faith, in the postconciliar period, in their 'Letter to the Bishops of the Catholic Church on Some Aspects of the Church as Communion', in such a way as to mean in practice more or less a U-turn."

yet afterward it nonetheless seems to be attributed to the letter of the Congregation for Doctrine, which thus necessarily appears to be an attempt at theological restoration and therefore a defection from the Second Vatican Council. This interpretative leap is astonishing, but there is no doubt it stands for a suspicion that is widespread; it gives expression to a complaint to be heard all around, and it probably also expresses a growing inability to imagine anything concrete at all under the heading of universal Church or that of the one, holy, catholic Church. The only elements still in the picture are the pope and curia, and if these are rated too highly from a theological point of view, then people are bound to feel threatened.[12]

Here, then, after a digression that is only apparent, we are concerned in a quite practical instance with the interpretation of the Council. The question facing us is now: What concept of the universal Church does the Council actually hold? There should, after all, be no need to state specifically that the letter of the Congregation for the Doctrine of the Faith does not "covertly identify" "the one universal Church . . . with the Roman Church, and, de facto, with the pope and the curia". This temptation arises if one has already identified the local Church of Jerusalem with the universal Church; that is to say, if one's concept of the Church has been reduced to the empirically visible congregations and the deeper theological dimension has been lost sight of. It is a good thing to turn

---

[12] Cardinal Kasper has in the meantime responded to the questions raised here in *Stimmen der Zeit* 218 (December 2000): 795–804, in an article entitled: "Das Verhältnis von Universalkirche und Ortskirche: Freundschaftliche Auseinandersetzung mit der Kritik von J. Kard. Ratzinger" [The relationship between the universal Church and the local Church: A friendly discussion of the criticisms of J. Cardinal Ratzinger]; this was also published in English translation in the American Jesuit periodical *America* (vol. 185, no. 4), to which I for my part reacted with a brief response (ibid., no. 16). This exchange of views has, thank God, led to an extensive rapprochement of our respective stances.

back to the Council's text with this question in mind. The
very first sentence of the Constitution on the Church makes
it clear that the Council does not regard the Church as a self-
contained reality; rather, it sees her from the perspective of
Christ: "Since Christ is the Light of the nations, this Council,
which is gathered together in the Holy Spirit, would like to
light all men with his splendor, which shines forth from the
face of the Church." [13] We can recognize in the background
the image from patristic theology that sees in the Church the
moon, which has no light of its own but gives out again the
reflected light of Christ the sun. [14] Ecclesiology appears as
dependent upon Christology, as belonging to it. Yet because
no one can talk correctly about Christ, the Son, without also
straightaway talking about the Father, and because no one can
talk about the Father and the Son without listening to the
Holy Spirit, then the christological aspect of ecclesiology is
necessarily extended into a trinitarian ecclesiology. [15] Talking
about the Church is talking about God and can be correct
only in that sense. In this trinitarian overture, which offers us
the key to a correct understanding of the text as a whole, we
learn to recognize what the one holy Church is, both beyond
and within all concrete historical forms of realization, what
"universal Church" means. That becomes clearer when, next,
the inner dynamic impulse of the Church toward the Kingdom of God is demonstrated. And precisely because the
Church is to be conceived as theo-logical, she is constantly
transcending herself; she is the gathering together for the
Kingdom of God, an opening up into that Kingdom. After
that, the particular images for the Church, which all refer to
the one Church, are briefly presented, whether by talking

---

[13] *Lumen gentium*, chap. 1, no. 1.

[14] See H. Rahner, *Symbole der Kirche: Die Ekklesiologie der Väter* [Symbols of
the Church: The ecclesiology of the Fathers] (Salzburg, 1964), pp. 89–173.

[15] *Lumen gentium*, nos. 2–4.

about that of the bride, that of the house of God, of his family, of the temple, of the holy city, of our mother, of the Jerusalem above, or of God's flock, and so on.

Finally this takes a more concrete form. We are given a quite practical answer to the question, What is this one universal Church, which is ontologically and temporally prior to the local Churches? What does she consist of? Where can we see her at work? The Constitution answers this when it talks to us about the sacraments.

First there is **baptism**: this is a trinitarian process, that is, one that is entirely theological—far more than a process of socialization in the local Church, as it is nowadays unfortunately so frequently misinterpreted. Baptism does not spring from the individual congregation; rather, in baptism the door is opened for us into the one Church: baptism is the presence of the one Church and can come only from her—from the Jerusalem that is above, from our new mother. The well-known ecumenist Vinzenz Pfnür has recently said about this: baptism implies being opened up

> toward the *one* body of Christ that was opened for us on the Cross (see Eph 2:16), into *which* we (and the others) are baptized through the Holy Spirit (1 Cor 12:13)—something substantially more than what is customarily proclaimed at baptism in many places: "We have . . . received into our congregation"—and *of which* we have become members—something not to be confused with membership of a local Church—and that with a view to *one* Bread (see 1 Cor 10:17), which is not the particular bread of a local Church, and that with a view to *one* bishop's office, in which one can only share (along with Cyprian) in fellowship with all the bishops.[16]

---

[16] V. Pfnür, "Communio und excommunicatio" [Communion and excommunication], in B. Hilberath and D. Sattler, eds., *Vorgeschmack: Ökumenische Bemühungen um die Eucharistie* [Foretaste: Ecumenical efforts for the Eucharist]: *Festschrift für Th. Schneider* (Mainz, 1995), pp. 277–92; quotation, p. 292.

In baptism the **universal Church** always takes priority over the local Church and is creating her. That is why the letter from the Congregation for the Doctrine of the Faith on "communion" is able to say that there are **no foreigners in the Church: everyone is at home everywhere, and not just a visitor. It is always the one Church, one and the same. Anyone baptized in Berlin is just as much at home in the Church in Rome or in New York or in Kinshasa or in Bangalore or wherever he may be as in the Church where he was baptized. He does not need to report his move; it is all the one Church**. Baptism springs from this Church and by it people are born into her.

Anyone who is talking about baptism is as a matter of course also dealing with the **Word of God**, which is but one for the whole Church and which repeatedly goes before her in every place, calls her together, and builds her up. This Word is set above the Church, and yet it is within her and is entrusted to her as a living agent. In order to be present and effective in history, the Word of God needs this agent, and yet the agent for her part cannot exist without the life-giving power of the Word—indeed, it is this that makes her a living agent. Whenever we talk about the Word of God, we mean also to include the Creed, which stands at the heart of the process of baptism; the Creed is the way in which the Church accepts and appropriates the Word, in certain respects the Word and the answer in one. There, too, is the universal Church, the one Church, in a quite practical and tangible fashion.

The Council's text proceeds from baptism to the **Eucharist**, in which Christ gives us his Body and, thus, makes us into his body. This Body and the body are one, and thus the Eucharist, again, is for each local Church the point at which people are drawn into the one Christ; **this is the process of all communicants becoming one in that universal com-**

munion which binds together heaven and earth; the living and the dead; past, present, and future; and opens up toward eternity. The Eucharist does not takes its origin from the local Church, nor does it end there. It always means that Christ is coming to us from without, passing through our locked doors; ever and again it comes to us from without, from the whole, one body of Christ, and draws us into that body.

This dimension of the sacrament *extra nos* is seen yet again in the **office of bishop and of priest**: the fact that the sacrament of priestly service is requisite for the Eucharist is founded upon the fact that the congregation cannot give itself the Eucharist; it has to receive it from the Lord by the mediation of the one Church. The apostolic succession, which constitutes the priestly office, comprehends both the synchronic and the diachronic aspects of the concept of the Church: both belonging to the whole history of the faith from the apostles onward and standing in fellowship with all those who let themselves be gathered together by the Lord to be his body. It is well known that the Constitution on the Church dealt with the office of bishop in the third chapter and explained its significance on the basis of the fundamental concept of the *collegium*. This concept, which makes only a marginal appearance in the tradition, serves to represent the inner unity of the episcopal office. One is a bishop, not as an individual, but in belonging to a body, to a college, which for its part signifies the historical continuity of the *collegium apostolorum*. To that extent, the office of bishop arises from the one Church and leads into her. Here in particular it becomes clear that there is no contradiction, theologically, between the local Church and the Church as a whole. The bishop, within the local Church, represents the one Church, and he builds up the one Church by building up the local Church and by rousing her particular gifts for the benefit of the body as a whole. The office of Peter's successor is a special instance of the office of bishop and is directed in a particular way toward responsibility for the unity of the whole Church. Yet this office of Peter and its responsibility could not exist if the universal Church had not existed before it. Otherwise it would be grasping at emptiness and would represent an absurd claim. There is no doubt that the correct reciprocal relationship of episcopacy and primacy has repeatedly had to be rediscovered, even through travail and suffering. Yet it is right for this struggle to be set in motion only when it is being seen from the viewpoint of the primacy of the real mission of the Church and is at all times a part of that and is subordinated to it: the point of view of the task of bringing God to men and men to God. What the Church is for is the gospel; and everything within her should revolve around that.

At this point I should like to break off our analysis of the concept of "communion" and at least briefly say how I stand in relation to perhaps the most controversial point in *Lumen gentium*: the meaning of that sentence already referred to, in *Lumen gentium*, number 8—that the one Church of Christ, which we confess in the Creed as being one, holy, catholic, and apostolic, **"subsists"** in the Catholic Church, which is led by Peter and by the bishops in communion with him. The Congregation for the Doctrine of the Faith found itself, in 1985, needing to declare its position in relation to this much-discussed text; this was occasioned by a book by Leonardo Boff in which the author propounded the thesis that just as the one Church of Christ subsists in the Roman Catholic Church, so it does also in other Christian churches.[17] Needless to say, what the Congregation for the

---

[17] "Notificazione sul volume: 'Chiesa: Carisma e potere: Saggio di Ecclesiologia militante' del P. Leonardo Boff OFM", in Congregatio pro doctrina fidei, *Documenta inde a Concilio Vaticano secundo expleto edita (1966–1985)* (Libreria Editrice Vaticana, 1985), pp. 286–94. What I am saying here is to a great extent

Doctrine of the Faith said was overwhelmed with sharp criticisms and then set aside. If we are trying to think about where we are today in the reception of the Council's ecclesiology, then the question of the interpretation of this *subsistit* is unavoidable, and in that case the only official pronouncement of the Magisterium concerning this expression since the Council, the *notificatio* to which we just referred, cannot be ignored. At a distance of fifteen years, it becomes clearer than it was at the time that this was not just a matter of a single theological writer; rather, it is a view of the Church current in a number of different variations and is just as much current today.

The 1985 clarification portrayed the context of Boff's thesis, which we have just briefly repeated, in some detail. We do not need to enter into all these particularities again here, as we are concerned with a more fundamental issue. The thesis of which Boff was at that time the representative might be characterized as ecclesiological relativism. It is justified by its adherents with the view that the "historical Jesus" himself did not think about a Church at all, still less found one. The concrete structure of the Church is said not to have developed until after the Resurrection, in the process of ridding Christianity of eschatology, through the more immediate sociological requirements of institutionalization; and it is said that at the beginning there was certainly no "catholic" Church, but merely various distinct local Churches with varying theologies, with offices that differed, and so on. No institutional Church therefore, it is said, can maintain that she is the one Church of Jesus Christ in accordance with God's will; for

the same as what I said in 1999, in the Vallombrosa Meeting (near San Francisco, California): "Deus locutus est nobis in Filio: Some Reflections on Subjectivity, Christology and the Church", in *Proclaiming the Truth of Jesus Christ: Papers from the Vallombrosa Meeting* (Washington, D.C., 2000), pp. 13–29, and on this point, pp. 23–29.

then all institutional structures have arisen through various sociological requirements and, hence, are all, as such, human constructions that in new situations may also be radically altered, perhaps indeed must be. They differ from one another in theological quality at a secondary level at most, it is said, and that is why one can say that the "one Church of Christ" subsists in them all, or at any rate in many of them—but the question here, of course, is what right anyone has, taking such a view of things, to talk about the Church of Christ at all.

The Catholic tradition, in contrast to that, has chosen a different starting point: it trusts the evangelists; it believes what they say. Then it is clear that Jesus, who was proclaiming the coming of the Kingdom of God, gathered disciples around himself for realizing that Kingdom in practice; that he not only imparted to them his message as a new interpretation of the Old Testament, but also gave them in the Sacrament of the Lord's Supper a new and unifying heart, through which everyone who confessed his name could become one with him in an entirely new way—so much so, that Paul could describe this fellowship as "being one body with Christ", as a spiritual union in the body. It is likewise then clear that the promise of the Holy Spirit was, not just a vague proclamation, but referred to the reality of Pentecost—and, thus, to the fact that the Church was not devised and built up by men but was created by the Holy Spirit and is and remains the creation of the Holy Spirit.

In that case, however, institution and spirit stand in a somewhat different relationship to one another in the Church than the representatives of those tendencies we have mentioned would like to persuade us. The institution is not then a structure we can rebuild or demolish just as we like, which has (allegedly) nothing at all to do with the business of believing. This kind of embodiment is then inherent in the Church herself. The Church of Christ is not hidden behind the multitude of human constructions, intangible and unattainable; she exists in reality as a corporal Church that shows her identity in the Creed, in the sacraments, and in the apostolic succession.

With the *subsistit* formula, Vatican II intended—in line with the Catholic tradition—to say something the exact opposite of "ecclesiological relativism": there is a Church of Jesus Christ. Hc himself willed her existence, and ever since Pentecost the Holy Spirit is constantly creating her, despite all human failures, and preserves her in her substantial identity. The institution is not an unavoidable—although theologically irrelevant or even damaging—external phenomenon; it is, in its essential core, a part of the concrete character of the Incarnation. The Lord is keeping his word: "The gates of hell shall not prevail against it."

At this point it becomes necessary to trace the term *subsistit* somewhat more carefully. With this expression the Council changed Pius XII's formulation, when he said in his encyclical *Mystici Corporis Christi*: The Catholic Church "is" (*est*) the one Mystical Body of Christ. The distinction between *subsistit* and *est* contains and conceals the entire difficulty of ecumenism. The term *subsistit* derives from classical philosophy, as it was further developed in Scholasticism. The Greek word corresponding to it is *hypostasis*, which plays a central role in Christology, for describing the unity between divine nature and human in the Person of Christ. *Subsistere* is a special variant of *esse*. It is "being" in the form of an independent agent. That is exactly what is concerned here. The Council is trying to tell us that the Church of Jesus Christ may be encountered in this world as **a concrete agent** in the Catholic Church. That can happen only once, and the view that *subsistit* should be multiplied fails to do justice to the particular point intended. With the term *subsistit*, the Council was trying to express the particular quality of the Catholic

Church and the fact that this quality cannot be multiplied: the Church exists as an active agent within historical reality.[18]

The distinction between *subsistit* and *est* does, however, imply the drama of the schism of the Church: although the Church is only one, and does really exist, there is being that is derived from the being of the Church, an ecclesiastical entity, even outside the one Church. Because sin is a contradiction, this distinction between *subsistit* and *est* is, in the end, something that cannot be entirely explained logically. Reflected in the paradox of the distinction between the uniqueness and the concrete existence of the Church, on the one hand, and, on the other, the continuing existence of a concrete ecclesiastical entity outside of the one active agent is the contradictory element of human sin, the contradictory element of schism. Such schism is quite different from the relativistic dialectic described above, in which the divisions between Christians are divested of their pain and are not really schisms at all but merely a representation of the multitudinous variations upon a theme, in which all the variations are in some sense right, and all in some sense wrong. There is not in that case actually any inner requirement to seek for unity, because even without it the Church is everywhere and nowhere. Christianity can then only exist at all in variations that are dialectically opposed to one another. Ecumenism then consists of everyone granting each other mutual recognition in some sense, because they are all merely fragments of what Christianity is. Ecumenism then consists in coming to terms with a relativistic dialectical process, because the historical Jesus belongs to the past, and truth in any case remains hidden.

---

[18] The Council Fathers, who were trained in neoscholastic philosophy and theology, were quite well aware that *subsistere* is a narrower concept than that of *esse*: while, in the *analogia entis*, *esse* includes the whole realm of being in all its modes and forms, *subsistere* is the form of existence of a being resting in itself, as in particular occurs in the case of an "active agent".

The Council's view is quite different: The fact that in the Catholic Church the *subsistit* of the one active agent, the Church, is present is in absolutely no way the achievement of Catholics but solely the work of God, which he maintains despite the persistent demerits of the human officeholders. They cannot take any credit for this; rather, they can simply marvel at it, with shame at their own sins, at the same time being filled with thanksgiving for the faithfulness of God. Yet the work of their own sins can be seen: the whole world is aware of that drama, in which divided Christian communities stand in opposition to one another, advance their opposing claims to truth, and thus apparently thwart what Christ was praying for on the night before his Passion. While schism is a historical reality anyone can grasp, it is only in faith that one can be aware of the continuing existence, as such, of the one Church in the concrete form of the Catholic Church.

It is because the Second Vatican Council comprehended this paradox that it declared that ecumenism, as a search for true unity, is a duty and handed this on to the Church of the future to be taken with her on the way.

I am coming to the end. No one who wants to understand the characteristics of the Council's ecclesiology can leave out chapters 4 through 7 of the Constitution, which talk about laymen, about the universal call to **holiness**, about religious, and about the eschatological orientation of the Church. In these chapters the inner reason for the Church's existence, what is essential in her life, once more makes its appearance: they are concerned with holiness, that is, with what is fitting for God—in order that space may be made in the world for God, so that he may dwell therein and the world may thus become his "Kingdom". Holiness is more than a moral quality. It is the dwelling of God with men, of men with God, the setting of God's "tabernacle" with us and among us (Jn 1:14). This involves the new birth—not of flesh and blood, but of

God (Jn 1:13). This orientation toward holiness is identical with the eschatological orientation of the Church, and that is, in fact, on the basis of Jesus' message, of fundamental importance for the Church. The Church is there in order that God may come to dwell in the world and in order that "holiness" may come about: that is what we should be competing for in the Church, not competing for more or less privilege, about sitting in the best places. All this is then summarized again in the last chapter of the Constitution, which deals with the Mother of the Lord.

At first sight, the choice made by the Council to treat **Mariology** under the heading of ecclesiology might seem more or less accidental. From a historical point of view, it is true that, as a matter of fact, the Fathers made this decision only by a very small majority. Yet from within, this decision entirely corresponds to the style of the Constitution as a whole: only when you have grasped this connection will you have correctly understood the picture of the Church that the Council was trying to portray. The researches of H. Rahner, A. Müller, R. Laurentin, and Karl Delahaye, in which Mariology and ecclesiology were both developed and renewed, bore fruit in this decision.[19] Hugo Rahner took the lead in showing from original sources, in the most marvelous way, how the whole of Mariology had first been thought out and given shape by the Fathers as ecclesiology: The Church is

---

[19] H. Rahner, *Maria und die Kirche* [Mary and the Church] (Innsbruck, 1951); A. Müller, *Ecclesia—Maria: Die Einheit Marias und der Kirche* [Ecclesia—Maria: The unity of Mary and the Church] (Fribourg, 1955); R. Laurentin, *Court traité de théologie mariale* [A brief treatise on Marian theology] (Paris, 1953); K. Delahaye, *Erneuerung der Seelsorgsformen aus der Sicht der frühen Patristik* [The renewal of pastoral practice from the perspective of early patristics] (Herder, 1958). Here I might also refer you to my little attempt at a systematic assessment of their conclusions in the light of the Second Vatican Council: *Die Tochter Zion*, 4th ed. (Johannes Verlag, 1990); Eng. trans.: *Daughter Zion* (San Francisco: Ignatius Press, 1983).

virgin and mother; she has been immaculately conceived and carries the burden of history; she suffers and yet has already been received into heaven. It gradually becomes clear in the course of development that the Church was anticipated by Mary, that she is personified in Mary, and vice versa, that Mary does not stand there as an isolated individual, closed up in herself, but carries within her the whole mystery of the Church. The person is not being understood as closed and individualistic, nor the community as collective and non-personal; the two merge inseparably together.

That is true of the apocalyptic woman who appears in the twelfth chapter of the Book of Revelation: it will not do for this woman to be understood exclusively and individualistically as Mary, because in her we are seeing the whole People of God, suffering and yet fruitful through their suffering, the old and the new Israel together; yet equally it will not do to keep Mary, the Mother of the Redeemer, purely separate from this picture. Thus, in the transition and fluidity between the person and the community, as we find it in this passage, the mutual indwelling of Mary and the Church is anticipated; this then gradually develops in patristic theology and is finally taken up again by the Council. The fact that later the two fell apart, that Mary was portrayed as an individual showered with privileges and thereby infinitely far removed from us, while the Church was seen as being nonpersonal and purely institutional, damaged both Mariology and ecclesiology in equal measure. Here the distinctions that Western thought has quite noticeably developed are having their effect, and there are certainly good reasons for these distinctions. Yet if we want to understand Mary and the Church properly, then we have to learn to get back behind these distinctions, in order to comprehend the supra-individual nature of the person and the supra-institutional nature of the community, at the very point at which both person and community are taken back to their origins through the power of the Lord, of the new Adam. The Marian view of the Church and the ecclesial and salvation-historical view of Mary lead us back in the end to Christ and to God the Trinity; because here it becomes clear what holiness means, what the dwelling of God in man, and in the world, actually is, and what we are to understand by the "eschatological" tension in the Church. Thus it is only with the chapter on Mary that the Council's ecclesiology is rounded out and brought back to its christological and trinitarian starting point.

So as to give you some taste of the patristic theology, I should like to close with a passage from Saint Ambrose, one of those selected by Hugo Rahner:

> Stand firm, then, in your inmost heart! . . . What it means to stand, the Apostle has taught us, and Moses wrote: "The place on which you are standing is holy ground." No one can stand who is not standing firm in faith. . . . And there is another saying written, "But you stand firm with me." You are standing firm with me when you are standing in the Church. The Church is the holy ground upon which we are to stand. . . . Stand firm, then, stand in the Church. Stand firm in that place at which I choose to appear to you; there I will stay with you. Where the Church is, there is the firm standing place for your heart. The foundations of your soul are resting in the Church. For in the Church I have appeared to you, as once I did in the thornbush. You are the thornbush, and I am the fire. I am the fire in the burning bush, in your flesh. I am fire to give you light; to burn away the thorny tangles of your sins; to bestow on you the favor of my grace.[20]

---

[20] Ambrose, *Epistle 63*, 41, 42 (PL 16, 1200 C/D), quoted and translated by H. Rahner, *Mater Ecclesia: Lobpreis der Kirche aus dem ersten Jahrhundert* [Mother Church: Praise of the Church from the first century] (Benziger, 1944), p. 64.

The Ministry and Life of Priests

When the Fathers of the Second Vatican Council were working on the Decree on the Ministry and Life of Priests, they were concerned above all, following the great debates about the office of bishop, after the important statements about the place of the layman in the Church and about the religious life, to give a word of encouragement to priests, too, who day by day bear the burden of the work in God's vineyard. It was clear that they could not make do there with just some pious address or other. After the bishops had thrown light upon the significance of their office and of its theological basis, the message to the priests would also have to have theological depth. Only in that way could it offer a convincing recognition of the part they played or encouragement in their work.

It was not just on the grounds of keeping a proportion between the two "classes" in the Church, however, that such a message to the priests was requisite. When the bishops were highlighting the independent importance of the episcopal office as opposed to the service of the succession of Peter, then they could be sure of finding widespread agreement in public opinion both in the Church and the world, and especially also in the ecumenical sphere of Christianity as a whole. The Catholic concept of what a priest is, on the other hand, had lost currency and acceptance as a self-evident concept,

153

even within the heart of the Church's consciousness; the crisis of this concept, which soon became evident following the Council and developed into a crisis of priestly life and priestly vocations, though it had not yet reached its full stature, was already under way. It was the result, on one hand, of a change in people's feeling about life, whereby what was sacral was less and less well understood and the functional category was becoming the only determinative one. It did, on the other hand, have real theological roots, which developed quite unexpected power and life from changed sociological circumstances. The interpretation of the New Testament itself seemed quite emphatically to support a nonsacral view of all ecclesiastical ministries. There was no continuity to be seen between the sacral offices of the Old Testament and the new ministries of the Church as she developed; still less was there any connection to be perceived with the pagan concepts of priesthood. The novelty of Christianity seemed to be portrayed, in particular, in the desacralizing of its offices. The servants of the Christian congregations were not called *sacerdotes* (*hiereis*), but *presbyter*—elder. It is clear that the Protestant origins of modern exegesis were substantially at work in this way of looking at the New Testament, yet that altered nothing about the obviousness that seemed attributable to such exegesis—on the contrary, it became a burning question as to whether Luther, as opposed to Trent, had not been right after all.

Thus, two entire conceptions of the priestly office stood, and still stand, in opposition to each other: on the one hand, a social and functional view, which described the nature of the priesthood with the word "ministry"—specifically, ministry to the congregation in carrying out a function in the social institution called the Church. On the other hand, there is a sacramental and ontological view, which obviously does not deny the ministerial character of the priesthood yet sees it as being rooted in the being of the one who ministers and, then again, is also aware that this being is determined by a gift that is granted by the Lord through the mediation of the Church and is called a sacrament. There is also a terminological shift associated with the functional view. It is noticeable that people avoid the sacrally influenced term "priest(hood)" and replace it with the neutral and functional word "office", which hitherto had hardly played any role in Catholic theology.

This real difference in understanding the nature of the priestly ministry further corresponds, to a certain extent, to a difference of emphasis in defining the tasks of the priest: as opposed to the view of the priest's life being centered on the Eucharist, in a way that has become classical in Catholicism (*sacerdos—sacrificium*), there emerged the primacy of the Word, which had hitherto been regarded as typically Protestant. A conception of the priesthood that is thought out on the basis of the primacy of the Word need not, of course, necessarily be antisacramental: Vatican II's decree on the priesthood demonstrates the contrary itself. **At this point the question arises of how far the alternatives outlined here are in any sense mutually exclusive and to what extent they complement and stimulate each other, so that any choice can be resolved from within.** It is the question prompted by Vatican II of how far the Tridentine image of the priest, which had become classical, can be extended and developed by the questionings of the Reformation, and on the basis of critical exegesis and of the modern attitude to life, without losing what is essential; and to what extent, on the other hand, the Protestant idea of "office" can be opened up to receive the living tradition of the Catholic Church of East and West. For in the matter of the priesthood there is no essential difference, even after Trent, between Catholicism and Orthodoxy.

1. On the Nature of the Priestly Office

The Second Vatican Council did not go into this question, which was at that time just coming to the fore; after the great discussions about the collegiality of the episcopate, about ecumenism, on freedom of religion, and about the questions posed by the modern world, there would have been no time or energy left for that. Thus it was that the synods of 1971 and 1990 took up the theme of the priesthood again and further developed what the Council had said; the Holy Thursday letters of John Paul II and the directory of the Congregation for the Clergy gave more concrete shape to that, as relating to the everyday life of priests. Yet even though the Council's decree does not explicitly take account of the current controversies, it does nonetheless give the basic outline upon which everything else can be built up.

So what answers do we find to the problems to which we have just referred? We should say straight off that the Council cannot be pinned down to a specific alternative. In the introductory definition of priesthood it is said that through ordination priests are appointed to serve Christ, who is Teacher, Priest, and King, and that they share in his office, through which the Church on earth is built up to be the People of God, the body of Christ, and the temple of the Holy Spirit (1). In number two it talks about the authority to present the sacrifice and to pronounce the absolution of sins. These, the particular tasks of the priest, are however most emphatically set in the context of a historical and dynamic view of the Church: in the Church, everyone has "a part in the mission" of the whole body, but "not all the members have the same function" (see Rom 12:4). Summing up our reflections thus far, we realize that the first chapter of the decree lays clear emphasis on the ontological aspect of priestly life, and in doing so it highlights the authority for sacrifice. At the beginning of the third section this is again described in these terms: "Priests . . . are taken from among men and ordained for men in the things that belong to God in order to offer gifts and sacrifices for sins; on this account all men meet them as brothers." What we may see as being new, by contrast with Trent, is **the marked insistence on interrelations in the Church and on the communal journey of the whole Church**, in the context of which this classic vision is set.

So much the more do we sit up and listen when at the beginning of the second chapter, which talks about the particular tasks of the priest, it is said that: "Priests, as co-workers with their bishops, have the primary duty of proclaiming the gospel of God to all" (4). This seems to give clear expression to the primacy of the Word, that is, of the ministry of preaching. The question thus arises: How are these two series of statements related to one another: *"able by the sacred power of orders to offer sacrifice"* and *"primary duty* [primum officium] *of proclaiming the gospel* [evangelium evangelizandi]*"*?

a. Laying a christological foundation

To discover the answer we first have to ask: **What does "evangelizing" actually mean?** What is happening when you do it? What is this gospel? In the first place, in order to find a basis for the primacy of preaching, the Council could very well have referred to the Gospels. I am thinking, for instance, of the very significant little episode at the beginning of the Gospel of Mark, when the Lord (who is being sought out by everyone on account of his miraculous power) retreats to a lonely place and prays there (Mk 1:35ff.). When he is pressed by "Simon and those who were with him", the Lord replies: Let us go somewhere else, to the nearby towns, that I may preach there also, "for that is why I came out" (1:38). As the actual reason for his coming, Jesus specifies the **preaching**

of the Kingdom of God. This must therefore rate as the first priority of all his servants: They go out to proclaim aloud the Kingdom of God—that is, to make the living, active, and immediately present God the most important thing in our own lives. Now, there are two further insights from this little story alone that can help us properly understand this matter of God taking first place: this preaching goes hand in hand with self-examination in the solitude of personal prayer. Such self-examination seems, indeed, to be the necessary condition for it. And it is associated with the "casting out [of] demons" (1:39); that is to say that these are not mere words but, at the same time, effective action. It takes place, not in a lovely world, but in a world dominated by demons and amounts to a liberating intervention in this world.

But we have to go one step farther and, besides this little story from Mark, pregnant with meaning, must keep in view the whole Gospel in order to understand Jesus' priorities correctly. He is preaching the Kingdom of God; he does this above all in parables, and he also does it in the form of signs, in which this Kingdom comes to men as a power that is present and immediate. Word and sign are indivisible. Whenever the signs are regarded as simple miracles, without the word that is within them, Jesus breaks off his activity. Nor, however, does he countenance his preaching being regarded as a merely intellectual matter, as material for discussion: his word demands a decision; it creates reality. In this sense it is an "incarnate" word; the relation of word and sign to each other shows a "sacramental" structure.[1]

We still have to go a step farther. Jesus does not communicate any contents that are independent of his own person, as a

---

[1] I have given a somewhat more complete picture of these interrelations in my little book *Evangelium—Katechese—Katechismus* (Munich, 1995), pp. 35–43; Eng. trans.: *Sidelights on the* Catechism of the Catholic Church (San Francisco: Ignatius Press, 1997), pp. 40–51.

teacher or a storyteller would usually do. He is more, and something other, than a rabbi. As his preaching continues, it becomes ever clearer that in his parables he is talking about himself, that the "Kingdom" and his own person belong together, that the Kingdom is coming in his own person. The decision he demands is a decision on how one stands in relation to him, like Peter makes when he says: You are the Christ (Mk 8:29). Finally, Jesus' own Paschal Mystery, the death and Resurrection awaiting him, emerges quite clearly as the content of the preaching of the Kingdom of God, as in the parable of the faithless tenants (Mk 12:1–11). And now message and reality interweave in a new fashion: the parable provokes the anger of his opponents, who do everything that was done in the story. They kill the Son. That means that the parables would have been empty, meaningless, without the living person of the incarnated Son who "came out" (Mk 1:38), who "was sent" (12:6) by the Father. They would be empty without the verification of the word in the Cross and Resurrection. Thus we now understand that Jesus' preaching should be termed "sacramental" in a still more profound sense than we could previously have seen: his message carries within it the concrete reality of the Incarnation and the theme of Cross and Resurrection. It is in this most profound sense a verbal action. And thus, for the Church, it points forward to the mutual relationship of preaching and the Eucharist and yet also that between preaching and a witness lived out in suffering.

From the paschal point of view, as it is presented to us in the Gospel of John, we have to take yet one step more. Jesus is the Christ, Peter had said. Jesus Christ is the Logos, John now adds. He himself is the eternal Word of the Father, who is with God and is God (Jn 1:1). In him this Word has become flesh and has dwelt among us (Jn 1:14). Christian preaching is a matter, not of words, but of *the* Word. "Therefore, when we are talking about the ministry of the Word of God, the

intratrinitarian relationships are thought of as being involved." [2] At the same time, it is true "that this ministry
participates in the function of becoming incarnate".[3] Our
attention has rightly been drawn to the fact that Jesus' sermons are fundamentally different from the rabbis' lectures in
that the first person of Jesus, he himself, stands at the center
of his message.[4] Yet at the same time we have to remember
that Jesus himself saw the fact that he was not speaking "in his
own name" (Jn 5:43; see 7:16) as the hallmark of his way of
speaking: his "I" is completely open to the "Thou" of the
Father; it does not stand alone; rather, it draws us into the
dynamics of the trinitarian relationship. For the **Christian
preacher**, this means that he **does not talk of his own
volition; rather, he makes himself the voice of Christ, so
as to make room for the Logos himself and, through
fellowship with the human Jesus, to draw people into
fellowship with the living God**.

And thus we come around again to Vatican II's decree on
the priesthood. It talks about the various ways of preaching
and then points out the one constant element in all these
forms: the priest should never teach his own wisdom but
always be concerned for the Word of God, which ever urges
us toward truth and holiness (4). The ministry of the Word
demands a profound self-denial on the part of the priest: he is
measured by the standard of Paul's saying: "It is no longer I
who live, but Christ who lives in me" (Gal 2:20). A little
incident from the early history of the Opus Dei comes to
mind. A young woman had the chance for the first time to

---

[2] F. Genn, *Trinität und Amt nach Augustinus* [Trinity and office according to
Augustine] (Einsiedeln, 1986), p. 181.

[3] Ibid., p. 183.

[4] See, for instance, R. Aron, *Die verborgene Jahre Jesu* [Jesus' hidden years]
(Frankfurt, 1962), pp. 237f.; J. Neusner, *A Rabbi Talks with Jesus* (Doubleday,
1993), p. 30.

attend lectures by the founder, Don Escrivá. She was tremendously eager to hear such a very famous speaker. Yet when she had taken part in the Mass with him—so she said later—she wanted no longer to listen to a human speaker but only to discern what was God's Word and his will. The ministry of the Word requires of the priest a sharing in the kenosis of Christ, dissolving oneself and submerging oneself in Christ. The requirement that he speak, not of his own volition, but as bringing someone else's message does not of course mean any lack of personal involvement—quite the opposite: it means losing oneself in Christ so as to accept the path of his Paschal Mystery, thus leading to true self-discovery and to fellowship with him who is the Word of God in person. This passional pattern of being "not me" and yet "wholly me" shows in itself how the ministry of the Word ultimately extends to involve our being, beyond any and every function fulfilled, and presupposes priesthood as being a sacrament.

b. Development in the tradition (Augustine)

Because we have now reached the central point of our question, I should like to try to elucidate this further with two series of images taken from the writings of Saint Augustine, images taken from meditation upon the Word of the Bible that have at the same time substantially influenced the dogmatic tradition of the Catholic Church.

First there is the term *servus Dei* or *servus Christi*, referring to the priest.[5] In the background of this way of speaking of the servant of Christ, current in ecclesiastical language at the time, is the hymn to Christ in Philippians 2:5–11: Christ, the Son who is equal to God, took on the form of a servant and

---

[5] See on this point Genn, *Trinität*, pp. 101–23; on the general use of the term *servus Dei* in Augustine's time: P. Brown, *Augustine of Hippo: A Biography* (New York: Dorset Press, 1986), pp. 132–37.

became a servant for us. We must leave aside here the profound theology of freedom and service that Augustine unfolds in this connection. What is important for our question is that the concept of *servant* refers to a relationship. Someone is a servant in relation to someone else. If the priest is defined as being a servant of Jesus Christ, this means that his life is substantially determined in terms of a relationship: being oriented toward his Lord as a servant constitutes the essence of his office, which thus extends to his very being. He is a servant of Christ, so as to be, on the basis of Christ, for his sake and along with him, a servant of men. The fact of being oriented toward Christ is not in contradiction to his relation to the congregation (to the Church) but is the basis of that relationship and is what gives it all its depth. Being oriented toward Christ means being received into his own life as a servant and being at the service of the "body", of the Church, with him. Precisely because the priest belongs to Christ, he belongs to men in a quite radical sense. Only in this way is he able to be so profoundly and so unconditionally dedicated to them. That, in turn, means that the ontological conception of the office of priest, as something extending to the very being of the person concerned, does not stand in opposition to the seriousness of the functional concept, the ministry to others, but gives to this service a radical dimension that would be unthinkable in the merely profane sphere.

Connected with the concept of "servant" is the image of the *indelible character*, which has become a part of the faith of the Church. In the language of late antiquity, "character" referred to the seal or stamp of possession with which a thing, an animal, or even a person was marked and which could then no longer be erased. Thus someone's property is irrevocably characterized as such and "calls after its master". We could say that "character" means a belonging that is a part of the person's very existence. To that extent the image of "character" expresses in its turn the same "being related to", "having reference to", that we were just talking about. And, indeed, this is a kind of belonging we can do nothing about; the initiative for this comes from the proprietor—from Christ. Thereby the nature of the sacrament becomes clear: I cannot simply declare myself as belonging to the Lord in this way. He must first accept me as one of his own, and then I can enter into this acceptance and accept it for my own part, learn to live it. To that extent, then, the term "character" describes the nature of the service of Christ that is contained in the priesthood as having to do with our being; and at the same time it makes clear what is meant by its being sacramental. Only from that standpoint can one understand how it is that Augustine describes the "character" in functional terms (and, at the same time, ontologically) as *ius dandi*, as the presupposition for the valid dispensing of the sacraments.[6] Belonging to the Lord who became a servant is belonging for the sake of those who are his. This means that **the servant can give, in the holy sign, what he is unable to give from his own resources**: he is dispensing the Holy Spirit; he is absolving people from sins; he is making present the sacrifice of Christ and Christ himself, in his sacred Body and Blood—all these are privileges reserved by God, which no man can get for himself and no congregation can delegate to him. If "character" is thus the expression of a fellowship of service, then, **on the one hand**, it shows how **ultimately the Lord himself is always acting** and how, **on the other hand, in the visible Church he nonetheless acts through men**. Thus the "character" guarantees the "validity" of the sacrament even when the servant is unworthy, but it is a

---

[6] Genn, *Trinität*, pp. 34, 63f.; on the ancient concept of "character" (corresponding to the Greek *Stigma, Sphragis*), see H. Schlier, *Der Brief an die Galater* [The Letter to the Galatians] (Göttingen, 1962), p. 284, with further literature cited.

judgment upon that servant and a demand for living out the sacrament.

A brief word more about a second series of images, with which Augustine tried to make clear, for himself and his faithful, the nature of priestly service. It came to him from meditation on the figure of John the Baptist, in whom he finds a prefiguring of the role of the priest.[7] He points out that in the New Testament John is described, with a saying borrowed from Isaiah, as a "voice", while Christ appears in the Gospel of John as "the Word". **The relation of "voice" (*vox*) to "word" (*verbum*)** helps to make clear the mutual relationship between Christ and the priest. The word exists in someone's heart before it is ever perceptible to the senses through the voice. Through the mediation of the voice, it then enters into the perception of the other person and is then present likewise in his heart, without the speaker's having thereby in any sense lost the word. Thus, the sensory noise—that is, the voice—that carries the word from one person to the other (or others) passes away. The word remains. Ultimately, the **task of the priest** is quite simply to be **a voice for the word**: "He must increase, but I must decrease"—the voice has no other purpose than to pass on the word; it then once more effaces itself. On this basis the stature and the humbleness of priestly service are both equally clear: the priest is, like John the Baptist, purely a forerunner, a servant of the Word. It is not he who matters, but the other. Yet he is, with his entire existence, *vox*; it is his mission to be a voice for the Word, and thus, precisely in his being radically referred to, dependent upon, someone else, he takes a share in the stature of the mission of the Baptist and in the mission of the Logos himself. Along the same lines, Augustine refers to the priest as the "bridegroom's friend" (Jn 3:29), who does

---

[7] *Sermo* 293, 1–3 (PL 38, 1327f.).

not take the bride for himself yet nonetheless shares, as a friend, in the joy of the wedding. The Lord has made the servant his friend (Jn 15:15), who is now a member of the household and stays in the house—from being a slave, he has become a free man (Gal 4:7; 4:21—5:1).[8]

2. Christology and Ecclesiology: The Ecclesial Character of the Priesthood

In everything we have said thus far, we have been talking about the christological character of the priesthood, which is always a trinitarian character, since the Son is in his nature coming from the Father and going toward him. He shares himself in the Holy Spirit, who is Love—and therefore giving—in person. But then the Council's decree goes a step farther and quite rightly emphasizes the ecclesial character of this office, something that cannot be separated from its christological and trinitarian basis. The Incarnation of the Word means that God does not merely want to come to the spirit of man, through the Spirit, but that he is seeking him through and in the material world, that he also in fact wants to encounter him as a social and historical being. **God wants to come to men through men.** God has approached men in such a way that through him, and on account of him, they can find their way to one another. Thus the Incarnation includes the **communal and historical aspects** of faith. Taking the way of the body means that the time, as a reality, and the social nature of man become features of man's relationship with God, features that are in turn based upon God's existing relationship with man. That is why Christology and ecclesiology are inseparable from each other: God's action brings

---

[8] Genn, *Trinität*, pp. 139ff.

into being "the People of God", and "the People of God", on the basis of Christ, become "the body of Christ", in accordance with the profound interpretation of the promise to Abraham offered by Paul in the Letter to the Galatians. This is made—thus it is that Paul reads the Old Testament—to "the seed" of Abraham: that is, not to many, but to one. God's action is aimed accordingly at getting us, the many, to be, not merely "at one", but "one"—sharing in his bodily life with Jesus Christ (Gal 3:16f., 28).

It is on the basis of this very ecclesial depth of Christology that the Council highlighted the dynamic effect in and on world history of the Christ event, in the service of which the priest is enlisted. The ultimate goal for us all is that of becoming happy. Yet **happiness** exists **only in company with each other**, and we can keep company **only in the infinity of love**. There is happiness only in the removal of the barriers of the self in moving into divinity, in becoming divine. Thus the Council agrees with Augustine in saying that the goal of history is that mankind become love: it is thus adoration, a living worship, "the city of God". And thus creation's inmost longing, that God may be everything to everyone, is fulfilled (1 Cor 15:28; *Decree on the Ministry and Life of Priests* 2:42–55; Augustine *De civ. Dei* X, chap. 6). What worship is, what sacraments are, can in the last analysis be understood only within this grand perspective.

It is this view, which points us toward the sublime and ultimate questions, that also leads us to quite practical matters: because that is how things are, Christian faith is never just spiritual and inward, never just a subjective or a personal and private relationship with Christ and his word, but is entirely concrete and ecclesial. On that basis, the Council's decree emphasizes, in a way that is perhaps a little forced, the dependent relationship of the priest to the bishop: the priests represent him; they act in his name and on his instructions. The sublime christological obedience, which reverses the disobedience of Adam, finds concrete form in **ecclesiastical obedience**, and for the priest, ecclesiastical obedience in turn is, in a quite practical fashion, obedience to his bishop. The Council could probably have more strongly emphasized that there must first of all be a **common obedience of all to the Word of God and to the way it is presented to us in the living tradition of the Church**. This shared obligation is also a freedom that all share; it protects us from arbitrary actions and decisions and ensures that ecclesiastical obedience has a truly christological character. Ecclesiastical obedience is not positivistic in type; it is not just the same as response to formal authority. It is obedience to someone who is himself obedient and who embodies the obedient Christ.

Yet this obedience is of course independent of the virtue and holiness of the officeholder, precisely because it relates to the objective existence of the faith that is the Lord's gift and that transcends all subjective considerations. To that extent, in the priest's obedience to the bishop there is always an element of transcending the local Church—this is a Catholic obedience: the bishop is being obeyed because locally he represents the Church as a whole. And this is an obedience that points beyond the immediate historical moment to the whole history of faith. It is based on everything that has grown up in the *communio sanctorum*, and in that very way it opens up toward the future in which God will be everything to everyone and we shall all be one. To that extent there is within the demand for obedience a serious demand made upon the person exercising authority. Yet that does not mean that this obedience is conditional: it is quite practical. I am not being obedient to a Jesus whom I (or others) think up out of Scripture; in that case, I would only be obeying my own favorite ideas, and in the picture of Jesus I had imagined I would be worshipping myself. No, obeying Christ means obeying his body, obeying him in his body. On the basis of the Letter to the Philippians, the obedience of Jesus, as a matter of overcoming Adam's disobedience, stands in the center of the saving event. In the priestly life, this obedience must be embodied as obedience toward the authority of the Church and, in practice, as obedience to the bishop. Only in that way can the renunciation of idolizing oneself be given concrete form. Only thus can Adam be overcome in us, too, and the way opened up to the new human life. In an age in which emancipation is regarded as the true heart of redemption, and freedom appears as the right to do everything I myself want to, and only that, the concept of obedience is, so to speak, anathematized. It has been excised, not merely from our vocabulary, but from our thinking. Yet this conception of freedom is the very thing that has made people incapable of living with one another, incapable of loving. It enslaves people. That is why obedience, correctly understood, has to be rehabilitated and be made effective in the heart of Christian and priestly spirituality.

3. Spiritual Applications

Whenever Christology is being understood in a pneumatological and trinitarian mode, and thus at the same time with an ecclesial dimension, then—as we have seen—the transition to spirituality, to the question of how faith is lived out, happens of its own accord. The Council's decree—after the dogmatic basis had indeed been laid down in advance in the Constitution on the Church—concentrated especially on this aspect, even making quite concrete practical statements. I should like to consider just one of the factors mentioned. In section fourteen, the decree talks about the difficult problem of how the priest, torn between the plethora of his often quite varied tasks, may be able to preserve the unity of his life—a problem that is threatening, with an increasing shortage of priests, to become the real crisis in the daily lives of priests. A parish priest who may today be in charge of three or four parishes is forever traveling from one place to another; this situation, well known to missionaries, is becoming more and more the rule in the heartlands of Christianity. The priest has to try to guarantee the availability of the sacraments to the communities; he is oppressed by administrative work; problems of all kinds make their demands on him in addition to the personal troubles of so many people, for whom he can often—because of all the rest—hardly find any time. Torn to and fro between such activities, he feels empty, and it becomes more and more difficult for him to find time for recollection, from which he can draw new strength and inspiration. Outwardly torn apart and inwardly emptied, he loses all joy in his calling, which ends by seeming nothing but a burden and scarcely bearable any longer. Escape increasingly seems the obvious course.

The Council offered three initiatives toward controlling this situation. The basic theme is inner fellowship with Christ, whose food was to do the will of the Father (Jn 4:34). It is important for the priest's ontological unity with Christ to be alive in his consciousness and, thus, in his actions: Everything I do, I do in fellowship with him. In the very act of doing it, I am with him. The great variety of my activities, and what are outwardly even contradictions in them, nonetheless amount to a calling: all of it is being together with Christ, acting with him as a tool in society.

And from that springs the second theme: the ascetic discipline of the priest is not to be set alongside the pastoral activity, as an additional burden and an extra program that overloads my day still further. In my work itself, I am learning to overcome myself, to let my life go and give it up to others;

in disappointment and failure, I am learning renunciation and the acceptance of pain, letting go of myself. In the joy of succeeding, I am learning thankfulness. When I celebrate the sacraments, I am inwardly receiving them along with the recipients; I am indeed not doing some outward work or other; I am talking with Christ and, through Christ, with God the Trinity, and thus I am praying with others and for them. There is no doubt that this asceticism of service or ministry, seeing ministry itself as the actual ascetic discipline in my life, is a most important theme, which does of course demand repeated and conscious practice, an inner ordering of my activity on the basis of who I am.

Thus a third theme is indispensable. Even if I am trying to live the ministry as a form of asceticism, and the sacramental actions as a personal encounter with Christ, I still need moments in which to catch my breath, so that this inner orientation can be put into effect at all. All this—the Council's decree says—can be achieved only if priests, through the lives they live, penetrate ever more profoundly into the mystery of Christ. What Saint Charles Borromeo says about this, from his own experience, is most impressive: If the priest wishes to achieve a true priestly life, then he has to use these means: fasting, prayer, avoiding the company of bad people, and, likewise, avoiding damaging and dangerous familiarity and confidences.

> If even a tiny spark of divine love has been kindled in you, then do not at once give it up, do not expose it to the wind . . . ; remain in a state of recollection with God. . . . You are a pastor? Do not omit the care you should take of yourself; do not dispense yourself so liberally that you have nothing left for yourself, since just as you have to think about the souls of those others, for whose sake you are there, so also you should not forget your own soul. . . . Whenever you are dispensing the sacraments, think upon what you are doing. If you are

celebrating the Mass, think upon what you are offering;
whenever you are praying the Psalms in the choir, think upon
what you are saying and to whom; if you are guiding souls,
think upon the blood with which they have been washed.[9]

The fourfold *meditare* (think upon) is itself enough to show
how essential, to this great pastor, was the inner depth that
should accompany our activity. And we know in this case
how radically Charles Borromeo gave of himself to people,
dying at the age of forty-six, having been entirely consumed
by his sacrificial service. This man, of all others, who truly
wore himself out for Christ and on behalf of Christ for other
people, teaches us that without the discipline and the refuge
of a true inner dimension of faith, such self-sacrifice is not
possible.

This is a point we have to learn anew. The inward dimension has in the last few decades been widely regarded as
promoting and indulging intimacy and privacy and has thus
been suspect. Yet ministry without an inner dimension becomes mere activism. The breakdown and failure of not a few
priests, who had approached their work with great idealism,
ultimately results from this suspicion of the inner dimension.
Making time for God ourselves, for inwardly standing before
him, is a pastoral priority that is equal to all other priorities—
has, indeed, in a certain sense precedence over the others.
This is not an additional burden but space for the soul to draw
breath, without which we necessarily become breathless—we
lose that spiritual breath, the breath of the Holy Spirit within
us. Other kinds of rest are important and make good sense,
but the most fundamental way of resting from our work and
learning how to love it again is that of inwardly seeking God's
face, which always restores to us our joy in God. One of the

---

[9] *Acta Ecclesiae Mediolanensis* (Milan, 1599), pp. 1177f.: the breviary reading
for November 4.

very humble parish priests of this century—and in his humility, great—Don Didimo Mantiero (1912–1992) of Bassano del Grappa, noted in his spiritual journal: "Converts were, and still are, acquired through the prayer and sacrifice of unknown faithful. Christ won souls, not by the power of his marvelous speeches, but rather by the power of his constant prayer. He preached by day, but by night he prayed." [10] Souls—that is to say, living people—cannot be brought over to God just by persuasion or discussion. They want to be asked of God in prayer, for God. That is why the Christian inner dimension is also the most important pastoral action. That ought to be much more seriously taken into consideration again in our pastoral planning. We finally have to learn again that we need less discussion and more prayer.

PROSPECT: THE UNITY OF
OLD AND NEW TESTAMENTS MEDIATED
BY CHRISTOLOGY

To conclude, I would like to come back to the problems outlined in the introduction: What does the priesthood of the Church mean, on the basis of the New Testament? Is there such a thing at all? The reproach of the Reformers was that the Church had betrayed the novelty of Christianity and had retreated from the new Christian path by making the presbyter into a sacerdotal priest again: Is that true? Ought not the Church to have stayed faithful to the function of the elder, without sacralizing and sacramentalizing it? If we want to give a proper answer to these questions, then mere terminological investigations concerning the initial difference and the later process of amalgamation of the concepts of *presbyter* and

---

[10] L. Grygiel, *La "Dieci" di don Didimo Mantiero* (Ed. San Paolo, 1995), p. 54.

hiereus (*sacerdos*) are not enough. We have to go deeper than that; the whole network of problems concerning the relationship between the Old and New Testaments is up for discussion here. Is the New Testament essentially a break with the Old or essentially its fulfillment, in which everything is taken up and transformed and, in the very fact of being renewed, preserved? Is grace opposed to law, or is there an inner connection between the two?

First, it can be established as a matter of history that in A.D. 70 the temple at Jerusalem was destroyed and that with it the entire sector of sacrifice and priesthood, which in some respects stands at the heart of the "law", disappeared. On one hand, Judaism tried to preserve this lost element by transferring the regulations for holiness in the temple to the life of Jews in general;[11] on the other, it gave a solid place in its spirituality to the lost heritage of the temple in the form of prayers and hope for the restoration of the Jerusalem cult. The synagogue, which is really just a place for meeting together for prayer and for proclaiming and listening to the word, is a fragment, in expectation of the greater whole. But an interpretation of the spiritual office and of Christian worship of strictly reformed type reduces Christianity to an image of the synagogue, to congregation, word, and prayer. The historicist interpretation of the once-for-all character of Christ's sacrifice banishes sacrifice and worship into the past and excludes priesthood, as it does sacrifice, from the present day. Meanwhile it is being perceived more and more, in the churches of the Reformation, that the sublimity and the depth of the event described in the New Testament are not thereby properly recognized. In that way, the Old Testament would certainly not be fulfilled. In the Resurrection of Christ, however, the temple is rebuilt through God's own power (Jn

---

[11] See Neusner, *Rabbi Talks with Jesus*, e.g., pp. 114f.

2:19!). This living temple—Christ—is himself the new sacrifice, which has in the body of Christ, the Church, its own
enduring "today". On the basis of this sacrifice, and with a
view to it, there is a true priestly ministry of the new cult in
which all the "figures" are fulfilled.

That is why any conception that presupposes a complete
break, in matters of worship and priesthood, with the pre-
Christian history of salvation and that denies any connection
between Old Testament priesthood and that of the New
Testament must be rejected. For in that case the New Testament would not be the fulfillment of the Old Covenant but
the contrary of it; the inner unity of the history of salvation
would be destroyed. Through the sacrifice of Christ and its
acceptance in the Resurrection, the entire cultic and sacerdotal heritage of the Old Covenant has been handed over to the
Church. This whole plenitude of the Christian affirmation
has to be highlighted, as against any possible reduction of the
Church to a kind of synagogue; only then can we grasp the
breadth and the depth of the office of the apostolic succession. In that sense, we must say, not with shame and with
excuses, but with all decisiveness and joy: Yes, the priesthood
of the Church is a continuation and an acceptance of the Old
Testament priesthood, which in this radically new and transformed state finds its true fulfillment. This view is likewise
important for the relationship of Christianity to the other
great religions of the world. However much Christianity is a
new beginning, however much it is what comes from God
and is greater than all else, it is still not a mere negation of
human seeking. The features of these religions that make
them forerunners, however distorted and misplaced they may
sometimes be, are not groping in the void. Such a conception
of the priesthood does not mean any devaluing of the priesthood of all believers. Again, it is Augustine who brought this
out very well when he said that all believers are servants of

God, but the priests are the servants of the servants, and from the perspective of his mission he calls the faithful his masters.[12] The New Testament priesthood stands in succession to the Lord who washes the disciples' feet: its greatness can consist only in its humility. Greatness and humble status are intermingled, since Christ, as the greatest of all, became the least; since he, the first, took the last place. Being a priest means entering into this fellowship of taking a humble place and thus taking a part in the shared glory of the redemption.

---

[12] Genn, *Trinität*, pp. 117f.

Church Movements
and Their Place in Theology

In his great missionary encyclical, *Redemptoris missio*, the Holy Father says:

> Within the Church, there are various types of services, functions, ministries, and ways of promoting the Christian life. I call to mind, as a new development occurring in many churches in recent times, the rapid growth of "ecclesial movements" filled with missionary dynamism. When these movements humbly seek to become part of the life of local churches and are welcomed by bishops and priests within diocesan and parish structures, they represent a true gift of God both for new evangelization and for missionary activity properly so-called. I therefore recommend that they be spread and that they be used to give fresh energy, especially among young people, to the Christian life and to evangelization, within a pluralistic view of the ways in which Christians can associate and express themselves.[1]

For me personally it was a marvelous event when at the beginning of the seventies I first came into close contact with movements like the Neo-Catechumens, Communione e Liberazione, and the Focolarini and thus experienced the enthusiasm and verve with which they lived out their faith and felt bound to share with others, from out of the joy of their faith, what had been vouchsafed to them. This was the

---

[1] No. 72.

time when Karl Rahner and others were using the expression the "winter period" in the Church; and indeed, after the great upsurge of the Council, a frost seemed to set in instead of springtime, weariness in place of the new dynamism. The dynamic impulse now seemed to be found somewhere quite different—where people set about shaping the better world of the future with their own resources, without making use of God. That a world without God could not be a good one, far less a better one, was obvious to anyone with eyes to see. But where was God? Was it not true that the Church, after many debates and the efforts to find new structures, was in fact tired and spiritually empty? What Rahner was saying could be understood perfectly; it was expressing an experience we all shared. Yet suddenly here was something nobody had planned on. The Holy Spirit had, so to say, spoken up for himself again. In young people especially, the faith was surging up in its entirety, with no ifs and buts, with no excuses or back ways out, experienced as a favor and as a precious life-giving gift. Many people, of course, felt they were being disturbed in their intellectual discussions or in making models of how a quite different church, created in their own likeness, could be constructed—how could it have been otherwise? The Holy Spirit, wherever he breaks into our lives, always hinders the plans man makes.

Yet there were, and still are, more serious difficulties. For these movements showed various infancy sicknesses. The power of the Spirit could be felt in them, but he works through men and does not simply free them from their weaknesses. There were tendencies toward being exclusive, toward having one-sided emphases and, thus, of being incapable of fitting into the life of the local Church. In their youthful impetus, they were convinced that the local Churches would have, as it were, to lift themselves up to their level, to share their form of life, not that they would have to allow themselves to be dragged into a framework that was sometimes really somewhat decrepit. It came to clashes in which, in differing ways, both sides were at fault. It became necessary to think hard about how these two entities, the new upsurge shaped by the situation and the continuing forms of Church life—that is, parishes and dioceses—could be set in the right relationship. This is to a great extent a matter of simply practical questions, which ought not to be elevated too far onto a theoretical level. Yet this is, on the other hand, a matter of a phenomenon that, in various forms, recurs from time to time in the history of the Church. There is a basic form of Church life that endures throughout and that expresses the continuity of the Church's historic institutions. And there are always the new interventions of the Holy Spirit, which ever again revive and renew this framework; yet this "making new" hardly ever happens without pain or without conflict. So we still cannot avoid asking the fundamental question of how the theological place can be correctly assigned to these "movements" in the continuity of the Church's institutions.

I. ATTEMPTS AT CLARIFYING THE QUESTION THROUGH A DIALECTIC OF PRINCIPLES

1. Institution and Charisma

The basic dual framework of institution and event, of institution and charisma, presents a first means toward solving the question. Yet when we try to examine the two concepts more closely so as to arrive at valid rules for determining the relation between them, we find something unexpected. The concept of "institution" falls apart in our hands if we try to define it exactly in theological terms. For what are the fundamental institutional elements in the Church, which constantly bring order in her life and make their mark on her? Certainly, sacramental office in its various grades—the office of bishop, priest, and deacon: the sacrament that most significantly goes by the name of *ordo* is the ultimate and only enduring and obligatory structure that constitutes, so to speak, the predetermined set form of organization in the Church and that makes her an "institution". Yet only in our own century has it become customary—perhaps for the practical purposes of ecumenism—to refer to the sacrament of *ordo* as "office", whereby it then appears entirely in the light of an institution, as being institutional. Yet this "office" is a "sacrament", and thereby we quite clearly pass beyond the normal sociological understanding of institutions. The fact that this, the sole enduring structural element in the Church, is a sacrament means at the same time that it is always having to be constituted anew by God. The Church cannot dispose of it as she wishes; it is not just there and cannot be set up or arranged by the Church out of her own resources. It comes into being only secondarily through the Church's call; primarily it is through God's call to this particular person and, thus, only charismatically and pneumatologically. It can therefore be accepted and lived out only on the basis of the way the calling is renewed, of the way the Spirit cannot be predicted or controlled. Because that is how it is, because the Church cannot simply of herself appoint "officials" but has to wait on God's call—and this is ultimately the only reason—there can be a shortage of priests. Hence it has always been the case that this office cannot simply be created by the institution but has to be asked of God in prayer. Jesus' saying has always been true: "The harvest is plentiful, but the laborers are few; pray therefore the Lord of the harvest to send out laborers into his harvest" (Mt 9:37f.). On that basis we can also understand how the calling of the Twelve was the fruit of a night in prayer by Jesus (Lk 6:12ff.).

The Latin Church explicitly emphasized the strictly charismatic character of the priestly ministry by linking priesthood (following in this a very old tradition in the Church) with celibacy, which quite clearly can be understood only as a personal charism, never simply as a quality of the office.[2] The demand for separating the two ultimately rests on the idea that priesthood ought to be regarded, not as charismatic, but—for the sake of the institution and its needs—purely as an office that can be assigned by the institution itself. If you want to take priesthood so entirely under your own management, with its accompanying institutional security, then the link with the charismatic aspect found in the demand for celibacy is a scandal to be removed as quickly as possible. In that case, however, the Church as a whole is being understood as a merely human organization, and the security you are aiming for does not bring the results it is supposed to achieve. From the fact that the Church is not our institution but is the breakthrough of something different, that she is in her nature *iuris divini*, it follows that we cannot ever simply constitute her ourselves. That means that we can never apply to her purely institutional criteria; it means that she is entirely herself at the very point at which the standards and methods of human institutions are broken through.

In the Church, besides this really basic order—the sacrament—there are of course also institutions of purely human

---

[2] The fact that the celibacy of priests is not an invention of the Middle Ages but stretches back to the earliest days of the Church has been clearly and persuasively shown by Cardinal A. M. Stickler, *Der Klerikerzölibat: Seine Entwicklungsgeschichte und seine theologische Grundlagen* (Abensberg: Kral, 1993; Eng. trans.: *The Case for Clerical Celibacy: Its Historical Development and Theological Foundations* [San Francisco: Ignatius Press, 1995]). See also C. Cochini, *Origines apostoliques du célibat sacerdotal* (Paris and Namur, 1981; Eng. trans.: *Apostolic Origins of Priestly Celibacy* [San Francisco: Ignatius Press, 1990]); S. Heid, *Zölibat in der frühen Kirche* (Paderborn, 1997; Eng. trans.: *Celibacy in the Early Church* [San Francisco: Ignatius Press, 2000]).

law for the many purposes of management, organization, and coordination, which may grow in accordance with the demands of the time and may have to grow. Yet we would have to say this: the Church needs such institutions of her own, yet if they become too numerous and too strong, then they threaten the order and the life of her spiritual essence. The Church always has to scrutinize her own institutional structure so that it does not become too heavy—lest it harden into an armor that stifles her actual spiritual life. One can of course understand that the Church, if she is deprived of spiritual vocations over a long period, might be tempted to create for herself a substitute clergy, so to speak, of purely human origin.[3] She has to set up emergency arrangements, too, and in the missions and in similar situations she has always managed this. We can only give hearty thanks to all those who have served, and serve today, as prayer leaders and heralds of the gospel in such emergency situations. Yet if on that account the prayer for sacramental vocations were to take a back seat, if the Church, here and there, were to start being self-sufficient in that way and making herself independent of the gift of God, so to say, then she would of course be acting like Saul, who when hard-pressed by the Philistines did indeed wait a long time for Samuel but who, when he did not appear and the people began running away, lost patience and presented the burnt-offering sacrifice himself. Since he had thought he could hardly do otherwise in an emergency, that he could and must take God's business into his own hands, he was now told that by doing that he had ruined his chances: to obey is better than sacrifice (see 1 Sam 13:8–14; 15:22).

Let us turn back to our question: What about the relation between enduring forms of Church order and occasional charismatic upsurges? The scheme contrasting institution and

---

[3] This is the question with which the Instruction on the service of laypeople in the Church, published in 1997, is ultimately concerned.

charism offers no answer to this question, because when the two entities are opposed, the Church is being inadequately described. We can, all the same, deduce a few rules from what we have said so far:

a. It is important that the spiritual office, the priesthood itself, be understood and lived as a charism. The priest himself should be a "pneumatic" Christian, a *homo spiritualis*, a person who has been roused and is being driven by the Holy Spirit. It is the task of the Church to take care that this charismatic character of the sacrament is seen and accepted. She should not, in her zeal for the progress and continuance of her arrangements, put numbers in first place and downgrade the demands of the spiritual aspect. In that way she would be making it impossible to see the point of having priests; a service badly done is more damaging than helpful. It blocks the path to priesthood and to faith. The Church has to be faithful and to recognize that God is the one who creates and maintains the Church. And she has to help those who are called to be faithful beyond the first impetus, in every possible way, so that they do not slowly suffocate in routine but more and more become truly spiritual men.

b. Whenever the spiritual office is thus being lived in pneumatic and charismatic fashion, there is no institutional hardening: there is an inner openness to the charism, a kind of "atmosphere" of the Holy Spirit. And then the charism can recognize its own origin in the person in office, and fruitful ways of working together are found in the discernment of spirits.

c. In some circumstances of special need, the Church has to make emergency arrangements. But these emergency arrangements have to be understood as being open to sacramental orders, as leading in that direction, not as leading away.

In general, the Church should keep the administrative arrangements she makes for herself as minimal as possible. She should not overinstitutionalize herself; rather, she should ever remain open to the unforeseen and unplanned call of the Lord.

2. Christology and Pneumatology

Yet the question now arises: If institution and charism can be seen only partially as opposites, and those twin concepts therefore bring only partial answers, are there perhaps other theological points of view more suited to this? In present-day theology the contrasting of christological with pneumatological views of the Church is quite noticeably coming to the fore. On that basis it is said that the sacrament lies in the line of Christology and incarnation, and that this necessarily pushes what is in the pneumatological and charismatic line to one side. What is right about this is that we have to distinguish Christ and the Pneuma. Yet just as one must not treat the three Persons of the Trinity like a fellowship, a "communion", of three gods, but must understand them as one single God in the relative trinity of Persons, just so Christ and the Spirit are properly distinguished only if, by considering their difference, we can learn better to understand their unity. We cannot properly understand the Spirit without Christ, nor indeed Christ without the Spirit. "The Lord is the Spirit", Paul tells us in 2 Corinthians 3:17. That does not mean that the two are the same as each other or the same person. But it does mean that **Christ as the Lord** can be there **among us and for us** only because the Incarnation was not his last word. The Incarnation is perfected in the death on the Cross and in the Resurrection. That means: Christ can come only **because he has gone before us in the way of life of the Holy**

Spirit and shares himself through him and in him. The pneumatological Christology of Saint Paul and of the farewell discourses in the Gospel of John have probably not yet taken enough of a place in our view of Christology or of pneumatology. The new presence of Christ in the Spirit is however the necessary presupposition for there being sacraments or any presence of the Lord in the sacraments.

So here again light is shed on the "spiritual" office in the Church and on its theological "locus", which the tradition has framed in the concept of *successio apostolica*. "Apostolic succession" certainly does not mean, as could seem to be the case, that we become independent of the Spirit, so to speak, through the unbroken chain of succession. The link with the line of *successio* means, on the contrary, that the sacramental office is never at our disposal but has to be given by the Spirit again and again, that it is the sacrament of the Spirit, which we can never provide and never institute for ourselves. Functional competence as such is not sufficient; the gift of the Lord is requisite. In the sacrament and in the symbolic actions of the Church on his behalf, he has reserved to himself the constant renewal and institution of the priestly ministry. The quite specific association of "once" with "always", which is true of the Mystery of Christ, here becomes beautifully clear. The "always" of the sacrament, the presence in all the ages of the Church of the historical origins, which is the work of the Spirit, presupposes the connection with the ἐφάπαξ, with the original once-for-all event. The connection to the origin, that peg in the ground of the once-only, unrepeatable event, is indispensable. We can never escape into a free-floating pneumatology, never leave behind the solid earth of the Incarnation, of God's action in history. But conversely, this once-for-all element is only mediated in the gift of the Holy Spirit, which is the Spirit of the risen Christ. It does not dwindle into what has been, into

what is gone for ever and cannot be recalled, but bears within it the power of being present, because Christ has passed through the "veil of the flesh" (Heb 10:20) and thus has set free, within what is once for all, what endures for ever. The Incarnation does not stop with the historical Jesus, with his *sarx* (2 Cor 5:16!). It is thus that the "historical Jesus" becomes forever significant, precisely on account of his "flesh" having been transformed in the Resurrection, so that now, in the power of the Holy Spirit, he can be present at all times and in all places, as Jesus' farewell discourses in John's Gospel marvelously demonstrate (see especially Jn 14:28, "I go away, and I will come to you"). On the basis of this synthesis of Christology and pneumatology, we may well expect that an investigation of the concept of "apostolic succession" could be genuinely helpful for the solution of our difficulty.

3. Hierarchy and Prophecy

Before we go farther into these ideas, we must just briefly mention a third method available for understanding the opposition between enduring forms of order in the Church and pneumatic upsurges: developing Luther's interpretation of Scripture as a dialectic between law and gospel, people nowadays like to contrast the cultic and sacerdotal thread in salvation history with the prophetic one. In that case, these movements would have to be counted as belonging to the prophetic thread. That too, like the other things we have considered, is not entirely wrong, but then again it is extremely inexact and thus of no practical use in this form. The problem it addresses is too great for us to deal with in detail here. In the first place it would have to be said that the law itself has the character of a promise. Only because that is so was it possible for it to be both fulfilled by Christ and, in being fulfilled, to be "abolished". And the scriptural prophets were never aiming to abrogate the Torah—on the contrary, they opposed misuses so as to ensure that its real meaning was applied. And finally it is significant that the prophetic call was always made to individuals and never became fixed into a "class". Insofar as prophets did appear as a "class" (and this did happen), it was no less sharply criticized by the scriptural prophets than was the "class" of the priests of the Old Covenant.[4] Seeing in the Church a left wing and a right wing, dividing her into the prophetic class of the orders or the movements on one side and the hierarchy on the other—nothing in Scripture authorizes us to do that. On the contrary, that is an intellectual construction quite contrary to the Church. She is constituted, not dialectically, but organically. What is correct is merely that there are **various functions** within her and that God **again and again arouses prophetic individuals—these may be laymen, religious, or even bishops and priests—who call out to her the right message, which does not in the ordinary workings of the "institution" attain sufficient strength**. I think it is quite evident that it is not possible to interpret the nature and task of the movements on that basis. They themselves do not understand themselves in that way at all.

Accordingly, the result of our reflections thus far is somewhat scant as a response to the question, yet important nonetheless. If anyone chooses a dialectic of principles as the starting point for an attempted solution, this will not achieve

---

[4] The classical confrontation between a prophet sent by God and the class of prophets is to be found in Amos 7:10–17. We meet a similar situation in 1 Kings 22, in the opposition between the four hundred prophets and Micaiah; and again in the book of Jeremiah, e.g., 37:19. See also J. Ratzinger, *Wesen und Auftrag der Theologie* (Einsiedeln, 1993), pp. 105ff.; Eng. trans.: *The Nature and Mission of Theology* (San Francisco: Ignatius Press, 1995).

our goal. Instead of trying to use a dialectic of principles, in my opinion one should choose a historical starting point, which corresponds to the historical nature of faith and of the Church.

II. THE PERSPECTIVES OF HISTORY: APOSTOLIC SUCCESSION AND APOSTOLIC MOVEMENTS

1. Universal and Local Offices

Let us then ask what this origin looks like. Anyone with even a modest knowledge of the discussions about the early development of the Church, on the basis of which all Christian churches and communities attempt to justify themselves, will also know that there seems no prospect of arriving at real answers to any such historical question. If nevertheless I dare to try to feel my way toward a solution on this basis, I am doing so with the presupposition of a Catholic view of the Church and of her origins, which, on the one hand, offers us a stable framework yet, on the other, does leave room for further thinking, the possibilities of which have by no means been exhausted. There is no doubt that the immediate agents of Christ's mission from Pentecost onward are the Twelve, who very soon are also met under the name of "apostles". It is their mission to carry the message of Christ "to the end of the earth" (Acts 1:8), to go to all nations and to make all men his disciples (Mt 28:19). The sphere of action allotted them is the world. Without any restriction as to locality, they work for the building up of the body of Christ, of the one People of God, of the one Church of Christ. The apostles were not bishops of particular local Churches but simply "apostles" and were commissioned as such for work in the whole world and in the whole of the Church to be built up in the world: the universal Church is prior to the local Churches, which come into being as local realizations of her.[5] To say this yet more clearly and unmistakably: Paul was never the bishop of any particular place and never wanted to be. The only division of responsibility there was in the early days is described by Paul in Galatians 2:9: We—Barnabas and I—would be for the Gentiles, and they—Peter, James, and John—would be for the Jews. This initial division was of course soon disregarded. Peter and John, too, were aware of being sent to the Gentiles and at once went beyond the bounds of Israel. James, the brother of the Lord, who after A.D. 42 became a kind of primate of the Jewish Church, was probably not an apostle.

Even without going into any further details, we can say that **the office of apostle is a universal office, directed toward the whole of humanity and thus toward the whole of the one Church**. The local Churches come into being through the missionary activity of the apostles, and they then need responsible leaders. They are responsible for guaranteeing unity of faith with the Church as a whole, for shaping the inner life of the local Churches, and for keeping the congregations open, so that they can grow further and can pass on to those of their fellow citizens who are still not believers the gift of the gospel. This office in the local Church, which first

---

[5] See: Congregazione per la Dottrina della Fede, *Lettera "Communionis notio"* (Libreria Editrice Vaticana, 1994), no. 9, pp. 29f.; and my introduction to this, pp. 8ff. I went into these matters in more detail in my little book *Zur Gemeinschaft gerufen* (Herder, 1991), pp. 40f., 70–97; Eng. trans.: *Called to Communion* (San Francisco: Ignatius Press, 1996), pp. 44, 75–103. The priority of the one Church, of the one Bride of Christ, in which the heritage of the people of Israel, of the "daughter" and "bride" of Zion, is carried forward, as against the empirical realization of the People of God in practice, is in fact so obvious, in Scripture just as in the writings of the Church Fathers, that I find it difficult to understand the oft-repeated views disputing this. One need only read again de Lubac's *Catholicisme* (1938) or his *Méditation sur l'Église* or the glorious passages that H. Rahner brought together in his book *Mater Ecclesia* (1944).

appears under a variety of titles, slowly takes a definite and uniform shape. Thus, in the early stages of development of the Church, there were quite clearly two systems of order existing side by side; and no doubt there were instances of transition between them, but we can still clearly distinguish them: on one hand, the ministries of the local Church, slowly developing into definite forms; on the other, the apostolic office, which was very soon no longer restricted to the Twelve. In the writings of Paul we can clearly distinguish two concepts of "apostle": on one hand, he highlights the uniqueness of his own apostolate with great emphasis, based as it is on a meeting with the Risen One that thus sets him on the same level as the Twelve. On the other hand, in I Corinthians 12:28, for instance, he sees "apostle" as an office that reaches far beyond this circle; in Romans 16:7, likewise, when he refers to Andronicus and Junia(s) as apostles, we find this second concept. We find a similar terminology in Ephesians 2:20, where, in talking about the apostles and prophets as the foundation of the Church, the Twelve are certainly not the only ones in mind. The prophets about whom the *Didachē* speaks at the beginning of the second century are quite clearly understood as having just such a supralocal missionary office. It is all the more interesting when it is said about them: "They are your high priests" (13:3).

We may therefore take it that the existence side by side of the two kinds of office—the universal and the local—continued well into the second century: that is, into a period when the question was quite seriously arising as to who was carrying on the apostolic succession. Various texts give us to understand that this existence of the two orders side by side was by no means entirely without conflict. The Third Letter of John shows us such a situation of conflict quite clearly. Yet as the message reached those "ends of the earth" that were accessible in those days, it became increasingly difficult to continue to ascribe a meaningful position to the "itinerants"; abuses of their office may have further contributed to its gradual disappearance. It was now the task of the local Churches and their leaders, who had in the meantime acquired a clear profile in the threefold offices of bishop—priest—deacon, to spread the faith in the area of each local Church in question. The fact that in the time of Emperor Constantine the Christians amounted to about eight percent of the population of the empire and that they were still in a minority at the end of the fourth century shows how great the task was. In those circumstances the leaders of the local Churches, the bishops, had to recognize that they had now become the successors of the apostles and that the apostles' task was now entirely borne on their shoulders.

The realization that the bishops, the leaders responsible for the local Churches, are the successors of the apostles took clear shape in the second half of the second century in the writings of Irenaeus of Lyons. This definition of the nature of the episcopal office comprises two basic elements:

a. Apostolic succession means first of all what is for us the current meaning: **guaranteeing the continuity and the unity of the faith—in a continuity we call sacramental**.

b. Linked with that, however, is a practical **task**, which reaches beyond the management of the local Churches: they now have to see to it that Jesus' commission, to make all peoples his disciples and to carry the gospel to the ends of the earth, is carried out. They are responsible—Irenaeus emphatically highlights this—for seeing **that the Church** does not become a sort of federation of local Churches, just existing as such side by side, but **retains her universality and unity**. They have to carry forward the universal impetus of what is apostolic.[6]

---

[6] Concerning this section, see Ratzinger, *Called to Communion*, pp. 83ff.

If at the beginning we talked about the danger that the priestly office might ultimately be understood in purely institutional and bureaucratic terms, and its charismatic dimension be forgotten, there now appears a second danger: the office of the apostolic succession might atrophy into a mere service undertaken in the local Church, the universality of Christ's commission might be lost from view and from within our hearts; the unrest that drives us to bring Christ's gift to others might die out altogether, in the standstill of a Church where everything is strictly ordered. I should like to put it drastically: Within the concept of apostolic succession there is a surplus that goes beyond the mere office in the local Church. That can never exhaust its meaning. The universal element, which transcends the ministry in the local Church, is always a necessary part of it.

2. Apostolic Movements in the History of the Church

We now have somewhat to develop this thesis, which anticipates my conclusions, and to apply it to more concrete instances in history. For it takes us directly to the place that movements have in the Church. I was saying that for various quite different reasons the universal type of ministries gradually disappeared during the second century and that the office of bishop took over all these offices. In many respects that was not just a historically inevitable development but was theologically necessary and clearly showed the unity of the sacrament and the inner unity of the apostolic ministry. Yet it was also—as we have said—a development that brought certain risks. That is why it was quite logical for there to appear in the life of the Church, as early as the third century, a new element that we may safely describe as a "movement": monasticism. Now, one may object that early monasticism had no apostolic or missionary character, that it was, on the contrary, a flight from the world into islands of holiness. At the outset, the lack of any inclination to missionary work, toward spreading the faith into all the world, can indeed be observed. The determinative motive in Anthony, whom we can clearly perceive as a historical personage at the beginning of monasticism, is the desire for the *vita evangelica*—the desire to live out the gospel radically, as a whole.[7] The story of his conversion has an astounding similarity to that of Saint Francis of Assisi. Here, as there, we meet with the same drive: to take the gospel quite seriously, to follow Christ in radical poverty, and to shape one's whole life upon him. The journey into the desert is a departure from the solid, interconnected structure of the local Church, a departure from a Christianity more and more adapted to the needs of worldly life, launching into a discipleship with no "ifs" or "buts". Now, however, a new spiritual fatherhood comes into being, which is indeed not directly missionary in character, yet supplements the fatherhood of the bishops and priests with the power of an entirely "pneumatic", spiritual life.[8]

In the writings of Basil, who gave to oriental monasticism its enduring shape, we can see quite clearly the outlines of the complex of difficulties that many movements today know they are liable to face. He by no means wanted to create his own institution alongside the ordinary Church. The first and one real "rule" that he wrote was intended—as von Balthasar expresses it—not to be the rule for an order, but a rule for the

---

[7] See Athanase d'Alexandrie, *Vie d'Antoine* [Life of Anthony], ed. G. Bartelink, Sources Chrétiennes 400 (Paris, 1994); in the introduction, especially the section "L'Exemple de la vie évangélique et apostolique" [The example of the evangelical and apostolic life], pp. 52f.

[8] On the theme of spiritual fatherhood, I should like to refer you to the sensitive little book by G. Bunge, *Geistliche Vaterschaft: Christliche Gnosis bei Evagrios Pontikos* [Spiritual fatherhood: Christian gnosis in the writings of Evagrius Ponticus] (Regensburg, 1988).

Church, the "Enchiridion of the committed Christian".[9] But that is how it is at the beginning of almost all movements, especially in our own century: people are not trying to start a separate community; they are trying to establish Christianity as a whole, the Church that is obedient to the gospel and lives on that basis. Basil, who was a monk first of all, accepted the office of bishop and thus emphasized the charismatic character of episcopal office, living out the inner unity of the Church in one's own life. The same thing happened to Basil as has happened to today's movements: he had to accept the fact that a movement of radical discipleship does not permit of its being entirely amalgamated with the local Church. In a second attempt at a rule, which Gribomont calls "the Little Asketikon", his idea emerges of a movement as a "transitional form, in between a group of committed Christians open to the Church as a whole and an order of monks that organizes itself and creates its own institutions".[10] It is again Gribomont who sees in the community of monks founded by Basil a "small group to give life to the whole" and who does not hesitate to address Basil "as the patron not only of the teaching and caritative orders, but also of the new communities who do not take vows".[11]

This much is clear: the **monastic movement** creates a new center of life that does not abolish the structure of local Churches in the postapostolic Church and yet does not simply coincide with it, rather, it works within it **as a stimulating**

---

[9] H. U. von Balthasar, *Die großen Ordensregeln* [The great "rules" for religious orders], 7th ed. (Einsiedeln, 1994), p. 47.

[10] J. Gribomont, "Les Règles morales de S. Basile et le Nouveau Testament" [The moral rules of Saint Basil and the New Testament], *Studia Patristica* 2 (1957): 416–26; von Balthasar, *Großen Ordensregeln*, pp. 48f.

[11] J. Gribomont, "Obéissance et Évangile selon S. Basile le Grand" [Obedience and the gospel according to Saint Basil the Great], *Vie Spirituelle*, suppl. no. 21 (1952): 192–215; on this point, p. 192; von Balthasar, *Großen Ordensregeln*, p. 57.

force and, at the same time, as a reservoir from which may come forth for the local Church truly spiritual clergy, in whom institution and charism are ever anew fused together. It is characteristic of this that the Eastern Church takes her bishops from among the monks and thereby defines the office of bishop as being charismatic, constantly renewing it, so to say, on the basis of apostolic life.

If one looks at Church history as a whole, it is clear that, on the one hand, the local Church, as shaped by the office of bishop, is the form that provides the fundamental framework that endures through the ages. Yet waves of movements are always sweeping through her that reinstate and reapply the **universalist aspect of the apostolic mission and the radical dimension of the gospel** and thus serve to promote the spiritual life and truth of the local Churches.

I should like briefly to mention five such waves that follow the monasticism of the early Church and in which the spiritual nature of what we may call "movements" becomes ever clearer, so that their ecclesiological place is progressively defined.

1. I would describe as the first wave the **missionary monasticism** that flourished especially from Gregory the Great (590–604) to Gregory II (715–731) and Gregory III (731–741). Pope Gregory the Great recognized the missionary potential in monasticism and made use of it by sending Augustine—later Archbishop of Canterbury—with his companions to the heathen Angles in the British Isles. Saint Patrick's Irish mission had already preceded them, and Patrick, too, had his spiritual roots in monasticism. Thus monasticism became a great missionary movement that brought the Germanic peoples to the Catholic Church and thus built up the new Christian Europe. Linking East and West together, in the ninth century the monks Cyril and Methodius, two brothers,

carried the Christian faith to the Slavic world. In all this, two of the constitutive elements of the thing we call a "movement" appear quite clearly:

a. The **papacy** did not bring the movement into being, but it was its essential anchor in the structure of the Church, its **ecclesial support**. The deepest significance and the true nature of the Petrine office as such becomes visible here: the Bishop of Rome is not just bishop of a local Church; his office always relates to the universal Church. To that extent it is, in one specific sense, apostolic in character. It has to keep alive the impulse, directed both outward and inward, of its mission. In the Eastern Church the emperor had at first laid claim to a kind of office of unity and universality; it was not by chance that Constantine was referred to as "bishop" for those outside and as "equal to an apostle". Yet that could at most be a matter of acting as substitute, and its dangers are obvious. It is no accident that from the middle of the second century onward, with the end of the old universal ministries, the claims of the popes to be particularly conscious of these components of the apostolic mission emerge ever more clearly. Again and again, movements that go beyond the sphere of the local Church and her structures go hand in hand with the papacy, and not by chance.

b. The theme of the evangelical life-style, which we meet right at the beginning of the monastic movement with Anthony of Egypt, remains determinative. Yet it now transpires that the *vita evangelica* includes the ministry of evangelism: the poverty and the freedom of the evangelical life-style are conditions requisite for a ministry of evangelism that goes beyond one's own homeland and home congregation, and this in turn is the aim and the inner basis for the *vita evangelica*, as we shall immediately see more clearly.

2. I would just briefly like to refer to the **Cluny reform movement**, which was influential in the tenth century and which with the support of the papacy achieved the emancipation of the *vita religiosa* from the feudal system and from the bishops as feudal lords. By bringing together individual monasteries into a congregation, this became a great movement for religious practice and renewal, within which the **idea of Europe** developed.[12] Out of the reforming power of Cluny emerged in the eleventh century the **Gregorian reform**,[13] which tore the papacy free when it was foundering in the quarrels of the Roman nobility and its worldliness and, more generally, took up the fight for the freedom of the Church in order to assert her own spiritual nature—though this did, of course, then largely degenerate into a power struggle between the pope and the emperor.

3. The spiritual power of the evangelical movement that broke forth in the thirteenth century with Francis of Assisi and Dominic is still at work in our own day. In Francis' case, it is quite clear that he did not intend to found a new religious order or to create a separate community. He simply wanted to call the Church back to living the whole gospel, to gather together the "new people", to renew the Church from the gospel. The two meanings of the term **"evangelical life"** pass into each other indivisibly: anyone who lives out the gospel, in the poverty of renunciation of worldly goods and of

---

[12] B. Senger, in LThK, 2nd ed., vol. 2, col. 1239, points out the connection between the Cluniac reform and the way the idea of Europe took shape and also makes us aware of the significance of the "legal independence and the aid of the popes".

[13] Even though P. Engelbert, in LThK, 3rd ed., vol. 2, col. 1236, is right in saying that "A direct influence of the C.R. [= Cluniac reform] on the Gregorian reform cannot be demonstrated", the remarks of B. Senger, in LThK, 2nd ed., vol. 2, col. 1240, to the effect that the C.R. had helped to prepare a suitable climate for the Gregorian reform, are still nonetheless valid.

descendants, must at the same time be proclaiming the gospel. There was at that time a need for the gospel, and Francis regarded it as his most essential task, with his brothers, to proclaim to men the simple core of the message of Christ. He and those who were with him wanted to be evangelists. And naturally this meant having to go beyond the borders of Christendom, having to carry the gospel to the ends of the earth.[14]

In his dispute with the secular clergy at the University of Paris, who, as representatives of a narrow-minded, closed system of local Churches, were opposed to the evangelizing movement, Thomas Aquinas summed up what was new and, at the same time, what was in keeping with Christian origins in these two movements and the form of religious life shaped by them. The secular priests were willing to recognize only the Cluniac type of monk, in its later ossified form: monasteries clearly separated from the local Church, living strictly within and unto themselves and serving only for contemplation. Those could not disturb or obstruct the local Church's organization, whereas with the new preachers there were inevitably clashes all over the place. Thomas Aquinas, in contrast to that, had emphasized Christ himself as the model and on that basis had defended the superiority of the apostolic life as against a purely contemplative life-style. "The active life, which suggests to others the truths attained through preaching and contemplation, is more perfect than

---

[14] The *Fonti francescane*, published by the Movimiento Francescano (Assisi, 1978), which set an ideal standard with their helpful introductions and bibliographical information, must remain normative for an understanding of Saint Francis. The article by A. Jotischky, "Some Mendicant Views of the Origins of the Monastic Profession", in *Christianesimo nella storia* XIX, 1 (Feruary 1998), pp. 31–49, is instructive on the way the mendicant orders understood themselves. The author shows how the mendicant writers referred to the early Church, and especially to the Desert Fathers, in order to portray their own origins and their significance within the Church.

the exclusively contemplative life." [15] Thomas was conscious
of being heir to the repeated renaissances of monastic life, all
of which referred to the *vita apostolica*.[16] Yet in the interpretation of the *vita apostolica*—coming to it from the experience
of the mendicant orders—he took an important new step,
which had indeed been at work in monastic tradition thus
far but had been little thought about. Everyone had referred
to the primitive Church for the *vita apostolica*; Augustine, for
example, had ultimately worked out his entire rule on the
basis of Acts 4:32: They were of one heart and soul.[17] Thomas Aquinas now added to this essential model Jesus' speech
when he sends out the apostles, in Matthew 10:5–15: the
true *vita apostolica* is the one that follows the teaching of Acts
4 *and* that of Matthew 10: "The apostolic life comprises the
way that the apostles, after they had left everything,
went through the world proclaiming the gospel and preaching, as is clear from Matthew 10, where they are given a rule
of life." [18] Matthew 10 now appears really like a religious rule,
or, to put it better: The rule of life and mission that
the Lord gave to the apostles is itself the enduring rule for the
apostolic life, which the Church always has need of. On the
basis of this rule the new evangelizing movement can be
justified.

---

[15] *Summa Theol.* III, q. 40, a. 1 ad 2. See J.-P. Torrell, *Magister Thomas: Leben
und Werk des Thomas von Aquin* [Magister Thomas: The life and work of Thomas
Aquinas] (Herder, 1998) (original French title: *Initiation à saint Thomas d'Aquin:
La Personne et son oeuvre*); see therein the stimulating and illuminating portrayal
of Saint Thomas' position in the dispute over the mendicant orders, esp. pp.
102–14.

[16] Thus Torrell, *Magister Thomas*, p. 108.

[17] See A. Zumkeller, in von Balthasar, *Großen Ordensregeln*, pp. 150–57. On
the place of the rule in Augustine's life and work, G. Vigini, *Agostino d'Ippona:
L'aventura della grazia e della carità* [Augustine of Hippo: The adventure of grace
and love] (Cinisello Balsamo, 1988), pp. 91–109.

[18] *Contra impugnantes Dei cultum et religionem* 4, quoted from Torrell, *Magister
Thomas*, p. 109.

The dispute at Paris **between the secular clergy and the representatives of the new movements**, in which context these passages originated, is of lasting significance. A narrow and impoverished idea of the Church, which assigns an absolute value to the structure of the local Church, cannot tolerate the new class of preachers, who for their part necessarily find their **anchor and support in the bearer of a universal office, in the pope, as the person who guarantees the missionary task and the building up of the one Church**. Thus it was logical that the great new impulse for the development of the doctrine of primacy came from this starting point and that it was thereby understood anew—over and beyond any contemporary coloring—on the basis of its apostolic roots.[19]

4. Since we are not concerned with Church history here but with understanding the forms of life within the Church, I must make do with just a brief mention of the sixteenth-century evangelizing movements. Among these the Jesuits, who then took up the **worldwide mission** in newly discovered America, in Africa, and in Asia, were outstanding; while Dominicans and Franciscans, with their continuing missionary dynamic, were not far behind them.

---

[19] I depicted the connection between the dispute over the mendicant orders and the doctrine of primacy in a study that first appeared in the *Festschrift* for Schmaus—*Theologie in Geschichte und Gegenwart* [Theology in history and in the present day] (1957)—which I then included, with some small additions, in my book *Das neue Volk Gottes* [The new People of God] (Düsseldorf, 1969), pp. 49–71. Y. Congar picked up my work, essentially worked out from Bonaventure and his interlocutors, and extended it across the whole area of relevant sources: "Aspects ecclésiologiques de la querelle entre mendiants et séculiers dans la seconde moitié du XIIIe siècle et le début du XIVe" [Ecclesiological aspects of the dispute between mendicants and seculars in the second half of the thirteenth century and the beginning of the fourteenth], AHD 28 (1961): 35–151.

5. Finally, we all know the new surge of movements that began in the nineteenth century. Strictly missionary congregations then arose, which from the outset were aiming less at inner renewal than at mission to those continents where Christianity had hardly taken hold at all. To that extent any clash with the organization of the local Church was largely avoided, and a fruitful teamwork developed, from which indeed the historic local Churches derived new strength, because the impulse toward spreading the gospel and for loving service animated them from within. Here appeared most powerfully an element that had by no means been lacking in the previous movements but that could nonetheless easily be overlooked: the apostolic movement of the nineteenth century was above all also a **women's movement**, in which, for one thing, there was more emphasis upon *caritas*, on caring for the suffering and the poor. We know how much the new women's orders meant—and still mean—for hospitals and for the care of those in need. Yet schools and education were also central here, and thus in the combination of teaching, education, and love the whole breadth of the gospel ministry was present. If we look back prior to the nineteenth century, we can see that women have always been an essential factor in helping to shape the apostolic movements. We may think of the adventurous women of the sixteenth century, such as Mary Ward or, on the other hand, Teresa of Avila; of women of the Middle Ages, such as Hildegard of Bingen and Catherine of Siena; the women in the circle around Saint Boniface; the sisters of the Church Fathers; and finally the women in Paul's letters and those around Jesus. The **women** were never in fact bishops or priests, but they were **among those who carried forward the apostolic life and its universal task.**

3. The Breadth of the Concept of Apostolic Succession

Following this tour through the great apostolic movements in Church history, let us return to the thesis I formulated after the brief analysis of the biblical evidence: **the concept of apostolic succession has to be understood more broadly and more profoundly if we want to do justice to the whole of the claim it makes**. What does that mean? First, as the central element in this concept, we keep hold of the sacramental structure of the Church, within which she receives ever anew the heritage of the apostles, the heritage of Christ. Through the sacrament of orders, in which Christ is acting through the Holy Spirit, she is distinguished from other institutions. The sacrament means that she lives as "a vessel of the Holy Spirit", founded on the Lord, and is constantly being re-created. Here the two inseparable components of the sacrament, about which we spoke earlier, must be kept in view: first there is the incarnational and christological element, that is to say, the Church's being linked to the "once only" element of the Incarnation and the Paschal events, the link with God's action in history. Yet at the same time there is the way that this event is made present now in the power of the Holy Spirit—that is, the christological and pneumatological component that guarantees both the newness and the continuity of the living Church.

This sums up what has always been taught in the Church as being the nature of the apostolic succession, the real heart of the sacramental conception of the Church. Yet this essential heart is impoverished, indeed it withers, if one is thinking only about the local Church structure. The office of the Petrine succession breaks open a structure based merely on the local Church; the successor of Peter is not merely the local Bishop of Rome; rather, he is bishop for the whole Church, and in the whole Church. Thereby he embodies one side of the essence of the apostolic mission that should never be absent within the Church. Yet the Petrine office, again, would not be rightly understood, and would become ossified as a monstrous exceptional case, if we were to load onto the person occupying that office sole responsibility for enforcing the universal dimension of the apostolic succession.[20] **There must always be in the Church ministries and missions that do not belong purely to the local Church but serve the task given the whole Church, the task of spreading the gospel.** The pope is dependent on these ministries, and they on him, and, in the existence side by side of the two kinds of mission, the symphony of Church life comes to fulfillment. The normative apostolic age exhibits in a way obvious to everyone how these components are indispensable for the life of the Church. The sacrament of orders, the sacrament of succession, is necessarily involved in this structural form, but—even more so than in the local Churches—it is surrounded by a multitude of ministries, and here the part taken by women in the Church's apostolate becomes impossible to overlook. Summing up the whole thing, we could even say that the primacy of the successor of Peter is there to guarantee the presence of these essential components of Church life and to bring them into an ordered relationship with the structures of the local Church.

So as to avoid any misunderstanding, I should say quite clearly here that the apostolic movements appear in history in forms that are ever new—necessarily so, because they are the

---

[20] People's aversion toward the primacy and the disappearance of their sense of the universality of the Church are no doubt connected in particular with the fact that the concept of the universal Church is to be found in fixed concrete form only in the papacy and that this, if isolated and deprived of the living matrix of realities within the Church as a whole, appears as a scandalous monolith that disturbs the picture of a church reduced to purely local ministries and the neighborly existence of congregations. This does not at all correspond to the reality of the early Church.

Holy Spirit's answer to the changing circumstances in which the Church is living. And just as vocations to the priesthood cannot be created, cannot be administratively determined, then movements most certainly cannot be organizationally introduced according to plans by the authorities. They have to be given to us, and they are given. We simply have to pay attention to them: by the gift of discernment, pick up what is right in them and learn to overcome what is not useful. Looking back on Church history, we may remark with thankfulness that through all the difficulties it has always been possible to make a place in the Church for the great new upsurges of life. We will of course be unable to avoid seeing all the series of movements that failed or that led to lasting division: Montanists, Cathars, Waldensians, Hussites, the Reformation movement of the sixteenth century. And we will probably have to talk about there being faults on both sides that left division here in the end.

III. DISTINCTIONS AND YARDSTICKS

Thus, our final task in this paper, the question of the criteria by which we should make distinctions, becomes unavoidable. In order to give a good answer we should first of all have to define the concept "movement" a little more closely, perhaps even to attempt a classification of movements. All that can obviously not be done here. We should also be wary of using too strict a definition, for the Holy Spirit always has further surprises in store, and it is only in looking back that we can recognize that there is some common nature amid all the great variety. I should like nonetheless to begin to clarify this concept by distinguishing from each other three different types we can observe in recent history, at any rate. I would give them the names of movement, trend, and action. The

Liturgical Movement of the first half of the twentieth century, and also the Marian movement that has become ever more prominent in the Church since the nineteenth century, I would characterize, not as movements, but as trends, which could have coalesced into the concrete form of movements like the Marian Congregation or groups of Catholic Youth but which nonetheless reached beyond those. The organized petitions for some dogmatic definition or for some change in the Church, which have become normal these days, are again not movements, but actions. We can perhaps see most clearly what a movement is in the Franciscan upsurge of the thirteenth century: movements mostly derive from a charismatic leader, taking shape in concrete associations, and these live the whole gospel in a new way on this basis and unhesitatingly recognize the Church as the foundation of their life, for without her they cannot exist.[21]

With this beginning of a definition—certainly quite inadequate—we have nevertheless already arrived at the **criteria** that will, so to speak, take the place of a definition. The essential yardstick has just emerged of its own accord: that of being rooted in the faith of the Church. Anyone who does not share the apostolic faith cannot claim to do apostolic work. Since the faith is one, for the whole Church—indeed, it constitutes her unity—the desire for unity is necessarily associated with the apostolic faith, the desire to stand within the living fellowship of the whole Church and, in concrete terms, to stand with the successors of the apostles and the successor of Peter, who is responsible for the interplay of local Churches and the universal Church as the one People of God. If the "apostolic" element is the place of movements in the

---

[21] For determining the nature of movements, A. Cattaneo, "I movimenti ecclesiali: Aspetti ecclesiologi" [Ecclesiastical movements: Some ecclesiological aspects], *Annales Theologici* 11 (1997): 401–27, and, on this point, pp. 406–9, is helpful.

Church, then the desire for the *vita apostolica* must be fundamental to her in all ages. The renunciation of property, of
descendants, of any effort to impose one's own idea of the
Church—that is, obedience in following Christ—have in all
ages been regarded as the essential elements of the apostolic
life, which cannot of course apply in the same way for all
those participating in a movement but which are in varying
ways points for orienting each person's own life that are
relevant for everyone. The apostolic life, in turn, is not an end
in itself; rather, it creates freedom to serve. An apostolic life
calls out for apostolic action: there is in the first place—again,
in varying fashion—the proclamation of the gospel as the
missionary element. In following Christ, evangelizing always
takes first place: *evangelizare pauperibus*—proclaiming the gospel to the poor. Yet this never takes place through words
alone: love, which constitutes its inner heart, both the center
of its truth and the heart of its activity, has to be lived out and
has in that sense to be a proclamation. Thus social service is
always associated with the gospel in some form or other. All
this presupposes—mainly on the basis of the charisma that has
kindled it all—a personal encounter with Christ at a deep
level. Becoming a community together, and building up the
community, does not exclude the personal element; rather, it
promotes its growth. Only when a person has been touched
by Christ and opened up by him in his deepest heart can the
other person also be touched in his heart; only in that case can
reconciliation be effected in the Holy Spirit; only then can
true community grow. Within this basic framework, christological, pneumatological, and existential, there can be most
varied accentuations and emphases, in which the novelty of
Christianity comes into being time and again, while again and
again the Church's "youth is renewed like the eagle's" by the
Holy Spirit (Ps 103:5).

On that basis both the **dangers** that there are in movements become visible and, likewise, the **paths of healing**. One-sided developments are a threat, through the overemphasis on the specific task that arises either in a given era or through a charismatic gift. If the spiritual upsurge is experienced, not as one form of Christian life, but as people's being struck by the simple entirety of the message, this can lead to their attributing an absolute value to the movement, which then understands itself as the Church herself, as the way for everyone, whereas this one way can in fact be shared with people in a variety of ways. Thus, on account of the freshness and the all-embracing nature of the spiritual upsurge, there is time and again, almost inevitably, a clash with the local congregation, in which there may be fault on both sides and by which both are therefore challenged spiritually. The local Churches may have come to a certain degree of conformity with the world; the salt may have become stale, as Kierkegaard depicted in bitter and caustic terms in his criticism of Christianity. Even when the drift away from the radical claims of the gospel has not attained the degree that Kierkegaard thus castigated, the irruption of a new element will nonetheless be experienced as something difficult and disturbing, especially if it appears with all kinds of youthful ailments and misplaced claims to absolute value, as happens far from rarely.

In that case, both sides have to accept lessons from the Holy Spirit and also from the Church authorities, have to learn a selflessness without which it is impossible to attain inner assent to the many forms in which the faith is lived out. Each side has to learn from the other, has to let itself be purified, must bear with the other and find its way to those attitudes of which Paul is speaking in his great hymn to love (1 Cor 13:4ff.). Thus movements—even if they have found the whole gospel on their path and are sharing it with others—must be warned that they are a gift made to the Church as a whole and that they need to submit to the demands of the whole in order to remain true to their own nature.[22] The local Churches too, however, and even the bishops, have to be told that they should not indulge in any pursuit of uniformity in their pastoral arrangements or planning. They should not set up their own pastoral plans as a yardstick of what the Holy Spirit is allowed to do: the Churches could quite possibly become impermeable to the Spirit of God through sheer planning, impermeable to the power from which they live.[23] It should not be the case that everything has to take its place within a single system of organization; far better less organization and more Spirit!

Above all, there must not be a concept of "communion" in which the avoidance of conflict becomes the prime pastoral value. Faith is always also a sword and may indeed promote conflict for the sake of truth and love (see Mt 10:34). Any concept of Church unity in which conflicts are a priori dismissed as polarization and peace within is bought at the price of renouncing witness to the whole gospel will soon prove to be illusory. Lastly, we should not set up a kind of blasé "enlightened" attitude that regards the zeal of those who have been seized by the Holy Spirit, and their uninhibited belief in the Word of God, as being equivalent to that fundamentalism which is anathema; an attitude that allows only that kind of faith for which "ifs" and "buts" become more important than the substance of what is believed itself. Finally, all of us must let ourselves be measured by the yardstick of our love for the unity of the *one* Church, which is but one single Church in all the local Churches and as such makes her appearance again in the apostolic movements. Time and again, local Churches and apostolic movements will have to recognize and accept that the same thing is true for both of them: "Ubi Petrus, ibi ecclesia—ubi episcopus, ibi ecclesia." The primacy and the

---

[22] See ibid., pp. 423–25.

[23] Cattaneo, ibid., pp. 413f. and p. 417, is insistent on this point.

episcopate, the structures of the local Church and the apostolic movements, all need one another: the primacy can live only through, and together with, a lively episcopate; the episcopate can maintain its dynamic and apostolic unity only in being ordered with reference to a primate. Whenever one of the two is weakened, the Church as a whole suffers.

After all these reflections, we should be left at the end, above all, with **gratitude** and **joy**. Gratitude that the Holy Spirit is quite obviously still at work in the Church today and endowing her with new gifts, through which she can relive the joy of her youth (Ps 42:4, Vulg.). Gratitude for the many people, young and old, who respond to the calling of the Holy Spirit and joyfully step out in the service of the gospel without turning back. Gratitude for those bishops who make themselves open to new ways, make a place for them in their local Churches, struggle patiently with them to overcome their one-sided attitudes, and guide them toward their true form. And above all, in this place and at this moment, we thank our Pope, John Paul II, who is ahead of us all in his capacity for enthusiasm, in his ability to become inwardly youthful through faith, in his discernment of spirits, in his humble and courageous struggle to achieve the fullness of ministries on behalf of the gospel, in his unity, in listening and advising, with the bishops of the whole world, who is for us all the guide toward Christ. Christ is alive, and he sends the Holy Spirit from the Father—that is the joyful and enlivening experience that is ours precisely in the encounter with the Church movements of our time.

Presentation of the Declaration
Dominus Iesus

In the press conference room of the Holy See,
on September 5, 2000

The following explanation is limited to outlining the circumstances giving rise to the declaration *Dominus Iesus* and its significance, since the talks that come afterward will explain the value, as well as the authority and status, of the document's teaching and, likewise, its particular contents in terms of Christology and ecclesiology.

1. In the current lively debate about the relationship of Christianity to other religions, the notion is becoming more and more widespread that all religions are of equal value for their adherents as paths to salvation. This conviction has meanwhile become accepted not only in the realm of theology, but also quite extensively among the Catholic public at large, and is being reinforced in particular by a cultural trend currently dominant in the West, that referred to as **relativism**.

The so-called **pluralist theology of religion**, although it has only recently attained substantial importance in the awareness of Christians, has gradually been gaining ground since the fifties of the twentieth century. The concepts current at any one time take many forms, and it would be a mistake to lump together all the theological positions we meet in this field. The declaration does not describe the essential characteristics of individual theological positions, nor does it attempt to sum them all up under a single formula. Rather, this document outlines some of the **philosophical and theological presuppositions** underlying the various pluralist theologies of religion:

—the belief that divine truth cannot be apprehended and is quite ineffable;

—the relativist attitude with regard to the truth, according to which what is true for some people is said to be not true for others;

—the radical opposition existing between the West's logical mode of thought and the symbolic mode of the East;

—the subjectivism of those who take human understanding to be the only source of knowledge;

—the metaphysical emptying of the mystery of the Incarnation;

—the eclecticism of those who in the course of theological research take over ideas from other philosophical and religious systems, regardless of their logic or of whether they can be reconciled with the Christian faith;

—finally, the tendency to interpret Holy Scripture without regard to the tradition or the teaching office of the Church (see declaration *Dominus Iesus*, no. 4).

What basic **consequences** does this way of thinking have for the heart and core of the Christian faith? Briefly, it is the **refusal to identify the unique historical figure of Jesus of Nazareth with the reality of God, the living God himself, since it is held that absolute being, or the absolute being, can never be completely and finally revealed in history**. In history, it is said, there are only models, ideal figures, who point us toward the Wholly Other, who as such cannot be apprehended historically. Some more moderate theologians do indeed recognize Jesus Christ as true God and true man but are of the opinion that on account of the limitations of the human nature of Jesus the revelation of God in him cannot be seen as final and complete but always has to be seen in relation to other possible revelations of God, like the great religious figures of mankind and the founders of religions. In this way, objectively speaking, the erroneous notion is introduced that the religions of the world are complementary to the Christian revelation. That means that the Church, dogma, and sacraments can have no absolute and necessary value. Attributing an absolute character to these limited media, and even regarding them as instruments for a real encounter with the truth of God, it is held, would mean elevating something particular to an absolute status and misrepresenting the reality of God, the Wholly Other who is never at our disposal.

In view of these objections, insisting that there is a universal, binding, and valid truth in history, which became flesh in Jesus Christ and is handed on through the faith of the Church, is regarded as a kind of fundamentalism, as an attack upon the modern spirit, and as a threat to tolerance and freedom. Here it becomes quite clear that **understanding through dialogue** has taken on a meaning that differs radically from the "understanding through dialogue" that the Second Vatican Council talked about. Dialogue—or, rather, the ideology of dialogue—has taken the place of mission and of the urgent call to conversion. Dialogue is no longer understood as a way to discover the truth, as a process through which one reveals to the other person the hidden depths of what he has learned in his religious experience and which is now being purified through the encounter with the final and complete revelation of Jesus Christ, thus finding its fulfillment. The new ideological form of dialogue, which unfortunately has found its way even within the Catholic Church and into certain theological and cultural spheres, aims at relativizing "dogma"—this is the opposite of "conversion" and "mission". What dialogue means, for relativist thinking, is this: setting one's own position, or one's own faith, and what the other person believes on the same level, so that everything is reduced to an exchange of opinions that are fundamentally relative and of equal value, with the aim of achieving a maximum of cooperation and integration between the different conceptions of religion.

The **dissolution of Christology, and of the ecclesiology that is subordinate to it yet indissolubly associated with it**, is the logical consequence of such a relativist philosophy, which, paradoxically, serves as a foundation both for the post-metaphysical thought of the West and for the negative theology of Asia. The result is that the figure of Jesus Christ loses its uniqueness and its character as being universally valid for salvation. The fact that relativism presents itself, under the banner of the encounter with other cultures, as the true and humane philosophy, as the only philosophy in a position to guarantee tolerance and democracy, leads in the end to the marginalizing of those who continue to defend the identity of Christianity and the claims of the universal saving truth in Jesus Christ. The truth is that this criticism of the absoluteness and finality of the claims made by the Christian faith on behalf of Christ's revelation is accompanied by a false concept of toleration. The principle of toleration, as the expression of respect for the freedom of conscience, of thought, and of religion, was defended and promoted by the Second Vatican Council and is set out again in this declaration; this is a fundamental ethical principle, which is a part of the Christian credo because it involves taking seriously the freedom to decide on one's faith. Yet this principle and respect for freedom are today being manipulated and inappropriately exaggerated if they are extended to include the acceptance of the contents of religious belief and if it is being maintained that all the contents of the various religions, and indeed nonreligious conceptions of life, are of equal value but that objective and generally valid truth, on the other hand, does not exist, because it is said that God, or the Absolute, reveals himself under countless names and that all these names are true. This false understanding of toleration is connected with the loss, or perhaps the **renunciation, of the question of truth**, which is indeed being dismissed by many people today as a meaningless question. In this way the intellectual weakness of present-day culture is becoming apparent. If the question of truth is no longer being considered, then what religion essentially is, is no longer distinguishable from what it is not; faith is no longer differentiated from superstition, experience from illusion. Unless claims to truth are considered, respect for other religions ultimately becomes contradictory and meaningless, because there is no criterion by which to distinguish what is of positive value in any religion and what is negative or is the product of superstition and deception.

2. In this connection, the declaration takes up something said in the encyclical *Redemptoris missio*: "Whatever the Spirit brings about in human hearts and in the history of peoples, in cultures and religions, serves as a preparation for the gospel" (no. 29). This passage refers explicitly to the action of the Spirit, not only "in human hearts", but also "in religions". The activity of the Spirit is connected to the inner mystery of Christ, and it should never be considered apart from that. Since the religions of the world are rooted in history and in the cultures of the various peoples, there is always a mixture of good and evil to be found in them. That is why not everything can be seen as *praeparatio evangelica*, but only "whatever the Spirit brings about". There is an important conclusion to be drawn from this fact: **The good that is present in the various religions offers paths toward**

salvation and does so as part of the activity of the Spirit in Christ, but the religions themselves do not. This is already being emphasized in the Second Vatican Council's declaration *Nostra aetate*, with reference to the seeds of truth and goodness that are present in other religions and cultures: "The Catholic Church rejects nothing that is true and holy in these religions. She regards with sincere reverence those ways of conduct and of life, those precepts and teachings that, though differing in many aspects from the ones she holds and sets forth, nonetheless often reflect a ray of that truth that enlightens all men" (no. 2). **All the truth and goodness that exist in other religions should not be lost but should rather be recognized and appreciated. Goodness and truth, wherever they may be, come from the Father and are the work of the Holy Spirit. The seeds of the Logos are cast abroad everywhere. Yet we cannot shut our eyes to the errors and illusions that are present in these religions.** The Second Vatican Council, in the Dogmatic Constitution on the Church, emphasizes that "often men, deceived by the Evil One, have become vain in their reasonings and have exchanged the truth of God for a lie, serving the creature rather than the Creator" (*Lumen gentium*, no. 16).

In a world that is growing ever closer together, the various religions and cultures naturally meet each other. That leads not only to people of various religions coming externally closer to one another, but also to a growing interest in religious worlds that were hitherto unknown to them. In that sense, with respect to the process of becoming mutually acquainted, it is legitimate to talk about its being mutually enriching. Yet that has nothing to do with giving up the claim of the Christian faith that in Christ we have received as a gift from God the final and complete revelation of the mystery of God's salvation. This way of thinking should be avoided, as it is imbued with a religious relativism that leads to the assumption that "one religion is just as good as another" (*Redemptoris missio*, no. 36).

That respect and regard for the religions and cultures of the world, which have brought an objective enriching in terms of promoting human dignity and the development of civilization, neither diminish the originality and unique status of the revelation of Jesus Christ nor restrict the missionary task of the Church: "She proclaims, and ever must proclaim, Christ 'the way, the truth, and the life' (Jn 14:6), in whom men may find the fullness of religious life" (*Nostra aetate*, no. 2). These simple words show at the same time what is the inner motive for the conviction that the revelation of God is full, universal, and final only as present in the Christian faith. This motive has its roots, not indeed in any presumption of superiority that might be ascribed to the Church's faithful or in the historical events in the course of the Church's earthly pilgrimage, but in the mystery of Christ, who is true God and true man. The claim that Christianity is unique and universal as a way of salvation essentially arises from the mystery of Jesus Christ, whose presence in the Church, his body and his bride, is enduring. That is why the Church sees herself as being, by her very nature, obliged to evangelize all peoples. Even in the present day, which is characterized by a religious pluralism and by the demand for freedom of choice and freedom of opinion, the Church is aware that she is called "to save and renew every creature, that all things may be restored in Christ and all men may constitute one family in him and one People of God" (*Ad gentes*, no. 1).

The declaration *Dominus Iesus* by the Congregation for the Doctrine of the Faith, which the Pope has affirmed "certa scientia et apostolica sua auctoritate", emphasizes the truths it presents and that the faith of the Church has always believed and firmly held and protects the faithful from widely disseminated errors or ambiguous interpretations. Thereby it fulfills two tasks: first it gives a renewed and most valuable witness to the world, showing "the glory of the gospel of Christ" (see 2 Cor 4:4), and then it officially lays down for the faithful as obligatory those fundamentals of teaching that can never be surrendered and that must guide, inspire, and direct, not only theological research, but also the pastoral and missionary activity of the faithful in the whole Catholic Church.

Exchange of Letters
between Metropolitan Damaskinos and
Cardinal Joseph Ratzinger

About the Declaration by the Congregation for the Doctrine of the Faith Dominus Iesus[1]
and about the Note by the Congregation for the Doctrine of the Faith Sister Churches[2]

METROPOLITAN DAMASKINOS OF SWITZERLAND

To His Eminence
Joseph Cardinal Ratzinger,
Prefect of the Congregation for the Doctrine of the Faith

Chambésy, October 30, 2000

Your Eminence,
My dear and respected Brother and Friend,
I am very happy to think back to our last unforgettable meeting from the fourteenth to the sixteenth of October in Tuscany, and I do so with gratitude.

---

[1] *Declaratio Dominus Iesus: De Iesu Christe atque Ecclesiae unicitate et universalitate salvifica*, Congregatio pro doctrina fidei (Libreria Editrice Vaticana, 2000); Eng. trans.: *Dominus Jesus* (London: Catholic Truth Society, 2000). On the Internet: ENGLISH TEXT: http://www.vatican.va/roman_curia/congregations/cfaith/documents/rc_con_cfaith_doc_20000806_dominus-iesus_en.html. LATIN TEXT: http://www.vatican.va/roman_curia/congregations/cfaith/documents/rc_con_cfaith_doc_20000806_dominus-iesus_lt.html.

[2] KNA Öki, Doc. no. 4, supplement to no. 38, 2000, of September 12, pp. 1–3; on the Internet: ENGLISH TEXT: http://www.vatican.va/roman_curia/congregations/cfaith/documents/rc_con_cfaith_doc_20000630_chiese-sorelle_en.html.

This meeting was an opportunity for us to reflect upon a great deal of what you, in your capacity as Prefect of the Congregation for the Doctrine of the Faith, had shortly before sent out as the official statement of the Roman Catholic Church to her bishops. I am thinking here of the declaration *Dominus Iesus* and especially of the *Note* of the Congregation for the Doctrine of the Faith about sister Churches.

When in 1999 I gave a lecture to the Roman Catholic Faculty of Theology at the University of Bonn about the contribution of the Greek Orthodox Church and Greek Orthodox theology in Europe today, I emphasized among other things that divine providence had so ordered matters that from 1959 onward, when I was continuing my studies in Germany with a scholarship from the Ecumenical Patriarch of Constantinople, I was able to have as my teacher and friend the young Professor Joseph Ratzinger. Our relationship was one of a growing and deepening fellowship. We discovered together what it means to belong to the Roman Catholic Church and to the Orthodox Church: two Churches that have rediscovered each other as sister Churches. Thus we helped each other prepare inwardly for the great event of the year 1965: the eradication of the excommunication from the memories of our Churches. In this fashion the passionate longing was awakened in us for the restoration of perfect unity between our Churches. We experienced the fact that we shared the same apostolic faith, and we followed the new epoch-making developments in our relations, from the *dialogue of love* right up to the official *theological dialogue*. We likewise felt that the mutual lifting of the excommunications did in fact create a new situation, which needed to be evaluated from a theological point of view.

This situation has a bearing upon psychological and ecclesiological dimensions far beyond the actual event, whose memory has faded. With time, it turned out that its echo among the people was wider and deeper than had been foreseen. Furthermore, this lifting of the anathemas produces, and must produce, a cleansing of memories that amounts to forgiveness. It has replaced the *symbol of division* with the *symbol of love*. It presumes the existence of a new ecclesiastical situation that will necessarily have increasing repercussions, at all levels, on each one of our local Churches. This reception is part of a process of drawing together and growth in understanding, for if it is true that there is an indissoluble link between theology and love, then the fact that we are both living out the Christian mystery that unites us will necessarily carry us farther. The Kingdom of God is being subjected to force.

I further recall the reflections you expressed on the occasion of our first ecclesiological meeting in Vienna, in 1974:

> By way of conclusion, let us ask again: What remains and what will be the consequences of the whole proceedings? The key event is this: the relationship "of a love grown cold", of "antitheses, mistrust, and antagonism", has been replaced by a relationship of love, of fraternity, the symbol of which is the fraternal embrace. The symbol of separation has been replaced by the symbol of love. Granted, the sacramental community has not yet been restored. But, after the "dialogue of love" has reached its first goal, the "theological dialogue" is expected to follow—not as a quiet academic skirmish that need arrive at no particular goal and is, basically, sufficient unto itself, but under the sign of "impatient expectation", which knows that "the hour has come". *Agape* and fraternal embrace are, in themselves, the *terminus* and *ritus* of eucharistic unity. Where *agape* is a reality in the Church, it must become a eucharistic *agape*. That must be the goal of every effort. That the goal may be reached, the most immediate result of the whole proceedings must be the unremitting

effort to bring about the "healing of memory". The legal fact of forgetting must be followed by the actual historical fact of a new memory. That is the inescapable challenge—at once legal and theological—that is inseparable from the event of December 7, 1965. [1]

We have learned together how *theology must be done* with reference to the special traditions of the West. We have experienced the way in which the revealed truth was differently received, lived out, and understood in East and West and that the variance in theologies can be understood as compatible within one and the same faith; and all the more, when a keen awareness for the transcendence of the mystery and for the mainly apophatic character that its human expression has to assume can leave free play for a legitimate pluralism of theologies within the bosom of the same traditional faith; and that one ought not to be a priori inclined to identify faith, and its expression, with particular theologies.

And we arrived together at the realization that East and West can meet and recognize one another again only if together they remember their original affinity and common past. As a first step, they would have to become aware of how East and West, despite all their differences, belong organically to one single Christendom. Together we arrived at the conclusion that our differences are to be understood in the sense of varying legitimate developments of one and the same apos-

---

[1] J. Ratzinger, "Das Ende der Bannflüche von 1054: Folgen für Rom und die Ostkirchen" [The ending of the anathema of 1054: Consequences for Rome and the Eastern Churches], *Internat. kathol. Zeitschrift Communio* 3 (1974): 289–303; reprinted in *Pro Oriente: Auf dem Weg zur Einheit des Glaubens* [Toward the East: On the way toward unity of belief] (Innsbruck, Vienna, and Munich, 1976), pp. 101–13, and in J. Ratzinger, *Theologische Prinzipienlehre: Bausteine zur Fundamentaltheologie* (Munich, 1982), pp. 214–30; quotation, pp. 229f.; Eng. trans.: *Principles of Catholic Theology* (San Francisco: Ignatius Press, 1987), pp. 217–18.

tolic faith in East and West, and not as divisions in the tradition of the faith itself. We also put the question differently: not only "Can we legitimately communicate with one another?", but also "Can we legitimately refuse Communion to one another?"

We felt, furthermore, that the *main obstacle* to the restoration of full communion is the pope's *primacy of jurisdiction.* The most difficult thing does in fact seem to be the question of Church order: on the one hand, for Rome, because it sees the primacy of the *Sedes Romana* as being constitutive for the unity of the Church; on the other hand, for the East, because it regards this very claim as being a change in the episcopal structure of the Church.

We asked ourselves how we can move forward in this, and we allowed ourselves to formulate a few possible perspectives—for example: if Rome resumed communion with the Eastern Churches without preconditions—with pan-Orthodox agreement, of course—then this is an explicit recognition of the legitimacy of the episcopal structure of the East. It includes a recognition that the East cannot be obliged to be part of the West's fully developed structure of primacy.

Conversely, the East would of course be recognizing that the West, in spite of the teaching on primacy, has not in principle strayed from the episcopal structure of the early Church, even if it has accepted an additional factor that from the point of view of the Eastern Church cannot be recognized as being necessary. The recognition of the continuing existence even in the West of the apostolic structure of the early Church could be made easier, on one hand, through the Second Vatican Council's efforts toward a clear restoration of episcopal order and, on the other, by the fact that the pope, whenever he communicates with the East, does not himself any longer advance the 1870 claim to primacy (*juridictio in omnes ecclesias*) in practice vis-à-vis the East.

Thus we have never abandoned hope that even the polarization with regard to the primacy of jurisdiction can be overcome so that the restoration of full communion, so deeply longed for, may soon become a reality. And there you, as Prefect of the Congregation for the Doctrine of the Faith, which has the mission of being "guardian of orthodoxy" and "defender of the faith", have a great part to play. May you be marked by the reflections and perspectives that you expressed in 1974, evaluating the reference to Ignatius of Antioch as quoted by Patriarch Athenagoras I when greeting Pope Paul VI:

> "Against all expectation the Bishop of Rome is in our midst, who is first in honor among us, 'he who has the presidency in love'" (Ignatius of Antioch, *To the Romans*: prologue; MPG 5, col. 801). It is clear that the Patriarch was not thereby departing from the Eastern Church's ground and recognizing the Western jurisdictional primacy. Yet he clearly sets forth what the Eastern Church has to say about the order in which the bishops of the Church, all equal in rank and in rights, stand, and it would indeed now be worthwhile reflecting whether this old confession, which has no awareness of "jurisdictional primacy", yet does recognize a first place in "honor" ($\tau\iota\mu\dot{\eta}$) and agape, might not be able to be evaluated as a view of the place of Rome in the Church that does justice to the heart of the matter—"sacred courage" demands "boldness" along with intelligence.[2]

All these views and reflections I am recalling here have made their mark on my life as a bishop and theologian. In the meantime, however, I have realized a number of things that

---

[2] Ibid., pp. 228f.

challenge me to put the question of whether there is any continuity between Professor Joseph Ratzinger and the Prefect of the Congregation for the Doctrine of the Faith. How do these statements I have just referred to relate to the following statements by Joseph Cardinal Ratzinger?

1. In the *Letter* of the Congregation for the Doctrine of the Faith "To the Bishops of the Catholic Church on Some Aspects of the Church as *Communion*", from 1992, the Orthodox Churches were referred to as "those venerable Christian communities" for whom "the current situation also means that their existence as particular Churches is *wounded*", since "communion with the universal Church, represented by Peter's successor, is, not an external complement to the particular Church, but one of her internal constituents" (§ 17). Thus, overcoming the state of being wounded through existing as only part of the Church presupposes the recognition of the jurisdictional primacy of the pope, without which no restoration of full communion appears to be conceivable.

2. In the *Note* of the Congregation for the Doctrine of the Faith about sister Churches, the following point is expounded: "In fact, in the proper sense, *sister Churches* are exclusively particular Churches (or groupings of particular Churches; for example, the Patriarchates or Metropolitan provinces) among themselves. It must always be clear, when the expression *sister Churches* is used in this proper sense, that the one, holy, catholic, and apostolic universal Church is not sister but mother of all the particular Churches" (§ 10).

3. In the Declaration *Dominus Iesus*, among other things, it is said:

Just as there is one Christ, so there exists a single body of Christ, a single Bride of Christ: "a single Catholic and apostolic Church". . . . "This Church, constituted and organized as a society in the present world, subsists in [*subsistit in*] the Catholic Church, governed by the successor of Peter and by the bishops in communion with him." With the expression *subsistit in,* the Second Vatican Council sought to harmonize two doctrinal statements: on the one hand, that the Church of Christ, despite the divisions that exist among Christians, continues to exist fully only in the Catholic Church and, on the other hand, that "outside of her structure, many elements can be found of sanctification and truth.". . . Therefore, there exists a single Church of Christ, which subsists in the Catholic Church, governed by the successor of Peter and by the bishops in communion with him. The Churches that, while not existing in perfect communion with the Catholic Church, remain united to her by means of the closest bonds, that is, by apostolic succession and a valid Eucharist, are true particular Churches. Therefore, the Church of Christ is present and operative also in these Churches, even though they lack full communion with the Catholic Church, since they do not accept the Catholic doctrine of the primacy, which, according to the will of God, the Bishop of Rome objectively has and exercises over the whole Church. (§§ 16 and 17)

a. I now permit myself to ask you how we could thoroughly rethink these "apparent contradictions", so that a whole series of misunderstandings, which have arisen on account of certain formulations and which do not appear to be fully in accord with the Second Vatican Council, can be dispelled. I am thinking of the exclusivity that is indissolubly associated with that "only", which the Second Vatican Council, with "*subsistit in*", was trying to avoid.

b. This "one single Church", which also calls herself "universal, one, holy, catholic, and apostolic Church", is described as the mother of all particular Churches and not as sister Church. And this "one single Church" in her plural form,

"Churches", is applicable only to the particular Churches. I now ask myself how it is that in chapter 4 of the declaration *Dominus Iesus*, the legitimate expression of the Nicene-Constantinopolitan Creed, which is binding on us all, had to be replaced with another formulation, from the great creed of the Armenian Church: "the one and only catholic and apostolic Church".

c. I have no wish to enter into the discussion about the theology and ecclesiology of particular Churches, since as far as I am aware what you are calling a "particular Church", that is, the local Church, can in the view of Orthodox theology lay claim to being the one, holy, catholic, and apostolic Church—on condition, of course, that she is living in *communion* with the other local Churches. And the fact that these local Churches are referred to and recognized as sister Churches among one another does *not* assume as a *conditio sine qua non* that the Church of Constantinople, the Ecumenical Patriarchate, is the mother of all of these Churches—this is not so in the case of all Orthodox local Churches—but simply the fact that they share the same faith, in the conviction that there is only one single Christ and only one single body of Christ, the one, holy, catholic, and apostolic Church.

Over and beyond this, the term "particular Church" as a concept interchangeable with "local Church" is liable to be moving toward a universalistically structured ecclesiology, which conceives of the local Churches as subordinate parts of the *Una Sancta*.

d. I deny that the concept "sister Church", as it occurs in the Brief *Anno ineunte* of Pope Paul VI to Patriarch Athenagoras I, may be restricted in the way that occurred in the *Note* on sister Churches. More precisely, "God is now granting us the grace, after long differences of opinion and disputes, of our Churches once more recognizing each other as sister Churches, despite the difficulties that have arisen between us in earlier ages." (I have replaced the word "opportunity" in the *Note* with the word "grace", in accordance with the official German translation of the *Tomos Agapis*: ". . . Dei beneficio fit ut nostrae ecclesiae se iterum sorores agnoscant".)[3]

This form of words may not only be applied as from the "particular Church" of Rome to the "particular Church" of Constantinople, but it also applies to the mutual recognition of the Roman Catholic Church and the Orthodox Church as sister Churches. That is why Father Emmanuel Lanne, at the Vienna Symposium of 1974, advanced the view that "if the Orthodox Churches as a whole are ready to recognize the [Roman] Catholic Church, just as she is, as the true Church of Christ and as sister to the Orthodox Churches . . . , [then] nothing more stands in the way of a resumption of canonical relations between the two Churches."[4]

e. The assertion that the use of the term "our two Churches" should be avoided on the grounds that this would "imply a plurality not merely on the level of particular Churches, but also on the level of the one, holy, catholic, and apostolic Church confessed in the Creed, whose real existence is thus obscured" (*Nota* § 11), appears among other things to contradict even the joint declaration of Pope Paul VI and Patriarch Athenagoras I, at the end of the Patriarch's visit to Rome on October 28, 1967. There, both primates give expression to their gladness

> that their meeting has been able to contribute to their Churches' greater ability to recognize each other again as

---

[3] *Tomos Agapis* (Vienna, 1978), p. 117.

[4] E. Lanne, "Schwesterkirchen—Ekklesiologische Aspekte des Tomos Agapis" [Sister churches: Ecclesiological aspects of the Tomos Agapis], in *Pro Oriente: Auf dem Weg zur Einheit des Glaubens* [Toward the East: On the way toward unity of belief] (Innsbruck, Vienna, and Munich, 1976), p. 74.

sister Churches. In their prayers, their public declarations and their private conversations, the Pope and the Patriarch wished to emphasize that a substantial contribution is made toward the restoration of full communion between the Roman Catholic Church, on one hand, and the Orthodox Church, on the other, by the renewal of the Church and of individual Christians, in faithfulness to the traditions of the Fathers and to the inspirations of the Holy Spirit, who is always present with the Church. . . . Pope Paul VI and the Ecumenical Patriarch Athenagoras I are convinced that the *dialogue of love* between their Churches must bear fruit in unselfish working together on the level of joint action in the pastoral, social, and intellectual spheres, in mutual respect for faithfulness *to their own Churches* on one side just as much as on the other.[5]

f. The use of the term "our two Churches" in no way relativizes the Roman Catholic Church's claim to be the Church in a complete and absolute sense, on one hand, or that of the Orthodox Church, on the other, in their claim to be, and to continue as, the one, holy, catholic, and apostolic Church. I permit myself to underline here a statement of their position by the pan-Orthodox Congress: "Conscious of the importance of the present structure of Christendom, our holy Orthodox Church, although she is the one, holy, catholic, and apostolic Church, not only recognizes the ontological existence of these ecclesial communities, but also firmly believes that all relations with them must be based on the quickest possible objective clarification of the ecclesiological problem and of their teaching as whole." What does that mean? Can any Church, so soon as she allows her own boundaries to be identified with those of the one, holy, catholic, and apostolic Church, recognize any other Church as Church, without giving up, or at least relativizing, her own

---

[5] *Tomos Agapis*, p. 121.

claim to continuity? Can we apply a "both-and" here, or does the canonical character of the Church oblige us to take "either-or" as our starting point? Both Churches take the view that they are continuations of the one, holy, catholic, and apostolic Church, without thereby being necessarily exclusive. In any case, one can in my view recognize the continuing existence even of an *ecclesia extra ecclesiam*, in the full sense of the word *ecclesia*, wherever there is unity in the essentials of the *pistis* (that is, of the great conciliar creeds) and wherever the fundamental ordering of the *ecclesia*, that is, the *successio apostolica*, has been preserved unbroken.

I thank God each time I think of you in my prayers, whenever I hear or read about your faith in our Lord Jesus Christ, in the Mother of God, who is also our mother, and in all the saints. In the fellowship of faith and love that unites us, I remain, in long-standing, thankful, and brotherly affection, Yours, † Metropolitan Damaskinos

JOSEPH CARDINAL RATZINGER

To His Eminence
Metropolitan Damaskinos of Switzerland

February 20, 2001

Your Eminence,
Dear Brother and Friend,
A long time has passed since we were able to spend those unforgettable days together in Tuscany and to talk about many things that concern us both in our care for the unity of the Church we are trying to serve. On October 30 you then wrote me a moving letter, as a result of our conversations, in which you explained in concrete terms all the questions we had been able only briefly to touch upon there. I am most

grateful to you for this, since openness is a basic necessity for ecumenical conversation, and our brotherly intimacy is so great and so deep-rooted that we need not be afraid to tell each other everything that moves us or disturbs us. I was unfortunately unable to answer at once, first because I wanted to think very carefully about the questions you put, but also because I was still holding my breath under the storm of criticism that broke over us following *Dominus Iesus*. Then came the avalanche of Christmas mail, which I was able to dig myself out of only with difficulty. Meanwhile came the sad news of your serious illness, which made me very anxious. You know that during this time I prayed for you quite specially, and now I am very happy to hear that you are on the way to recovery. I do not really need to tell you that I am continuing to be with you in prayer, asking that the Lord may restore you to full health. So it seems to me that the time has now come for me to try to get the answer to your letter under way.

I was very moved by the way you portrayed our path in theology together, in the course of which we became ever more dramatically aware of the urgent necessity of achieving unity between East and West, and, at the same time, some theological illumination appeared, so as to show us the way we should go in order to arrive, with God's help, at this great goal. Nothing of all that has been revoked; on the contrary, I have become still more clearly aware that the Orthodox Church and the Catholic Church belong to one another and that none of the doctrinal questions that appear to divide us is insoluble. In this connection you put the question of whether there is any continuity between Professor Joseph Ratzinger and the Prefect of the Congregation for the Doctrine of the Faith, of how those theological statements of mine that you quoted relate to various texts of the Congregation for the Doctrine of the Faith that raise questions for you. I would say to that: The Professor and the Prefect are the same person, but the two terms refer to two offices that correspond to different tasks. In that sense, then, there is a difference but no contradiction. The Professor (and I am still the Professor) is concerned with knowledge, and in his books and lectures he presents what he thinks he has found and opens himself not only to other theologians disputing it but also to the judgment of the Church. He is trying, in being responsible for the truth of the faith and conscious of his own limitations, to reach insights that will help us along the path of faith and the path to unity. What he writes or says springs from his personal journey of faith and understanding and locates him in the shared journey of the Church. The Prefect, on the other hand, is not supposed to expound his personal views. On the contrary, he has to leave them in the background so as to make room for the common message of the Church. He does not, as the Professor does, write texts based on his own research and findings; rather, he must see to it that the organs of the teaching Church carry on their work with a high degree of responsibility, so that in the end a text is purged of everything that is merely personal and truly becomes the common message of the Church.

The occasion for writing a document at all is given by questions coming from within the Church, perceptions being developed from many sides and making it clear that a statement of clarification is required. Many and various contacts with our brother bishops are a part of the process by which this develops, as are, also, the classic instruments: commissions, the *consulta* (regular meetings of the standing advisors to the Congregation), and finally the work of the "Congregation" in the proper sense, a collegial instrument consisting of a number of bishops, some of whom work in Rome in the various curial departments, while some are diocesan bishops from all over the world. There is a plenary meeting of the

Congregation about every year and a half, to which only big projects (such as *Dominus Iesus*) can be submitted, and the meeting convened about every fortnight, in which the Roman members, and normally a few members from neighboring European countries, take part. At the same time the Pope is regularly informed about progress.

While the Pope, as chief pastor of the Church, tries to speak as directly as possible to the faithful, and therefore chooses something like "pastoral" language, the Congregation's task is more limited: it has to put down markers at critical points, to show where the realm of theological debate—which it is not allowed to hinder—begins and where it is that the faith itself is at stake, that faith which is the basis of all theology. Thus, through a long struggle (many documents take ten years, hardly any less than two years), a text takes shape in which no one can set down his personal opinion, in which, rather, so far as possible, the common yardstick of the faith should emerge. The Congregation's documents are not infallible, yet they are still more than contributions to the discussion—they are signposts intended to speak to the believing consciences of pastors and teachers. Thus it is clear that the Congregation's texts cannot and should not be Professor Ratzinger's texts, for he is in the service of something greater than himself and is, moreover, conscious of his responsibilities, trying to be aware of his role as moderator. Even if the texts, because of their character, are different from what I personally could or should write, it is clear that I do and say nothing as Prefect that I cannot be responsible for personally as well, both as counsel to myself and as a message to the Church and on behalf of the Church.

And now, before I come to the questions you raise about content, I should like to emphasize two points from your introductory reflections that seem to me important. One is the healing of memory. In meeting with the bishops who come *ad limina apostolorum*, I repeatedly find how much there still is to do, how deeply the hurts of the centuries have sunk into the memory of the Churches, and it is not unusual for them to poison mutual relations. I have always thought, and now even more so, that what stands between the Orthodox and Catholic Churches is far less questions of doctrine than the memory of old hurts that alienate us from each other: the power of the confused tangles of history seems to be stronger than the light of faith that ought to be transforming them into forgiveness. It is precisely against this background that I would like to reemphasize your formulation, to the effect that we ought not really to be asking: "Can we legitimately communicate with one another?"—but rather: "Can we legitimately refuse Communion to one another?" In this area we have, praise God, made some progress together. The two codes of canon law of the Catholic Church and her Ecumenical Directory show that under certain conditions admission to Communion between East and West is permissible or even positively recommended. An agreement is about to be concluded between the "Assyrian" and the "Chaldean" Churches about mutual admission to Communion in the wide areas of the diaspora, where very often only one of the two has a priest available. This case needed special studies to be made, because the Anaphora of Addai and Mari most commonly in use by the Assyrians does not include an institution narrative. But these difficulties were able to be overcome, and thus in general, despite many problems, there are now and again little bits of encouragement that give us hope.

And so at last I come to your questions, and I am beginning with the "main obstacle" to the full restoration of unity, the pope's **primacy of jurisdiction**, where you highlighted in particular the difficulties in the formula *iurisdictio in omnes* *ecclesias*. I should like to distinguish two aspects of this thorny problem, which we certainly cannot resolve in our exchange of letters.

First, there is, it seems to me, above all a **problem of language**. The concept of a jurisdiction over the whole Church, and, indeed, the legal terminology of the second millennium as such, is foreign to the East and disturbs people whenever they are aware of it. I believe it is right and also possible to trace the essential concepts, and especially those that are proving to be an obstacle, back to their basis in patristic theology and, in that way, not only to make them more comprehensible, but also of course to discover starting points for a usage more in keeping with the thinking of the Fathers. You remind me of the unforgettable address of Patriarch Athenagoras, on the occasion of Pope Paul VI's visit to Phanar, when the Patriarch applied to the Pope the titles from the patristic era, "first in honor" and "president in love". I believe that we could correctly define "jurisdiction over the whole Church" on that basis: the "honor" of the first is not, indeed, to be understood in the sense of the honor accorded by worldly protocol; honor in the Church is service, obedience to Christ. Then again, *agape* is not just a feeling entailing no obligations, still less a form of social organization, but is in the final analysis a eucharistic concept, which is as such connected to the theology of the Cross, since the Eucharist is based on the Cross; the Cross is the most extreme expression of God's love for us in Jesus Christ.

If the Church in the very depth of her being coincides with the Eucharist, then the presidency of love carries with it a responsibility for unity, which has a significance within the Church yet, at the same time, is a responsibility for "distinguishing what is Christian" as against worldly society, and therefore it will always bear a martyrological character. You know that a little while ago (in the course of the dispute over women's ordination), I tried to interpret the ministry of the pope as a ministry of obedience, with him as the guarantor of obedience: the pope is not an absolute monarch whose will is law, but quite the opposite—he always has to try to resist arbitrary self-will and to call the Church back to the standard of obedience; therefore, however, he must himself be first in obedience. In a period when the secular temptations to theology are growing in every area, it seems to me that this kind of common responsibility for the obedience of the Church toward tradition is of great significance; its being consistent with Christ is borne out by the way that it stands as a witness of suffering for and with Christ, over against the disobedience of unauthorized behavior in the world. A patristic interpretation of the primacy is in any case encouraged by the First Vatican Council itself, when it says that the constant practice of the Church stands for the teaching proclaimed there, as do the ecumenical councils, especially those in which East and West met together in unity of faith and love; here Vatican I refers to the Fourth Council of Constantinople (DS 3065f.).

The second point I should like to mention here concerns the distinction between theory and practice—or perhaps, better, **the span of dogma in practice**. In his encyclical *Ut unum sint*, the Pope pointed this out and asks for suggestions for a renewal of the practice of primacy. Here, as ever, history is instructive. R. Schieffer, who presided over the *Monumenta Germaniae historica*, writes in one place in this connection, "that at the moment of passing from the first to the second millennium of Church history a qualitative leap was made, not in the theory of primacy, but in the way people dealt with it." [1]

---

[1] R. Schieffer, "Natur und Ziel primatialer Interventionen des Bischofs von Rom im ersten Jahrtausend" [The ways in which the Bishop of Rome intervened as primate during the first millennium and his purpose in doing so], in *Il Primato del Successore di Pietro* [The primacy of Peter's successor] (Vatican City, 1998), pp. 348f.

You will permit me to add one more personal reflection. The primacy—Paul VI himself said it—is in certain respects the "main obstacle" to the restoration of full communion. Yet it is at the same time the main opportunity for this, because without it the Catholic Church would long ago have fallen apart into national churches and churches of this or that rite, which would make it quite impossible to gain any general view of the ecumenical landscape, and because the primacy makes it possible to take definite steps toward unity. You recently referred to this yourself in an important article, pointing out that it will be of decisive importance to the future of Orthodoxy to find an appropriate solution to the problem of autocephalous Churches, so that Orthodoxy's inner unity and its capacity for common action should not be lost or, perhaps, that it may be restored. I believe that the problem of autocephalous Churches shows the **necessity for an instrument of unity**, which must of course be **correctly balanced with the independent responsibility of the local Churches**: the Church cannot and should not be a papal monarchy but has her points of orientation in the communion of the bishops, within which there is a ministry of their unity among themselves—that is, a ministry that does not do away with the responsibility of the bishops but is directed toward that end. I believe that the more realistic we are in speaking with one another, on the basis of the concrete data of history and of the present day and also, on the other hand, on that of the theological breadth and depth of the doctrinal texts, the closer we shall get to answers that make unity possible for us.

I now come to the first question in your letter, the difficulties with the word "wounded" in describing the particular Churches because of their being separated from Peter's successor, as the *Communionis notio* says; the same text does, however, say explicitly that of course the Roman Catholic Church, too, is wounded by this separation, because she cannot fully represent unity in history. If we take a look at the reality of the Church and the Churches, then who could doubt that all of them—in varying ways—are wounded? It seems to me that theology was far more realistic in describing their historical impoverishment before the fractures of modern times. I would remind you, just as an example, of the *Horologium Sapientiae* of Henry Suso (first half of the fourteenth century), which describes the Church, in a vision, as a city of which some parts have been destroyed by enemies, while other parts have fallen into ruin through the inhabitants' neglect. "Animals appeared in the city—sea monsters in human form, by whom any pilgrims who asked for help were turned away and despised." [2] Yes, division is a wound, and we ought to admit it to each other in a spirit of penitence and ask for help, struggle to get help.

And that brings me to the dispute about the use of the term **"sister Churches"**. The letter about this from the Congregation for the Doctrine of the Faith, as you know, points out explicitly that particular Churches, even across lines of division, can be—and are—sister Churches to one another, as for instance Constantinople and Rome, Rome and Antioch, Antioch and Constantinople, and so on. The letter does not in any case consider it appropriate to refer to the Orthodox Church as a whole and the Roman Catholic Church as a whole as "our two Churches" or as two "sister Churches". Why? This is a matter of setting the plural "the Churches" and the singular "the Church" in the right relationship to each other. In the common Creed of the Church we confess

---

[2] Quoted from A. M. Haas, "Vorwort" [Preface], in *Wer ist die Kirche?* [Who is the Church?], Symposium for the tenth anniversary of the death of Hans Urs von Balthasar (Johannes Verlag, 1999), p. 7.

that there is ultimately only *one* Church of Christ, which does of course in concrete terms exist in many particular Churches, and yet these are in fact particular Churches, part Churches, of the one Church. If, however, we were to speak of the Orthodox Church and the Catholic Church as two sister Churches, then we would be setting up a plural above and beyond which no singular is apparent. A dualism would remain at the ultimate level of the concept of "Church", and the one Church would thus become a phantom, a utopia, whereas bodily existence is the very thing that is essential to her.

The fact that in the fourth chapter of *Dominus Iesus* the great creed of the Armenian Church has been quoted does not signify, naturally, any departure from the Constantinopolitan-Nicene Creed, which is, and remains, our common and binding creed. The difference between the two in the article concerning the Church is indeed very small; the word "holy" is missing from the Armenian creed, but the word μονή is there over and above what is in the Nicene Creed, although this only emphasizes the μία and adds nothing to it. To be quite honest, I had not noticed this quotation at all, and in practice the text would not lose anything by its absence. It is obvious that this variant in the tradition was used here only in order to emphasize the unity of the Church, which in itself can clearly be deduced from Scripture and from our common Creed. In this connection, I find H. Legrand's suggestion, in his letter to you of October 6, which you have most kindly made available to me, well worth considering. Legrand first refers to the way that the Greek delegate in Baltimore decidedly refused to regard the Catholic Church as the sister Church of the Orthodox Church and, from that starting point, asks whether it would not be possible for the Orthodox Church, not to recognize as a sister Church the Catholic Church as such, but to recognize the Catholic (particular)

Churches as sisters of the Orthodox local Churches. That is an attempt at a terminological solution that both sides should think carefully about and that might perhaps point toward a way out of a dualistic understanding of "Church" and that might nonetheless give appropriate verbal expression to the common sisterly relationship of all Orthodox and Catholic Churches with one another. I do not believe that the brief *Anno ineunte* intended to canonize the terminology referring to our two Churches as "sister Churches". There it is directly based upon the meeting between Rome and Constantinople, so as to expand and comprehend the whole sphere of the Catholic and Orthodox local Churches, a terminological anticipation that is open to development in further conversations (I refer to pages 5 and 6 of your letter).

Let us stay with the question of terminology. If I have rightly understood, you have reservations about the concept of **"particular Churches"**. Vatican II alternates between using the terms "local Church" and "particular Church" without any clear distinction; H. de Lubac has shown that the concept of "particular Church" is preferable, and that has largely been taken up both by theology and by the Magisterium. But we could devote further discussion to this terminology.

And then there is the other difficulty, the concept of the **"Mother Church"**. I think it is important to distinguish, here again, the two levels of the concept of "Church". There is, first of all, the level at which the plural may correctly be used—that of the Churches within the Church. On this level, the Church of Rome is the Mother Church of the Churches in Italy, but not of course the Mother Church of all the others. Jerusalem is the Mother Church of many Churches; Antioch and Constantinople are Mother Churches. Yet this "motherhood" can be only an image of the real "Mother

Church"—the "Jerusalem above" that Paul talks about (Gal 4:26), of which the Fathers speak so movingly. I might remind you of the wonderful collection of passages made by H. Rahner: *Mater Ecclesia* (1944).

As I can see from a whole number of publications by Catholic theologians, the term **"universal Church"** is also very often wrongly interpreted. The fact that *Communionis notio* talks about the ontological and temporal precedence of the universal Church before the particular Churches is interpreted as a declaration in favor of Roman centralism. That, of course, is complete nonsense. For the local Church of Rome is a local Church that has been entrusted, as we are persuaded, with a special responsibility for the whole Church, but she is not herself the universal Church. Maintaining that the universal Church takes precedence over the particular Churches is not a declaration in favor of any particular form of distribution of responsibility within the Church, not a declaration that the local Church of Rome should seek to acquire as many privileges as possible. That kind of interpretation completely misjudges the level of the question. Anyone who always just turns straight to the question of the distribution of power has utterly missed the mystery of the Church. No, this is strictly a matter of theology, not of juridical questions or of Church politics: the fact that God's idea of the Son's one bride, eschatologically oriented toward the eternal wedding feast, is the first and the one essential idea of God that is at stake in matters to do with the Church, while the concrete realization of the Church in local Churches constitutes a second plane that is subsequent to the first and always remains subordinated to it. I do not think there can be any quarrel about that.

And finally we come to the thorny question of the *subsistit in*, which is of course in some sense underlying all the previous questions. In order to make clear what is meant I find the text of a pan-Orthodox statement that you quoted on page 6 and following of your letter most helpful. Because it seems so important to me, I should like—presuming I have your permission—to reproduce it here: "Conscious of the importance of the present structure of Christendom, our holy Orthodox Church, although she is the one, holy, catholic, and apostolic Church, not only recognizes the ontological existence of these ecclesial communities, but also firmly believes that all relations with them must be based on the quickest possible objective clarification of the ecclesiological problem and of their teaching as a whole." I should be very grateful to be able to look at the entire text of this statement, which seems to me of great significance for the further progress of our discussions. This text expresses, in somewhat different but nonetheless related terminology, the very ecclesiological paradox that *Dominus Iesus* is also trying to express. It clearly states that the Orthodox Church is "the one, holy, catholic, and apostolic Church"; it is thus assigning a quite concrete embodiment and place to the theological singular of "Church". Yet it nonetheless adds to this the recognition of the ontological existence of these ecclesial communities and, on that basis, formulates the task of clarifying the ecclesiological problem and the teaching as a whole. Following *Lumen gentium*, number 8, *Dominus Iesus* replaced *esse* (is) with *subsistit in* (subsists in) so as to build the ontological bridge, so to speak, toward the existence of other Church communities and thus to take a step toward the "clarification of the ecclesiological problem" that your text recommends.

No doubt, this step does not resolve the paradox, but it renders it still more striking. To us it is not given to resolve the paradox of the faithfulness of God and the faithlessness of men ("If we are faithless, he remains faithful"—2 Tim 2:13!); our task is rather to suffer it and, thus, contribute in our own measure to a resolution: this is ultimately a problem of life itself, not of concepts. I understand *Dominus Iesus* as intending to transform the indifference with which all churches are regarded as different but equally valid, so that the validity of faith itself disappears in scepticism, once more into a lively suffering and thus to kindle anew the true fervor of ecumenism. Whenever everything is equally valid, everything becomes indifferent, unimportant. This text caused people pain, and man's first reaction to pain is always to protest, and the less he wants to be hindered by faith, the more he will do so. When the first disturbing pain turns to a willingness to suffer for the truth, this text will begin to serve its true purpose.

Dear Friend and Brother, we are both suffering from the fact that we are not permitted to celebrate the Eucharist with one another, and this itself unites us. The way that you have remained close to me in this suffering we share, and in the hidden joy of the hope of a more profound unity, is the great achievement of many decades of friendship, for which today, just for once, I should like to offer you my thanks quite explicitly. I hope you will see from these few lines—however inadequate they may be in many ways—that this passion, sharing in which we discovered one another more than forty years ago, has remained alive within me. I hope that this knowledge will be of help to you in your present suffering and that you will soon be able once more to be entirely at the service of the one Church of God.

　　With this in mind, and with my sincere gratitude and best wishes, very affectionately

　　　　Your Friend and Brother
　　　　† Joseph Card. Ratzinger

Exchange of Letters between Provincial Bishop Johannes Hanselmann[1] and Joseph Cardinal Ratzinger

About the communication from the Congregation for the Doctrine of the Faith to the bishops of the Catholic Church, On Some Aspects of the Church Understood as Communion,[2] *of May 28, 1992*

DR. JOHANNES HANSELMANN
PROVINCIAL BISHOP OF THE
LUTHERAN-EVANGELICAL CHURCH IN BAVARIA

To His Eminence
Joseph Cardinal Ratzinger,
Congregation for the Doctrine of the Faith

February 5, 1993

Dear and Most Reverend Cardinal,
I should honestly like to thank you for your brotherly letter of January 21, 1993. I can understand, of course, that in the

---

[1] Provincial Bishop Dr. Hanselmann, D.D., as head of Catholica for the VELKD, quoted passages from this correspondence in his report to the Ninth General Synod of the VELKD, on October 19, 1993 (see *Una Sancta* 40 [1993]: 347–51).

[2] Congregazione per la dottrina della fede, *Communionis notio: Lettera e commenti* (Libreria Editrice Vaticana, 1994). Text on the Internet: LATIN TEXT: http://www.vatican.va/roman_curia/congregations/cfaith/documents/rc_con_cfaith_doc_28051992_communionis-notio_lt.html. ENGLISH TEXT: http://www.vatican.va/roman_curia/congregations/cfaith/documents/rc_con_cfaith_doc_28051992_communionis-notio_en.html.

plethora of your engagements you had no time available for a meeting when I was in Castelgandolfo in November last year. I am only the more grateful that you are giving me this opportunity to formulate some questions that were raised about the letter on Communion.

Not all of them are my personal questions. I must nonetheless express them, because as head of Catholica for the United Evangelical and Lutheran Church of Germany [German initials: VELKD] I should like to give as genuine an answer to them as possible, whenever—as happens repeatedly—I am asked. In my report on Catholica to the General Synod of the VELKD in Dresden, in October 1992—I enclose a copy of this—I expressed myself as cautiously as possible, first, in order to do no violence to the "Letter on Communion" (henceforth I call this "the document"), and, on the other hand, because I did not wish to start by narrowing down the area in which contentious problems, or those not yet clarified, might be discussed. To my great surprise, this step aroused less criticism than I had anticipated.

But now for particular points:

1. In the process of dialogue between our churches, the concept of "communion" (*koinonia*) has led to a greater degree of understanding and cooperation. Can it be expected that the fundamental decision made by the Roman Catholic Church with respect to this concept will still correspond in the future to the understanding of "communion" that has played a role in our dialogue and has found expression in our working reports?

2. How should we evaluate the accusation—which comes solely from the Lutheran side—that numbers 1 to 16 of the document have a different concept of "communion", that is, a somewhat more juridical one in the style of the CIC, and is a regression from the Vatican II Decree on Ecumenism?

3. In number 5 it says: "Ecclesial communion, into which each individual is introduced by faith and by baptism, has its root and center in the holy Eucharist." Would one not have to conclude from that that Churches and ecclesial communities who, in the words of number 17, "have not preserved a valid Eucharist" are cut off from the root and the heart of ecclesial fellowship—although we have previously stated together that—despite the divisions that still exist—we are received by baptism and by faith into a fellowship with one another, whose heart is the gospel of Jesus Christ himself?

4. We understand what is said in the first clause of number 9 in the sense that the one Church is present in particular Churches and that none of the historical entities entirely comprehends the "one, holy, catholic, and apostolic Church". This common understanding has drawn us closer to one another in our conversations. In his message of greetings for the commemoration of the Augsburg Confession, in 1980, Pope John Paul II recognized with thanksgiving that the fundamental pillars of our churches have continued to exist, even if the bridge between them is missing. That is why the sentence, "according to the Fathers, *ontologically*, the Church-mystery, the Church that is one and unique, precedes creation", has astonished people. Instead of argument from the Bible, an ontological argument is used here. Is this convincing? Is not the concept of revelation, in consequence, being applied to the Church instead of to the gospel of Christ?

5. Number 11 talks about unity being founded in the "eucharistic sacrifice". Does this expression perhaps touch on the consensus achieved in our conversations, that the sacrifice of the Lord was offered once and for all when he offered himself on the Cross? Or is a connection being made here with the old Roman Catholic doctrine of sacrifice?

6. In number 12 we read about "a Church that is *Head* of the Churches, which is precisely the Church of Rome". In our conversations there was a consensus that Jesus Christ is the head of the Church. In that sense, we as a Lutheran Church are standing in the tradition of the apostolic witness (Eph 4:15). Is this consensus under threat?

7. In our conversations we recognized that the office of pope is subordinate to Holy Scripture and has a duty toward it. With this presupposition, the recognition of this office as a Petrine ministry for the unity of the Church becomes conceivable. Now we read, in number 13, "The primacy of the Bishop of Rome and the episcopal College are essential elements of the universal Church"; and the conclusion is drawn: "The ministry of the primacy involves, in essence, a truly episcopal power, which is not only supreme, full, and universal, but also *immediate*, over everybody". Can this be justified from the Bible?

8. We have to conclude from number 17 that we are reckoned among the "ecclesial communities" whose wound is "still deeper yet". We are familiar with the reproach that we have not preserved the apostolic succession, but we have repeatedly maintained that the determinative content, that is to say our profound commitment to the *successio veritatis*, takes a decisive priority for us over the formal element. As far as the valid Eucharist is concerned, the "Lord's Supper" has met with broad agreement—the problem has been hitherto the link made between the priestly ordination and a valid Communion. Can we not make another single step of progress here, if for instance we undertake a comparative study and discussion of ordination to the priesthood in the Roman Catholic Church and ordination in the Lutheran Church?

9. Number 18 talks of how, "through a new conversion to the Lord, all may be enabled to recognize the continuity of the primacy of Peter in his successors, the Bishops of Rome, and to see the Petrine ministry fulfilled, in the manner intended by the Lord." We are in agreement that unity can be achieved only through penance and through the conversion of all Churches to the Lord. Yet where is the biblical foundation for "in the manner intended by the Lord"?

Dear and most reverend Cardinal, please forgive me for the way that a fairly long catalogue of questions has developed. I can assure you that the reason for this is to be found, not in a love of criticism, but in a genuine concern for much that seemed to have been achieved thus far in interconfessional conversations. We are truly concerned that we should follow the Lord obediently in the fellowship of our Churches and should accept the unity that is granted us in him. That is why we do want—see number 18—to give priority of place in this ecumenical undertaking to prayer, to penance, to study, to dialogue, and to working together.

With this in mind, with gratitude and respect, and in the hope that I am not asking too much of you with this inquiry,

Yours sincerely,
Dr. Johannes Hanselmann

P.S.
I take the liberty of enclosing my letter to all the congregations for Passiontide (the "Lenten Letter") for this year.

JOSEPH CARDINAL RATZINGER

Dr. Johannes Hanselmann,
Provincial Bishop of the Evangelical Lutheran Church
in Bavaria

March 9, 1993

Dear Provincial Bishop,

My heartfelt thanks for your letter of February 5, marked as it is by a great sense of ecumenical responsibility and by an inner concern for moving closer to unity. Since in the meantime I had to travel to Hong Kong for a week-long meeting with the chairmen of the Asian bishops' conferences and commissions of faith, my reply has unfortunately been delayed. Nor can it be as detailed a reply as I would wish; but I do hope to be able to set out the essential points. I have to say in advance that this document should of course be understood in the context of the whole of Catholic official teaching, especially that of Vatican II. The Congregation has not the authority to change any teaching, much less to "correct" a council; it can only establish what are the existing teachings, and clarify them, in a corresponding situation. That is why interpretations that try to set the "Letter" in opposition to the Second Vatican Council or to papal doctrinal statements of an earlier or later date must be excluded from the start, simply on the basis of our official task. The letter takes the Council for granted and has to be read within the matrix of its texts.

1. As applied to your first question, what I have just said means that our letter is situated within the realm of the Catholic Church's *doctrina recepta*, of which of course her ecumenical obligations are an essential part. Accordingly, it is only building upon those texts that are in some way a part of the body of official teaching (Scripture, councils, Fathers),

and from these elements—using Vatican II as a hermeneutic "key"—it puts together the picture of "communion". It is accordingly unable to make a part of its statement any reports of the dialogues or of working parties that have not as yet been accorded official recognition by the Church. Yet it does not contradict them, insofar as they are not intended to be in direct contradiction to the sources I have mentioned—and one would certainly not assume that they were. The text, by the very fact of being limited in its application, leaves room for further theological development.

2. And thereby question 2 has probably been answered. The strong emphasis on the vertical dimension, as on the interrelationship of the visible and the invisible Church, excludes any narrowly juridical sense.

3. Of course the fellowship with Jesus Christ himself, and with his saving Word, based on baptism, is and remains as important as it was portrayed by the Council's Decree on Ecumenism; no one intends to call that into question. The "eucharistic ecclesiology" that is taken up in the document presupposes baptism and reinforces the christological center. Besides, I reckon as one of the important results of ecumenical conversations particularly the realization that the question of the Eucharist cannot be restricted to the problem of "validity". Even a theology along the lines of the concept of succession, as is in force in the Catholic and in the Orthodox Church, should in no way deny the saving presence of the Lord in the Evangelical Lord's Supper. The place of the Eucharist is of course seen differently within the framework of the ecclesiology of the Reformed tradition from how it is seen in the Catholic and the Orthodox tradition. There is no doubt that the dialogues still have a great deal of work before them here. Yet this difference, and the questions it implies, cannot diminish what has so far been found on the path of ecumenism.

4. Number 9 of our text says that the one, holy, catholic, and apostolic Church is not the result of adding together individual churches that already exist and might unite in some kind of federation; rather, it says that the one Church is ontologically and temporally prior to the individual churches. I cannot imagine anyone defending the contrary theory, that is, the view that the Church as a whole consists only of the sum of a number of particular churches, that it is thus a matter external to the nature of the Church. In that case, indeed, the whole business of ecumenism would merely be a matter of human ingenuity, of managing to get as wide as possible a process of merging. The fact that the one Church is a theological entity, and not the subsequent empirical uniting of many churches, certainly emerges convincingly from the New Testament itself. In this case the Letter to the Ephesians is only making quite clear what the whole of the New Testament is saying. This theological priority is what is meant by the "ontological" priority, which the Fathers then portray—following analogous Jewish traditions—as a kind of preexistence of the Church. In doing so, they are able to refer to Galatians 4:26, as also to Ephesians and Colossians. What is essential, however, is not the question of "preexistence" or temporal priority, which is an image, but the question of inner (= theological—"ontological") precedence. This, again, expresses itself, as our text says, in the temporal precedence of the Church as a whole: the first congregation in Jerusalem is not just the "local Church" of Jerusalem, but an anticipation of the universal Church: the twelve apostles are the responsible representatives of the universal Church; Luke expresses that in the image of many languages. First the Church as a whole is there; and then she forms individual Churches; and it is not the individual Churches that gradually come together into one Church. So I cannot see how the concept of revelation is in any way being

redirected from the gospel to the Church here; and I cannot see that arguing on a biblical basis is being abandoned in favor of ontological argument.

5. Nothing new is being said in our text about the sacrificial character of the Eucharist; it is not as such discussed at all. The entire paragraph is exclusively directed to showing that the Eucharist always involves the self-transcendence of any individual congregation in the vertical sense as in the horizontal.

6. The concept of a chief or "head" Church [*Hauptkirche* in German] does not of course imply that this Church is the head of "the Church" (in the singular), as only Christ is that, but merely that among the local Churches (plural) there is one chief Church, just as there are metropolitan Churches, and so on.

7. The sentence quoted from number 13 is taken almost word for word from Vatican I and Vatican II; it merely repeats what is said at length there in the same terms. On this point in particular we kept most carefully to the Council texts. The question about the biblical basis of the doctrine on the primacy of the two Vatican Councils is a classical point of controversy that has been a matter of debate for a long time and certainly needs to be debated further. A document from the Congregation had no business intervening in this debate, but it could, quite properly, repeat the doctrine as given, without changing the theological task associated with it.

8. In framing your question, you have yourself kindly made it clear that at this particularly painful point, our document, once again, is merely taking up the existing doctrine and the existing difficulties of the apostolic succession—certainly the most painful point, and the most troublesome, in the dialogues between Catholics and those Christians whose

faith is based on the Reformation. Here I may refer you to what I said under point 3. The fact that the burdensome question of succession does not detract from the spiritual dignity of Evangelical Christianity, or from the saving power of the Lord at work within it, has been very nicely elucidated in the Decree on Ecumenism, especially in number 23, so it seems to me. The ecumenical dialogues you refer to in this connection do of course have to seek farther and do more work to open up paths to unity. I think that in number 17 here we have taken a step beyond the Decree on Ecumenism, in talking about wounds on both sides, which may be of different kinds but are still quite real on both sides; it seems to me that this had never before been articulated in this way.

9. All in all, number 17 is attempting a significant step forward, of which people do not yet seem to have been sufficiently aware in their reception of this text. For here—in keeping with the fact that there are wounds on both sides—it talks about the way that all of us, turning anew in conversion to the Lord, must go forward and, thus, move toward each other. It talks about the variety of ways the Petrine office has been exercised in historical practice, whereby possibilities open up for the future that we cannot yet visualize at all. And for these future possibilities there is a yardstick given: May it become what corresponds to the Lord's will even in its practice (not just in its basic nature) and be able to be perceived by all as consistent with Christ. In that sense one might say that the text ends with a prayer. It is not just appealing here to the well-known Catholic scriptural proof texts for the institution of the Petrine office by the Lord; rather, it is asking that the way that office is exercised may become so transparent that the will of Christ may become visible in this. This petition is a hope, and the hope is a prayer: that the Petrine ministry may be entirely consistent with Christ and may thus become for

everyone a point of reference for unity. I do not know how one could talk more appropriately about the difficult ecumenical problem of the primacy.

Dear Provincial Bishop, my letter has become longer than I thought, and I have also simply set it down in the matter-of-fact language of theological reflection, so as not to let it become longer still. I hope it may be helpful for you and may thus help in our struggle for unity. With this in mind, I remain, with sincere thanks for your brotherly fellowship and with best wishes for blessings during the Easter season,

Yours in the Lord,
Joseph Cardinal Ratzinger

On the Ecumenical Situation

Thirty years after the Second Vatican Council, ecumenism is looking for new visions. The setting out toward Christian unity that took place in that great assembly of the bishops of the Catholic Church had awakened far-reaching hopes. The end of divisions seemed to have come. After the millennium of divisions, people expected a new phase of Christian unity. Paul VI and Patriarch Athenagoras believed they were on the very threshold of the restitution of communion between East and West. Both of them hoped to be able to drink together from the same cup. Yet the relationship with the Reformed communities had also quickly begun to move. Statements of consensus on the most difficult subjects of controversy—justification, the Eucharist, Church office—were put together; the barriers that the sixteenth century had erected seemed almost to have been overcome. Yet there was always somewhere some element remaining unresolved: for all the convergences, it never came to actual union.

THE CLASSICAL MODEL OF ECUMENISM

Why not? That is the question no one who is concerned about faith, and thus about the unity of the faithful, can evade. It is quite clear that accusations are of no avail; they just make the whole thing more difficult and could draw us back into the old polemics. Thus the radical question arises,

directed to everyone: Where did we go wrong? Do we need
other methods, other working models? Which ones? Such
questions as these, going to the heart of the matter, have
arisen not only because the efforts thus far made for ecumenism, for all the positive things they have brought, have
found that the "success" they expected has been denied them;
new questions also arose independently, because in the meanwhile a great deal has changed within the churches themselves. Their inner understanding of what the Church is, and
thus also of what even should be sought as unity, is in many
cases simply not the same as before. If Vatican II saw the
Church as being essentially founded upon creed and sacraments, it could count on agreement about this basic approach
not only from Orthodox Christianity, but also from the
greater part of the ecclesial communities arising from the
Reformation.[1] But if the Church is defined by creed (faith)
and sacrament, then at the same time a certain understanding
of the way God acts in history is being assumed here, which
in turn is based on faith in Christ as true man and true God.
It is assumed that God himself is an active agent in history, not
merely the concluding concept of a certain view of the world
or the conceptualization of the goal of a history that is pro-
gressing toward the omega of a better world. What gives the
Church significance is, in the view of faith, the fact that she is
more than the result of purposeful human activity plus historical development. She represents, rather, the sphere of a
concrete encounter between God and man in this world; an

---

[1] The shared presuppositions for ecumenical dialogue are illuminatingly set
forth in E. Herms' book *Von der Glaubenseinheit zur Kirchengemeinschaft: Plädoyer
für eine realistische Ökumene* [From unity of faith to church fellowship: The
argument for realistic ecumenism] (Marburg, 1989); see Herms, "'Grund,
Wesen und Struktur der Kirche' aus der Sicht eines katholischen Theologen"
(= M. M. Garijo-Guembe) ["The foundation, the nature and the structure of
the Church" in the view of a Catholic theologian], *Theologische Rundschau* 67
(1992): 188–223.

encounter that not only brings individuals to God, but at the same time leads them to one another, makes them into a new family.

What makes the Church the Church, accordingly, are those elements that do not derive from merely human activity. They alone distinguish the Church from all other communal groupings and accord her the quality of being unique, being irreplaceable. Division within the Church thus consists of a split in the confession of faith, the creed, and in the administration of the sacraments themselves; all other differences do not ultimately count: there can be no objection to them; they do not divide us in the heart of the Church. Division within that central sphere, on the other hand, threatens the real reason for the Church's existence, her very being.

From this basic understanding of unity arose two tasks for ecumenism. It had first of all to distinguish purely human divisions from the real theological divides. Purely human divisions, in particular, like to give themselves the importance of something essential; they hide themselves, so to speak, behind this: what is human, what we have made for ourselves, is declared obligatory, as being divine. The silent divinization of what is our own, which is the everlasting temptation for man, easily spreads. In a high proportion of church schisms, such divinizing of what is ours, the self-assertion of some human or cultural form, has played a significant role. Ecumenism demanded, and still demands, the attempt to free ourselves from such distortions, which are often subtle. Then it follows that the variety by no means needs to disappear, because it does not detract from the nature of the Church: this can be special in some way and that can be different, but these things do not have to be compulsory for everyone. A tolerance for different things had to be aroused, not founded on indifference concerning the truth, but on the distinction between truth and mere human tradition.

The first task of ecumenism, as I have outlined it, was therefore concerned with perceiving the limits of the demand for unity; with recognizing what was variable as such and learning to live with a multitude of historically developed forms side by side. This demanded a process of unification that would constantly stand at new beginnings. Thus, for instance, the unexpected return of freedom to the Uniate Christians of the East suddenly turned a process of human and spiritual education of that kind into an urgent challenge. All theological consensuses that have been achieved will falter if we do not rise to this challenge. The fact that theology does not, of itself, bring the requisite human reconciliations has become clear once more in a most disturbing fashion. Thus there is concrete evidence that the first task we have described is quite inseparable from the second, which relates to divisions in the confession of faith and in the sacraments themselves.

Now, almost all divisions will straightaway be justified on the grounds of faith. Establishing whether or not this is well founded is the first question of ecumenism. As we have shown, it looks for the nontheological factors producing division. But the allegation that someone else is ascribing to God what he himself has invented can only become a shared conviction in the case of some of the questions facing us. The really hard cases of division are only those in which one or more of the parties is convinced that they are not defending their own ideas but are standing by what they have received from revelation and cannot therefore manipulate. The consensual statements mostly related to the area of these questions. The aim of the dialogues is then to perceive how positions that are apparently opposed may be compatible at a deeper level and, in doing so, of course, to exclude everything that derives only from certain cultural developments. The demands that such dialogues make on the individual participants are extraordinarily high. People are not simply exchanging their own ideas. What is at stake is not just consensus within the group; and inventing new mediating positions is no solution. Each person is challenged in his inmost conscience. Each has to give way before what is not his own choice: first before what he himself recognizes as the Word of God; yet at the same time he has to respect the conscience of the other person who cannot agree with his faith. Thus it is clear that ecumenical dialogues face a very different task from philosophical discussions, for instance, and certainly different from that of political negotiations. Their ultimate goal is in fact sharing a common faith. Since, however, faith is not a mere construct of human thought but has been vouchsafed as a gift, sharing it in common cannot ultimately result from an intellectual act; rather, it can only, in its turn, be given. Because the goal is the correct apprehension of God's Word, however, and distinguishing it from mere human words, we cannot leave God out of account here.

It is at this point, again and again, that all attempts at reunion founded on negotiations and dialogues have ground to a halt, not least of all in the twentieth century. The truth cannot be decided by majority vote. Either something is true, or it is not. It is not because a majority of qualified representatives have decided something that councils are binding on us. How could people decide what is going to be true? Councils are based on the principle of moral unanimity, and that in turn does not simply appear as an especially strong majority. It is not consensus that offers a basis for the truth, but the truth that offers one for consensus: the unanimity of so many people has always been regarded as something that is humanly impossible. Whenever it occurs, this makes manifest how people have been overpowered by truth itself. Unanimity is not the basis of binding authority but is a sign of the manifestation of truth, and it is from this latter that the authority derives. In this self-understanding of the councils, which at the same time sets a limit to all conciliar decisions, God is presupposed as being a real active agent. It thus corresponds to the belief that the Church is not just a consensus-based community; rather, she is living out a unity that derives from a higher power.[2]

Yet what if, despite all efforts, such ultimate unity does not come about? Some years ago I believed it permissible, in this connection, to interpret 1 Corinthians 11:19 to the effect that division represents not only an evil we have created, and which we ought therefore also to clear away again, but something wherein there can be an element of divine "necessity": division is necessary for purifying us.[3] We have to do everything to become once more capable and worthy of unity, so as not to need any more, so to speak, the scourge of division. But we cannot simply manipulate things so that it is now at an end. In saying this—and inwardly close to Oscar Cullmann's ideas—I tried to outline a model of ecumenism of which the acceptance of division, and drawing close to one another even while separated, was an essential element.[4] In that sense I could accept slogans like "unity through diversity", "unity in diversity", and "a reconciled diversity".

---

[2] The reversal of the relationship between truth and consensus has been worked out above all in the philosophy of Habermas but is also fundamental as a constitutive element for the discursive ethic developed by K. O. Apel. See on this point E. Arens, "Kommunikative Ethik und Theologie" [Communicative ethics and theology], *Theologische Revue* 88 (1992): 441–54. M. Kriele, *Befreiung und politische Aufklärung* [Liberation and political enlightenment](Freiburg, 1980), pp. 91–99, is directed against Habermas. V. Hösle, *Die Krise der Gegenwart und die Verantwortung der Philosophie* [The present-day crisis and the responsibility of philosophy] (Munich, 1990), also takes up an opposing position.

[3] In my book *Kirche, Ökumene und Politik: Neue Versuche zur Ekklesiologie* (Einsiedeln, 1987), pp. 128–34; on the problem of ecumenism as a whole, see pp. 65–134 [Eng. trans.: *Church, Ecumenism and Politics: New Essays in Ecclesiology* (New York: Crossroad, 1988)].

[4] O. Cullmann, *Einheit und Vielfalt* [Unity and diversity], 2nd ed. (Tübingen, 1990).

A NEW ECUMENICAL "PARADIGM"?

In the meantime, then, ecclesial and ecumenical developments have taken place that give a whole new meaning to such formulae. The renunciation of what is called, in a derogatory sense, "consensus ecumenism" has meanwhile become widespread and, now and then, somewhat too hasty, with too much taken for granted, as well. People talk about changes in ecumenical paradigms.[5] The new direction in people's thinking, on which this new view is based, reaches far beyond purely theological questions. In view of the disputes about the confession of faith and, thereby, the doubtful nature of the truth therein expressed, for many people the concept of truth itself has become questionable. Can this be the determinative standard in our searching at all? "Henceforth truth, justice, and humanity are always plural", says one of the leaders of the so-called postmodernists.[6] One would like immediately to ask in response: "What is this business, then, of various humanities? Is there really no longer any common standard of humanity? What can we still expect of one another, then?" The same is true in the case of different kinds of justice: Can what is injustice for one person be

---

[5] K. Raiser, *Ökumene im Übergang: Paradigmenwechsel in der ökumenischen Bewegung* [Ecumenism in transition: Changing paradigms in the ecumenical movement] (Munich, 1989), esp. pp. 51ff.

[6] G. Scobel: "Postmoderne für Theologen? Hermeneutik des Widerstreits und bildende Theologie" [Postmodernism for theologians? The hermeneutics of dispute and theology as a cultural force], in H. J. Höhn, ed., *Theologie, die an der Zeit ist* [Theology that is up-to-date] (Paderborn, 1992), pp. 175–229; quotation from p. 224. This is quoted here from H. Wagner, "Ekklesiologische Optionen evangelischer Theologie als mögliche Leitbilder der Ökumene" [Ecclesiological options from evangelical theology as possible guiding models for ecumenism], *Cath.* 47 (1993): 124–41. This article, with its wealth of material, carefully weighed, seems to me most significant for the rethinking now due in ecumenism.

justice for another? Where truth is concerned, we already hesitate to put the same question quite so readily, but it is no less justified and necessary: Can something be true for one person, then, when it is untrue for another? Is not truth indivisible?

Nonetheless, the experiences of so-called consensus ecumenism have shown how difficult it is to do justice to the demands of truth, have shown how far beyond our capacities it is, time and again. So it is that people are often inclined to invert the relationship between consensus and truth: It is not, they say, truth that creates consensus but consensus that is the only concrete and realistic court of judgment to decide what shall now hold good. The confession of faith, too, would not then express the truth but would have significance as an achievement of consensus. Yet thereby the relationship between truth and action ("praxis") is also reversed. Action becomes the standard for truth. The most varied movements and tendencies find themselves increasingly at one today in this giving preeminence to action. Action is becoming the actual hermeneutic of unity. And at the same time ecumenism thereby transcends the limits of Christian denominations and becomes an ecumenism of religions. According to this view, Christianity and all the other religions should be measured by their contribution to the liberation of man, by their "liberating practice". Justice, peace, and the conservation of creation are now being regarded as the real heart of credal belief.[7] Serving these ends appears as the common purpose of all religions. In terms of theological concepts this

---

[7] See H. Wagner, "Ekklesiologische Optionen", p. 132: "The new ecumenical paradigm implies the transition from the classical perspective of the reign of Christ to the messianic perspective of the Kingdom of God, that is, from a sacramental and christological ecclesiology to a messianic, prophetic, and theocratic ecclesiology. That also means dismissing previous conceptions of unity. Instead of 'unity', one should talk rather of 'community'."

means that the idea of the Kingdom of God takes the place of Christology and ecclesiology, though from this starting point it is usually just referred to as "the kingdom". People are in fact intending to leave open the question of a personal or nonpersonal conception of the idea of God. In ecumenism as apprehended under the primacy of action, the distinction between the one and only God, who has revealed himself by name, and the nameless unknown can no longer necessarily be an ultimate criterion.[8]

At this point it becomes clear how from this point of view many previous efforts toward unity become redundant. If it is no longer ultimately of relevance for unity whether God is a person in the sense of Christian trinitarian belief or whether he is just as validly described under the cipher of "nirvana" in the sense of the Buddhist traditions, then pluralism can basically comprehend everything, whether in the question of religious convictions or as concerns the activity of worship. One should not of course conceive of the new ecumenical "paradigm" as a single and fully worked out way of looking at things; it can be associated with widely differing positions, both moderate and radical. We find the essence of it precisely expressed by Konrad Raiser, who says: "A new ecumenical paradigm would have to release a vision of ecumenism that would take seriously the contradictions, conflicts and dangers of the interdependent world situation and the historical social forms of church." [9] Ecumenical work then relates, "not so much to convergences and consensuses at which to aim, but is rather concerned with the worldwide solidarity and coexistence of Christians, indeed, of all men".[10]

---

[8] That became quite clear in the discussions at the Munich Church Assembly in 1993.

[9] Raiser, *Ökumene*, p. 134; see Wagner, "Ekklesiologische Optionen", p. 136.

[10] See Wagner, "Ekklesiologische Optionen", pp. 129f.

I probably need hardly say that I cannot accept this "paradigm" as such. It is easy to formulate the great goals—peace, justice, the conservation of creation. Yet if justice falls apart into many justices, and all this occurs only in the plural form, which can never be transcended, then these become empty goals. Almost inevitably they are taken over by the contemporary party attitude, by the dominant ideologies. Ethos without logos cannot endure; that much the collapse of the socialist world, in particular, should have taught us. Such criticism by no means implies, however, that the new model should be rejected lock, stock, and barrel. On the contrary, I am convinced that there is much to be learned from it that can be of help to us at the present moment. We have decidedly to reject the relativism in relation to doctrine and credal statements that is more or less clearly at work here. Yet we should nonetheless try—without being indifferent—to find a new patience with each other and for each other in this sphere; a new capacity to permit things and people who are different; a new readiness to distinguish the different levels of unity, so as to realize those elements of unity that are now possible and to leave what is not now possible in the sphere of pluralism, which can also have a positive significance. Through such divisions that cannot at present be overcome, we can time and again be a reminder to each other and bring one another to search our consciences; we very often need the call of this difference that cannot for the present be overcome so as to be purified by the objections and called back from one-sided developments.

Although I decidedly deny that practice should be given priority over logos, I see in the emphasis given to the ethical dimension another important element that has to be picked up. According to the words of Jesus, the whole of the law and the prophets depend on the twin commandment to love God and our neighbor (Mt 22:14). "Love is the fulfilling of the law" is how Paul expresses the same idea (Rom 13:10). If, then, on one hand, Christianity can be entirely defined on the basis of belief, on the other hand, it can equally be determined completely on the basis of love. Bearing witness to this common center of the law and the prophets, which is also the heart of Jesus' own message, remains an urgent task for the whole of Christendom: this heart would in fact have to be that ecumenical formula that is beyond any dispute. So it should in fact be the urgent subject matter of ecumenical dialogues to discover what the commandment of love means in practice at the present time. In that sense, an ecumenism of practice is clearly demanded not only by the historical moment in which we find ourselves, but also on the basis of the word of the Bible. We may presume that the resolute determination to obey the commandment to love will then also appreciably purify our belief and will help us to distinguish what is essential from what is not.

THE PATH OF ECUMENISM TODAY AND TOMORROW

What does all this imply for the path of ecumenism today? What vision can lead us forward? I have already mentioned the limitations of the new "paradigm". The very first fundamental condition is that the confession of belief in the one living God should remain unqualified. Whenever the distinction between the personal, revealed God, on whom we can call, and the nonpersonal, inconceivable mystery disappears, then the distinction between God and the gods, between worship and idolatry, likewise disappears. At this point revelation allows us no ambiguities. We cannot put philosophical profundity in the place of the word that has been uttered and the rationality proper to it. God has spoken—if we think we know better, then we get lost in the darkness of our own

opinions; we lose unity instead of moving toward it. Yet that
then means that we cannot work out an ethic without logos.
If we try it, there are no standards of judgment; we end up in
an ideological moralizing with a tendency to enthusiasm or
to fanaticism.[11] Besides that, consensus in ethics is perhaps
even more difficult to achieve than consensus in the great
questions of belief: the discussions about moral theology in
the Catholic Church and the worldwide discussion of ethics
demonstrate that abundantly. The neglect of what is distinc-
tively Christian and the further inner fragmentation of the
churches, which according to the new "paradigm" are supposed to live in multifarious circles and forms of social group-
ing, are liable to lead to new instances of people shutting
themselves off, new oppositions, which by no means calmly
and serenely take their place in a great pluralistic symphony.
The renunciation in this way of any unity determined by
content, or even one shaped by rules, is liable to give free rein
to sectarian and syncretistic tendencies that can then no
longer be kept in touch with the ethos shared in common.

Belief and sacrament remain constitutive for the Church.
Otherwise she just gets lost. And then she no longer has
anything to offer to mankind. She draws her life from the
Logos having become flesh, from the truth having become a
way. The view of the Church developed from the Bible and
the Fathers is more than a "paradigm", more than one era's
view of life and the world. Here we are led out of all the
paradigms into contact with the truth itself (see Mk 4:18; Jn

---

[11] R. Guardini clearly showed the primacy of logos over ethos in a mag-
nificent and most definite fashion in his early book *Vom Geist der Liturgie* (1918;
Eng. trans.: *The Spirit of the Liturgy* [1930]; reprinted with intro., New York,
1998), which has remained of fundamental importance; see on this point H.-B.
Gerl, *Romano Guardini* (Mainz, 1985), pp. 119f. In the first volume of his
memoirs (*Noch wußte es niemand* [No one yet knew] [Munich, 1976], pp. 69f.),
J. Pieper shows us how the encounter with Guardini and with what he said
about logos and ethos had a fundamental effect on his own path.

16:25). That in fact is what "revelation" consists of; this is the core of our liberation—being led out from that cabinet of mirrors of images and historical points of view and into the encounter with the reality that is vouchsafed to us in Christ. That is why ecumenism will always be a seeking after unity in belief, not just a striving for unity of action. Nevertheless, the new vision—as we have already said—can substantially broaden the images with which we envisage our ecumenical aims in practice and, in part, reshape them—and, indeed, must do so. We had in fact overrated our own capacities if we believed that theological dialogues could, within a fairly brief time span, restore the unity of belief. We had lost our way if we got it into our heads that this goal must be reachable within deadlines we laid down. For a little while we were confusing theology with politics, confusing dialogues about belief with diplomacy. We wanted to do ourselves what only God can do. That is why we have to learn to be prepared to keep on seeking, in the knowledge that the seeking itself is one way of finding; that being on a journey and traveling on, without stopping to take rest, is the only appropriate attitude for the person who is on a pilgrimage toward eternity. Augustine found some wonderful words with which to comment on the saying from a psalm, "Forever seek his face": Even in eternity the seeking will not stop, because love for the Infinite is an eternity of seeking and discovering.[12] This eternal seeking, which does signify at the same time an eternity of already having been found, is of course something different from our

---

[12] *Ennarationes in Ps.* 104:3 (CChr. Ser. Lat., 40, 1537); in Gregory of Nyssa's interpretation of the Song of Songs, the idea of never-ending discovery is a central theme; see H. U. von Balthasar's introduction to his German translation of the text: *Gregor von Nyssa: Der versiegelte Quell* [Gregory of Nyssa: The sealed spring] (Einsiedeln, 1984), pp. 7–26. See also W. Löser, *Im Geist des Origenes: H. U. von Balthasar als Interpret der Theologie der Kirchenväter* [In the spirit of Origen: H. U. von Balthasar as interpreter of the theology of the Fathers] (Frankfurt, 1976), pp. 107–9.

bungling search, which is so often a groping in the dark and so often represents, not the unending path of love, but the all-too-finite path of our own egotism. And yet in this readiness to keep on searching together and to accept ourselves and each other in our provisional form, there is an assent to the inexhaustibility of the mystery of God; this may be an act of humility by which we accept our limitations and in that very act appropriate for ourselves God's greater truth.

In that sense, I would say that theological dialogues, as a search for unity of belief, should certainly continue. But the actual meetings should be carried on in a much more relaxed way, less oriented toward success, in a more "humble" way, with more serenity and patience. Statements of consensus do not have to be their product every time. It is enough if many and varied forms of witnessing to belief thus develop, through which everyone can learn a little more of the wealth of the message that unites us. From the "praxeological model" (as I should like to call it for the moment) we should learn dogmatic patience but without declining into indifference toward the truth and its verbal expression. We should take from it a readiness to countenance a far-reaching multiplicity of forms without encouraging self-sufficiency or self-satisfaction. We should always take care lest hard-won unity be lost, lest Church fellowship slip away into "do as you like". Its demands, comprehending times and places, must remain clear; it must remain clear that we ourselves do not make the Church but that she is shaped by HIM in word and sacrament and that what will endure is only what is his.

We should therefore liberate ourselves, time and again, from our own institutions, that what is essential may appear in its full stature and proportion. Then there can be freedom in many ways, which we should open up our hearts and accept, without any schemes for pastoral uniformity. All this is on condition that these forms developed in human terms are not seen as absolute but are open to what is shared in common and what is essential. Thus there will be crosslinking between groups set up in the individual churches and communities that resemble each other, as is the case today, for instance, in the Focolarini movement or in the relationship between Evangelical brotherhoods and Catholic religious orders. Finally, we ought always to be subjecting ourselves to the yardstick of the love of God and of our neighbor, so as to try to meet the great challenges of our time on this basis. It will be too late if we do not look for forces of reconciliation until the moment of conflict, as for instance in the former Yugoslavia or in Ireland or in the countries that made up the former Soviet Union. Faith must be a matter of constant education for loving, for reverence before someone else's belief, for tolerance, for working together while remaining diverse, for renunciation, for an active readiness for peace. As just such a practical force for good it has to be practiced and lived out, that the forces of salvation may be ready in the moment of crisis. More important than any goals immediately in the sphere of Church politics is the daily growth of what is essential: a faith that works through love (Gal 5:6). It seems to me, then, that there are a good many practical things in which the so-called new paradigm can show us new ways forward, on condition that it is set free from its ideology, with its tendency to relativism.

A FINAL REFLECTION:
SOLOVIEV'S VISION OF ESCHATOLOGICAL UNITY

As I reflect on the situation for ecumenism and the situation of Christianity as such, Soloviev's story of the Antichrist has recently been coming to mind with increasing frequency. It appears in this story that, in the moment of final decision in all three communities, those of Peter, of Paul, and of John, there are living followers of the Antichrist, who play into his hands and submit to him; yet at the same time it appears that in all three there are true Christians, who keep faith with the Lord right up to the hour of his coming. In the face of Christ, the divided groups around Peter, Paul, and John recognize one another as brothers; the true Christians, though divided, recognize that they have always been one, just as, conversely, the host of the Antichrist are convicted of their lies. By the light of the Redeemer it becomes clear who was, and are, members of the one group or the other.[13]

It would be utterly mistaken to suppose that this vision of the passionate advocate of ecumenism, Soloviev, postpones the whole matter of Christian unity to the end of the ages or in any way to the realm beyond time. In Soloviev's vision, eschatology is correctly understood in the biblical sense: it is not later in a chronological sense, something that with the succession of days will sometime arrive in an indefinitely distant future and is just not here yet today. No, what is eschatological is what is genuinely real, which will at some time be revealed as such but already sets its mark upon all our days. The vision shows, rather, that this unity is "eschatological" in the true sense of the term: already present and yet within time never perfected, never simply frozen into the state of a complete empirical fact. What becomes visible in the light of Christ when he comes again exposes the truth of our time, that of each and every time. In all three of the great communities there are true Christians; but in all three, likewise, the Antichrist has his followers, and always even among those occupying the highest spiritual offices. Already at the present time, however, we are to know about these hidden

---

[13] See the edition translated, with commentary, by L. Müller: W. Solowjev, *Kurze Erzählung vom Antichrist* [A short tale about the Antichrist], 6th ed. (Munich, 1986), pp. 44f. and 131ff.

things, to bring us comfort and a healthy fear. Already we are to encounter the eschatological view of it and to carry within us the joy of what will in the future be known.

Therefore, we should already, and always, be motivated by concern lest, with big Christian words and wrapped in a cloak of Christianity, we become servants of the Antichrist, who wants to set up his kingdom in this world and to render the future kingdom of Christ redundant. Peter, Paul, and John are inseparable. Together with them, taught by them, we must ever anew seek the face of the Lord. Only in his light can we know ourselves, can we know each other. Ecumenism is really nothing other than living at present in an eschatological light, in the light of Christ who is coming again. It thus also signifies that we recognize the provisional nature of our activity, which we ourselves cannot finish; that we do not want to do for ourselves what only Christ, when he comes again, can bring about. On our way toward him, we are on our way toward unity.

The Heritage of Abraham[1]

At Christmastime we give each other presents to give one another pleasure and thus to share in the joy that the angel choir proclaimed to the shepherds. In doing this, we remember the gift par excellence that God vouchsafed to mankind when he gave us his Son Jesus Christ. This had been **prepared for** by God **in a long history**, in which—as Saint Irenaeus says—God became accustomed to being with men, and men became accustomed to fellowship with God.

This history begins with the faith of Abraham, father of those who believe, also father of the faith of the Christians and, through faith, our father.

The history continues with the blessing of the patriarchs, with the revelation to Moses, and with Israel's exodus to the Promised Land. A new stage begins with the promise to David and his seed of an everlasting kingdom. The prophets, for their part, interpret history, call people to penitence and repentance, and thus prepare the hearts of men to receive the highest gift of all.

Abraham, the father of the people of Israel, the father of faith, is thus the root of the blessing in which "all the families of the earth shall bless themselves" (Gen 12:3). The task of the

---

[1] Published in Italian in the *Osservatore Romano* of December 29, 2000, and in a German translation by Dr. Titus Lenherr (Rome) in: *Heute in Kirche und Welt: Blätter zur Unterscheidung des Christlichen* [Today in Church and world: Notes toward distinguishing what is Christian], year 1, no. 2 (February 2001): 1–2.

Chosen People is therefore to make a gift of their God, the one true God, to all the other peoples, and we Christians are in fact inheritors of their faith in the one God.

We therefore have to thank our Jewish brothers, who despite all the difficulties of their history have maintained to this day their faith in this God and bear witness to him before other peoples, who without knowledge of the one God "sit in darkness and in the shadow of death" (Lk 1:79).

The God of the Jews' Bible—which, together with the New Testament, is also the Christians' Bible—who is sometimes a God of infinite tenderness, sometimes so strict as to instill fear, is also the God of Jesus Christ and of the apostles. The Church of the second century had to resist the rejection of this God on the part of the Gnostics, and above all by Marcion, who set in opposition to the God of the New Testament a demiurge, a creator-god from whom the Old Testament supposedly derived; the Church, on the other hand, always held fast to the **faith in the one and only God, Creator of the world and Author of both the Testaments**.

The New Testament perception of God, which culminates in the Johannine definition "God is love" (1 Jn 4:16), is not in contradiction with the past, but rather it comprehends within itself the entire history of salvation, of which Israel was at first the pioneer. That is why, from the earliest days up to the present, the voices of Moses and the prophets are heard in the Church's liturgy; Israel's Book of Psalms is also the Church's great prayer book. Consequently, the early Church did not set herself against Israel; rather, she believed herself, in all simplicity, to be Israel's rightful continuation.

The marvelous picture in the twelfth chapter of the Revelation of John of a woman clothed in the sun and crowned with twelve stars, who is pregnant and suffering the pangs of childbirth, is that of Israel, who is bearing the one who "shall rule the nations with a rod of iron" (Ps 2:9); and this woman is nevertheless transformed into the New Israel, the mother of new peoples, and is personified in Mary, the Mother of Jesus. This uniting of the three meanings—Israel, Mary, the Church—shows how Israel and the Church, for the Christian faith, were and are inseparable.

We know that every birth is difficult. Certainly, the relationship between the developing Church and Israel was, from the beginning, often defined by conflict. The Church was regarded by her mother as an unnatural daughter, while the Christians regarded the mother as blind and obstinate. Down through the history of Christianity the already difficult relationship further deteriorated and led in many cases to downright anti-Jewish attitudes, which produced in history lamentable acts of violence. Even if the final, horrific experience of the Shoah took place in the name of an anti-Christian ideology, which was aiming to hit at the Christian faith through its Abrahamic roots in the people of Israel, we cannot deny that a certain inadequacy on the part of Christians in their opposition to these atrocities may be explained by the anti-Jewish heritage present in the minds of not a few Christians.

Precisely on account of the dramatic nature of this final tragedy, perhaps, **a new vision of the relationship between the Church and Israel** has arisen, a sincere intention of overcoming every kind of anti-Jewish attitude and of beginning a constructive dialogue in pursuit of knowledge of one another and of reconciliation. Such a dialogue, in order to be fruitful, has to start with a prayer to our God that he should above all grant to us Christians a greater esteem for this people, the Israelites, a greater love for them, for "to them belong the sonship, the glory, the covenants, the giving of the law, the worship, and the promises; to them belong the patriarchs, and of their race, according to the flesh, is the Christ, who is God over all, blessed for ever. Amen" (Rom 9:4–5).

And this is true not only with regard to the past; it is also true in the present, "For the gifts and the call of God are irrevocable" (Rom 11:29). We will also pray that he may vouchsafe to the sons of Israel a greater knowledge of Jesus of Nazareth, their son, the gift they have made to us. Since both of us are awaiting redemption at the end of time, let us pray that our paths may lie along converging lines.

It is obvious that the dialogue of us Christians with the Jews takes place on a different plane from dialogue with other religions. **The faith to which the Bible of the Jews, the Christians' Old Testament, bears witness is not a different religion for us; rather, it is the basis for our own faith.** That is why Christians read and study these books of Holy Scripture—and nowadays they are doing it more and more in cooperation with their Jewish brethren—with such great attention and as part of their own heritage. It is true that Islam, too, regards itself as a son of Abraham and has inherited from Israel and the Christians the same God, yet it walks by another path, which requires different standards for dialogue.

To come back to the exchanging of presents at Christmas, with which I began this meditation: we must above all recognize that everything we have and do is a **gift from God**, which we receive with the help of humble and sincere prayers, a gift **that we are to share with various ethnic groups, with religions that are seeking greater knowledge of the divine mystery, with nations seeking after peace, and with peoples who desire to establish a society in which justice and love prevail.** That is the program that the Second Vatican Council drew up for the Church of the future. And we Catholics ask the Lord to help us to follow faithfully on this way.

The Church's Guilt

Presentation of the document Remembrance and Reconciliation *from the International Theological Commission*

To help people understand the document *Remembrance and Reconciliation: The Church and the Faults of the Past*, it may be helpful first of all to introduce its authors. The joint authors are the **International Theological Commission**, which was set up in 1969 by Pope Paul VI following a suggestion of the synod of bishops. At that time the bishops had expressed the desire that the cooperation between the Magisterium and theologians all over the world, so fruitful at the Council, should continue and should preferably be given an institutional form that might then in the future function as the instrument of this standing cooperation. The Pope took up this suggestion and, thus, the International Theological Commission came into being. It consists of thirty members, whose names are proposed by the various bishops' conferences and who are then appointed for a five-year period by the pope; they may be confirmed in their appointment for a further five years. At present we are in the sixth five-year period of this commission, which brings together theologians from all parts of the world. These theologians enjoy the confidence of their bishops and thus reflect a little of the international community of theologians and what their thinking is at any particular time. The commission is free to conduct its research. According to the statutes its chairman is the Prefect of the Congregation for the Doctrine of the Faith, but he acts as moderator, being responsible for the work's being carried on in orderly fashion and representing the commission to the outside world. As a rule the commission chooses for itself which tasks it wishes to work on. There is, however, also the possibility that other bodies of the Holy See (perhaps at the suggestion of bishops) may invite them to work on a particular subject that is important to the Magisterium in some given situation.

As far as concerns our present theme, the apostolic letter *Tertio millennio adveniente* had made known the Pope's wish that the Holy Year should not only be the occasion for individual penitence, but would also have to signify a "purifying of conscience" for the Church, in which she should bring to mind the **faults of the past**, which weigh heavily on the history of the Church. A subject was thereby proposed for theology that in this form was new: The many kinds of sin and failure that Church history tells us about—who is to blame for them? Can perhaps the Church herself be to blame? What kind of confession, of penitence, of forgiveness is possible here? I felt the ideas expounded by the Pope were a substantial challenge to theology; and in conversation with them I had seen that the members of the Theological Commission had similar thoughts. That is why I made the suggestion of reflecting on the problem together, and this brought an immediate positive response from the members of the Commission. What was new in the Pope's ideas and in the liturgy of penitence he was planning for the Church set the theologians the task of reflecting on the theological significance of such a procedure, of looking for its internal connections in the history of faith, and thereby also of clarifying its significance for the faith and life of the Church today and tomorrow.

That is how the document before you came into existence. I do not want to analyze here the text of this little book, as Father Cottier explains it more detail. Instead, I should like to give a brief outline of my own reflections on this subject, as inspired by the debates of the Theological Commission over which I presided.

It seemed to me—and I felt my view was confirmed by the theologians' work—that the Pope's gesture, in the form of the penitential liturgy in Saint Peter's, is new, and yet it stands in profound continuity with the Church's history, with her understanding of herself, with her response to God's action. In their dealings with the history of faith, other people will find other elements there in advance; for my part, I became aware of three strands of thought and behavior that have expressed this theme in the faith and life of the Church from the beginning.

In the newspapers people quite rightly talk about the Pope's **"mea culpa"** in the name of the Church. They are thereby quoting from a liturgical prayer, the *Confiteor*, which is used every day in introduction to the celebration of the liturgy. The priest, the pope, the laymen all confess with their "I"—each one of them and all together before God and in the presence of their brothers and sisters—that they have sinned, with their own sin, their own most grievous sin. Two aspects of this opening of the holy liturgy seem important to me. On one hand, we speak in the first person singular; "*I*" have sinned; I am not confessing the sins of other people; I am not confessing the anonymous sins of a collective entity; I am myself confessing with my "I". Yet at the same time it is all the people at prayer who with their "I" are saying, "I have sinned." The entire living Church, in her living members, is saying this: "I have sinned." Thus in this fellowship of confession is expressed that image of the Church which was formulated by the Second Vatican Council in *Lumen gentium*, chapter 1, number 8: "Ecclesia . . . sancta simul et semper purificanda, poenitentiam et renovationem continuo prosequitur": the Church is at the same time holy and constantly in need of purification; she is always treading the path of penitence and of renewal. This picture of the Church, formulated by Vatican II and put into practice daily in the liturgy, for its own part reflects the Gospel parables of the darnel growing amid the corn and of the fishing net that catches all kinds of fish, good and bad. In all generations the Church has recognized these parables as being the Lord's way of expressing in anticipation her own experiences. Again and again there have been tendencies toward forming a church of the wholly pure, a church in which there would be no sinners allowed. Over against such programs, which are entirely understandable, stood the recollection that the Lord came to seek sinners and that he sat with them at their table. The Church always knew that Christ's table-fellowship with sinners continues unbroken in her and that this very thing is the hope we all share. The Church of Jesus Christ cannot separate herself from sinners; she has to accept that there are all kinds of fish in her net and that in her field the darnel is always growing along with the corn.

Three things are important in this first chain of thought. The agent who does the confessing is I—I am confessing, not the sins of other people, but my own. However—second—I am confessing my sins **in fellowship with other people**, before them and before God. And finally, I am asking **God** for forgiveness, since he alone can grant it. Yet in doing so, I am asking my **brothers and sisters** to pray for me in this, and thus in God's forgiveness I am also looking for reconciliation with my brothers and sisters.

The second strand of thought and behavior before my eyes is that of the **penitential psalms of the Old Testament**: these are Israel's prayers first of all, in which the People of

God, in the depths of its suffering and distress, confesses the sins of its history, the sins of the fathers, the constant rebellion from the beginning of the story up to this day. There is a similarity we cannot overlook between these penitential psalms of Israel, which were thoroughly rooted in their liturgy, and the penitential liturgy that the Pope celebrated in Saint Peter's, Rome, on March 12, with and for the Church. For there, too, a story of the sins of the fathers is brought before God in prayer. If, in the psalms, Israel recalled again and again, together with and alongside the history of God's saving acts, the history of its own failure, too, then it was not in order to condemn those others, their fathers, but so as to recognize in the story of this sinning its own situation and so as to prepare itself for repentance and forgiveness. Christians have always prayed these psalms with Israel and have thus renewed the same kind of awareness. That means that our history, too, is of the kind the psalms are describing—a history of rebellion, of sins, of shortcomings. And we, too, confess this, not so as to condemn other people, not to set ourselves as judges over others, but so as to recognize ourselves and to open ourselves up for the purifying of our memory and for our being renewed. We could list many examples of this attitude in the history of the Church. I should like to give just one instance here: Maximus the Confessor (ca. 580–662), in his *Liber asceticus* (Guidance in the Christian life), applied the self-accusations of the Old Testament to us Christians. Just a couple of examples: "That is why the great Isaiah laments aloud over us"—"Jeremiah complained about us. . . . I also hear Moses talking about us. . . . Micah, too, laments. . . . The Psalmist, too, talks about us in a similar way: Save me, O Lord, for there is no holy man"—"Woe unto us, therefore, for we have fallen into the utmost evil. . . . Are we, who now bear the great name of Christ, not worse than the Jews, then? No one should be angry when he hears the truth"—"That is why any and every pious practice, if lacking in love, has nothing to do with God."[1]

I see a third model upon which the penitential liturgy of March 12 could build, in the prophetic warnings to the seven churches in the Apocalypse—warnings that from the beginning were seen as exemplary of the prophetic warnings necessary for local Churches in all ages and, thus, for the universal Church. This model of the prophetic reprimand, already provided in the New Testament itself, has been taken up again and again in the history of the Church, in the most varied forms and ways. The criticism of the hierarchy offered by such great theologians and Doctors of the Church as Albert the Great and Bonaventure can hardly be surpassed in its severity. An impressive example of this grappling with the sins of the Church is offered by Dante in the thirty-second canto of his *Purgatory*: he sees how first of all a fox slinks into the carriage of the Church, then—an image of the "donation of Constantine"—an eagle, finally a dragon. The way Philip the Fair of France used force to dominate the Church is pictured in the horrific image of a whore in the holy carriage. "At her side I saw a giant. . . . And from time to time the two of them kissed each other. Yet when her lascivious, wandering eyes fastened upon me, then her furious lover flogged her from head to toe." The Theological Commission's document quotes Hadrian VI's confession of guilt. In a more recent period we might perhaps think of Rosmini's "five wounds of holy Church".

When we look at this constant story of "mea culpa" in the Church, we may ask ourselves—and I, too, have asked myself this—what exactly is surprising about it, what is new about this Holy Year? My impression—and I should like to offer this

---

[1] *Maximi Confessoris Liber Asceticus*, ed. Peter van Deun, CChr. Ser. Graec. 40 (Turnhout and Louvain, 2000), vv. 669–71, 563–77, 596–615, 714–16.

for discussion here—is that something changed at the beginning of the modern era, when Protestantism created a new kind of **church history**, with the aim of showing that the Catholic Church was not merely stained with sin, as she has always known and said, but that she was, allegedly, completely corrupted and ruined and no longer the Church of Christ; rather, she has, on the contrary, become an instrument of the Antichrist. Consequently—since she was corrupt through and through—she was said to be no longer the Church but an anti-church. At this point, something had obviously changed. A Catholic historiography now necessarily grew up in opposition to this picture, with the aim of showing that the Catholic Church—despite those sins that could not be denied and were more than obvious—was nonetheless the Church of Christ and remained the Church of the holy saints, the holy Church. At that time when two kinds of historiography were opposed to each other and when the Catholic historians felt obliged to write apologetics to demonstrate that in spite of everything the quality of holiness still remained in the Church, then necessarily the voice in which sins are confessed in the Church becomes more quiet.

The position became still worse in the course of the Enlightenment; let us recall Voltaire's "Écrasez l'Infâme!" Ultimately, the accusations were growing in scope right up to those of Nietzsche, in which the Church appears, no longer as merely failing to do the will of Christ, but as the great evil of all evils afflicting mankind, as effecting the alienation of man from himself, something from which he must finally be liberated in order to become once more himself. We see the same theme, differently worked out, in Marxism. For Marxism, too, the Church, Christianity as such, alienates man from himself, gives its sanction to oppression, and stands in the way of progress. Since the Enlightenment, many deplorable historical realities have been exaggerated into real myths—the

Crusades, the Inquisition, the burning of witches—and these have grown far beyond the historical facts into mythical bugbears that not merely justify but positively demand the rejection of the Church. Any attempt to see history as being a little less black and white, to distinguish a little more clearly the various ways in which different people were responsible, to see the complexity of these phenomena and to see what the various people responsible were trying to do, is condemned beforehand as a concession to inhumanity. When certain distressing facts grow into a kind of negative confession of faith and are no longer able to be seen in the context of forces and effects that can be distinguished from one another, then it becomes more difficult for the faithful to join in the confession of being at fault: it would now seem necessary to make clear that the Church, in spite of it all, has been and still remains an instrument of salvation, a force for good and not for the destruction of man.

Today we find ourselves in a new situation, in which the Church can, with greater freedom, invite us to return to the confession of sins and can thus also invite other people to confession and to a more profound reconciliation. We have seen the enormous destruction wrought by various kinds of atheism, which brought forth a new level of anti-humanism, of the destruction and ruin of man. The atrocities that the atheistic systems of the twentieth century have invented and practiced cast all previous horrors into the shadows; we cannot take them in without shuddering. The rejection of the Church, the rejection of God and of Christ, does not save anyone; on the contrary—we can see what appalling capacities it unchains within man. The question is once more posed for everyone: Where are we? What can save us? Thus, we can admit to guilt with a new openness and, at the same time, recognize with a new gratitude the gift of the Lord, which he grants to us through the Church and which all the sins in her have never been able and never will be able to ruin or spoil.

To end with, I should like very briefly to formulate three **criteria** for dealing correctly with the Church's guilt and for the right way to purify our memory.

The first criterion: The present-day Church cannot set herself up as a tribunal to deliver judgments on previous generations—even though sins of the past are necessarily implicated in the "mea culpa"; for without the sins of the past, we are unable to understand the situation of today. It is neither possible nor permissible for the Church to dwell arrogantly in the present day, to feel herself exempt from sins and to make out that it is the sins of others, of the past, that are the source of evil. The confession of the sins of other people does not set us free from acknowledging the sins of the present day. Rather, it helps to awaken our own consciences and to open up the way toward conversion for us all.

A second criterion: Confessing, according to Augustine, means: "Doing the truth".[2] That is why it demands, above all, the discipline and the humility belonging to truth, not to deny all the evil that has been carried out in the Church, yet also to avoid marking up against ourselves, in false modesty, sins that were never committed or concerning which there is no historical certainty.

Third criterion: Again in accordance with Augustine, we have to say that a Christian *confessio peccati* always has to go hand in hand with a *confessio laudis*. In any honest examination of conscience we can see that for our part in every generation we have done much that is evil. Yet we can also see that, in spite of our sins, God has always purified and renewed the Church and has always entrusted great things to fragile vessels.

---

[2] See on this point J. Ratzinger, "Originalität und Überlieferung in Augustins Begriff der *confessio* [Originality and tradition in Augustine's concept of *confessio*], *Rev. Études Aug.* 3 (1957): 375–92, esp. p. 385.—ED.

And who could fail to recognize how much good has been done, for example, in the past two centuries by new religious congregations and by lay movements in the sphere of education, in the social sector, in efforts on behalf of the weak, the sick, the poor, and the suffering, even while those centuries were at the same time ravaged by the atrocities of the atheistic systems? It would be failing in honesty to see only our evil and not the good that God has effected through the faithful—in spite of their sins. The Church Fathers saw this paradox of guilt and grace as being summed up in the words of the Bride in the Song of Songs: "Nigra sum sed formosa" (Song 1:4). "I am stained with sins, yet beautiful"—beautiful through your grace and through what you have done. The Church is able to confess the sins of the past and of the present in all openness and confidence, in the knowledge that evil will never completely ruin her; in the knowledge that the Lord is stronger than our sins and renews his Church again and again, that she may continue to be the instrument of God's good works in our world.

The Church on the Threshold
of the Third Millennium

I recently read in a newspaper of a German intellectual who said about himself that where the question of God was concerned, he was an agnostic: It was just not possible, he said, either to demonstrate the existence of God or absolutely to exclude it, so the matter would remain undecided. He said he was utterly convinced, on the other hand, of the existence of hell; a glance at the television was enough for him to see that it existed. While the first half of this confession corresponds entirely with modern consciousness, the second appears strange, indeed, incomprehensible—at least when you first hear it. For how can you believe in hell if there is no God? When you look closer at it, this statement turns out to be entirely logical: hell is, precisely, the situation in which God is absent. That is the definition of it: Where God is not there, where no glimmer of his presence can any longer penetrate, that place is hell. Perhaps it is not actually our daily look at the television that shows us that, but certainly a look at the history of the twentieth century, which has left us terms like Auschwitz and the Gulag Archipelago and names like Hitler, Stalin, and Pol Pot. Anyone who reads the witnesses' accounts of those anti-worlds will encounter visions that for atrocities and destruction in no way yield to Dante's descent into hell, are indeed even more frightful, because there appear dimensions of evil that Dante could have had no way of perceiving in advance. These hells were constructed in order to be able to bring about the future world of the man who was his own master, who was no longer supposed to need any God. Man was offered in sacrifice to the Moloch of that utopia of a God-free world, a world set free from God, for man was now wholly in control of his destiny and knew no limits to his ability to determine things, because there was no longer any God set over him, because no light of the image of God shone forth any more from man.

Wherever God is not, hell comes into existence: it consists simply in his absence. That may also come about in subtle forms and almost always does so under cover of the idea of something beneficial for people. If nowadays there is a traffic in human organs, if fetuses are being formed to provide a supply of such organs or in order to further research into health and sickness, it is for many the humanitarian content of these actions that is apparent; yet with the contempt for human beings that is inherent in them, with this way of using people, and even using them up, we are in fact, after all, again on our way down to hell. That does not imply that there cannot be—as in fact there are—atheists with high ethics. Yet I venture to maintain that these ethics are based on the lingering glimmer of the light that once came from Sinai—the light of God. Far-distant stars, now already dead, may still be shining upon us. Even when God seems to be dead, his light may still be around. Yet Nietzsche rightly pointed out that the moment when the news that God is dead has reached everywhere, the moment in which his light would finally be extinguished, can only be frightful.

Why am I saying all this in a meditation on the question of what we Christians have to do today, in this historic moment of ours at the beginning of the third millennium? I am saying it because it is on that very basis that our task as Christians becomes clear. It is both simple and very great: It is a matter of witnessing to God, of opening up the barred and darkened windows so that his light may shine among us, that there may be room for his presence. For it is true, conversely, that where God is, there is heaven: there, even in the tribulations of our daily living, life becomes bright. Christianity is not a complicated philosophy that has in the meanwhile also become obsolete, not a package of dogmas and rules beyond being grasped as a whole. **Christian faith is being touched by God and witnessing to him.** That is why Paul, on the Areopagos, described his task and his intention as wishing to make known to the Athenians, whom he addressed as representative of the peoples of the world, the unknown God—the God who had emerged from his hiddenness, who had made himself known, and who could therefore be proclaimed by him (Acts 17:16–34). The reference to the expression "the unknown god" presupposes that man, in not knowing, still does know about God in some way; it responds to the situation of the agnostic, who does not know God personally and yet cannot exclude him. It presupposes that man is in some sense waiting for God and yet cannot of his own resources reach him, so that he is in need of preaching, of the hand that helps him over into the sphere of his presence.

Thus we can say: **the Church is there so that God, the living God, may be made known—so that man may learn to live with God, live in his sight and in fellowship with him. The Church is there to prevent the advance of hell upon earth and to make the earth fit to live in through the light of God.** On the basis of God's presence, and only through him, is it humanized. We may also formulate this from the third petition of the Our Father: "Thy will be done on earth, as it is in heaven." Wherever God's will is carried out is heaven, and there earth can become heaven. That is why it is a matter of making it possible to discern God's will and of bringing man's will into harmony with God's will. For one cannot know God in a merely academic way; one cannot merely take note of his existence, as for instance I may note the existence of distant stars or that of the data of past history. Knowledge of God may be compared to the knowledge of someone in love: it concerns me as a whole; it also demands my will; and it comes to nothing if it does not attain this all-embracing assent.

But in saying this I have anticipated. For the moment, let us note that for the Church, it is never merely a matter of maintaining her membership or even of increasing or broadening her own membership. **The Church is not there for her own sake.** She cannot be like an association that, in difficult circumstances, is simply trying to keep its head above water. She has a task to perform for the world, for mankind. The only reason she has to survive is because her disappearance would drag humanity into the whirlpool of the eclipse of God and, thus, into the eclipse, indeed the destruction, of all that is human. We are not fighting for our own survival; we know that we have been entrusted with a mission that lays upon us a responsibility for everyone. That is why the Church has to measure herself, and be measured by others, by the extent to which the presence of God, the knowledge of him, and the acceptance of his will are alive within her. A church that was merely an organization pursuing its own ends would be the caricature of a Church. To the extent to which she is revolving around herself and looks only to the aims necessary for maintaining herself, she is rendering herself redundant and is in decline, even if she disposes of considerable means and skillful management. She can live and be fruitful only if the primacy of God is alive within her.

The Church is there, not for her own sake, but **for mankind.** She is there **so that the world may become a sphere for God's presence, the sphere of the covenant between God and men.** Thus, that is what the creation story is saying (Gen 1:1–2:4): the way that the text moves toward the Sabbath is trying to make clear that creation has an inner basis and purpose. It is there in order that the covenant may come to be in which God freely gives his love and receives the response of love. The idea that the Church is there for mankind has recently been appearing in a variant that makes sense to us but jeopardizes the essence of the matter. People are saying that in recent times the history of theology and of the Church's understanding of herself has passed through three stages: from ecclesially centered to being Christ-centered and, finally, God-centered. This, it is said, represents progress, but it has not yet reached its final stage. It is clear, people say, that ecclesially centered theology was wrong: the Church should not make herself the center of things; she is not there for her own sake. Therefore we moved on to Christ-centered thinking; Christ was supposed to be at the heart. Then, however, it was recognized—they say—that Christ, too, points above and beyond himself to the Father, and thus we arrived at theocentric, God-centered thinking, and this signified at the same time an opening up of the Church to the outside, to other religions: The Church divides people, but Christ also divides, so people say. And then people add: God, too, divides people, since people's images of God contradict one another, and there are religions without a personal God and ways of understanding the world without God. Thus, as a fourth stage, the centrality of the kingdom is postulated, and though this is apparently a development from the gospel, people call it, no longer the Kingdom of God, but just simply "the kingdom", as a cipher for the better world that is to be built up.

The centrality of the kingdom is supposed to mean that everyone, reaching beyond the boundaries of religions and ideologies, can now work together for the values of the kingdom, which are, to wit: peace, justice, and the conservation of creation. This trio of values has nowadays emerged as a substitute for the lost concept of God and, at the same time, as the unifying formula that could be the basis, beyond all distinctions and differences, for the worldwide community of men of goodwill (and who is not one of them?) and thus might really be able to lead to that better world. That sounds tempting. Who is there who does not feel bound to support the great aim of peace on earth? Who would not be bound to strive for justice to be done, so that finally the glaring differences between classes and races and continents might disappear? And who would not see the need today to defend creation against the modern forms of destruction it suffers? Has God become superfluous, then? Can this trio of values take his place? Yet, how do we know what will bring peace? Where do we find a standard for justice and a way of distinguishing paths that lead there from paths that turn aside? And how are we to know when technology is appropriate to the claims of creation and when it is becoming destructive? Anyone who sees how this trio of values is handled, worldwide, cannot hide the fact that it is increasingly becoming a hotbed of ideologies and that without an all-embracing standard of what is consistent with existence, what is appropriate to creation, and what is humane, it cannot survive intact. Values cannot replace truth; they cannot replace God, for they are only a reflection of him, and without his light their outline becomes blurred.

Thus, we are left with this: **Without God, the world cannot be bright, and the Church is serving the world by the fact that God lives within her and that she is transparent for him and carries him to mankind.** And thereby we come at last to the quite practical question: How does that happen? How can we ourselves recognize God, and how can we bring him to other people? I think that for this purpose, several different ways must be interwoven. First there is the way that Paul adopted on the Areopagos—**the reference to the capacity to know God that is buried within men,**

appealing to reason. "[God] is not far from each one of us",
Paul says there. "In him we live and move and have our
being" (Acts 17:27–28). In the Letter to the Romans, we
meet the same idea, still more strongly expressed: "Ever since
the creation of the world [God's] invisible nature, namely, his
eternal power and deity, has been clearly perceived in the
things that have been made" (1:20). Christian faith appeals to
reason, to the transparency of creation in revealing the Creator. The Christian religion is a **logos-religion**: "In the beginning was the Word" is how we translate the first sentence
of the Gospel of John, which is consciously referring, for its
part, to the first sentence of the Bible as such, the account of
the creation being carried out through the Word. Yet "word"
(logos), in the biblical sense, also means reason, with its creative power.

Meanwhile, however—is that sentence about the beginning of the world in the Word, thus understood, still acceptable today? Can the Church still join the Bible today in
appealing to reason, in referring to the way creation transpar-
ently reveals the creative spirit? There is today a materialistic
version of the theory of evolution that presents itself as being
the last word in science and lays claim to have made the
creative spirit superfluous through its hypotheses, indeed, to
have excluded it definitively. Jacques Monod, who elaborated
this theory with admirable logical consistency, has com-
mented on his own theory with typical honesty: "The
miracle has indeed been 'explained', and yet it remains for us
a miracle." And then he quotes the comment that François
Mauriac delivered about his theories: "What this professor
says is much more incredible yet than what we poor Christians believe." And he responds, "That is just as true as the fact
that we cannot succeed in forming a satisfying mental picture
of certain abstractions of modern physics. Yet at the same
time, we know that such difficulties cannot stand as an argu-

ment against a theory that has in its favor the certainties of experience and logic." [1] At that point one must inquire: Which logic? I cannot—and do not want to—take up this dispute here, but I will say only that faith has no reason to quit the field here: The option of thinking that the world originates from reason, and not from unreason, can be rationally maintained even today, though it must of course be formulated in conversation with the genuine findings of natural science. That is one task the Church has today: to revive the argument about the rationality of belief or unbelief. Belief is not an opponent of reason, but the advocate of its true stature, as the Pope has depicted with passionate commitment in his encyclical *Faith and Reason*. **The struggle for the new presence of the rationality of faith** is what I regard as an **urgent task for the Church in our century.** Faith should not withdraw into its own shell, behind a decision for which it gives no further reason; it should not shrink into being no more than a kind of system of symbols, in which people can make themselves at home but which would ultimately remain a random choice among other visions of life and the world. It needs the wide realm of open reason; it needs the confession of faith in the Creator God, for without this confession of faith even Christology is diminished; it then talks only indirectly about God, by referring to a particular religious experience, while this, however, is necessarily limited and would then become just one experience among others.

The appeal to reason is a great task for the Church, especially today, for whenever faith and reason part company, both become diseased. Reason becomes cold and loses its standards of judgment; it becomes cruel, because nothing is superior to

---

[1] J. Monod, *Le Hasard et la nécessité* (1957; reprinted, Paris: France Loisirs, 1989); Eng. trans.: *Chance and Necessity* (Harmondsworth: Penguin, 1997); German trans.: *Zufall und Notwendigkeit* (Munich, 1971); quotations from pp. 171f. of the German ed.

it any more. The limited understanding of man is now making decisions alone about what should happen to creation in the future, about who is allowed to live and who is being shut out from the banquet of life: the path to hell, as we have seen, then lies open. Yet faith, too, becomes diseased without the wide realm of reason. What dreadful destruction can then come forth from a sick religiosity we can see in abundance in our own present-day society. It is not without reason that the Apocalypse portrays sick religion, which has taken leave of the dimension of belief about creation, as the genuine power of the Antichrist.

It remains true, of course, that the revelation in creation to which Paul refers in the Areopagos speech and in the Letter to the Romans is not in itself sufficient really to bring man into relationship with God. **God has come to meet man. He has shown him his face, opened up his heart to him.** "No one has ever seen God; the only-begotten Son, who is in the bosom of the Father, he has made him known", says the Gospel of John (1:18). The Church has to make him more widely known; she has to bring men to Christ and Christ to men, so as to bring God to them and them to God. Christ is not just some great man or other with a significant religious experience; he is God, God who became man to establish a bridge between man and God and so that man may become truly himself. Anyone who sees Christ only as a great religious person is not truly seeing him. The path from Christ and to Christ has to arrive at the point at which the Gospel of Mark ends up, at the confession of the Roman centurion before the Crucified One: "Truly this man was the Son of God!" (15:39). It has to arrive at the point where the Gospel of John ends up, in the confession of Thomas: "My Lord and my God!" (20:28). It has to stride along the great arch that the Gospel of Matthew sets up from the Annunciation story to the missionary speech of the Risen One. In the story of the

Annunciation, Jesus is heralded as the "God with us" (1:23). And the final saying in the Gospel takes up this message: "Behold, I am with you always, to the close of the age" (28:20). In order to know Christ, we have to join in following the path along which the Gospels lead us.

The great and central task of the Church today is, as it ever was, to show people this path and to offer a **pilgrim fellowship** in walking it. I said just now that we know God, not simply with our understanding, but also with our will and with our heart. Therefore the knowledge of God, the knowledge of Christ, is a path that demands the involvement of the whole of our being. The most beautiful portrayal of the way we are traveling is offered by Luke in the story of the disciples going to Emmaus. This is **traveling together with Christ the living Word, who interprets for us the written word, the Bible, and turns that into the path, the path along which our heart starts to burn and thus our eyes are finally opened**: Scripture, the true tree of knowledge, opens our eyes for us if at the same time we are eating of Christ, the tree of life. Then we become truly able to see, and then we are truly alive. Three things belong together on this path: the fellowship of the disciples, the Scriptures, and the living presence of Christ. Thus, this journey of the disciples to Emmaus is at the same time a description of the Church—a description of how knowledge that touches on God grows and deepens. This knowledge becomes a fellowship with one another; it ends up with the Breaking of Bread, in which man becomes God's guest and God becomes man's host. Christ— that becomes clear here—is not someone we can have for ourselves alone. He leads us, not just to God, but to each other. That is why Christ and the Church belong together, just as the Church and the Bible belong together. Giving actual form to this great fellowship in the concrete individual fellowships of diocese, of parish, of ecclesial movements, is and remains the central task of the Church, yesterday, today, and tomorrow. It must become possible to experience this fellowship as a pilgrim fellowship with our cares, with the word of God, and with Christ, and it has to lead us onward to the gift of the Sacrament, in which the marriage feast of God with mankind is ever and again anticipated.

If we look back at our reflections thus far, we can say this: The theme of Christ is ultimately not a separate, second theme beside the theme of God; rather, it is the way in which the theme of God becomes for us entirely concrete, the way it makes its presence felt, rubbing shoulders with us, as it were, and getting through to our mind. And the theme of the Church, in turn, is not a separate, third theme; rather, it is woven in support of the theme of Christ: **the Church is a pilgrim fellowship with him and toward him**, and it is only if she remains in this supporting role that we understand her aright; then, we can truly love her, as one loves companions on a journey.

The individual **elements of this traveling** ought actually now to be expounded in somewhat more detail. The Pope, in his apostolic letter *Novo millennio ineunte*, has said everything that is essential on this subject, so in the closing part of these reflections I should like to make do with a couple of footnotes to this. In this text the Pope speaks at length about the **meaning of prayer**, which is what really makes the Christian a Christian. In prayer, he says, we experience the primacy of grace: God is always there before us. Christianity is not moralism, not our own construct. First, God moves to meet us, and then we can go along with him; then our inner powers are freed. And prayer, he continues, makes it possible for us to experience the primacy of Christ, the primacy of inwardness and of holiness. At this point the Pope adds a question well worth pondering: "When this principle is not being respected, is it surprising if pastoral projects fail and we are left with a feeling of depression and frustration?" (38). Over and above all our activism, we have to learn anew the primacy of inwardness—the mystical component of Christianity has to gain renewed force.

From personal prayer, the Pope quite logically moves on to shared liturgical prayer, above all to the Sunday Eucharist. **Sunday, as the day of the Resurrection, and the Eucharist, as a meeting with the Risen One**, belong together. Time needs to have its inner rhythm. It needs the correspondence between the everyday period of our work and the solemn encounter with Christ in church, in the Sacrament. The Pope quite rightly views winning back Sunday as a pastoral task of the first order. In that way time is given its inner ordering; God once more becomes the starting point of time and the point at which it is aiming. This is also at the same time the day of human fellowship, the family's day (on a small scale), and also the day on which the great family, the family of God, takes form in the Church and the Church becomes something we experience. If anyone knows the Church only from committee sessions and papers, they do not know her. Then she becomes an offense, because she either becomes the object of our own constructive activities, or she appears as something imposed upon us from outside, something alien. We know the Church from within only if we experience her at that moment when she is transcending herself, when the Lord enters into her and makes her his dwelling and, thereby, makes us his brothers and sisters. That is why the dignified celebration of the Eucharist is so important, a celebration in which the Church's dispossession of herself must appear. We do not make the liturgy ourselves. We do not think something up, as profane festival committees do, in the way that quizmasters proudly present something. The Lord comes. The liturgy derives from him, has grown up from the apostles in the faith of the Church; we enter into it; we do not construct it. That is the only way there can be celebration, and celebration—as an anticipation of future freedom—is essential for man. We could go so far as to say: This is **the Church's task, to vouchsafe us the experience of celebration**. Celebration, festivals, have arisen throughout the whole history of mankind as cultic events and are unthinkable without the divine presence. Celebration attains its full stature when God truly becomes our guest and invites us to share in his banquet.

There are two more points I should like to mention. The Pope moves on from the Sunday liturgy to the **sacrament of reconciliation**. No sacrament has become so alien to us, in recent decades, as this one has. And yet, who could fail to be aware that we need reconciliation? That we have a need for forgiveness, for inner cleansing? Meanwhile, we have switched to psychotherapy and psychoanalysis, and I would not quarrel with their tasks or their capacities. Yet without the word of reconciliation that comes from God, our attempts to repair sick spirits remain inadequate. That leads me to a second comment. I had said that the whole of man is required for the knowledge of God—understanding, will, and heart. In practice this means that we cannot know God unless we are prepared to accept his will, to take it as the yardstick and the orientation for our lives. In still more practical terms, that means that living in accordance with the Commandments is a part of belonging to the pilgrim fellowship of faith, the fellowship of those traveling toward God. That is not a heteronomous rule being imposed upon man. It is in assenting to the will of God that our being made truly similar to God is actually effected, and we become what we are: the image of God. And because God is love, that is why the **Commandments**, in which his will is made known, are the essential variations of the single theme of love. They are the practical **rules of love** for God, for my neighbor, for creation, for ourselves. And because, again, there exists in Christ the entire assent to God's will, the full stature of being in God's image, that is why living in accordance with love and within the will of God is following Christ, moving toward him and walking together with him.

Reference to the Commandments has become quite muted, even in the Church, in the last few decades; suspicion of legalism and moralism has risen so high. And indeed, what the Commandments say remains external if it is not illuminated by the inwardness of God within us and by the way Christ has gone ahead on behalf of us all. It remains moralistic if it is not standing in the light of the grace of forgiveness. Israel was proud of knowing God's will and, thus, knowing the way of life. Psalm 119 as a whole is an ever-repeated outbreak of joy and thankfulness at knowing **God's will**. We know this will now as **having become flesh in Jesus Christ, showing us the way and at the same time showing compassion, time and again picking us up and leading us on**. Should we not rejoice anew for this, in the midst of a world filled with darkness and confusion? **The reawakening of joy in God, joy in God's revelation and in friendship with God, seems to me an urgent task for the Church in our century.** For us, too, in particular, the saying is true that Ezra the priest cried out to the people of Israel when their courage had ebbed after the exile: The joy of the Lord is your strength (Neh 8:10).

I should like to close with an image from Dante's *Divine Comedy*. We started from the descent into hell, into a world without God. Dante portrays the path of purification, the way to God, as the ascent of a mountain. The external path becomes a symbol of the inner way to the real heights, the heights of God. At first, the climbing becomes infinitely difficult for the earth-bound man. In Dante's poetic vision, after the first stage of the path, an angel blots out from the climber's forehead the sign of pride, and now a strange feeling comes over him as he pursues his way: "Already we were mounting up the holy cliffs, and to me it was as if I had become far lighter than I had felt myself to be previously, on level ground. So I spoke: 'Master, say, what heavy load has been taken from me, that it scarcely feels much trouble when I walk, any more?'" (II, 12, ll. 115–20). Being freed from pride means being able to overcome our difficulties. Our own thoughts, such as arrogance, greed, ambition, and whatever else dark and evil there is dwelling in our souls—these are like lead weights that hinder our upward climb, that make us unable to reach the heights. "The purer man becomes, the more closely is he related to him who is above. He loses weight, he has more strength for climbing. . . . Freedom grows; it is complete when the will becomes one with the demand." [2] The **pilgrim fellowship of faith**, which we call the Church, should be a fellowship in climbing, a fellowship in which those processes of cleansing are effected in us that render us capable of the true heights of human existence, of fellowship with God. In the same measure as we are cleansed, the climbing, which is at first so difficult, rapidly becomes a joy. This joy must more and more shine forth from the Church into the world.

---

[2] R. Guardini, *Der Engel in Dantes göttlicher Komödie* [The angel in Dante's *Divine Comedy*], 3rd ed. (Mainz and Paderborn, 1995), pp. 48f.

Joseph Cardinal Ratzinger: Bibliography

As of February 1, 2002

PRELIMINARY REMARKS

In *Weisheit Gottes—Weisheit der Welt: Festschrift für Joseph Cardinal Ratzinger* [Wisdom of God—Wisdom of the World: Essays presented to Joseph Cardinal Ratzinger], published on behalf of the association of his former students (St. Ottilien, 1987), H. Höfl published a bibliography that ran up to the year 1986. This also lists book reviews, sermons, and addresses, and likewise radio broadcasts by Joseph Cardinal Ratzinger. Besides this, it records scholarly discussion with him in the form of reviews. In the collection of pieces published ten years later, on the occasion of his seventieth birthday: Joseph Cardinal Ratzinger, *Vom Wiederauffinden der Mitte: Grundorientierungen: Texte aus vier Jahrzehnten* [Rediscovering the Center: Basic orientations: Texts from four decades] (Freiburg, 1997), there is a selective bibliography put together by V. Pfnür, arranged by subject, which runs up to 1997, and also a collection of secondary literature put together by Monsignor H. Moll, which offers a view of the "Reception of and Discussion with the Theological Work of Joseph Cardinal Ratzinger". The bibliography we offer here includes separate publications, the Cardinal's work as an editor, and also articles in collective works and periodicals, up to January 2002. It includes, however, the entire period of publication. Thus we are able to draw attention to recent translations of what was published in earlier years; we would not, of course, claim that this is exhaustive. Further bibliographical information can be found on the Internet or especially in the following works: Aidan Nichols, O.P., *The Theology of Joseph Ratzinger* (Edinburgh, 1988); A. F. Utz, ed., *Glaube und demokratischer Pluralismus im wissenschaftlichen Werk von Joseph Kardinal Ratzinger* [Faith and democratic pluralism in the scholarly work of Joseph Cardinal Ratzinger] (Bonn, 1989; 2nd ed., 1991); T. Weiler, *Volk Gottes—Leib Christi* [People of God—Body of Christ] (Mainz, 1997).

The abbreviations conform to the list of abbreviations in the third edition, edited by W. Kasper, of the *Lexikon für Theologie und Kirche* (Freiburg, 1993), and otherwise that of International List of Abbreviations IATG (Berlin and New York, 1974), compiled by S. Schwertner.

I.

SEPARATE PUBLICATIONS

Volk und Haus Gottes in Augustins Lehre von der Kirche. MThS.S 7.
Munich, 1954. Unamended reprint, with a new preface. St.
Ottilien, 1992.
Italian: Popolo e casa di Dio in S. Agostino. Milan, 1979.

Die Geschichtstheologie des heiligen Bonaventura. Munich, 1959.
Unamended reprint, with a new preface. St. Ottilien, 1992.
American: The Theology of History in St. Bonaventure. Chicago,
1971; 2nd ed., 1989.
French: La Théologie de l'histoire de saint Bonaventure. Paris, 1988.
Italian: La teologia della storia di San Bonaventura. Milan, 1978,
1991.

Der Gott des Glaubens und der Gott der Philosophen. Munich, 1960.
Spanish: El dios de la fe y el dios de los filósofos. Madrid, 1962.
Russian: Bog very i Bog filosofov. Leningrad, 1977 (samizdat).

Die christliche Brüderlichkeit. Munich, 1960. First appeared in *Der
Seelsorger* 26 (1958): 387–429.
French: Frères dans le Christ: L'Esprit de la fraternité chrétienne. Paris,
1962.
Italian: Fraternità cristiana. Rome, 1962.
Dutch: De Christelijke broederlijkheid. Hilversum and Antwerp,
1963.
Greek: 'Αδελφοσύνη. Athens, 1964.
English: Christian Brotherhood. London, 1966.
American: The Open Circle: The Meaning of Christian Brotherhood.
New York, 1966.
Spanish: La fraternidad cristiana. Madrid, 1966.
Hungarian: Guardini, Pieper, Ratzinger, Rahner, Balthasar, and
Varvier. *A szeretetről,* pp. 207–72. Budapest, 1987.
Also in *Japanese* (Tokyo, 1972).

(Together with Karl Rahner) *Episkopat und Primat.* QD 11. Freiburg, 1961; 2nd ed., 1963.
English/American: *The Episcopate and the Primacy.* London, Edinburgh, and New York, 1962.
Spanish: *Episcopado y Primado.* Barcelona, 1965.
Italian: *Episcopato e primato.* Edited by A. Bellini. Brescia, 1966.

Die erste Sitzungsperiode des 2. Vatikanischen Konzils: Ein Rückblick. Cologne, 1963.
English: in *The Furrow* 14 (1963): 267–88.
Spanish: *La Iglesia se renueva.* Buenos Aires, 1965.
American: in J. Ratzinger. *Theological Highlights of Vatican II.* New York, 1966.

Das Konzil auf dem Weg: Rückblick auf die zweite Sitzungsperiode. Cologne, 1964.
Italian: *Concilio in cammino—Sguardo retrospettivo sulla seconda sessione.* Rome, 1965.
Spanish: *La Iglesia se mira a si misma.* Buenos Aires, 1965.
American: in J. Ratzinger. *Theological Highlights of Vatican II.* New York, 1966.

Der gegenwärtige Stand der Arbeiten des Zweiten Vatikanischen Konzils. Lecture given on October 1, 1964. Bonn: Katholische Rundfunk- und Fernseharbeit in Deutschland, 1964.

Ergebnisse und Probleme der dritten Konzilsperiode. Cologne, 1965.
Spanish: *Resultados y perspectivas en la Iglesia conciliar.* Buenos Aires, 1965.
Italian: *Problemi e resultati del concilio Vaticano II.* Brescia, 1966.
American: in J. Ratzinger. *Theological Highlights of Vatican II.* New York, 1966.

(Together with Karl Rahner) *Offenbarung und Überlieferung.* QD 25. Freiburg, 1965.
Dutch: *Openbaring on overlevering.* Hilversum, 1965.
American/English: *Revelation and Tradition.* New York and London, 1965.
Italian: *Rivelazione e Tradizione.* Brescia, 1970.

Spanish: *Revelación y tradición*. Barcelona, 1970.
French: *Révélation et tradition*. Paris, 1972.
Also in **Portuguese** (1970).

Probleme der Vierten Konzilsperiode. Lecture given on October 28, 1965, in Rome. Bonn: Katholische Rundfunk- und Fernseharbeit in Deutschland, 1965.

Vom Sinn des Christseins: Drei Adventspredigten. Munich, 1965; 2nd ed., 1966; 3rd ed., 1971.
Italian: *Il senso dell'esistenza cristiana*. Catania, 1966; 2nd ed., 1974.
Spanish: in *Ser cristiano*. Salamanca, 1967; 2nd ed., 1972 (includes *Die sakramentale Begründung christlicher Existenz*, 1966, and *Meditationen zur Karwoche*, 1969).
American: *Being Christian*. Chicago, 1970.
French: *Un seul Seigneur, une seule foi*. Paris, 1971; Tours, 1973.

Die letzte Sitzungsperiode des Konzils. Cologne, 1966.
Italian: *Problemi e risultati del concilio Vaticano II*. Brescia, 1966.
Spanish: *La Iglesia en el mundo de hoy*. Buenos Aires, 1968.
American: in J. Ratzinger, *Theological Highlights of Vatican II*. New York, 1966.

Die sakramentale Begründung christlicher Existenz. Meitingen and Freising, 1966; 2nd ed., 1967; 3rd ed., 1970; 4th ed., 1973.
French: *Sacrements et existence chrétienne*, in *Prière et vie* 142 (1967): 277–85 and 341–50.
Spanish: in *Ser cristiano*. Salamanca, 1967; 2nd ed., 1972.
Italian: *Il fondamento sacramentale dell'esistenza cristiana*. Brescia, 1971.

Das Problem der Dogmengeschichte in der Sicht der katholischen Theologie. Arbeitsgemeinschaft für Forschung des Landes Nordrhein-Westfalen. Geisteswissenschaften, no. 139. Cologne and Opladen, 1966.
Italian: in *Testimonianze* 13, no. 126 (1970): 510–34.

Einführung in das Christentum: Vorlesungen über das Apostolische Glaubensbekenntnis. Munich, 1st–5th eds., 1968; 6th–9th eds., 1969; 10th and 11th eds., 1970; 12th ed., 1977; pocket edition: 1971; 2nd ed., 1972; 3rd ed., 1977; 4th ed., 1980; paperback edition: 1974; 2nd ed., 1976; 3rd ed., 1977; 4th ed., 1980; 5th ed., 1985; 6th ed., 1990; 7th ed., 1998; new edition, unamended but with a new introduction, Munich, 2000.

English: Introduction to Christianity. London, 1969; 2nd ed., 1985.

French: Foi chrétienne, hier et aujourd'hui. Paris and Tours, 1969; 2nd ed., 1985.

Dutch: De kern van ons geloof. Tielt and Utrecht, 1st–3rd eds., 1970.

Italian: Introduzione al cristianesimo. Brescia, 1969; 5th ed., 1974; 7th ed., 1984; 9th ed., 1990.

American: Introduction to Christianity. New York, 1970; 2nd ed., 1979; San Francisco, 1990; new edition, 2004.

Croatian: Uvod u kršćanstvo: Predavanja o apostolskom vjeroranju. Zagreb, 1970.

Polish: Wprowadzenie w chrześcijaństwo. Kraków, 1970; 2nd ed., 1994.

Portuguese: Introdução ao cristianismo. São Paulo, 1970.

Spanish: Introducción al cristianismo. Salamanca, 1969; 2nd ed., 1970; 3rd ed., 1976; 4th ed., 1979; 5th ed., 1982; 6th ed., 1987; 8th ed., 1996; 9th ed., 2001 (with a new foreword).

Japanese: Kirisutokyô Nyûmon. Tokyo, 1973.

Korean: Geuriseudo sinang. Seoul, 1974; 2nd ed., 1983.

Hungarian: A keresztény hit: Gondolatok az Apostoli Hitvallás nyomán. Vienna, 1976.

Also in *Slovenian* (1975), *Russian* (Brussels, 1988), *Czech* (Brno, 1991), *Lithuanian* (Vilnius, 1991), *Arabic* (Beirut, 1993), *Norwegian* (Oslo, 1993).

Meditationen zur Karwoche. Meitinger Kleinschriften. Meitingen and Freising, 1969; 2nd and 3rd eds., 1970; 4th ed., 1973; 5th ed., 1974; 6th ed., 1978; 7th ed., 1980.

Spanish: in Ser cristiano. Salamanca, 1967; 2nd ed., 1972. Partly reprinted (Holy Saturday) in Humanitas 12 (1997): 116–23.

Das neue Volk Gottes: Entwürfe zur Ekklesiologie. Düsseldorf, 1969; 2nd ed., 1970; pocket edition, 1972; 2nd ed., 1977.
French: *Le Nouveau Peuple de Dieu.* Paris, 1971 (partial translation).
Italian: *Il nuovo popolo di Dio.* Brescia, 1971; 2nd ed., 1972; 3rd ed., 1984.
Spanish: *El nuevo pueblo de Dios.* Barcelona, 1972.
Portuguese: *O novo povo de Deus.* São Paulo, 1974.
Also in *Polish* (Poznań, 1975).

Glaube und Zukunft. Munich, 1970; 2nd ed., 1971.
American: *Faith and Future.* Chicago, 1971.
French: *Foi et avenir.* Paris, 1971.
Dutch: *De toekomst van het geloof.* Tielt and Utrecht, 1971.
Italian: *Fede e futuro.* Meditazioni teologiche 49. Brescia, 1971; 2nd ed., 1984.
Spanish: *Fe y futuro.* Salamanca, 1973.
Polish: *Wiara i przyszłość.* Warsaw, 1975.
Also in *Japanese* (Tokyo, 1971) and *Portuguese* (1971).

(Together with H. Maier) *Demokratie in der Kirche: Möglichkeiten, Grenzen, Gefahren.* Limburg, 1970. New edition, with additional contributions from both authors: *Demokratie in der Kirche: Möglichkeiten und Grenzen.* Limburg and Kevelaer, 2000.
Italian: *Democrazia nella chiesa: Possibilità, limiti, pericoli.* Rome, 1971.
Spanish: *¿Democracia en la Iglesia?* Madrid, 1971.
French: *Démocratisation dans l'Église? Possibilités, limites, risques.* Paris, 1972; Sherbrooke (Canada), 1973.
Portuguese: *Democracia na Igreja: Possibilidades, limites, perigos.* São Paulo, 1976.

(Together with Cardinal J. Höffner) *Die Situation der Kirche heute: Hoffnungen und Gefahren.* Kölner Beiträge 1. Cologne, 1st–4th eds., 1970; 5th ed., 1971; 6th ed., 1973; 7th slightly amended edition, 1977, Rufe in die Zeit 4 (without any contribution from Cardinal J. Höffner).

(Together with H. U. von Balthasar) *Zwei Plädoyers: Warum ich noch Christ bin:Warum ich noch in der Kirche bin*. Munich, 1st and 2nd eds., 1971; an excerpt in *Die Furche*, 1975, no. 36, 10.

American: *Two Say Why: Why I Am Still a Christian:Why I Am Still in the Church*. Chicago and London, 1971.

Italian: *Perché sono ancora cristiano: Perché sono ancora nella Chiesa*. Brescia, 1971.

French: "Église du Christ, bien de ma foi". In G.-M. Garonne, J. Daniélou, J. Ratzinger, H. U. von Balthasar. *Je crois en l'Église, que je n'en sois jamais séparé*, pp. 79–109. Tours and Paris, 1972.

Spanish: *¿Por qué soy cristiano? ¿Por qué permanezco todavía en la Iglesia?* Salamanca, 1st and 2nd eds., 1974; 3rd ed., 1975.

Die Einheit der Nationen: Eine Vision der Kirchenväter. Salzburg and Munich, 1971.

Spanish: *La unidad de las naciones*. Aportaciones para una teología política. Madrid, 1972.

Italian: *L'unità delle nazioni: Una visione dei padri della Chiesa*. Brescia, 1973.

Also in *Portuguese* (São Paulo, 1975).

Teología y historia: Notas sobre el dinamismo histórico de la fe. Salamanca, 1971.

Italian: *Storia e dogma*. Milan, 1971.

Die Hoffnung des Senfkorns. Meitinger Kleinschriften 27. Meitingen and Freising, 1973; 2nd ed., 1974; 3rd ed., 1978.

Italian: *Speranza del grano di senape*. Brescia, 1974.

Spanish: in *El rostro de Dios*. Salamanca, 1983.

Also in *Hungarian* (1979).

Dogma und Verkündigung. Munich and Freiburg, 1973; 2nd ed., 1974; 3rd ed., 1977.

Italian: *Dogma e predicazione*. Brescia, 1974.

Spanish: *Palabra en la Iglesia*. Salamanca, 1976.

Portuguese: *Dogma e Anunciação*. São Paulo, 1977.

American: *Dogma and Preaching* (selective edition). Chicago, 1985.

(Together with U. Hommes) *Das Heil des Menschen: Innerwelt-lich—christlich.* Munich, 1975.

Italian: *La Salvezza dell'uomo.* Brescia, 1976.

Der Gott Jesu Christi: Betrachtungen über den Dreieinigen Gott. Munich, 1976; 2nd ed., 1977.

French: *Le Dieu de Jésus-Christ: Méditations sur Dieu-Trinité.* Paris, 1977.

American: *The God of Jesus Christ: Meditations on God in the Trinity.* Chicago, 1978.

Italian: *Il Dio di Gesù Cristo.* Brescia, 1978.

Spanish: *El Dios de Jesucristo: Meditaciones sobre el Dios uno y trino.* Salamanca, 1978; 2nd ed., 1980.

Polish: *Bóg Jezusa Chrystusa: medytacie o Bogu Trói.* Kraków, 1995.

(Together with Karl Lehmann) *Mit der Kirche Leben.* Freiburg, 1st–4th eds., 1977.

American: *Living with the Church.* Chicago, 1978.

French: *Vivre avec l'Église.* Paris, 1978.

Italian: *Vivere con la Chiesa.* Brescia, 1978.

Eschatologie—Tod und ewiges Leben. KKD, vol. 9. Regensburg, 1st and 2nd eds., 1977; 3rd–5th eds., 1978; amended version, Leipzig, 1981; 6th, enlarged ed., Regensburg, 1990.

French: *La mort et l'au-delà: Court traité d'espérance chrétienne.* Paris, 1979; 2nd ed., 1994.

Italian: *Escatologia—morte e vita eterna.* Assisi, 1979.

Spanish: *Escatología: La muerta y la vida eterna.* Barcelona, 1979; 2nd ed., 1984.

Polish: *Eschatologia—śmierć i życie wieczne.* Poznań, 1984; Warsaw, 2nd ed., 1986; 3rd ed., 2000.

American (enlarged edition): *Eschatology, Death and Eternal Life.* Chicago, 1988.

Lithuanian: *Eschatologija.* Vilnius, 1996.

Erlösung, mehr als eine Phrase? Steinfelder Kleinschriften 3. Steinfeld, 1977.

Die Tochter Zion: Betrachtungen über den Marienglauben der Kirche.
Einsiedeln, 1st and 2nd eds., 1977; 3rd ed., 1978; 4th ed.,
1990.
Italian: La figlia di Sion: La devozione a Maria nella Chiesa. Milan,
1979.
American: Daughter Zion. San Francisco, 1983.
Hungarian: in *Jézus és az Egyház Anyja,* pp. 24–62. Eisenstadt,
1987.
Polish: Córa Syjonu. Warsaw, 1997.
Also in *Korean* (1990).

Gottes Angesicht suchen: Betrachtungen im Kirchenjahr. Theologie
und Leben 46. Freising, 1978; 2nd ed., 1979.
American: Seeking God's Face (together with *The Lesson of the
Christmas Donkey,* by Pope John Paul I). Chicago, 1982.
Spanish: in *El rostro de Dios.* Salamanca, 1983.
Italian: in *Cerco il tuo volto Dio.* Milan, 1985.

Licht, das uns leuchtet: Besinnungen zu Advent und Weihnachten
(together with the meditation *Die Lektion des Weihnachtsesels*
[The lesson of the Christmas donkey], by Pope John Paul I).
Freiburg, 1st–4th eds., 1978; 5th and 6th eds., 1979; 7th ed.,
1982; new edition (without Pope John Paul I's meditation),
1999.
Spanish: in *El rostro de Dios.* Salamanca, 1983.
Italian: in *Cerco il tuo volto Dio.* Milan, 1985.

Eucharistie—Mitte der Kirche. Munich, 1978. Reprinted in *Gott ist
uns nah: Eucharistie: Mitte des Lebens.* Augsburg, 2001.

Mitarbeiter der Wahrheit: Gedanken für jeden Tag. Edited by Sr. Irene
Grassl. With pictures by R. Seewald. Munich, 1979; new,
revised, and enlarged 2nd ed., Würzburg, 1990; 3rd ed.,
1992.
*French: Vivre sa foi: Méditations pour chaque jour de l'année sur des
thèmes spirituels et théologiques.* Paris, 1979.
Polish: Służyć Prawdzie. Poznań, Warsaw, and Lublin, 1983;
Wrocław, 2001.

American: *Co-Workers of the Truth: Meditations for Every Day of the Year*. San Francisco, 1992.
Italian: *Collaboratori della verità*. Cinisello Balsamo, 1994.

A Mustármag remény. Eisenstadt, 1979. (A selection of various pieces.)

"Ich glaube": Strukturen des Christlichen. Edited by W. Kraning. Leipzig, 1979. (A selection from various works.)

Zum Begriff des Sakramentes. Eichstätter Hochschulreden 15. Munich, 1979.

(Together with H. U. von Balthasar) *Maria—Kirche im Ursprung*. Freiburg, 1980; 4th enlarged ed., Einsiedeln and Freiburg, 1997.
Russian: *Marija—praobraz Cerkvi*. Leningrad, 1980 (samizdat).
French: *Marie, première Église*. Paris, 1981; 2nd ed., 1987; enlarged 3rd ed., 1998.
Italian: *Maria, Chiesa nascente*. Rome, 1981; new enlarged ed., 1998.
Spanish: *María, primera Iglesia*. Madrid, 1982; new enlarged ed., 1999.
Polish: *Dlaczego właśnie Ona*. Warsaw, 1991.

Konsequenzen des Schöpfungsglaubens. Salzburger Universitätsreden, no. 28. Salzburg, 1980.

Glaube—Erneuerung—Hoffnung: Theologisches Nachdenken über die heutige Situation der Kirche. Edited by W. Kraning. Leipzig, 1981. (A selection from various works.)

Umkehr zur Mitte: Meditationen eines Theologen. Edited by G. Nachtwei. Leipzig, 1981.

Das Fest des Glaubens: Versuche zur Theologie des Gottesdienstes. Einsiedeln, 1981; 2nd ed., 1982.
Italian: *La festa della fede*. Milan, 1984.
French: *La Célébration de la foi: Essai sur la théologie du culte divin*. Paris, 1985.

American: *The Feast of Faith*. San Francisco, 1986.
Spanish: *La fiesta de la fe: Ensayo de Teología Litúrgica*. Bilbao, 1999.

Christlicher Glaube und Europa: 12 Predigten. Munich: Pressereferat der Erzdiözese München-Freising, 1981; 2nd ed., 1982; 3rd ed., 1985.

Theologische Prinzipienlehre: Bausteine zur Fundamentaltheologie. Munich, 1982; 2nd ed., 1983.
French: *Les Principes de la théologie catholique: Esquisse et matériaux*. Paris, 1985.
Spanish: *Teoría de los principios teológicos*. Barcelona, 1985.
Italian (partial translation): *Elementi di teologia fondamentale: Saggi sulla fede e sul ministero*. Brescia, 1986.
American: *Principles of Catholic Theology*. San Francisco, 1987.

Zeitfragen und christlicher Glaube: Acht Predigten aus den Münchner Jahren. Würzburg, 1982; 2nd ed., 1983.

(Together with H. Schlier) ***Lob der Weihnacht***. Freiburg, 1982.

Die Krise der Katechese und ihre Überwindung: Rede in Frankreich. (With talks by D. J. Ryan, G. Danneels, F. Macharski.) Einsiedeln, 1983.
French: *Transmettre la foi aujourd'hui: Conférences données à Notre-Dame de Paris*. Paris, 1983.

Demokratie, Pluralismus, Christentum. Deutsche Sendungen im Radio Vatikan. Leutesdorf, 1984. (Opening address at the International Congress of the Hanns-Martin-Schleyer Foundation and the Papal Council for Culture, given on April 24, 1984, in Munich.)

Schauen auf den Durchbohrten: Versuche zu einer spirituellen Christologie. Einsiedeln, 1984; 2nd ed., 1990.
American: *Behold the Pierced One: An Approach to a Spiritual Christology*. San Francisco, 1986.
Also in *Czech* (Brno, 1996).

Suchen, was droben ist: Meditationen das Jahr hindurch. Freiburg, 1985.

American: *Seek That Which Is Above*. San Francisco, 1986.
Italian: *Cercate le cosi di lassù*. Milan, 1986.

Il cammino pasquale: Corso di Esercizi Spirituali tenuti in Vaticano alla presenza di S.S. Giovanni Paolo II. Milan, 1985; 2nd ed., 1986; 3rd (new) edition, 2000.
Portuguese: *O Caminho Pascal*. São Pauolo, 1986.
French: *Le Ressuscité*. Paris, 1st and 2nd eds., 1986.
American: *Journey towards Easter*. New York, 1987; 2nd ed., 1996.
English: *Journey towards Easter*. Middlegreen, 1987.
Spanish: *El camino pascual*. Madrid, 1990.
Polish: *Droga Paschalna*. Kraków, 2001.

Rapporto sulla fede: Vittorio Messori a colloquio con Joseph Ratzinger. Turin, 1st and 2nd eds., 1985.
American: *The Ratzinger Report*. San Francisco, 1985; 2nd ed., 1986.
German: *Zur Lage des Glaubens*. Munich, 1985.
French: *Entretien sur la foi*. Paris, 1985.
Portuguese: *A fé em crise?* São Paulo, 1985.
Spanish: *Informe sobre la fe*. Madrid, 1st–10th eds., 1985; 11th ed., 1986.
Hungarian: *Beszélgetés a Hitröl*. Budapest, 1985, 1990.
Polish: *Raport o stanie*. Kraków and Warsaw, 1986.
Also in **Korean** (Seoul, 1993; new eds., 1994 and 1995); and in **Croatian** (1998).

Im Anfang schuf Gott: Vier Predigten über Schöpfung und Fall. Munich, 1986; 2nd enlarged ed., Einsiedeln and Freiburg, 1996.
French: *Au commencement, Dieu créa le ciel et la terre*. Paris, 1986.
Italian: *Creazione e peccato*. Milan, 1986.
American: *"In the beginning . . .": A Catholic Understanding of the Story of Creation and the Fall*. Huntington, Ind., 1990; new ed., 1995.
Spanish: *Creación y pecado*. Pamplona, 1992; *En el principio creó Dios: Consecuencias de la Fe en la Creación*. Valencia, 2001.

Politik und Erlösung: Zum Verhältnis von Glaube, Rationalität und Irrationalem in der sogenannten Theologie der Befreiung. Rheinisch-Westfälische Akademie der Wissenschaften Vorträge, G 279. Opladen, 1986.
Spanish: in *Tierra nueva* 16 (1987): 38–51.

Iglesia Comunicadora de Vida: Conferencias y Homilías pronunciadas en su visita al Perú. Lima, 1986.

Kirche, Ökumene und Politik: Neue Versuche zur Ekklesiologie. Einsiedeln, 1987.
French: *Église, oecuménisme et politique.* Paris, 1987.
Italian: *Chiesa, ecumenismo e politica: Nuovi saggi di ecclesiologia.* Milan, 1987.
Spanish: *Iglesia, ecumenismo y politica: Nuevos ensayos de eclesiología.* Madrid, 1987.
English: *Church, Ecumenism and Politics: New Essays in Ecclesiology.* Middlegreen, 1988.

Abbruch und Aufbruch: Die Antwort des Glaubens auf die Krise der Werte. Eichstätter Hochschulreden 61. Munich, 1988.
Italian: in *Avvenire,* March 1988; in booklet form ("Il tramonto dell'uomo"), Padua, 1988.
Spanish: in *ABC,* March 31, 1988, pp. 27–29; April 1–2, 1988, pp. 25–27.

Diener eurer Freude: Meditationen über die priesterliche Spiritualität. Freiburg, 1988.
English: *Ministers of Your Joy.* Slough, 1989.
American: *Ministers of Your Joy.* Ann Arbor, 1989.
Italian: *Servitore della vostra gioia.* Milan, 1989.
French: *Serviteurs de votre joie: Méditations sur la spiritualité sacerdotale.* Paris, 1990.
Also in *Polish* (1990) and *Spanish* (1989).

Auf Christus schauen: Einübung in Glaube, Hoffnung, Liebe. Freiburg, 1989; 2nd ed., 1990.
Italian: *Guardare Cristo: Esercizi di Fede, Speranza e Carità.* Milan, 1989.

Slovenian: *Zazrti v Kristusa*. Ljubljana, 1990.

Spanish: *Mirar a Cristo: Ejercicios de fe, esperanza y amor*. Valencia, 1990.

Polish: *Patrzč na Chrystusa*. Warsaw, 1991.

American: *To Look on Christ: Exercises in Faith, Hope, and Love*. New York, 1991.

French: *Regarder le Christ: Exercices de foi, d'espérance et d'amour*. Paris, 1992.

Zur Gemeinschaft gerufen: Kirche heute verstehen. Freiburg, 1991.

Italian (enlarged version): *La Chiesa: Una comunità sempre in cammino*. Milan, 1991.

Portuguese: *Questões sobre a Igreja*. Lisbon, 1991. *Compreender a Igreja hoje*. Petropolis, 1992.

Spanish: *La Iglesia: Una comunidad siempre en camino*. Madrid, 1992.

French: *Appelés à la communion: Comprendre l'Église aujourd'hui*. Paris, 1993.

Polish: *Kościół wspólnotą*. Lublin, 1993.

Slovenian: *Poklicani v občestvo: Današnji prgled na Cerkev*. Ljubljana, 1993.

American: *Called to Communion*. San Francisco, 1991; 2nd ed., 1996.

Swedish: *Kallad till gemenskap*. Malmö, 1997.

Also in *Czech* (Prague, 1995).

Conscience and Truth. New Haven, Conn., 1991.

Spanish: in *Boletín oficial del Arzobispo di Toledo*, 1991, pp. 528–49.

English: with discussion, in *Catholic Conscience Foundation and Formation*, pp. 7–27; dialogue, pp. 29–35 and 279–89. New Haven, Conn.: Pope John Center, 1992.

Wendezeit für Europa? Diagnosen und Prognosen zur Lage von Kirche und Welt. Einsiedeln and Freiburg, 1991; 2nd ed., 1992.

Italian: *Svolta per l'Europa? Chiesa e modernità nell'Europa die rivolgimenti*. Milan, 1992.

Spanish: *Une mirada a Europa*. Madrid, 1993. *Iglesia y Modernidad*. Buenos Aires, 1992.

American: *A Turning Point for Europe?* San Francisco, 1994.
French: *Un tournant pour l'Europe?* Paris, 1996.
Polish: *Czas przemian w Europie.* Kraków, 2001.

Église et théologie. Paris, 1992.

Wesen und Aufgabe der Theologie. Einsiedeln and Freiburg, 1993.
Italian: *Natura e compito della Teologia: Il Teologo nella disputa contemporanea: Storia e dogma.* Milan, 1993. (Constituting also a new ed. of *Storia e dogma,* 1971.)
American: *The Nature and Mission of Theology.* San Francisco, 1995.

Wahrheit, Werte, Macht: Prüfsteine der pluralistischen Gesellschaft. Freiburg, 1993; 2nd ed., 1994; 3rd ed., 1995; new ed., Frankfurt, 1999.
Spanish: *Verdad, valores, poder: Piedras de toque de la sociedad pluralista.* Madrid, 1995; 2nd ed., 1998; 3rd ed., 2000.
Italian: *Cielo e terra: Riflessioni su politica e fede.* Casale Monferrato, 1997.
Polish: *Prawda, wartości władza.* Kraków, 1999.
Also in *Czech* (1996).

Evangelium—Katechese—Katechismus: Streiflichter auf den Katechismus der katholischen Kirche. Munich, 1995.

Ein neues Lied für den Herrn: Christusglaube und Liturgie in der Gegenwart. Freiburg, 1995.
French: *Un Chant nouveau pour le Seigneur: La Foi dans le Christ et la liturgie aujourd'hui.* Paris, 1995.
Italian: *Cantate al Signore un canto nuovo.* Milan, 1996.
American: *A New Song for the Lord: Faith in Christ and Liturgy Today.* New York, 1997.
Polish: *Nowa pieśń dla pana: Wiara w Chrystusa a liturgia dzisiaj.* Kraków, 1999.
Spanish: *Un canto nuevo para el Señor: La fe en Jesucristo y la liturgia hoy.* Salamanca, 1999.

Ser cristiano en era neopagana. Madrid, 1995.

Salz der Erde: Christentum und katholische Kirche an der Jahrtausendwende: Ein Gespräch mit Peter Seewald. Stuttgart, 1st–5th eds., 1996; 6th–9th eds., 1997; 10th ed., 1998; pocket ed., Munich, 1998.

Spanish: *La Sal de la Tierra: Cristianismo y Iglesia católica ante el nuevo milenio: Una conversación con Peter Seewald.* Madrid, 1997.

Dutch: *Zout der aarde: Christendom en katholieke kerk aan het einde van het millennium: Een gesprek mit Peter Seewald.* Barn, 1997.

Portuguese: *O Sal da terra: O Cristianismo e a Igreja Católica no Liminar do Terceiro Milénio: Uma Entrevista com Peter Seewald.* Lisbon, 1997.

Polish: *Sól ziemi: Chrześcijaństwo i kościoł katolicki na przełomie tysiącleci.* Kraków, 1997.

Slovakian: *Sol Zeme: Krestanstvo a katolicka cirkev na prelone tisícrocí: Rozhovor a Petrom Seewaldom.* Trnava, 1997.

American: *Salt of the Earth: Christianity and the Catholic Church at the End of the Millennium: An Interview with Peter Seewald.* San Francisco, 1997.

Slovenian: *Sol zemlje: Krščanstvo in katoliška Cerkev ob premolu tisočletja: Pogovor s Petrom Seewaldom.* Ljubljana, 1998.

Norwegian: *Jordens Salt: Kristendom og Den Katolske Kirke ved Årtusenskiftet.* Oslo, 1998.

Also in **Croatian, Hungarian, French, Italian, Czech** (all in 1997), **Chinese** (1998), and **Korean** (Seoul, 2000).

La via della fede: Le ragioni dell'etica nell'epoca presente. Milan, 1996.

Spanish: *La fe como camino: Contribución al ethos cristiano en el momento actual.* Barcelona, 1997.

Bilder der Hoffnung: Wanderungen im Kirchenjahr. Freiburg, 1st–3rd eds., 1997.

Hungarian: *A Remény Forrásai.* Budapest, 1997.

Croatian: *Slike nade.* Zagreb, 1998.

Spanish: *Imágenes de la esperanza.* Madrid, 1998.

Polish: *Obrazy Nadziei.* Poznań, 1998.

Italian: *Immagini di speranza.* Milan, 1999.

Heiligenpredigten. Edited by S. Horn. Munich, 1997.
 Spanish: *De la mano de Cristo: Homilías sobre la Virgen e algunos Santos.* Pamplona, 1998.

Cielo e terra: Riflessioni su politica e fede. Casale Monferrato, 1997.

La mia vita: Ricordi (1927–1977). Milan, 1997.
 Spanish: *Mi vida: Recuerdos (1927–1977).* Madrid, 1997.
 German: *Aus meinem Leben: Erinnerungen (1927–1977).* Stuttgart, 1st–3rd eds., 1998; pocket ed., Munich, 2000.
 French: *Ma vie: Souvenirs (1927–1977).* Paris, 1998.
 American: *Milestones: Memoirs (1927–1977).* San Francisco, 1998.
 Also in *Polish* (1998) and *Czech* (Brno, 1999).

Die Vielfalt der Religionen und der eine Bund. Hagen, 1st and 2nd eds., 1998.
 French: *"L'Unique Alliance" de Dieu et le pluralisme des religions.* Saint-Maur, 1999.
 American: *Many Religions—One Covenant: Israel, the Church, and the World.* San Francisco, 1999.
 Italian: *La Chiesa, Israele e le religioni del mondo.* Cinisello Balsamo, 2000.

Vom Wiederauffinden der Mitte: Grundorientierungen: Texte aus vier Jahrzehnten. Published by the association of former students. Edited by S. O. Horn, V. Pfnür, V. Twomey, S. Wiedenhofer, J. Zöhrer. Freiburg, Basel, and Vienna, 1997; 2nd ed., 1998.

La fede e la teologia ai giorni nostri: Guardare Cristo: Coscienza e verità. Milan, 1997.

Weihnachtspredigten. Munich, 1998.
 Polish: *Wczas Bożego Narodzenia.* Kraków, 2001.

Il Sabbato della Storia. (With illustrations by W. Congdon.) Milan, 1998.
 Spanish: *El sábado de la historia.* Madrid, 1998.
 American: *The Sabbath of History.* Washington, D.C., 2000.

(In collaboration with others) *Giovanni Paolo II: Vent'anni nella storia.* Cinisello Balsamo, 1998.

Polish (together with F. Macharski): *20 lat w historii Kościoła i świata*. Częstochowa, 1999.

French: *Jean Paul II: Vingt ans dans l'histoire*. Paris, 1999.

Spanish: *Juan Pablo II: Un Papa entre dos milenios*. Buenos Aires, 2000.

Portuguese: *João Paulo II: Vinte anos na história*. Lisbon, 2001.

Der Geist der Liturgie: Eine Einführung. Freiburg, Basel, and Vienna, 1st–5th eds., 2000; 6th ed., 2002.

American: *The Spirit of the Liturgy*. San Francisco, 2000.

Italian: *Introduzione allo spirito della liturgia*. Cinisello Balsamo, 1st–3rd eds., 2001.

Croatian: *Duh Liturgije: Temeljna promišljanja*. Mostar and Zagreb, 2001.

Portuguese: *Introdução ao espírito da liturgia*. Lisbon, 2001.

Spanish: *El espíritu de la Liturgia: Una introducción*. Madrid, 2001.

French: *L'esprit de la liturgie*. Geneva, 2001.

(Together with H. Maier) *Demokratie in der Kirche: Möglichkeiten und Grenzen*. Limburg and Kevelaer, 2000. A new edition, with further contributions from both authors, of *Demokratie in der Kirche: Möglichkeiten, Grenzen, Gefahren*. Limburg, 1970.

Berührt vom Unsichtbaren: Jahreslesebuch. Freiburg, Basel, and Vienna, 2000.

Gott und die Welt: Glauben und Leben in unserer Zeit: Ein Gespräch mit Peter Seewald. Stuttgart, 1st and 2nd eds., 2000; 3rd ed., 2001.

Italian: *Dio e il mondo: In colloquio con Peter Seewald*. Cinisello Balsamo, 2001.

French: *Voici quel est notre Dieu: Croire et vivre aujourd'hui: Conversations avec Peter Seewald*. Paris, 2001.

Polish: *Bóg i świat kardynałem Josephem Ratzingerem rozmawia Peter Seewald*. Kraków, 2001.

American: *God and the World: Conversations with Peter Seewald*. San Francisco, 2002.

Gott ist uns nah: Eucharistie: Mitte des Lebens. Edited by S. O. Horn and V. Pfnür. Augsburg, 2001.

American: *God Is Near Us*. San Francisco, 2003.

II.

J. RATZINGER AS EDITOR OR CO-EDITOR

Studium Generale: Zeitschrift für die Einheit der Wissenschaften. Edited together with many other scholars. From no. 14 (1961) until its closure in 1971.

Einsicht und Glaube: Festschrift für Gottlieb Söhngen zum 70. Geburtstag. Edited together with H. Fries. Freiburg, 1962; 2nd ed., 1963.

Münsterische Beiträge zur Theologie. Edited together with B. Kötting. From no. 28 (1965).

Theologische Quartalschrift. Edited together with other scholars. Nos. 146 (1966) to 149 (1969).

Theologie im Wandel: Festschrift zum 150jährigen Bestehen der katholisch-theologischen Fakultät an der Universität Tübingen: 1817–1967. Edited together with J. Neumann. Munich and Freiburg, 1967.

Ökumenische Forschungen. Edited together with H. Küng. Freiburg, 1967–1970.

Zweites Vatikanisches Konzil: Dogmatische Konstitution über die Kirche. Latin-German. Münster, 1st–5th eds., 1965; 6th revised ed., 1965; 7th ed., 1966; 8th ed., improved and with index, 1966.

Lexikon für Theologie und Kirche: Das Zweite Vatikanische Konzil: Konstitutionen, Dekrete und Erklärungen. Latin-German and commentaries. Supplementary vols. 1, 2, 3. Edited together with H. S. Brechter, B. Häring, J. Höfer, et al. 2nd completely revised ed., Freiburg, 1966–1968.

Kleine Katholische Dogmatik. Edited together with J. Auer. 9 vols. Regensburg, 1970ff.

Internationale katholische Zeitschrift Communio. Edited together with other scholars. Nos. 1 (1972) to 11 (1982).

Die Frage nach Gott. QD 56. Freiburg, 1972.
Spanish: *Dios como problema.* Madrid, 1973.
Italian: *Saggi sul problema di Dio.* Brescia, 1975.

Aktualität der Scholastik? Regensburg, 1975.

Prinzipien christlicher Moral. Kriterien 37. Edited together with H. Schürmann and H. U. von Balthasar. Einsiedeln, 1st and 2nd eds., 1975; 3rd ed., 1981.
French: *Principes d'éthique chrétienne.* Paris, 1979.
American: *Principles of Christian Morality.* San Francisco, 1986.
Polish: *Podstawy moralności chrześcijańskiej.* Poznań, 1999.

Mysterium der Gnade: Festschrift für Johann Auer zum 65. Geburtstag. Edited together with H. Rossmann. Regensburg, 1975.

Salvezza cristiana tra storia e aldilà. Edited together with L. Sartori. Rome, 1976.

Dienst an der Einheit: Zum Wesen und Auftrag des Petrusamtes. Düsseldorf, 1978.

Wege zur Wahrheit: Die bleibende Bedeutung von Romano Guardini. Düsseldorf, 1985.

Schriftauslegung im Widerstreit. QD 117. Freiburg, 1989.

III.
PIECES IN COLLECTIVE WORKS AND PERIODICALS

— 1954 —

"Herkunft und Sinn der Civitas-Lehre Augustins". In *Augustinus Magister* 2:965–79. Paris, 1954. And in *Geschichtsdenken und Geschichtsbild im Mittelalter*, edited by W. Lammers, pp. 55–75. Darmstadt, 1961.

— 1956 —

"Beobachtungen zum Kirchenbegriff des Tyconius im 'Liber regularum'". *REAug* 2 (1956): 173–85. Reprinted in *Das neue Volk Gottes* (see under section I).

"Die Kirche als Geheimnis des Glaubens". *LebZeug* 4 (1956/57): 19–34. Reprinted in *Das neue Volk Gottes* (see under section I).

— 1957 —

"Der Einfluß des Bettelordenstreites auf die Entwicklung der Lehre vom päpstlichen Universalprimat". In *Theologie in Geschichte und Gegenwart: Festgabe für Michael Schmaus zum 60. Geburtstag*. Edited by J. Auer, pp. 697–724. Munich, 1957. Reprinted in *Das neue Volk Gottes* (see under section I).

"Originalität und Überlieferung in Augustins Begriff der confessio". in *REAug* 3 (1957): 375–92.

— 1958 —

"Offenbarung—Schrift—Überlieferung: Ein Text des hl. Bonaventura und seine Bedeutung für die gegenwärtige Theologie". *TThZ* 67 (1958): 13–27.

"Gedanken zur Krise der Verkündigung". *KlBl* 38 (1958): 211f. and 235ff.

"Vom Sinn des Advents". *KlBl* 38 (1958): 418–20. Reprinted in *Dogma und Verkündigung* (see under section I).

"Die neuen Heiden und die Kirche". *Hochl* 51 (1958/59): 1–11. Reprinted in *Das neue Volk Gottes* (see under section I).

— 1959 —

"Das Geheimnis der Osternacht". *KlBl* 39 (1959): 101–2. Reprinted in *Dogma und Verkündigung* (see under section I).

"Tod und Auferstehung: Erwägungen zum christlichen Verständnis des Todes". *KlBl* 39 (1959): 366–70. Enlarged in *Dogma und Verkündigung* (see under section I).

"Auferstehung und ewiges Leben". *Tod und Leben: Von den letzten Dingen.* LuM 25. 1959. Pp. 92–103. Reprinted in *Dogma und Verkündigung* (see under section I).

"Emélkedések Nagypéntektöl Mennybemenetelig" (from *Dogma und Verkündigung*). In *Munkátalok, Magyar Egyházirodalmi Iskolája*, pp. 37–50. Készült, 1959.

"Primat, Episkopat und successio apostolica". *Cath* 13 (1959): 260–77; also in *ThJb(L)* 1962, pp. 118–33.

"Das unbesiegte Licht: Eine Ansprache". *Hochl* 52 (1959/60): 97–100. Reprinted in *Dogma und Verkündigung* (see under section I).

"Paulinisches Christentum? Zu G. Schneider: Kernprobleme des Christentums". *Hochl* 52 (1959/60): 367–75.

— 1960 —

"Zum Problem der Entmythologisierung des Neuen Testamentes". *Rhs* 3 (1960): 2–11.

"Theologia perennis? Über Zeitgemäßheit und Zeitlosigkeit in der Theologie". *WuW* 15 (1960): 179–88.
English: (extract) in *ThD* 10 (1962): 71–76.

"Der Mensch und die Zeit im Denken des hl. Bonaventura". In *L'Homme et son destin d'après les penseurs du moyen âge*, pp. 473–83. Louvain and Paris, 1960.

"Grundgedanken der eucharistischen Erneuerung des 20. Jahrhunderts". *KlBl* 40 (1960): 208–11.

"Licht und Erleuchtung: Erwägungen zu Stellung und Entwicklung des Themas in der abendländischen Geistesgeschichte". *StGen* 13 (1960): 368–78.

"Wesen und Weisen der auctoritas im Werk des hl. Bonaventura". In *Die Kirche und ihre Ämter und Stände: Festgabe für Kardinal Frings*, edited by W. Corsten, A. Frotz, and P. Linden, pp. 58–72. Cologne, 1960.

— 1961 —

" 'Wiedervereinigung im Glauben' in katholischer Sicht". *KlBl* 41 (1961): 25–28.

"Christozentrik in der Verkündigung". *TThZ* 70 (1961): 1–14; also in *KatBl* 86 (1961): 299–310; and in *ThJb(L)* 1962, pp. 437–49. Considerably altered in *Dogma und Verkündigung* (see under section I).

"Bewußtsein und Wissen Christi: Zu E. Gutwengers gleichnamigem Buch". *MThZ* 12 (1961): 78–81.

"Der Tod und das Ende der Zeiten". In *Die Kirche und die Mächte der Welt: Seelsorge für morgen*, edited by K. Rudolf, pp. 97–107. Vienna, 1961. Partially reprinted as "Der Tod im Leben des Christmenschen". *Christophorus* 6/7 (1962): 25–28.

"Der Eucharistische Weltkongreß im Spiegel der Kritik". In *Statio orbis*, vol. 1, edited by R. Egenter, O. Pirner, and H. Hofbauer, pp. 227–42. Munich, 1961.

"Die Kirche in der Frömmigkeit des hl. Augustinus". In *Sentire ecclesiam: Das Bewußtsein von der Kirche als gestaltende Kraft der Frömmigkeit: Festschrift für P. Hugo Rahner*, edited by J. Daniélou and H. Vorgrimler, pp. 152–75. Freiburg, 1961. Reprinted in *Das neue Volk Gottes* (see under section I).

"Menschheit und Staatenbau in der Sicht der frühen Kirche".
StGen 14 (1961): 664–82. Included in *Die Einheit der Nationen*
(see under section I).

"Eine Theologie über Fatima: Zu Virgil Marions gleichnamigen
Buch". *MThZ* 12 (1961): 305–7.

"Christlicher Universalismus: Zum Aufsatzwerk H. U. von
Balthasars". *Hochl* 54 (1961/62): 68–76.

"Zur Theologie des Konzils". *Militärseelsorge* 4 (1961/62): 8–23;
also, with slight alterations, in *Cath* 15 (1961): 292–304. And
in *Vaticanum secundum*, vol. 1, *Die erste Konzilsperiode*, edited
by O. Müller, pp. 29–39. Leipzig, 1963. Extensively reworked
in *Das neue Volk Gottes* (see under section I).

— 1962 —

"Kritik an der Kirche? Dogmatische Bemerkungen: Kirche der
Heiligen—Kirche der Sünder". *Test. Zeugnisse studentischer
Sozialarbeit* 3 (1962): 22–25.

"Mariä Heimsuchung: Eine Homilie". *BiLe* 3 (1962): 138–40.
Reprinted in *Dogma und Verkündigung* (see under section I).

"Gratia praesupponit naturam: Erwägungen über Sinn und
Grenze eines scholastischen Axioms". In *Einsicht und
Glaube: Festschrift für Gottlieb Söhngen zum 70. Geburtstag*, ed-
ited by J. Ratzinger and H. Fries, pp. 135–49. Freiburg, 1962.
Reprinted in *Dogma und Verkündigung* (see under section I).

"Freimut und Gehorsam: Das Verhältnis des Christen zu seiner
Kirche". *WuW* 17 (1962): 409–21. In *English* in *The Church
Readings in Theology*, pp. 194–217. New York, 1963. An ex-
tract in *ThD* 13 (1965): 101–6. Reprinted in *Das neue Volk
Gottes* (see under section I).

"Der Stammbaum Jesu: Eine Homilie". *BiLe* 3 (1962): 275–78.
Reprinted in *Dogma und Verkündigung* (see under section I).

"Vom Ursprung und Wesen der Kirche". *Humanitas christiana:
Werkblatt für das Erzbischöfliche Abendgymnasium Collegium*

Marianum Neuss 6 (1962): 2–11. Essentially identical to "Die Kirche als Geheimnis des Glaubens". *LebZeug* 4 (1956/57): 19–34.

"Vom Geist der Brüderlichkeit". *Horizonte* 1 (1962): 1–2. Reprinted in *Dogma und Verkündigung* (see under section I).

— 1963 —

"Die Vision der Väter von der Einheit der Völker". *KathGed* 19 (1963): 1–9. Included in *Die Einheit der Nationen* (see under section I).

"Erwägungen zur dogmatischen und aszetischen Bedeutung der christlichen Brüderlichkeit". *Korrespondenzblatt des Collegium Canisianum* 97 (1963): 2–14; enlarged as "Bruderschaft und Brüderlichkeit". *Pastoralkatechetische*, no. 22 (1964): 9–35.

"Wesen und Grenzen der Kirche". In *Das Zweite Vatikanische Konzil*, edited by K. Forster, pp. 47–68. Studien und Berichte der Katholischen Akademie in Bayern, no. 24. Würzburg, 1963. Reprinted in *Das neue Volk Gottes* (see under section I).

"Der Wortgebrauch von Natura und die beginnende Verselbständigung der Metaphysik bei Bonaventura". In *MM II: Die Metaphysik im Mittelalter*, pp. 483–98. Berlin, 1963.

"Eine deutsche Ausgabe der Franziskuslegende Bonaventuras". *WiWei* 26 (1963): 87–93.

"Sentire ecclesiam". *GuL* 36 (1963): 321–26.

"Das geistliche Amt und die Einheit der Kirche". *Cath* 17 (1963): 165–179. Reprinted in *Die Autorität der Freiheit*, vols. 1 and 2, edited by J. C. Hampe, pp. 417–33. Munich, 1967. Also in *ThJb(L)* 1969, pp. 405–18; and in *Das neue Volk Gottes* (see under section I).
English: in *JES* 1 (1964): 42–57.

"Theologische Fragen auf dem II. Vatikanischen Konzil". In *Protokoll der Dechanten-Konferenz vom 4.–6. Juni 1963* (Münster), pp. 10–15.

— 1964 —

"Atheismus". *Rhs* 7 (1964): 1–6. Also in *Wahrheit und Zeugnis*, edited by M. Schmaus and A. Läpple, pp. 94–100. Düsseldorf, 1964.

"Glückwünsche für Karl Rahner". *Der christliche Sonntag* 16 (1964): 75f.

"Der christliche Glaube und die Weltreligionen". In *Gott in Welt: Festgabe für Karl Rahner*, edited by J. B. Metz, W. Kern, A. Darlapp, and H. Vorgrimler, pp. 287–305. Freiburg, 1964. Reprinted in *Vom Wiederauffinden der Mitte* (see page 299).

"Zeichen unter den Völkern". In *Wahrheit und Zeugnis*, edited by M. Schmaus and A. Läpple, pp. 456–66. Düsseldorf, 1964.

"Die Kirche und die Kirchen". *Reformatio* 13 (1964): 85–108.

"Papst, Patriarch, Bischof". In *Ende der Gegenreformation? Das Konzil: Dokumente und Deutung*, edited by J. C. Hampe, pp. 155–63. Stuttgart, Berlin, and Mainz, 1964.

"Zurück zur Ordnung der alten Kirche", ibid., pp. 183f.

"Zur Katechismuslehre von Schrift und Tradition". *ThRv* 60 (1964): 217–24.

"Zur Konzilsdiskussion über das Verhältnis von Schrift und Überlieferung". In *Das Zweite Vaticanum: Dritte Konzilsphase*, edited by F. Buschmann, pp. 147–55. Gießen, 1964.

"Naturrecht, Evangelium und Ideologie in der katholischen Soziallehre". In *Christlicher Glaube und Ideologie*, edited by K. von Bismarck and W. Dirks, pp. 24–30. Stuttgart and Mainz, 1964.

— 1965 —

"Die pastoralen Implikationen der Lehre von der Kollegialität der Bischöfe". *Conc(D)* 1 (1965): 16–29 (simultaneously in *English, French, Italian, Spanish,* and *Portuguese*). Reprinted in *Das neue Volk Gottes* (see under section I).

"Nachfolge Christi". *KlBl* 45 (1965): 140f., and in *Die Funk-postille, ein Querschnitt durch das Wortprogramm des Saarländischen Rundfunks,* 1964/65, pp. 99–104. Reprinted in *Dogma und Verkündigung* (see under section I).

"Das Problem der Mariologie: Überlegungen zu einigen Neuer-scheinungen". *ThRv* 61 (1965): 73–82.

"Angesichts der Welt von heute: Überlegungen zur Konfron-tation mit der Kirche im Schema XIII". *WuW* 20 (1965): 493–504. An extended version under a different title in *Welt-verständnis im Glauben,* edited by J. B. Metz, pp. 143–60. Mainz, 1965. Another new version in *Dogma und Verkün-digung* (see under section I).

"Das Geschick Jesu und die Kirche" (based on the outline of a lecture, prepared for publication by W. D. Theurer). In *Kirche heute,* edited by V. Schnurr and B. Häring, pp. 7–18. *Theo-logische Brennpunkte 2.* Bergen-Enkheim, 1965; 2nd ed., 1985.

"Over het Kerkbegrip der Vaders". In *Veranderd Kerkbewustzijn,* pp. 18–30. Doc dossiers 4. Hilversum, 1965.
Italian: in *La fine della chiesa come società perfetta,* pp. 47–64. Milan, 1969.
French: in *Pour une nouvelle image de l'Église,* pp. 31–48. Rome and Geneva, 1970.

"Salus extra Ecclesiam nulla est". In ibid., pp. 42–50; extensively reworked in *Das neue Volk Gottes* (see under section I).
Portuguese: in *O Mistério da Igreja: Temas Conciliares,* 1:57–67. Lisbon, 1965.
Italian: in *La fine della chiesa come società perfetta,* pp. 65–77. Milan, 1969.
French: in *Pour une nouvelle image de l'Église,* pp. 51–61. Rome and Geneva, 1970.

"Die sakramentale Begründung christlicher Existenz". *"Blätter":* Zeitschrift für Studierende (Vienna) 20 (1965/66): 22–27 (see also under section I).

— 1966 —

"Zum Personverständnis in der Dogmatik". In *Das Person-verständnis in der Pädagogik und ihren Nachbarwissenschaften,* edited by J. Speck, pp. 157–71. Münster, 1966. Slightly re-worked in *Dogma und Verkündigung* (see under section I). *American:* in *Communio* 17 (Fall 1990): 439–54.

"Die bischöfliche Kollegialität: Theologische Entfaltung". In *De Ecclesia,* edited by G. Baraúna, 2:44–70. Freiburg and Frankfurt, 1966. Reprinted in *Das neue Volk Gottes* (see under section I).

"Kommentar zu den 'Bekanntmachungen' " (= "Nota praevia explicativa, *Konstitution über die Kirche"*). *LThK. E I* (1966): 348–59.

Vorwort: P. Hacker, *Das Ich im Glauben bei Martin Luther,* pp. 7–9. Graz, 1966.

"Ecclesiologische aantekeningen betreffende het schema 'over de bisschoppen' ". In *Primaat, Collegialiteit, Bisschoppencon-ferenties,* pp. 152–65. Doc dossiers 6. Hilversum, 1966. *Portuguese:* in *Novas Estruturas na Igreja: Temas Conciliares,* 4:183–202. Lisbon, 1966.

"Weltoffene Kirche?" In *Umkehr und Erneuerung: Kirche nach dem Konzil,* edited by T. Filthaut, pp. 273–91. Mainz, 1966. Re-printed in *Das neue Volk Gottes* (see under section I).

"Was heißt Erneuerung der Kirche?" *Diakonia* 1 (1966): 303–16. Reprinted in *Das neue Volk Gottes* (see under section I).

"Der Katholizismus nach dem Konzil—Katholische Sicht". In *Auf Dein Wort hin: 81. Deutscher Katholikentag,* pp. 245–66. Paderborn, 1966. Reprinted in many German periodicals; enlarged version in *Das neue Volk Gottes* (see under section I). *French:* in *La Documentation catholique* 63 (1966): 1557–76. *English:* in *The Furrow* 18 (1967): 3–23. *Italian:* (extract) in *StCatt* 69 (1966): 44–47.

— 1967 —

"Kardinal Frings: Zu seinem 80. Geburtstag". *Christ in der Gegenwart* 19 (1967): 52.

"Christi Himmelfahrt". *GuL* 40 (1967): 81–85. Reprinted in *Dogma und Verkündigung* (see under section I).

"Das Menschenbild des Konzils in seiner Bedeutung für die Bildung". In *Christliche Erziehung nach dem Konzil*, pp. 33–67. Berichte und Dokumentationen, Kulturbeirat beim Zentralkomitee der Deutschen Katholiken. Cologne, 1967.

"Ist die Eucharistie ein Opfer?" *Conc(D)* 3 (1967): 299–304. (At the same time in *English, French, Italian, Spanish,* and *Portuguese*).

"Gottlieb Söhngen". *Christ in der Gegenwart* 19 (1967): 182f.

"Das Problem der Transsubstantiation und die Frage nach dem Sinn der Eucharistie". *ThQ* 147 (1967): 129–58. Reprinted in *ThJb(L)* 1969, pp. 281–301.
Italian: in J. Ratzinger and W. Beinert, *Il problema della transsustanziazione e del significato dell'Eucaristia*, pp. 7–58. Rome, 1969.

"Das Problem der Absolutheit des christlichen Heilsweges". In W. Böld et al., *Kirche in der außerchristlichen Welt*, pp. 7–29. Regensburg, 1967. Reprinted in *Das neue Volk Gottes* (see under section I).
English: in *Teaching All Nations* 4 (1967): 183–197.

"Konzilsaussagen über die Mission außerhalb der Missionsdekrete". In *Mission nach dem Konzil*, edited by J. Schütte, pp. 21–47. Mainz, 1967. At the same time in *French*. Reprinted in *Das neue Volk Gottes* (see under section I).

"Heilsgeschichte und Eschatologie: Zur Frage nach dem Ansatz des theologischen Denkens". In *Theologie im Wandel: Festschrift zum 150jährigen Bestehen der Katholisch-Theologischen Fakultät an der Universität Tübingen, 1817–1967)*, edited by J.

Neumann and J. Ratzinger, pp. 68–89. Munich and Freiburg, 1967. Reprinted in *ThJb(L)*, 1970, pp. 56–73, and in *Theologische Prinzipienlehre* (see under section I).

"Einleitung zum Kommentar zur Offenbarungskonstitution des II.Vaticanums und Kommentar zu Kap. 1, 2 und 6 der Konstitution". *LThK. E II* (1967): 498–528 and 571–81.

— 1968 —

" 'Vielleicht ist es aber wahr': Von der Unabweisbarkeit des Glaubens". *Orien* 32 (1968): 5–7.

" 'Von dannen er kommen wird, zu richten die Lebenden und die Toten' ". Hochl 60 (1968): 493–98.

"Die Bedeutung der Väter für die gegenwärtige Theologie". *ThQ* 148 (1968): 257–82; reprinted in *Kl* 1 (1969): 15–38. Published together with a discussion in *Geschichtlichkeit der Theologie*, edited by T. Michels, pp. 63–81; discussion, pp. 81–95. Salzburg and Munich, 1970.
Spanish: (extract) in *SelTeol* 31 (1969): 265–72.

"Zur Frage nach dem Sinn des priesterlichen Dienstes". *GuL* 41 (1968): 347–376.
Italian: as a booklet, *Il senso del ministero sacerdotale*. Trento, 1969.
American: in *Emmanuel* 76 (1970); also as a booklet in 1971.
Spanish: in *Liturgia* 3 (Argentina, 1972): 82–94.

"Schöpfungsglaube und Evolutionstheorie". In H. J. Schultz, *Wer ist das eigentlich—Gott?* pp. 232–45. Munich, 1969. Reprinted in *Dogma und Verkündigung* (see under section I).

"Kommentar zu Art. 11–22 der Pastoralkonstitution Gaudium et spes". *LThK. E III* (1968): 313–54.

"Tendenzen in der katholischen Theologie der Gegenwart". *Attempto*, no. 29/30 (1968): 46–51.
Spanish: in *Revista de Occidente*, no. 76 (July 1968): 23–38.

"Schwierigkeiten mit dem Apostolicum: Höllenfahrt—Himmel-fahrt—Auferstehung des Fleisches". In *Veraltetes Glaubens-bekenntnis?* edited by P. Brunner, pp. 97–123. Regensburg, 1968.

Italian: (the entire book) Assisi, 1971; also in *Spanish* (1971).

"Zur Frage nach der Geschichtlichkeit der Dogmen". In *Martyria: Liturgia: Diakonia: Festschrift für Hermann Volk zum 60. Geburtstag*, edited by O. Semmelroth, pp. 59–70. Mainz, 1968.

— 1969 —

"Zur Theologie der Ehe". *ThQ* 149 (1969): 53–74. Also in *Theologie der Ehe*, edited by G. Krems and R. Mumm, pp. 81–115. Regensburg and Göttingen, 1969. Reprinted in W. Ernst, *Moraltheologische Probleme in der Diskussion*, pp. 246–65. Leipzig, 1971.

"Theologische Aufgaben und Fragen bei der Begegnung lutherischer und katholischer Theologie nach dem Konzil". In *Oecumenica: Jahrbuch für ökumenische Forschung*, edited by F. W. Kantzenbach and V. Vajta, pp. 251–70. Gütersloh, 1969. Reprinted in *Das neue Volk Gottes* (see under section I).

"De relatione inter conceptum historiae salutis et quaestionem eschatologicam". In *Acta congressus internationalis de theol. Conc. Vat. II*, edited by D. Schönmetzer, pp. 484–89. Rome, 1969.

"Kommentar zu Art. 26 der Kirchenkonstitution". In P. Foot et al., *Church*, p. 57. New York, 1969.

"Gibt es eine Zukunft—was kommt nach dem Tod?" In *Dialog mit dem Zweifel*, edited by G. Rein, pp. 108–13. Stuttgart, 1969. Also reprinted in *Deutsche Zeitung*, 1972; in *Die Furche*, no. 17 (April 28, 1973): 8. In *An die Hinterbliebenen: Gedanken über Leben und Weiterleben*, edited by W. Erk, pp. 206–11. Stuttgart, 1973. Also in *Dogma und Verkündigung* (see under section I).

"Der Priester im Umbruch der Zeit". *KlBl* 49 (1969): 251–254. Reprinted with some changes in *Civitas* 25 (1969): 251–61. *Italian*: in *StCatt* 108 (1970): 183–89.

"Glaube, Geschichte und Philosophie: Zum Echo auf 'Einführung in das Christentum' ". Hochl 61 (1969): 533–43. *Italian*: in *IDOC internazionale* 1 (1969), Courrier IDOC.

"Bemerkungen zur Frage der Charismen in der Kirche". *Korrespondenzblatt der Priestergemeinschaft des Collegium Canisianum zu Innsbruck* 104 (1969/70): 12–22. Somewhat enlarged in *Die Zeit Jesu: Festschrift für Heinrich Schlier zum 70. Geburtstag*, edited by G. Bornkamm and K. Rahner, pp. 257–72. Freiburg, 1970.

" 'Nachwort des Theologen' zu Karl Hummel, Was Theologen nicht mehr sagen sollten". *ThQ* 149 (1969): 336–49.

"Heil und Geschichte: Gesichtspunkte zur gegenwärtigen theologischen Diskussion des Problems der 'Heilgeschichte' ". *Regensburger Universitätszeitung* 5 (1969): 11:2– 7; also in *WuW* 25 (1970): 3–14. An extract (in *Spanish*) in *SelTeol* 40 (1971): 314–22. Extensively reworked in *Theologische Prinzipienlehre* (see under section I).

"Der Verstand, der Geist und die Liebe". *Rheinische Post* (May 24, 1969), no. 119. Reprinted in *Dogma und Verkündigung* (see under section I).

— 1970 —

"Die Zeit der vierzig Tage: Predigt zum Aschermittwoch der Künstler in München". *KlBl* 50 (1970): 75ff. Reprinted in *Dogma und Verkündigung* (see under section I).

"Vom Alpha zum Omega:Von der Vergöttlichung des Menschen im Opfer". *Die Presse* (Vienna), March 28/29, 1970, XV. Reprinted in *Dogma und Verkündigung* (see under section I).

"Il ministero sacerdotale". *OR* 110 (May 28, 1970): 3 and 8.

"Schlußwort zu der Diskussion mit W. Kasper". *Hochl* 62 (1970): 157ff.

"Die anthropologischen Grundlagen der Bruderliebe". *Caritasdienst* 23 (1970): 45–49. Reprinted in *Pro Filia* 58 (1970): 109–18; also in *Dogma und Verkündigung* (see under section I).

"Der Holländische Katechismus: Versuch einer theologischen Würdigung". *Hochl* 62 (1970): 301–13; reprinted in *Dogma und Verkündigung* (see under section I). *Swedish*: in *Katolsk informationsjänst* (1970), pp. 363–68, 390–93. *English*: in *The Furrow* 22 (1971): 739–54.

"Der Weg der religiösen Erkenntnis nach dem heiligen Augustinus". in *Kyriakon: Festschrift für Johannes Quasten*, edited by P. Granfield and J. A. Jungmann, pp. 553–64. Münster, 1970.

"Kirche—Dienst am Glauben". In *Offene Horizonte*, edited by E. Spath, pp. 119–24. Freiburg, 1970. Reprinted in *Dogma und Verkündigung* (see under section I).

— 1971 —

"Widersprüche im Buch von Hans Küng". In *Zum Problem der Unfehlbarkeit: Antwort auf die Anfrage von Hans Küng*, edited by Karl Rahner, pp. 97–116. QD, no. 54. Freiburg, 1971.

"Das Ganze im Fragment: Gottlieb Söhngen zum Gedächtnis". *Christ in der Gegenwart* 23 (1971): 398f.; under a different title in *Cath* 26 (1972): 2–6.

"Primacy and Episcopacy". *ThD* 19 (1971): 200–207 (taken from *Das neue Volk Gottes*; see under section I).

— 1972 —

"Einheit der Kirche—Einheit der Menschheit: Ein Tagungsbericht". *IKaZ* 1 (1972): 78–83.

"Die Auferstehung Christi und die christliche Jenseitshoffnung". In *Christlich—was heißt das?* edited by G. Adler, pp. 34–37. Düsseldorf, 1972.

"Was eint und was trennt die Konfessionen? Eine ökumenische Besinnung". *IKaZ* 1 (1972): 171–77.

"Opfer, Sakrament und Priestertum in der Entwicklung der Kirche". *Cath* 26 (1972): 108–25. Extract in *ThD* 21 (1973): 100–105.

"Zur Frage nach der Unauflöslichkeit der Ehe: Bemerkungen zum dogmengeschichtlichen Befund und zu seiner gegenwärtigen Bedeutung". In *Ehe und Ehescheidung: Diskussion unter Christen*, edited by F. Henrich und V. Eid, pp. 35–56. Munich, 1972.

"Wozu noch Christentum?" In *Lebendige Kirche: Mitteilungen des Diözesanrates im Erzbistum Köln*, pp. 6–9. 1972. Reprinted in *OR(D)* 2, no. 23 (1972): 10. Extracts distributed by KNA to several weeklies. Reprinted in *Dogma und Verkündigung* (see under section I).

"Jenseits des Todes". *IKaZ* 1 (1972): 231–44. Reprinted in *Leben nach dem Sterben*, edited by A. Rosenberg, pp. 15–31. Munich, 1974. Abridged in *SelTeol* 13 (1974): 204–11.

"Die Christologie im Spannungsfeld von altchristlicher Exegese und moderner Bibelauslegung". In *Urbild und Abglanz: Festgabe für Herbert Doms zum 80. Geburtstag*, edited by J. Tenzler, pp. 359–67. Regensburg, 1972.

"Metanoia als Grundbefindlichkeit christlicher Existenz". In *Buße und Beichte: Drittes Regensburger Ökumenisches Symposion*, edited by E. C. Suttner, pp. 21–37. Regensburg, 1972. Given a different title in *Theologische Prinzipienlehre* (see under section I).

"Taufe und Formulierung des Glaubens". *Didaskalia* 2 (1972): 23–34; also in *EThL* 49 (1973): 76–86. Given a different title in *Theologische Prinzipienlehre* (see under section I).

"Das Gewissen in der Zeit". *IKaZ* 1 (1972): 432–42; the same in *Reinhold-Schneider-Gesellschaft e. V.*, vol. 4 (July 1972): 13–29; and in *Kirche, Ökumene, Politik* (see under section I).

"Der Priester als Mittler und Diener Christi". In *100 Jahre Priesterseminar in St. Jakob zu Regensburg 1872–1972*, edited by P. Mai, pp. 53–68. Regensburg, 1972. Given a different title in *Theologische Prinzipienlehre* (see under section I).

"Die Bedeuting der Ökumene am Ort". *OR(D)* 2, no. 49 (1972): 8–10. Reprinted in *Theologische Prinzipienlehre* (see under section I). Extended version in *Cath* 27 (1973): 152–65.

"Die Legitimität des christologischen Dogmas". *EE* 47 (1972): 487–503.

— 1973 —

"Abschied vom Teufel?" In various diocesan newsletters (Regensburg, Munich, Passau, Bamberg, Rottenburg, Würzburg, Aachen, Speyer) in early 1973. Reprinted in *Dogma und Verkündigung* (see under section I).

Antwort: *Wer ist Jesus von Nazaret—für mich? 100 zeitgenössische Antworten*, edited by H. Spaemann, pp. 23–26. Munich, 1973. Reprinted in *Dogma und Verkündigung* (see under section I). *Portuguese* in *Questões actuais de Cristología*, edited by J. E. M. Terra, pp. 66–69. São Paulo, 1985.

"Noch einmal: 'Kurzformeln des Glaubens': Anmerkungen". *IKaZ* 2 (1973): 258–64.

"Les 'Sources Chrétiennes' et la 'source unique' ". *Bulletin des amis de "Sources chrétiennes"*, no. 29 (May 1973): 28–32.

"Verkündigung von Gott heute". *IKaZ* 2 (1973): 342–55. Reprinted in *Dogma und Verkündigung* (see under section I). Extract in *ThD* 22 (1974): 196–201. Again reprinted in *ThJb(L)* 1975, pp. 336–48.

"Vom Sinn des Kirchbaus". In *Kirchenbau in Diskussion: Austellungskatalog* (pages not numbered, but following p. 16). Munich, 1973. Reprinted in *Dogma und Verkündigung* (see under section I).

"Fragen zur Apostolischen Nachfolge: Zum Memorandum der sechs ökumenischen Universitätsinstitute". *Suchen und finden: Der katholische Glaube* 22 (1973): 172–77, previously distributed through KNA.

"Einleitung und Kommentar zu den Thesen I–VIII und X–XII". In *Die Einheit des Glaubens und der theologische Pluralismus*, edited by the Internationale Theologenkommission, pp. 11–51 and 61–67. Einsiedeln, 1973.
Italian: *Unità della fede e pluralismo teologico*. Bologna, 1978.
Spanish: *El pluralismo teológico*. Madrid, 1976.
French: *L'Unité de la foi et le pluralisme théologique*. 1978.

"È partendo da Cristo che l'altro diventa prossimo". *Settimana del clero*, November 1973, no. 40.

"Vorfragen zu einer Theologie der Erlösung". In *Erlösung und Emanzipation*, edited by L. Scheffczyk, pp. 141–55. Freiburg, 1973.

— 1974 —

"Der Heilige Geist als communio: Zum Verhältnis von Pneumatologie und Spiritualität bei Augustinus". In *Erfahrung und Theologie des Heiligen Geistes*, edited by C. Heitmann and H. Mühlen, pp. 223–38. Hamburg and Munich, 1974.

"Tradition und Fortschritt". *Ibw-Journal* 12 (1974): 1–7. Also in *Freiheit des Menschen*, edited by A. Paus, pp. 9–30. Graz, 1974. Reprinted in *ThJb(L)* 1979, pp. 189–203; given a different title in *Theologische Prinzipienlehre* (see under section I).
American: in *Communio* 25 (Summer 1998): 325–39.

"Ökumenisches Dilemma? Zur Diskussion um die Erklärung 'Mysterium Ecclesiae'". *IKaZ* 3 (1974): 56–63. Reprinted in *OR(D)* 4 (1974): 6f. Given a different title in *Theologische Prinzipienlehre* (see under section I).

"Das Ende der Bannflüche von 1054: Folgen für Rom und die Ostkirchen". *IKaZ* 3 (1974): 289–303. Also in *Pro oriente:Auf dem Weg zur Einheit des Glaubens*, pp. 101–13. Innsbruck, Vienna, and Munich, 1976. Given a different title in *Theologische Prinzipienlehre* (see under section I).

French: in *Istina*, 1975, pp. 87–99.

"Zur theologischen Grundlegung der Kirchenmusik". In *Gloria Deo—Pax hominibus: Festschrift zum 100jährigen Bestehen der Kirchenmusikschule Regensburg*, edited by F. Fleckenstein, pp. 39–62. Regensburg, 1974. Partially reprinted in *Österr. KlBl* 108 (1975): 127, and in *OR(D)* 5 (1975): 7. Complete reprint in *KlBl* 5 (1975): 263–67, and in *Das Fest des Glaubens* (see under section I).

"Kirchliches Lehramt—Glaube—Moral". First in *Italian* in *OR* 114 (December 15, 1974): 3f.; in German in *OR(D)* 5, no. 4 (1975): 8f. Extended version in *Prinzipien christlicher Moral* (see under II).

American: in *The Distinctiveness of Christian Ethics*, edited by C. E. Curran and R. McCormick, pp. 174–89. Readings in Moral Theology no. 2. New York, 1980.

Spanish: in J. Ratzinger, Hans Urs von Balthasar, Heinz Schürmann, *Principios de moral cristiana compendio*, pp. 43–69. Valencia, 2000.

(Together with S. Horn) **"Die Struktur der Kirche".** In *Japanese*, in *Fides et theologia*, edited by L. Elders and H. Van Straelen, pp. 43–71 (Tokyo, 1974).

— 1975 —

" 'Ich glaube an Gott den allmächtigen Vater' ". *IKaZ* 4 (1975): 10–18; also in *Ich glaube*, edited by W. Sandfuchs, pp. 13–24. Würzburg, 1975. Reworked version in *Brückenbau im Glauben*, ed. W. Sandfuchs, pp. 17–29. Leipzig, 1979. And in *Theologische Prinzipienlehre* (see under section I).

Italian: in *Communio* 4 (1975).

Spanish: in *SelTeol* 15 (1976): 254–59; in entirety in *Yo creo*, ed. J. Auer et al. Madrid, 1981.

French: in *Je crois: Explication du symbole des apôtres*. Paris, 1978.

Vorwort: Stylianos Harkianakis, *Orthodoxe Kirche und Katholizismus: Ähnliches und Verschiedenes*, pp. 7–10. Munich, 1975.

"Institución, Carisma, Sacramentos". In Conferencia Episcopal de Colombia, *Cuestiones actuales de Teología*, pp. 55–118. Bogotà, 1974.

"Theologie und Ethos". In *Die Verantwortung der Wissenschaft*, edited by K. Ulmer et al., pp. 46–61. Bonn, 1975.

"Bedarf der Christ des Alten Testaments? Eine Anmerkung zu Meinrad Limbecks gleichnamigen Artikel". *HerKorr* 29 (1975): 253f.

"Der Weltdienst der Kirche: Auswirkungen von 'Gaudium et spes' im letzten Jahrzehnt". *IKaZ* 4 (1975): 439–54. Reprinted in *Zehn Jahre Vaticanum II*, edited by A. Bauch et al., pp. 36–53. Regensburg, 1976.

"Bildung und Glaube in unserer Zeit: Drei Thesen zur christlichen Bildung". *Ibw-Journal* 13 (1975): 113–16.

"Gebet und Meditation". In *Beten—leben—meditieren*, edited by W. Rupp, pp. 76–81. Würzburg, 1975.

" 'Auferbaut aus lebendigen Steinen' ". In *Kirche aus lebendigen Steinen*, edited by W. Seidel, pp. 30–48. Mainz, 1975. Also in *Ein neues Lied für den Herrn* (see under section I).

"Was ist für den christlichen Glauben heute konstitutiv?" In *Mysterium der Gnade: Festschrift für J. Auer*, edited by H. Rossmann and J. Ratzinger, pp. 11–19. Regensburg, 1975. Reprinted in *Theologische Prinzipienlehre* (see under section I).

"Christ sein—plausibel gemacht". *ThRv* 71 (1975): 353–64. Reprinted in *Unsere Seelsorge* 26 (1976): 28–33.
English: in *DoLi* 27 (1977): 3–17.
French: in *Communio* 3 (1978): 84–95.

"Theologische Fakultät und Seelsorge". *KlBl* 55 (1975): 39.

— 1976 —

"Wer verantwortet die Aussagen der Theologie? Zur Methodenfrage". In H. U. von Balthasar et al., *Diskussion über Hans Küngs "Christ sein"*, pp. 7–18. Mainz, 1976. *French*: in *Comment être chrétien?* edited by J. R. Armogathe, pp. 69–86. Paris, 1979.

"Kirchenmusikberuf als liturgischer und pastoralischer Dienst". In *Kirchenmusik im Gespräch*, edited by F. Fleckenstein, pp. 24–27. Bonn, 1976.

"Taufe, Glaube und Zugehörigkeit zur Kirche". *IKaZ* 5 (1976): 218–34; extract in *ThD* 25 (1977): 126–31, and in *SelTeol* 16 (1977): 237–48. *French*: in *Communio* 1 (1976): 9–21. *Italian*: in *Communio* 5 (1976): 22–39.

"Die kirchliche Lehre vom sacramentum ordinis". In *Pluralisme et oecuménisme en recherches théologiques: Mélanges offertes au R. P. Dockx O.P.*, pp. 155–66. BeThL 43. Paris, 1976. Also in *IKaZ* 10 (1981): 435–45, and in *Theologische Prinzipienlehre* (see under section I).

"Meditationen". *Pastoralblatt für die Diözesen Aachen, Berlin, Essen, Köln, Osnabrück* 28 (1976): 1, 33, 65, 97, 129, 161, 193, 225, 257, 289, 321, 353. A selection in *Die Hoffnung des Senfkorns* and in *Gottes Angesicht suchen* (see under section I).

"Prognosen für die Zukunft des Ökumenismus". *Bausteine für die Einheit der Christen* 17, no. 65 (1977): 6–14; also in *Ökumenisches Forum: Grazer Hefte für konkrete Ökumene* 1 (1977): 31–41. Reprinted in *Pro oriente: Ökumene—Konzil—Unfehlbarkeit*, pp. 208–15. Innsbruck, 1979. Likewise in *Theologische Prinzipienlehre* (see under section I) and in *Vom Wiederauffinden der Mitte* (see under section I). *French*: in *Proche Orient Chrétien* (Jerusalem) 26 (1976): 206–19. *English*: (extract) in *ThD* 25 (1977): 200–205.

"Stimme des Vertrauens: Kardinal Frings auf dem Zweiten Vatikanum". In *Ortskirche im Dienst der Weltkirche: Festgabe für die Kardinäle Höffner und Frings*, edited by N. Trippen and W. Mogge, pp. 183–90. Cologne, 1976.

— 1977 —

"Il sacerdozio dell'uomo: un'offesa ai diritti della donna?" *OR* 117 (March 26, 1977).

German: in *KlBl* 57 (1977); in *LS* 27, no. 2 (1977): 1–4; and in *OR(D)*.

Spanish: in *Misión de la mujer en la Iglesia*, pp. 149–60. Madrid, 1978. Reprinted in Congregatione per la Dottrina della Fede, *Dall' "Inter insigniores" all' "Ordinatio sacerdotalis": Documenti e commenti*, pp. 150–58. Vatican City, 1996.

"Eschatologie und Utopie". *IKaZ* 6 (1977): 97–110. Also in *Abschied von Utopia? Anspruch und Auftrag der Intellektuellen*, edited by O. Schatz, pp. 193–210. Graz, 1977. And in *Kirche, Ökumene, Politik* (see under section I).

In *English*, *French*, and *Italian*, in the various editions of *Communio*.

"Alcune forme bibliche ed ecclesiali di 'presenza' dello Spirito nella storia". In *Spirito santo e storia*, edited by L. Sartori, pp. 51–64. Rome, 1977.

"Die Gabe der Weisheit". In *Die Gaben des Geistes: Acht Betrachtungen*, edited by W. Sandfuchs, pp. 35–48. Würzburg, 1977.

"Der Stärkere und der Starke: Zum Problem der Mächte des Bösen in der Sicht des christlichen Glaubens". In M. Adler et al., *Tod und Teufel in Klingenberg: Eine Dokumentation*, pp. 84–101. Aschaffenburg, 1977.

"Gestalt und Gehalt der eucharistischen Feier". *IKaZ* 6 (1977): 385–96.

French: in *Communio* 2 (1977): 31–32.

English: (extract) in *ThD* 26 (1978): 117–21.

Again in *French* in *L'Eucharistie*, pp. 34–51. Paris, 1981.

"Liturgie—wandelbar oder unwandelbar? Fragen an J. Ratzinger". *IKaZ* 6 (1977): 417–27.
  French: in *L'Eucharistie*, pp. 161–76. Paris, 1981.

"Wissenschaft—Glaube—Wunder". In *Jenseits der Erkenntnis*, edited by L. Reinisch, pp. 28–44. Frankfurt, 1977.

"Kirche als Heilssakrament". In *Zeit des Geistes: Zur heilsgeschichtlichen Herkunft der Kirche*, edited by J. Reikerstorfer, pp. 59–70. Vienna, 1977.

"Meditationen". *Pastoralblatt für den Diözesen Aachen, Berlin, Essen, Köln, Osnabrück* 29 (1977): 1, 33, 65, 97, 129, 161, 193, 225, 257, 289, 321, 353. A selection in *Die Hoffnung des Senfkorns* and in *Gottes Angesicht suchen* (see under section I).

"Ist der Glaube wirklich 'Frohe Botschaft'?" In *In libertatem vocati estis: Miscellanea Bernhard Häring zum 65. Geburtstag*, edited by H. Boelaars and R. Tremblay, pp. 523–33. StMor 15. Rome, 1977.
  Italian: in *Chiamati alla libertà*, pp. 149–61. Rome, 1980.

"Zum Zölibat der katholischen Priester". *StZ* 195 (1977): 781–83.
  Hungarian: in *Szolgalat* 37 (1978): 73–75.

— 1978 —

"Wandelbares und Unwandelbares in der Kirche". *IKaZ* 7 (1978): 182ff.

"Der Primat des Papstes und die Einheit des Gottesvolkes". In *Dienst an der Einheit* (see under II); also in *Kirche, Ökumene, Politik* (see under section I).

"Vom Verstehen des Glaubens: Anmerkungen zu K. Rahners Grundkurs des Glaubens". *ThRv* 74 (1978): 177–86.

"Kirche und wissenschaftliche Theologie". In *Die Kirche*, edited by W. Sandfuchs, pp. 83–95. Würzburg, 1978. Reprinted in *Theologische Prinzipienlehre* (see under section I).
  American: in *Communio* 7 (1980): 332–47.

"Anmerkungen zur Frage einer 'Anerkennung' der Confessio Augustana durch die katholische Kirche". *MThZ* 29 (1978): 225–37; *Theologische Prinzipienlehre* (see under section I).

"Zur Frage nach der Struktur der liturgischen Feier". *IKaZ* 7 (1978): 488–97; and in *Das Fest des Glaubens* (see under section I).
Italian: in *Communio* 7 (1978): 177–86.

"Theologische Probleme der Kirchenmusik". In *Kirchenmusik eine geistig-geistliche Disziplin: Gastvorträge an der kath. Kirchenmusikabteilung der Staatl. Musikhochschule Stuttgart*, no. 1, edited by R. Walter. Rottenburg, 1978. Reprinted in *MS(D)* 99 (1979): 129–35, and in *IKaZ* 9 (1980): 148–57.
English: in *Crux et cithara*, edited by R. A. Skeris, pp. 214–222. Altötting, 1983. Reprinted in *Musicae Sacrae Ministerium* 26–27 (1989/90): 44–54.
French: in *Communio* 4 (1979): 84–93.

"Intervenciones". In *Congreso Mariano Nacional: Memorias*, 2:21–44. Guayaquil, 1978.

"Aus meinem Leben". In *Kardinal Ratzinger: Der Erzbischof von München und Freising in Wort und Bild*, edited by K. Wagner and A. H. Ruf, pp. 54–67. Munich, 1978.

"Zum Geleit". In R. Graber, *Stärke deine Brüder*, pp. 17f. Regensburg, 1978.

— 1979 —

"Was ist Theologie? Rede zum 75. Geburtstag von Hermann Kardinal Volk". *IKaZ* 8 (1979): 121–28, reprinted in *Theologische Prinzipienlehre* (see under section I).
French: in *Communio* 4 (1979): 89–96, and in H. Volk, *La Foi comme adhésion*, pp. 149–68. Paris and Namur, n.d. [1980].

"Europa—Verpflichtendes Erbe für die Christen". Munich: Kath. Akademie in Bayern, 1979. Also printed in *Zur debatte* 9 (1979): 1–4. Reprinted in *Europa: Horizonte der Hoffnung*,

edited by F. König and K. Rahner, pp. 61–74. Graz, 1983.
Also in *Kirche, Ökumene, Politik* (see under section I).

French: in *RevSR* 54 (1980): 41–54. Again in J. Ratzinger, *Damaskinos métropolite de Suisse, l'héritage chrétien de l'Europe*, pp. 9–26. Thessalonika, 1989.

Portuguese: in *Communio* 3 (1986): 101–13.

Hungarian: in *Mérleg*, 1989, no. 4, pp. 376–88.

"Kleine Korrektur: Zur Frage der Eucharistie". *IKaZ* 8 (1979): 381f. Extended in *Das Fest des Glaubens* (see under section I).

"Erwägungen zur Stellung von Mariologie und Marienfrömmigkeit im Ganzen von Glaube und Theologie". In *Maria die Mutter des Herrn*, pp. 13–27. Bonn: Sekretariat d. Dt. Bischofskonferenz, 1979. Reprinted in *Maria—Kirche im Ursprung* (see under section I); and in *ThJb(L)* 1983, pp. 137–66.

Préface: Commission théologique internationale: P. Delhaye, W. Ernst, et al., *Problèmes doctrinaux du mariage chrétien*, pp. 7–12. Louvain-la-Neuve, 1979.

— 1980 —

"Erfahrung und Glaube: Theologische Bemerkungen zur katechetischen Dimension des Themas". *IKaZ* 9 (1980): 58–70; reprinted in *Theologische Prinzipienlehre* (see under section I).

"Zwischen Tod und Auferstehung". *IKaZ* 9 (1980): 209–33; *ThJb(L)* 1984, pp. 274–87.

French: in *Communio* 5 (1980): 4–19.

Spanish: (extract) in *SelTeol* 21 (1982): 37–46.

"La sinfonia della Croce: 'La conoscenza di Dio che rifulge sul volto di Cristo' ". *Anton* 55 (1980): 280–86.

Geleitwort: H. Schlier, *Der Geist und die Kirche*, pp. vii–x. Freiburg, 1980.

"Das 'Vater unser' sagen dürfen". In *Sich auf Gott verlassen: Erfahrungen mit Gebeten*, edited by R. Walter, pp. 64–69. Freiburg,

1980. Reprinted in *Mit tausend Flügeln trägst du mich*, edited by A. L. Balling, pp. 15–22. Freiburg, 1986; 2nd ed., 1987.

"Theologie und Kirchenpolitik". *IKaZ* 9 (1980): 425–34. Reprinted in *Wem nützt die Wissenschaft?* edited by L. S. Schulz, pp. 106–17. Munich, 1981. Also in *Kirche, Ökumene, Politik* (see under section I).
Italian: in *Communio* 9 (1980): 60–71.
French: in *Communio* 6 (1981): 29–40.

"Gemeinde aus der Eucharistie". In *800 Jahre St. Martini Münster*, edited by W. Hülsbusch, pp. 32–34. Münster, 1980. Also in *Vom Wiederauffinden der Mitte* (see under section I).

"Lehramt schützt den Glauben der Einfachen". *Bausteine* 20, no. 80 (1980): 3–10.

"Dorothea von Montau". In *Zeugen der Wahrheit*, edited by W. Herbstrith, pp. 63–66. Munich, 1980.

"Worte der Widmung". In *Gottesherrschaft—Weltherrschaft: Festschrift für Bischof Rudolf Graber*, edited by J. Auer, J. Mussner, and G. Schweizer, pp. 7–9. Regensburg, 1980.

"Wort bei der Schlußversammlung der Augsburger CA-Festtage". *US* 35 (1980): 199.

"Europa: Erstanden aus dem christlichen Glauben". In *Eine Pilgerreise durch Polen*, edited by R. Hammerschmid, pp. 55–64. Kevelaer, 1980.

(Together with the International Theological Commission) "Quaestiones selectae de christologia". *Gr* 61 (1980): 609–32.

— 1981 —

"L'essentiel des propositions élaborées par le Synode". In *Aujourd'hui la famille*, edited by J. Potin, pp. 281–303; with "Rapport d'introduction", pp. 25–43, and "Deuxième rapport", pp. 221–32. Paris, 1981. Also in *EeV* 91 (1981): 241–52; abridged in *Louvain* 1 (1981): 8–23.

Geleitwort: L. Weimer, *Die Lust an Gott und seiner Sache*, pp. 5f. Freiburg, 1981.

"Freiheit und Bindung in der Kirche". In *Die Grundrechte des Christen in Kirche und Gesellschaft*, edited by E. Corecco et al. Fribourg, Freiburg, and Milan, 1981. And in *Verein der Freunde der Universität Regensburg* 7: 5–21; also in *Kirche, Ökumene, Politik* (see under section I).

Dutch: in *Communio* 7 (1982): 386–400.

French: in *StMor* 22 (1984): 171–88.

"Das I. Konzil von Konstantinopel 381: Seine Voraussetzungen und seine bleibende Bedeutung". *IKaZ* 10 (1981): 555–63; reprinted in *Theologische Prinzipienlehre* (see under section I).

"Sicherheit im Aspekt der Sozialethik". In *Sicherheit—verwirklichbar, vergleichbar, tragbar?* edited by P. C. Compes, pp. 17–27. Gesellschaft für Sicherheitswissenschaften, Wuppertal, 1981. Also in *IkaZ* 11 (1982): 51–57. And in *Technik und Ökonomie im Lichte sozialethischer Fragestellungen*, edited by M. Spangenberger, pp. 24–34. Beiträge zur Gesellschafts- und Bildungspolitik: Institut der deutschen Wirtschaft 106. Cologne, 1985.

American: in *Communio* 9 (1982) 238–46.

"Misterio Pascual y culto al Corazón de Jesus". *Tierra nueva* 11 (1982): 77–86.

French: in *Le Coeur de Jésus coeur du monde*, pp. 141–56. Paris, 1982.

Dutch: in *De Volheid van Gods Genade*, pp. 75–97. Bruges, 1982.

German: in J. Ratzinger et al., *Entwicklung und Aktualität der Herz-Jesu-Verehrung*, pp. 128–44. Aschaffenburg, 1984. Also in *Schauen auf den Durchbohrten* (see under section I).

"Hort des Glaubens und der Hoffnung". In *Benedikt 480–1980: Ettal 1330–1980: Festschrift zum Ettaler Doppeljubiläum 1980*, edited A. Kalff, pp. 50–53. Sondernummer Ettaler Mandl 59. Ettal, 1981.

"Theologische Grundlagen der Kirchenmusik". In *Das christliche Universum*, edited by B. Moser, p. 362. Munich, 1981.

— 1982 —

" 'Wähle das Leben': Eine Firmhomilie". *IKaZ* 11 (1982): 444–
49.

French: in *Communio* 7 (1982): 65–69.

Italian: in *Communio* 11 (1982): 40–46.

"Matrimonio e famiglia nel piano di Dio". In *La "Familiaris
consortio"*, pp. 77–88. Vatican City, 1982.

German: in *OR(D)* 12, no. 25 (1982): 8f.

Geleitwort: *Episcopale munus: Recueil d'études sur le ministère episcopal
offertes en hommages à son Excellence Msgr. J. M. Gijsen*, edited
by P. Delhaye and L. Elders, pp. xi–xvi. Assen, 1982.

"Interpretation—Kontemplation—Aktion: Überlegungen zum
Auftrag einer kath. Akademie". Special issue no. 7 of the
Katholische Akademie in Bayern. Munich, 1982. Also in
IKaZ 12 (1983): 167–79; and in *Wesen und Auftrag der Theologie*
(see under section I).

"Stellungnahme zum offiziellen orthodox-katholischen Dialog". *Ut omnes unum* 45 (1982): 154–58.

"Über die Wurzeln des Terrors in Deutschland". In *Almanach für
das Erzbistum Köln*, second series, edited by D. Froitzheim
and A. Wienand, pp. 99–103. Cologne, 1982.

"Was feiern wir am Sonntag?" *IKaZ* 11 (1982): 226–31.

— 1983 —

"Transmission de la foi et sources de la foi". Special offprint,
Paris, 1983. Also in D. J. Ryan et al., *Transmettre la foi
aujourd'hui*, pp. 41–61. Paris, 1983.

Italian: in *Cristianità—Organo ufficiale di Alleanza Cattolica* 11,
no. 96 (1983): 5–11.

American: in *The Wanderer*.

American: in *Communio* 10 (1983): 17–34.

Spanish: in *Scripta theologica* 15 (1983): 9–29.

Portuguese: in *Communio/Brasil* 3 (1984): 177–201.

"Anglican–Catholic Dialogue: Its Problems and Hopes". *Insight: A Journal for Church and Community* 1 (1983): 2–11.

German: in *IKaZ* 12 (1983): 244–59; also, with afterword, in *Kirche, Ökumene, Politik* (see under section I).

"L'eucaristia al centro della communità e della sua missione". Special offprint, Collevalenza, 1983. Reworked version in *Schauen auf den Durchbohrten* (see under section I).

"Schwierigkeiten mit der Glaubensunterweisung heute: Interview mit F. Greiner". *IKaZ* 12 (1983): 259–67; reprinted in *Pastoralblatt* 35 (1983): 196–203.

American: in *Communio* 11 (1984): 145–56.

"'Auf Dein Wort hin': Eine Meditation zur priesterlichen Spiritualität". In J. Ratzinger, H. Volk, B. Henrichs, *"Auf Dein Wort hin"*, pp. 15–36. Kölner Beiträge, new series, no. 9. Cologne, 1983.

"La speranza elemento fondamentale che definisce l'esistenza del cristiano". *OR* 123 (June 10, 1983): 5.

French: in *L'Homme nouveau* 37, no. 837/838 (July 3–17, 1983): 7–9 (= shorter version of "Sulla speranza", see below).

"Orientaciones Cristológicas". In Consejo Episcopal Latino-americano—CELAM, *Cristo el Señor: Ensayos Teológicos*, pp. 5–22. 1983. A new reworked version included in *Schauen auf den Durchbohrten* (see under section I).

"Luther und die Einheit der Kirchen". *IKaZ* 12 (1983): 568–82; with an afterword, in *Kirche, Ökumene, Politik* (see under section I).

American: in *Communio* 11 (1984): 210–26.

French: in *La doc. cath.* (1984): 121–28.

"Erwägungen zur Stellung von Mariologie und Marienfrömmigkeit im Ganzen von Glaube und Theologie". *ThJb(L)* 1983, pp. 137–66 (from *Maria—Kirche im Ursprung*; see under section I).

— 1984 —

"Sulla speranza". In *La speranza*, edited by B. Giordani, vol. 2. Brescia and Rome, 1984. (Shorter version appeared earlier in *OR*, see above.)
German: in *IKaZ* 13 (1984): 293–305; also in other editions of *Communio*.

"Vi spiego la teologia della liberazione". *30 giorni* (February 1984): 48–55; published in various periodicals in different languages.

"Obispos, Teólogos y Moralidad." In *Teología moral hoy*, edited by J. Lozano Baragan, pp. 23–52. Mexico, 1984.
French: in *Communio* 9 (1984): 21–40; also in *Bulletin de la conférence épiscopale française*, no. 17 (1984).
German: in *IKaZ* 13 (1984): 524–38; also in other editions of *Communio*.
Italian: as a special offprint, CRIS, *Documenti* 54. Rome, 1985.

"Der Streit um die Moral: Fragen der Grundlegung ethischer Werte". Festvortrag Regensburger Fortbildungstagung für Ärtzte, 1984; also in *Ibw journal* 10 (1985): 1–11.
Italian: in *Vita e pensiero* 1989, pp. 173–84; also in *Studi sociali* 29 (1989): 9–23.
Czech: in *Studie II–III*, 1989, Cislo 122–23, pp. 84–95.
French: in *Sources* 16 (1990): 1–12.

"Kirchenverfassung und Umkehr: Fragen an Joseph Kardinal Ratzinger". *IKaZ* 13 (1984): 444–57; much abbreviated in *Ein neues Lied für den Herrn* (see under section I).

"Problemas principales de la teología contemporanea". *La Revista Católica* 84, no. 1063/64 (1984): 13–23.

"Christliche Orientierung in der pluralistischen Demokratie?" In *Pro fide et iustitia: Festschrift für Kard. Casaroli zum 70. Geburtstag*, edited by H. Schambeck, pp. 747–61. Berlin, 1984. Also in *Das europäische Erbe und seine christliche Zukunft*, edited by N. Lobkowicz, pp. 20–25. Cologne, 1985. Likewise in *Kirche, Ökumene, Politik* and in *Vom Wiederauffinden der Mitte* (see under section I).

Spanish: Universidad del Norte (Chile), *Teología* (1985); also in *ScrTh* 16 (1984): 815–29; in *Communio/America Latina* 3 (1985): 52–63; and in *Hablan tres Cardenales* (Santiago, 1986). *Polish*: in *Znak: Czasu*, no. 12 (1988): 90–102.

"Gesicht und Aufgabe einer Glaubensbehörde: Ein Gespräch mit Joseph Kardinal Ratzinger über die Römische Glaubenskongregation". *HerKorr* 38 (1984): 360–68.

"Intrução sobre a Teologia da libertação". *REB* 44 (1984): 691–95.

(Collaboration) "Teología de la liberacíon: Documentos sobre una polémia". San José, Costa Rica, 1984.

"Die Theologie der Befreiung". *NOrd* 38 (1984): 285–95.

— 1985 —

"Glaube, Philosophie und Theologie". *IKaZ* 14 (1985): 56–66. *American*: in *Communio* 1985. And in *Pope John Paul II Lecture Series*, College of St. Thomas, pp. 10–14. 1985. *French*: in *Communio* 10 (1985): 24–37.

"Scopi e methodi del Sinodo dei vescovi". In *Il Sinodo dei vescovi: Natura—metodi—prospettiva*, edited by J. Tomko, pp. 45–58. Vatican City, 1985. Reworked in *Kirche, Ökumene, Politik* (see under section I).

"Zum Sinn des Sonntags". *Pastoralblatt für den Diözesen Aachen, Berlin, Essen, Hildesheim, Köln, Osnabrück* 37 (1985): 258–69; also in *FoKTh* 1 (1985): 161–75; also in *KlBl* 65 (1985): 209–14; and in *Ein neues Lied für den Herrn* (see under section I). *Spanish*: in *La Revista Católica* 88/1078 (1988): 135–46.

"Von der Liturgie zur Christologie: Romano Guardinis theologischer Grundansatz und seine Aussagekraft". In *Wege zur Wahrheit* (see under II), pp. 121–44. "Vorwort" in ibid., p. 7.

"L'ecclesiologia del Vaticano II". In J. Ratzinger et al., *La Chiesa del Concilio*, pp. 9–24. Milan, 1985.

German: in *IKaZ* 15 (1986): 41–52; *OR(D)* 15, no. 4 (1985): 4ff.

Pastoralblatt für den Diözesen Aachen, Berlin, Essen, Hildesheim, Köln, Osnabrück 38 (1986): 130–39; *KlBl* 1986; with an appendix in *Kirche, Ökumene, Politik* (see under section I).
Spanish: in *Iglesia comunicadora de vida* (see under section I).

"La celebrazione del sacramento con assoluzione generale". In *La "reconciliatio et paenitentia"*, pp. 136–45. Vatican City, 1985.
German: in *OR(D)* 15, no. 10 (1985): pp. 1f.

"Unità e pluralismo nella Chiesa dal Concilio al post-Concilio". *Orientamenti pastorali* 12 (1985): 125–44. (First appeared in *Bolletino diocesano per gli ufficiali e le attività pastorali dell'arcidiocesi di Bari* 61 [1985], no. 1.)
German: in *FoKTh* 2 (1986): 81–96.
French: in *StMor* 24 (1986): 299–318.

"Pourquoi la foi est en crise". *PenCath* 1985, no. 214, pp. 22–58.

Préface: J.-H. Nicholas, *Synthèse dogmatique*, pp. v–vi. Fribourg and Paris, 1985.

"Zuversicht für ein Leben in Freiheit: Das Ende des Krieges im Mai 1945". *OR(D)* 15, no. 18 (1985): 11.

— 1986 —
"Liturgie und Kirchenmusik". *OR(D)* 16, no. 6 (1986): 10–12; also in *MS(D)* 106 (1986):. 3–12; and in *IKaZ* 15 (1986): 243–56; as a separate offprint by Musikverlag Sikorski (Hamburg, 1987); and in *Ein neues Lied für den Herrn* (see under section I).
English: in *Sacred Music* 112 (1985): 13–22; also *American*: in *Homiletic and Pastoral Review* 86 (1986): 10–22.
French: in *Una voce*, no. 126 (January-February 1986): 13–22 (extracts).
Italian: in *Bollettino Ceciliano* 81 (1986): 99–112.
Italian, German, English, French, Spanish: in *Christus in Ecclesia cantat*, edited by J. Overath, pp. 47–114. Rome, n.d. [1986].
Spanish: in *Gladino* (Buenos Aires) 9/1987, pp. 5–22.

"Kirche und Wirtschaft in der Verantwortung für die Zukunft der Weltwirtschaft". In *Technik und Mensch* (together with *Renovatio*) 1 (1986): 7–9; also in *Kirche und Wirtschaft in der Verantwortung für die Zukunft der Weltwirtschaft*, edited by G. Fels, pp. 29–37. Cologne, 1987. *American*: in *Communio* 13 (1986): 199–204. Reprinted in *Church and Economy: Common Responsibility for the Future of the World Economy*, edited by J. Thesing, pp. 21–27. Mainz, 1987.

"Teses de Cristologia". In *Novo Testamento e Cristo*, edited by J. E. M. Terra, pp. 3–5. São Paulo, 1986. (From *Dogma und Verkündigung*; see under I.)

"A Cristologia nasce da oração". In *Questões actuais de Cristologia*, edited by J. E. M. Terra, pp. 52–65. São Paolo, 1985. (From *Orientaciones Cristológicas*, 1983, see above).

"Theologie und Kirche". *IKaZ* 15 (1986): 515–33.
Italian: in *Communio* 15 (1986): 92–111.
Canadian: separate offprint, St. Michael's College. Toronto, 1986.
Spanish: in *Tierra nueva* 16 (1987): 5–19.

"Freiheit und Befreiung: Die anthropologische Vision der Instruktion 'Libertatis conscientia'". *IKaZ* 15 (1986): 409–24.
Italian: in *Il nuovo Areopago* 5 (1986): 7–24.
Hungarian: in *Mérleg* (1987/3), pp. 219–36.
Polish: in *Znak* 40, no. 388 (1988): 4–20.

Geleitwort: R. Spaemann, R. Löw, P. Koslowski, *Evolutionismus und Christentum*, pp. vii–ix. Weinheim, 1986.

"Zum Fortgang der Ökumene". *ThQ* 166 (1986): 243–48; also in *Kirche, Ökumene, Politik* (see under section I).

"Wie sollte heute ein Bischof sein? Gedanken aus Anlaß eines Jubiläums". *Der Bischof in seiner Zeit: Festgabe für Joseph Kardinal Höffner*, edited by P. Berglar and O. Engels, pp. 469–75. Cologne, 1986.

"Le Baptême et la foi". *Al-Liqâ/Communio* 1 (1986): 15–24.

"Marktwirtschaft und Ethik". In *Stimmen der Kirche zur Wirtschaft*, edited by L. Roos, pp. 50–58. Cologne, 1986.

— 1987 —

"Omelia in occasione della festa di S. Tommaso d'Aquino". *Ang* 64 (1987): 189–92.

English: in *New Blackfriars* 68 (1987): 113–15.

"Buchstabe und Geist des Zweiten Vatikanums in den Konzilsreden von Kardinal Frings". *IKaZ* 16 (1987): 251–65; and in *Kölner Beiträge*, new series 12 (1987).

American: in *Communio* 14 (1988): 131–47.

"Das Zeichen der Frau". In Papst Johannes Paul II, *Maria—Gottes Ja zum Menschen: Enzyklika "Mutter des Erlösers"*, pp. 105–28. Freiburg, 1987.

Italian: *Maria il Sì di Dio all'uomo*, pp. 7–37. Brescia, 1987.

American: *Mary: God's Yes to Man*, pp. 9–40. San Francisco, 1988.

"Pater Rupert Mayer—Zeuge der Wahrheit". *IKaZ* 16 (1987): 357–63; also in *Predigtsammlung zur Seligsprechung von P. Rupert Mayer SJ*, pp. 24–32. Munich, 1987.

"Omelia, 11.4.87". *Romana: Bollettina della Prelatura della Santa Croce e Opus Dei* 3 (1987): 114–17.

"Sintesi sull'Enciclica 'Redemptoris Mater' ". In J. Ratzinger et al., *La Madonna a vent'anni dal Concilio*, pp. 13–22. Naples and Rome, 1987. Also in *Una luce sul cammino dell'uomo*, pp. 3–12. Vatican City, 1988.

Lithuanian: in *Jonas Paulius II, Enciklika Redemptoris Mater*, in *Logos Knyga*, 1992, pp. 81–98.

"Gottes Macht—unsere Hoffnung". *KlBl* 67 (1987): 343–47; also in *Pastoralblatt für den Diözesen Aachen, Berlin, Essen, Köln, Osnabrück* 40 (1988): 71–83; and in *Kirche, Ökumene, Politik* (see under section I).

— 1988 —

Geleitwort: *M. J. Scheeben—teologo cattolico d'ispirazione tomista*, pp. 9–13. Vatican City, 1988. In *Italian*, pp. 14–18.

Prefazione: *Incontrare Cristo nei sacramenti*, edited by H. Luthe, pp. 5–9. Cinisello Balsamo, 1988.

"Biblical Interpretation in Crisis: On the Question of the Foundations and Approaches of Exegesis Today: Erasmus Lecture 1988". *This World: A Journal of Religion and Public Life* 22 (Summer 1988): 1–19. Again in *Biblical Interpretation in Crisis: The Ratzinger Conference in Bible and Church*, edited by R. J. Neuhaus, pp. 1–23. Michigan, 1989. *Italian*: in I. de la Potterie et al., *L'esegesi cristiana oggi*, pp. 93–125. Casale Monferrato, 1991.

"Homilie zum Heimgang von H. U. von Balthasar". *IKaZ* 17 (1988): 473–76. Reprinted in *Hans Urs von Balthasar: Gestalt und Werk*, edited by K. Lehmann and W. Kasper, pp. 349–54. Cologne, 1989.

"El cisma de Lefèbvre". *La revista Católica* 88, no. 1079 (1988): 224–28. Translated into various languages, such as in *Cuestiones actuales de Cristología y Eclesiología*, pp. 27–31. Bogotà, 1990.

"Dieci anni di pontificato". In *Giovanni Paolo II pellegrino per il Vangelo*, pp. 17–21. Rome, 1988.
Polish: in *Ethos Rok* 1, no. 4 (1988): 5–11.
Also in *Spanish* (1989).

Presentazione: G. Vigini, *Agostino d'Ippona*, pp. 5f. Milan, 1988.

"Uno sguardo teologico sulla procreazione umana". *Medicina e morale* 3/4 (1988): 507–21.
German: in *IKaZ* 18 (1989): 61–71; reprinted in *Bioethik*, edited by R. Löw, pp. 28–47. Cologne, 1990.
Spanish: in *Ecclesia* 3 (1989): 159–74.
Polish: in *Ethos Rok* 1, no. 4 (1988): 134–47.

" 'Du bist voll der Gnade': Elemente biblischer Marienfrömmigkeit". *IKaZ* 17 (1988): 540–50.
American: in *Communio* 16 (1989): 54–68.
Italian: private printing, Cinisello Balsamo, 1990.
Spanish: in *Cuestiones actuales de Cristología y Ecclesiología*, pp. 11–23. Bogotà, 1990.
Portuguese: in *Communio/Brasil* 8 (1991): 455–67.

"Die Frau, Hüterin des Menschen". In *Die Zeit der Frau: Apostolisches Schreiben "Mulieris dignitatem" Papst Johannes Pauls II*, pp. 109–20. Freiburg, 1988.
Italian: in *Il tempo della donna*, pp. 5–17. Brescia, 1990.

— 1989 —
Vorwort and "Schriftauslegung im Widerstreit: Zur Frage nach Grundlagen und Weg der Exegese heute". In *Schriftauslegung im Widerstreit* (see under II). (Extended version of *Biblical Interpretation in Crisis*; see above, section for 1988.)
Italian: in *L'esegesi cristiana oggi*, pp. 93–125. Casale Monferrato, 1991.
Spanish: *La interpretación biblica en crisis*. Lima, 1995.
French: in R. Guardini et al., *L'Exégèse chrétienne aujourd'hui*, pp. 63–109. Paris, 2000.

"Omelia in occasione della festa delle stimmate di S. Francesco nel santuario della Verna". *StFr* 85 (1988): 395–99.

"Ce que croire veut dire". *Sources* 14 (1989): 49–63.

"Der Auftrag der Religion angesichts der gegenwärtigen Krise von Friede und Gerechtigkeit". *IKaZ* 18 (1989): 113–22.
Reprinted in *Der konziliare Prozeß—Utopie und Realität*, edited by P. Beyerhaus and L. von Padberg, pp. 124–36. Aßlar, 1990.
Italian: in *Mondo e missione*, December 1989, pp. 656–60.
American: in *Communio* 16 (Winter 1989): 540–51.
Spanish: in *Communio/Chile* 7 (1990): 5–13.

"Anstelle eines Festschriftbeitrages: Brief an Helmut Kuhn". In ΑΝΟΔΟΣ: *Festschrift für Helmut Kuhn*, edited by R. Hofmann et al., pp. 1–3. Weinheim, 1989.

"Difficoltà di fronte alla fede oggi in Europa". *OR* 139 (June 30/July 1, 1989): 7; translated in the various editions of *OR*; reprinted in various periodicals.

"Der Heilige Geist und die Kirche". In *Servitium pietatis: Festschrift für Hans Herrmann Kard. Groer*, edited by A. Coreth and I. Fux, pp. 91–97. Maria Roggendorf, 1989. Also in *Bilder der Hoffnung* (see under section I).

Introduzione: Congregazione per la Dottrina della Fede, *"Mysterium Filii Dei": Dichiarazione e commenti*, pp. 9–24. Vatican City, 1989.

— 1990 —
"Perspektiven der Priesterausbildung heute". In *Unser Auftrag*, edited by K. Hillenbrand, pp. 11–38. Würzburg, 1990. Also in *Ein neues Lied für den Herrn* (see under section I).
   French: in J. Ratzinger et al., *Mission et formation du prêtre*, pp. 1–24. Namur, 1990.
   American: in *The Catholic Priest*. San Francisco, 1990.

"Jesus Christus heute". *IKaZ* 19 (1990): 56–70.
   Spanish: in Universidad Complutense, *Jesucristo hoy: Cursos de Verano*, pp. 297–316. El Escorial, 1989.
   American: in *Communio* 16 (1990): 68–87.
   Italian: in *Communio* 19 (1990): 121–39; also in *Rivista Cistercense* 7 (1990): 223–37.
   Portuguese: in *Communio* 14 (1997): 202–18.

"Perspectivas y tareas del Catolicesimo en la Actualidad y de cara al futuro". In *Catolicismo y cultura*, pp. 89–115. Madrid, 1990. Reprinted in revised form in *Communio/Chile* 7 (1990): 79–90.
   Italian: in *Il nuovo Areopago* 9, no. 2 (1990): 7–24. In revised form, under the title *Le vie della fede nell'attuale momento della svolta*. Private printing, Rome, 1990.

Joseph Cardinal Ratzinger: Bibliography 355

"Die Aktualität der Gestalt Pius' V. (1566–1572)". In *Pax et Iustitia: Festschrift für Alfred Kostelecky zum 70. Geburtstag*, edited by H. W. Kaluza et al., pp. 623–29. Berlin, 1990.

"Ein Katechismus für die Weltkirche?" *HerKorr* 44 (1990): 341ff.

Presentazione: Congregazione per la Dottrina della Fede, *"Donum vitae": Instruzione e commenti*, pp. 5–10. Vatican City, 1990.

"Glaube—eine Antwort auf die Urfrage des Menschen: Die Instruktion über die kirchliche Berufung des Theologen". *OR(D)* 20, no. 27 (1990): 6–7; also in *OR* 140 (June 27, 1990): 1, 6; and in *IKaZ* 19 (1990): 561–65.

"Entgegnung zu Th. Schneider, Römisch (und) Katholisch?" *OR* 39 (1990): 318–20.

"Una compagnia sempre riformanda". *Litterae Communionis, Quaderni* 24, 1990; also in *Communio* 19 (1990): 91–105 (reprinted several times).

"Europa—Hoffnungen und Gefahren". Separate offprint, Speyer, 1990.

"Discorso introduttivo alla III giornata del Simposio di Newman". *ED* 43 (1990): 431–36.
German: in *J. H. Newman, Lover of Truth*, edited by K. Strolz and M. Binder, pp. 141–46. Rome, 1991.

"Capire e valutare il Sacerdozio". In *Vivere* 18 (1990): 17–26.
German: in *Amtsblatt der Österreichischen Bischofskonferenz* 4 (1990): 7–12.
American: in *Communio* 17 (1990): 617–27.

"Chiara, 'silenziosa parole' di vita per la Chiesa". In *Forum Sororum* 4–5 (1990): 234–39.
Spanish: in *Selecciones de Francescanesimo* 30 (1992): 268–74.

— 1991 —

"Le Primat de Pierre et l'unité de l'Église". *PenCath* 46 (1991): 11–25.

Spanish: in *Selecciones de Francescanesimo* 30 (1992): 268–74.

Portuguese: in *Communio/Brasil* 7 (1990): 249–60.

Italian: in *ED* 44 (1991): 158–76.

English: (some extracts) in *Sceptre Bulletin* 17 (1992): 3–9.

"Origem e natureza da Igreja". *Communio/Brasil* 7 (1990): 234–48.
Spanish: in *Ecclesia* 5 (1991): 7–23.

"Igreja universal e Igreja particular: A missão do bispo". *Communio/Brasil* 7 (1990): 261–72.

"Biblische Vorgaben für die Kirchenmusik". In *Brixener Initiative Musik und Kirche: 3. Symposion "Choral and Mehrstimmigkeit" 1990*, pp. 9–21. Brixen, 1991. Also in *Ein neues Lied für den Herrn* (see under section I).

"Omelia per il IX Centenario della nascita di S. Bernardo". *Riv. Cistercense* 7 (1990): 219–22.

Presentazione: M. Di Ruberto, *Bibliografia del Card. Pietro Parente*, pp. 3–6. Vatican City, 1991.

Introduzione: Congregazione per la Dottrina della Fede, *"Orationis Formas": Lettera e commenti*, pp. 9–13. Vatican City, 1991.

"The Nature of Priesthood". *Faith* 23 (1991): 13ff.

Presentazione: *Santi e santità dopo il Concilio Vaticano II*, edited by F. Peloso, pp. 5f. Rome, 1991.

"'Vorsitz in der Liebe': Der Cathedra-Altar von St. Peter zu Rom". In *Kirche im Kommen: Festschrift für J. Stimpfle*, edited by E. Kleindienst and G. Schmuttermayr, pp. 423–29. Berlin, 1991. Also in *Bilder der Hoffnung* (see under section I).

Geleitwort: P. Berglar, *Vom Fischer zum Stellvertreter*, pp. 7f. Munich, 1991.

— 1992 —

Vorwort: J.-B. d'Onorio, *Le Pape et le gouvernement de l'Église*, pp. 9f. Paris, 1992.

Presentazione: Giovanni Paoli II, *I dieci commandamenti,* edited by D. del Rio, pp. 5ff. Cinisello Balsamo, 1992.

"Predigt am Fest des hl. Augustinus". In *Buße—Umkehr: Formen der Vergebung,* edited by F. Breid, pp. 250–56. Steyr, 1992.

Geleitwort: *Enchiridion familiae,* edited by A. Sarmiento and J. Escrivà Ivars, 1:cvx–cxx. Madrid, 1992.

"Die Bedeutung religiöser und sittlicher Werte in der pluralistischen Gesellschaft". *IKaZ* 21 (1992): 500–512; also in *Wahrheit, Werte, Macht* (see under section I).
Italian: in *Communio* 22 (1993): 372–89.
French: in *Communio* 19 (1994): 50–66.

"Gewissen und Wahrheit". In *Fides quaerens intellectum: Beiträge zum Fundamentaltheologie: M. Seckler zum 65. Geburtstag,* edited by M. Kessler et al., pp. 293–309. Tübingen and Basel, 1992. Much abridged in *Die Weltfriedensbotschaften Papst Johannes Pauls II,* edited by D. Squicciarini, pp. 289–300. Berlin, 1992. Reprinted in *Der Wahrheit verpflichtet,* edited by S. Rehder and M. Wolff, pp. 135–58. Würzburg, 1998. Also in *Wahrheit, Werte, Macht* and in *Vom Wiederauffinden der Mitte* (see under section I).
Polish: in *Ethos* 15/16 (1991): 171–84.
German: in *Ethos* 1 (1993): 131–66.
French: in *Communio* 21 (1996): 93–114.
American: in *Crisis of Conscience,* edited by J. M. Haas, pp. 1–20. New York, 1996.

" 'Daß Gott alles in allem sei': Vom christlichen Glauben an das ewige Leben". *KlBl* 72 (1992): 203–7. Reprinted in N. Kutschki and J. Hoeren, *Kleines Credo für Verunsicherte,* pp. 121–40. Freiburg, 1993.
Italian: in *Palestra del Clero* 71 (1992): 7–20; separate offprint, Adria/Rovigo, 1992.

"Communio—ein Programm". *IKaZ* 21 (1992): 454–63; in various editions of *Communio.*

"Thorn in the Flesh". *The Catholic World Report* (1992): 48–54.

"Probleme von Glaubens- und Sittenlehre im europäischen Kontext". In J. Ratzinger et al., *Zu Grundfragen der Theologie heute*, pp. 7–17. Paderborn, 1992. Also in *Ein neues Lied für den Herrn* and in *Vom Wiederauffinden der Mitte* (see under section I).

"Der Mensch—Objekt oder Person? Christliche Erwägungen zu Fragen der Bioethik". *Christliches Krankenhaus* 31 (1992): 12–22.
Italian: in *Bioetica fondamentale e generale*, edited by G. Russo, pp. 325–29. Turin, 1995.

"Bioética e Moral Cristã". *Leopoldianum/Santos-Brasil* 18 (1992): 121–30.

— 1993 —
Introduzione: *Il Catechismo del Vaticano II*, pp. 5–13. Cinisello Balsamo, 1993.

"Der christliche Glaube vor der Herausforderung der Kulturen". In *Evangelium und Inkulturation (1492–1992): Salzburger Hochschulwochen 1992*, edited by P. Gordan, pp. 9–26. Graz, 1993. Also in KNA, *Öki* 52/53 (December 1992): 5–15.
Spanish: in *Ecclesia* 7 (1993): 369–86; in *Mercurio* (1993).
Italian: (revised version) in *Nuova umanità* 16 (1994): 95–118.
English: (extended version) in *Origins: Christ, Faith, and the Challenge of Cultures* 24 (1995): 678–86. The same version (*Spanish*) in *Communio* 18 (1996): 152–70.

"Igreja e Europa". *Communio* 9 (1992): 540–47.

"Natura e finalità del Catechismo della Chiesa cattolica e inculturazione della fede". In *Un dono per oggi: Il catechismo della Chiesa cattolica: Riflessioni per l'accoglienza*, edited by T. Stenico, pp. 29–39. Milan, 1992.

"L'educazione dei figli di Dio". *Il nuovo Areopago* 11 (1992): 110–12.

"Réponse". In Institut de France. Académie des sciences morales et politiques, *Installation du Card. Ratzinger*, pp. 19–23. Paris, 1992. Also in *Acta philosophica* 2 (1993): 301–6.
Hungarian: in *Mérleg* 1993/1, pp. 15–19.
Portuguese: in *Communio/Brasil* 10 (1993): 430–34.

Presentazione: L. Giussani, *Un avvenimento di vita cioè una storia*, edited by C. Di Martino. Rome, 1993.

"Qué cree la Iglesia". *Communio* 15 (1993): 93–98.
Italian: in *Sinodo Romano: La fede della Chiesa di Roma: Quaderni nuovi*, series 2 (1993), pp. 57–63. Also in *Il Catechismo della Chiesa Cattolica*, pp. 7–13. Vatican City, 1993.

Introduzione: Congregazione per la Dottrina della Fede, *"Mysterium Ecclesiae": Dichiarazione e commenti*, pp. 7–15. Vatican City, 1993.

"Il Catechismo della Chiesa cattolica e l'ottimismo dei redenti". *Communio* 22 (1993): 8–23.

"Wollen, was Gott will: Der selige Josemaría Escrivá". In *Die Welt—eine Leidenschaft: Chance und Charisma des Seligen Josemaría Escrivá*, edited by K. M. Becker and J. Eberle, pp. 10–17. St. Ottilien, 1993.

"Presentación del Catecismo de la Iglesia Católica". *Ecclesia* 7 (1993): 131–36.

"Hinführung zum Katechismus der katholischen Kirche". In J. Ratzinger and C. Schönborn, *Kleine Hinführung zum Katechismus der katholischen Kirche*, pp. 9–34. Munich, 1993.
Spanish: in *El Catechismo postconciliar*, edited by O. González de Cardedal and J. A. Martínez Camino, pp. 47–64. Madrid, 1993.
American: in *Communio* 19 (1993): 469–84. And in *Introduction to the Catechism of the Catholic Church*, pp. 11–36. San Francisco, 1994.
Polish: in *Wprowadzenie do Katechizmu Kościoła katolickiego*, pp. 9–22. Warsaw, 1994.

French: in *Introduction au Catéchisme de l'Église catholique*. Paris, 1995.
Also in *Catalan* (1995) and *Slovakian* (1995).

"L'attualità di S. Brigida di Svezia". In *Santa Brigida profeta di tempi nuovi*, pp. 71–81. Rome, 1993. *English*: ibid., pp. 82–92.

"Glaube als Weg: Hinführung zur Enzyklika des Papstes über die Grundlagen der Moral". *IKaZ* 22 (1993): 564–70. *Italian*: in *Medicina e morale*, no. 6 (1993): 1101–110. Also in *Veritatis splendor: Testo integrale e commento filosofico-teologico*, edited by A. Lucas, pp. 5–9. Milan, 1994. And in *Veritatis splendor*, edited by G. Russo, pp. 9–19. Rome, 1994. *American*: in *Communio* 20 (1994): 199–207.

Geleitwort: F. Mußner, *Maria, die Mutter Jesu im Neuen Testament*, pp. 7–12. St. Ottilien, 1993.

Introduzione: Congregazione per la Dottrina della Fede, *"Donum Veritatis": Istruzione e commenti*, pp. 9–14. Vatican City, 1993.

— 1994 —

"Un passato che non li riguarda". (Text of the interview in *Time*.) Supplement to *30 Giorni*, January 1, 1994, pp. 3–30.

"Mein Bruder, der Domkapellmeister". In *Der Domkapellmeister: Georg Ratzinger—ein Leben für die Regensburger Domspatzen*, edited by P. Winterer, pp. 11–23. Regensburg, 1994.

"Evangelisierung, Katechese und Katechismus". Separate off-print, Paderborn, 1994. Also in *ThGl* 84 (1994): 273–88. *Italian*: in *Vivens homo: Rivista teologia Fiorentina* 5/1 (1994): 5–19.

"La lettera Apostolica 'Ordinatio Sacerdotalis'". *CivCatt* 145 (1994): 61–74; in various versions, also in *OR* in *Italian, English, French, German*; also in *IKaZ* 23 (1994): 337–45. Reprinted in Congregazione per la Dottrina della Fede, *Dall' "Inter insigniores" all' "Ordinatio Sacerdotalis": Documenti e commenti*, pp. 9–23. Vatican City, 1996.

Swedish: in *Svensk Pastoralstidskrift* 5 (1995): 69–74.

"**Israel, the Church and the World**". *Catholic International* 5 (1994): 309–14.

German: in *Homiletisch-liturgisches Korrespondenzblatt*, new series, 11 (1993/94): 233–44; separate offprint, Regensburg, 1994. Included in *Evangelium, Katechese, Katechismus* (see under section I).

Italian: in *Palestra del Clero* 73 (1994): 169–80; the first part in *Le Porte d'Oriente: Newsletter* II, 3 (1994): 15–23.

Spanish: in *Communio* 17 (1995): 216–28.

"**Glaubenskraft und Glaubenszweifel**". In *Lebens-Gesätze*, edited by K. Hurtz, pp. 11–17. Regensburg, 1994.

"**In der Spannung zwischen Regensburger Tradition und nachkonziliarer Reform**". *MS(D)* 114 (1994): 379–89; also in *Ein neues Lied für den Herrn* (see under section I).

English: in *Sacra musica* 122 (1995): 5–17.

"**Dio nel libro di Giovanni Paolo II**". *Communio* 23 (1994): 81–86.

American: in *Communio* 22 (1995): 107–12.

French: in *Communio* 20 (1995): 113–19.

Introduzione: Congregazione per la Dottrina della Fede, "*Communionis notio*": *Lettera e commenti*, pp. 7–12. Vatican City, 1994.

— 1995 —

"**La nuova Alleanza: Sulla teologia dell'Alleanza nel Nuovo Testamento**". *Rassegna di teologia* 36 (1995): 9–22. Extract in *L'Homme nouveau* 46 (April 16, 1995): 7f.

French: in *Revue des sciences morales et politiques* 150 (1995): 17–36; also in *Communio* 22 (1997): 93–112.

German: in *IKaZ* 24 (1995): 193–208.

Portuguese: in *Communio* 12 (1995): 395–409.

American: in *Communio* 22 (1995): 635–51.

"**Et incarnatus est de Spiritu Sancto ex Maria Virgine**". *30 Giorni*, April 1995, pp. 65–73.

German: in *KlBl* 75 (1995): 107–10; also in *Gott ist uns nah* (see under section I).

Italian: in *Maria nel mistero del Verbo incarnato: Theotokos: Rivista interdisciplinare di Mariologia* 3 (1995): 291–302.

"Zur Lage der Ökumene". In *Perspectives actuelles sur l'oecuménisme*, edited by J.-L. Leuba, pp. 231–44. Louvain-la-Neuve, 1995.

"A proposito de la 'Evangelium vitae'". *Communio* 24 (1995): 167–73.
Italian: in *Presenza pastorale* 65 (1995): 569–76. Also in *Il vangelo della vita*, edited by S. De Giorgi, pp. 51–58. Rome, 1995. And in Pont. Academia vitae, *Evangelium vitae: Enciclica e commenti*, pp. 153–60. Vatican City, 1995.

Prefazione: L. Grygiel, *La "Dieci" di don Didimo Mantiero*, pp. 5–9. Milan, 1995.

Vorwort: Johannes Paul II, *Aus der Kraft der Hoffnung leben*. Freiburg, 1995.

"La nuova evangelizzazione". In *Leonianum*, pp. 43–50. Anagni, 1995. Also in *Università, cultura, evangelizzazione*, edited by P. Poupard, pp. 24–37. Rome, 1997.
Spanish: in *Ecclesia* 10 (1996): 351–61.

"Verantwortung für Kirche und Welt in dieser Zeit: Hommage an Kardinal König". In *30 Jahre Pro oriente: Kard. König zu seinem 90. Geburtstag*, edited by A. Stirnemann and G. Wiflinger, pp. 42–44. Innsbruck and Vienna, 1995.

Prefazione: *Paolo VI: Un credo per vivere*, pp. 5–17. Milan, 1995.

"Un instancabile maestro della 'lectio divina'". In *Carlo M. Martini da 15 anni sulla cattedra di Ambrogio*, pp. 101–3. Milan, 1995.

Introduzione: Congregazione per la Dottrina della Fede, *Cura Pastorale delle persone omosessuali: Lettera e commenti*, pp. 7–13. Vatican City, 1995.

"Freiheit und Wahrheit". *IKaZ* 24 (1995): 526–42. Again in *1848: Erbe und Auftrag*, edited by O. Scrinzi and J. Schwab, pp. 83–99. Graz, 1998.

Italian: in *Communio* 24 (1995): 9–28; also in *StCatt* 40 (1996): 820–30.

American: in *Communio* 23 (1996): 16–35.

French: in *Communio* 24 (1999): 83–101.

Spanish: in *Humanitas* 14 (1999): 199–222.

— 1996 —

"Il ministero e la vita dei presbiteri". In Congr. pro Clericis, *Sacrum ministerium*, 2:7–21. 1996. Also in *StCatt* 40 (1996): 324–32. And in I. Sanchez and C. Sepe, *Un amore più grande*, pp. 89–104. Milan, 1996.

German: in *Eucharisteria: Festschrift für Damaskinos Papandreou*, edited by M. Brun and W. Schneemelcher, pp. 125–37. Athens, 1996.

French: in *Nova et vetera* 71 (1996): 6–19.

English: in *Position paper* 286/287, pp. 285–92, 323–29. Dublin, 1997.

"Die Weihnachtsbotschaft in der Basilika Santa Maria Maggiore". In *Ab oriente et occidente (Mt 8:11): Kirche aus Ost und West: Gedenkschrift für W. Nyssen*, edited by M. Schneider and W. Berschin, pp. 361–66. St. Ottilien, 1996. Also in *Bilder der Hoffnung* (see under section I).

Presentazione: J. Tscholl, *Dio e il bello in S. Agostino*, pp. 5–7. Milan, 1996.

Presentazione: G. Codias, *I Padri nella liturgia delle ore*. Vatican City, 1996.

"Zur lage von Glaube und Theologie heute". *IKaZ* 25 (1996): 359–72; also in the various editions of *OR*. And in *Stets war es der Hund, der starb*, edited by M. Müller, pp. 33–53. Aachen, 1998.

Spanish: in *Ecclesia* 10 (1996): 485–502; also in *Communio* 19 (1997): 13–27; and in *Humanitas* 12 (1997): 280–93. An extract

in *Enciclopedia del Cristianesimo*. Navarre, 1997. And again in
Consejo Episcopal Latino americano, *Fe y teología en America
Latina*, pp. 13–36. Bogotá, 1997. And in *Gladius* 43 (1998):
13–27.
Italian: in *CivCatt* 147 (1996): 477–90.
French: in *Communio* 22 (1997): 69–88; and in *Documentation
catholique*.
Portuguese: in *Communio/Brasil* 17 (1998): 185–201.

"O Sinat de Caná: Homilia". *Communio* 13 (1996): 553–58.

Introduction: R. Guardini, *The Lord*, pp. xi–xiv. Washington,
1996.

Introduzione: Congregazione per la Dottrina della Fede, *Dall'
"Inter insigniores" all' "Ordinatio Sacerdotalis"*: *Documenti e com-
menti*, pp. 9–23. Vatican City, 1996.
Spanish: in Congr. para la Doctrina de la Fe, *El Sacramento del
Orden y la Mujer: De la Inter insigniores a la Ordinatio sacerdotalis:
Introducción y comentarios*, pp. 17–33. Madrid, 1997.

— 1997 —

"Ein Demütiger für die Demütigen: Laudatio auf Erzbischof
Tamkevicius". *Akademische Monatsblätter*, January 1997, pp.
3–5.

"Portiunkula—Einladung ins Gebet". *Heilen* 16 (1997): 31–37.

"La grandezza dell'essere umano è la sua somiglianza con
Dio". *Dolentium hominum* 12 (1997): 16–20.
Spanish: in *Educación medical, Universidad Católica de Chile* 16
(1998): 18–22.

"La Angustia de una Ausencia: Meditación sobre el Sábado
escrita por el Cardenal Prefecto para la Doctrina de la
Fe". *Humanitas* 12 (1997): 116–23.

Préface: M. Schooyans, *L'Évangile face au désordre mondial*, pp. i–iv.
Paris, 1997.

"Il quinto sigillo". *La guida* 16 (1997): 11–13.

"Le Dialogue interreligieux et la relation judéo-chrétienne".
Revue des sciences morales et politiques, 1997, pp. 127–40; extract
in *Géopolitique* 58 (1997): 46–53.
German: in *IKaZ* 26 (1997): 419–29.
American: in *Communio* 25 (1998): 29–41.
Spanish: in *Communio* 20 (1999): 199–210; also in *Reseña Bíblica*
26 (2000): 15–26.
Polish: in *Ethos* 49–50 (2000): 202–13.

"Guardare Cristo". In C. Ruini et al., *Dialoghi in Cattedrale*, pp.
89–111. Milan, 1997.
German: in *Diakon Anianus*, no. 26 (November 1997): 6–15.
Also in *Stets war es der Hund, der starb*, edited by M. Müller, pp.
375–93. Aachen, 1998.
Spanish: in *Humanitas* 18 (2000): 202–20.

"Eucaristia come genesi della missione". *Il Regno* 42 (1997):
588–93; also in *Ecclesia orans* 15, no. 2 (1998): 137–61.
Spanish: in *Communio* 19 (1997): 495–513.
German: in *FoKTh* 14 (1998): 81–98.
Portuguese: in *Communio/Brasil* 17 (1998): 64–84.
English: in *ThQ* 65 (2000): 245–64.

Presentazione: M. Thurian, *Passione per l'unità e contemplazione del
mistero*, edited by Matthias R. Richter and Mario Russotto,
pp. 5–11. Vatican City, 1997.

Grußwort: For *Die heilige Liturgie*, edited by F. Breid, pp. 9–12.
Steyr, 1997.

— 1998 —

"¿Qué es propriamente le Teología?" In *El Cardenal Ratzinger en
la Universidad de Navarra: Discursos, Coloquios y Encuentros*, pp.
23–30. Pamplona, 1998.
Polish: in *Ethos* 5/4 (1999): 19–23.
German: in *Die Weite des Mysteriums: Christliche Identität im Dialog: Für Horst Bürkle*, edited by K. Krämer and A. Paus, pp.
14–19. Freiburg, 2000.

Introduzione: Congregazione per la Dottrina della Fede, *Dichiarazione sull'Aborto procurato: Testo della Dichiarazione e Documenti degli Episcopati*, pp. 7–18. Vatican City, 1998.

Introduzione: Congregazione per la Dottrina della Fede, *Sulla Pastorale dei Divorziati risposati: Documenti, commenti e studi*, pp. 7–29. Vatican City, 1998.

Spanish: in Congr. para la Doctrina de la Fe, *Sobre la atención pastoral de los divorciados vueltos a casar: Documentos, comentarios y estudios*, pp. 9–35. Madrid, 2000.

"Glaube zwischen Vernunft und Gefühl". In *Mitteilungen des Übersee-Club Hamburg 1998* (separate offprint); also in *Die neue Ordnung* 52 (1998): 164–77; and in *Konferenzblatt für Theologie und Seelsorge* (Brixen) 110 (1999): 133–44.

Polish: in *Ethos* 44 (1998): 59–72.

Italian: in *Archivio Teologico Torinese* 1 (1999): 7–19.

"Movimenti ecclesiali e loro collocazione teologica". *Il Regno* 43 (1998): 399–407; also in *Orientamenti pastorali* 6/98, pp. 8–30; and in *Communio* 27 (1998): 65–83. Likewise in Pontificium Consilium pro Laicis, *I movimenti nella Chiesa*, pp. 23–51. Vatican City, 1999. In *Nuova Umanità* 21 (1999): 511–38; in *Rassegna di Teologia* 40 (1999): 805–26; in *IusE* 12 (2000): 3–28. And in F. González Fernández, *I movimenti: Dalla Chiesa degli apostoli a oggi*, pp. 303–36. Milan, 2000.

German: in *IKaZ* 27 (1998): 431–48. Also in *Lebensaufbrüche: Geistlicher Bewegungen in Deutschland*, edited by Peter Wolff, pp. 23–56. Vallendar-Schönstatt, 2000.

American: in *Communio* 25 (1998): 480–504. Also in Pontificium Consilium pro Laicis, *Movements in the Church*, pp. 23–51. Vatican City, 1999.

Spanish: in *Communio* 21 (1999): 87–108.

French: in *Communio* 24 (1999): 77–103. Also in *Don de l'Esprit, Espérance pour les hommes*, pp. 25–50. Nouan-le-Fuzelier, 1999.

"L'apertura degli Archivi del Sant'Uffizio". *Atti dei Convegni Lincei* 142 (Rome, 1998): 181–89.

"Culto divino e responsibilità politica". In J. Ratzinger et al., *I cattolici e la politica oggi: Quaderni del Centro Pastorale Cremona 6* (1998): 7–18; reprinted in *Notiziario della Banca Popolare di Sondrio*, no. 78 (December 1998): 1–7.
German: in *Kölner Beiträge*, new series, 20 (Cologne, 1998).

— 1999 —

"Stellungnahme". *StZ* 124 (1999): 169–71. *"Schlußwort"*. Ibid. 420–22.
Spanish: in *SelTeol* 152 (1999): 303–4.

"Culture and Truth: Reflections on the Encyclical". *Origins* 28 (1999): 625–31; also in *Sacerdos* 26 (2000): 19–28.
German: "Die Einheit des Glaubens und die Vielfalt der Kulturen: Reflexionen im Anschluß an die Enzyklika 'Fides et ratio'". *ThGl* 89 (1999): 141–52. In *Wahrheit, die uns trägt*, pp. 24–40. Paderborn, 1999. And in *IKaZ* 28 (1999): 289–305.
Italian: in *Per una lettura dell'Enciclica Fides et ratio: Quaderni de "L'Osservatore Romano"* 45 (Vatican City, 1999): 9–15, 245–59. Also in *Fides et ratio: Lettera enciclica di Giovanni Paolo II*, edited by R. Fisichella, pp. 117–28. Cinisello Balsamo, 1999.
Portuguese: in *Communio* 16 (1999): 464–72, 557–68.
Spanish: (extensively reworked version) in *Alfa y Omega/ Documentos* (= supplement to *ABC*), no. 200 (February 17, 2000): 1–18.
Polish: in *ACra* 32 (2000): 231–46.

"La nuova Evangelizzazione". In *Terzo Millenio: Ipotesi sulla parrochia*, edited by G. Tangorra and C. Zucarro, pp. 105–14. Rome, 1999.

"Das Ende der Zeit". In *Das Ende der Zeit? Die Provokation der Rede von Gott*, edited by T. R. Peters and C. Urban, pp. 13–31. Mainz, 1999.
Italian: in *Nuntium* 8 (1999): 31–47.

Einleitung: *Johannes Paul II—Zeuge des Evangeliums: Perspektiven des Papstes an der Schwelle des dritten Jahrtausends*, edited by S. O. Horn and A. Riebel, pp. 16–17. Würzburg, 1999.

"Das Problem der christlichen Prophetie: Nils Christian Hvidt im Gespräch mit Joseph Kardinal Ratzinger". *IKaZ* 28 (1999): 177–88.

"Il magistero dei Padri nell'Enciclica 'Fides et ratio'". *Per la Filosofia: Filosofia e insegnamento* 45 (1999): 3–7.

Presentazione: *Dilexit Ecclesiam: Studi in onore del prof. Donato Valentini*, edited by G. Coffele, pp. 5–8. Rome, 1999.

"O nihilizmie, piekle i kryzysie w Kościele: Rozmowa z Kardynałem Josephem Ratzingerem". *Fronda*, no. 15/16 (Warsaw, 1999): 6–21; an extract in *Rzeczpospolita* 10–11 lipca 1999, D4. *German*: in *Die Tagespost*, October 23, 1999, pp. 5–6.

"Dialog jest koniecznością: Kardynał Joseph Ratzinger odpowiada na pytania 'Znaku'". *ZNAK Miesięcznik Rok LI, Kraków LISTOPAD* (534, 11/1999): 4–24.

"Il mistero e l'operazione della grazie: Intervista con Gianni Cardinale". *30 Giorni*, June 1999, pp. 11–14. *German*: in *30 Tage*, June–July 1999, pp. 9–12.

"Dio dà inizio a una storia: Dall'intervento del Card. Ratzinger alla Pontificia Università Lateranense il 15. dicembre 1998". *30 Giorni*, July–August 1999, pp. 42–45. *German*: in *30 Tage*, August 1999, pp. 54–57.

"La sorpresa di un incontro: Ratzinger al Seminario dei vescovi sui movimenti: due ore di domande". *Tracce—Litterae communionis* 7 (1999): 48–50.

Geleitwort: R. Cantalamessa, *Komm, Schöpfer Geist: Betrachtungen zum Hymnus Veni Creator Spiritus*, pp. 11–14. Freiburg, 1999. Also in *Kirche heute*, June 2000, pp. 8–9.

"Für ein Christentum, das trägt: Predigt anläßlich des Hauptfestes der Priesterbruderschaft St. Salvator am 30. August 1998". *Communio* (Mitteilungen an die Freunde und Förderer der Priesterbruderschaft St. Salvator in Straubing, Diözese Regensburg) 2 (1999): 2–3.

"Predigt von S. Em. Kardinal Ratzinger am 17. April 1999 in Weimar". *Pro Missa Tridentina*, no. 17 (September 1999): 3–6.

"Église universelle et Église particulière: La Charge épiscopale". In *L'Évêque et son ministère*, pp. 27–40. Vatican City, 1999.

"Życie—fundamentalną wartością i nienaruszalnym prawem człowieka" (Polish translation of the lecture "Il rispetto sulla vita" given on December 19, 1987, in the Augustinianum, Rome). In *Medycyna i prawo: za czy przeciw życiu?* edited by E. Sgreccia et al., pp. 20–25. Lublin, 1999.

" 'Teologia sapienziale': Sollecitudine di Giovanni Paolo II per il 3° millennio". In *Fede di Studioso e Obbedienza di Pastore: Atti del Convegno sul 50° del Dottorato di K. Wojtyła e del 20° Pontificato di Giovanni Paolo II*, edited by E. Kaczyński, pp. 77–88. Rome, 1999.
Slovenian: in *Communio* 2 (1999): 97–105.

"La speranza nella luce della Fede". (Written for the occasion of the special European Synod of Bishops, October 8, 1999.) *Il Regno* 19 (1999): 609.

"Peccato e redenzione". (From J. Ratzinger, *Creazione e peccato* [Cinisello Balsamo, 1986].) In S. Ragusa and A. Savorana, *Da duemila anni Cristo, compagnia di Dio all'uomo*, pp. 59–61. Milan, 1999.

"Hinweise zum Motu proprio 'ad tuendam fidem' und zum 'Lehrmäßigen Kommentar' der Glaubenskongregation". In *Gott—ratlos vor dem Bösen?* edited by W. Beinert, pp. 224–27. Freiburg, Basel, and Vienna, 1999.

"Vérité du Christianisme?" Lecture given on November 27, 1999, at the Sorbonne, Paris; extracts in *Le Monde, La Croix* (1999); complete text in *La Documentation catholique*, no. 1, 2000, pp. 29–35; in *30 Jours*, January 2000, pp. 33–44.
German: (extract) in *Frankfurter Allgemeine Zeitung*, January 8, 2000; also (complete text) in *30 Tage* (January 2000), pp. 33–

44. In *Weg und Weite: Festschrift für Karl Lehmann*, edited by A. Raffelt, pp. 631–42. Freiburg, 2001.
Italian: in *30 Giorni*, January 2000, pp. 49–60; also in the *English*, *Portuguese*, and *Spanish* editions of *30 Giorni/30 Days*; likewise in *Vita e Pensiero* , no. 1, 2000, pp. 1–16; in *Nuova umanità* 22 (2000): 187–202; and in *MicroMega: Almanacco di filosofia*, no. 2, 2000, pp. 41–53.
Polish: in *Christianitas*, no. 3, 2000, pp. 11–23; also in *Ethos* 53–54 (2001): 79–90.
Hungarian: (extract, as in *Frankfurter Allgemeinen Zeitung* of January 8, 2000) in *Mérleg*, 2000, pp. 292–301.

"Foi, raison et institutions de l'Église". A reply to the "reader's letter" from Cardinal Eyt (*La Croix*, December 9, 1999), in *La Croix*, December 30, 1999; also in *30 Jours*, February 2000, pp. 33–35.
German: in *30 Tage*, February 2000, pp. 33–35; also in the *English*, *Italian*, *Portuguese*, and *Spanish* editions of *30 Giorni/30 Days*.

"Introducción: El viernes santo". In J. Ratzinger et al., *Via Crucis*, pp. 9–16. Madrid, 1999.

— 2000 —

"Meine Buchempfehlung für Jahr 2000". *Christ in der Gegenwart* 42 (1999): 345.

"Deus locutus est nobis in Filio: Some Reflections on Subjectivity, Christology, and the Church". In *Proclaiming the Truth of Jesus Christ: Papers from the Vallombrosa Meeting*, pp. 13–30. Washington, D.C., 2000.

"Il santo viaggio: Pellegrinaggio e vita cristiana". *Il Regno* 45 (2000): 29–31.

"L'Ecclesiologia della Costituzione Lumen Gentium". *OR* 140 (March 4, 2000): 6–8. Also in *Il Concilio Vaticano II: Recezione e attualità alla luce del Giubileo*, edited by R. Fisichella, pp. 66–81. Cinisello Balsamo, 2000. And in *Nuova umanità* 129/130 (2000): 383–407.

German: in *Die Tagespost*, special supplement, March 2000, pp. 1–8; part published in *Frankfurter Allgemeine Zeitung*, December 22, 2000, p. 46.

Spanish: in *La Eclesiología de la Lumen Gentium*. Lima, 2001.

English: in *OR(E)*, September 19, 2001, pp. 5–8.

"Das Christentum wollte immer mehr sein als nur Tradition". (Interview with P. Bahners and C. Geyer.) *Frankfurter Allgemeine Zeitung*, March 8, 2000.

Italian: in *MicroMega: Almanacco di folosofia*, no. 2, 2000, pp. 53–64; also (an extract) in *Tracce—Litterae Communionis*, no. 4, 2000, pp. 90–91.

Dutch: in *Kwartana*, no. 3 (September 2000): 3–7.

"Presentazione del Documento 'Memoria e riconciliazione: La Chiesa e le colpe del passato' ". *OR*, March 9, 2000, p. 8; also in *30 Giorni*, March 2000, pp. 18–21.

German: (extract) in *KNA* (*Dokumentation*), March 11, 2000, pp. 1–4; full text in *OR(D)*, March 17, 2000, pp. 11–12; also in *30 Tage*, March 2000, pp. 20–23; also in the *English*, *French*, *Portuguese*, and *Spanish* editions of *30 Giorni/30 Days*.

" 'Solo il fatto del perdono permette il riconoscimento del peccato': Le risposte del cardinale Joseph Ratzinger alle domande dei giornalisti durante la conferanza stampa". *30 Giorni*, March 2000, pp. 22–25.

German: in *30 Tage*, March 2000, pp. 24–27; also in the *English*, *French*, *Portuguese*, and *Spanish* editions of *30 Giorni/30 Days*.

"Fe, verdad y cultura: Reflexions a propósito de la Encíclica 'Fides et ratio' ". *RET* 40 (2000): 7–27.

Italian: in *Tracce*, special supplement, no. 3, 2000, pp. 5–30; also in *MicroMega*, no. 3, 2000, pp. 207–24.

"La Trinità fonte, modello y traguardo della Chiesa". *Ho theológos: Rivista della Facoltà Teologica di Sicilia*, no. 1, 2000, pp. 134–47.

"Die Kardinalfrage: Warum mußte Christus sterben? Ein Gespräch mit Joseph Kardinal Ratzinger, dem obersten

Glaubenshüter der katholischen Kirche". *Süddeutsche Zeitung Magazin*, no. 16 (April 20, 2000).

"La morte, una nube sconfitta solo dalle potenza di Dio". (Abbreviated text from *Il cammino pasquale*; see under section I.) *L'Avennire*, April 22, 2000, p. 15.

"Ein Spiegel der europäischen Geistesgeschichte: Überlegungen aus Anlaß der Öffnung des Archivs der Glaubenskongregation". *Frankfurter Allgemeine Zeitung*, May 22, 2000.

"Bleiben und Reifen—Formen christlicher Existenz: Predigt von Joseph Kardinal Ratzinger zum silbernen Bishofsjubiläum von Kardinal Meisner, Weihbischof Dick und Weihbischof Plöger am 21. Mai". *OR(D)* 22 (June 2, 2000): 12; also in *KlBl* 80 (2000): 147–48.

"La presentazione del Documento 'Il Messagio di Fátima': L'intervento del Cardinale Joseph Ratzinger". *OR* 147 (June 26/27, 2000): 9.

"Theologischer Kommentar". In Kongregation für die Glaubenslehre, *Die Botschaft von Fatima*, pp. 32–43. Vatican City, 2000. Also in *Italian, English, French, Portuguese*, and *Spanish*. *Italian: Il Messaggio di Fatima*, supplement to *OR* 147 (June 26/27, 2000): 32–44. In *Le profezie di Fatima: L'amore della Madre nel cuore di un secolo*, edited by L. Lincetto et al., pp. 73–90. Padua, 1st and 2nd eds., 2000.
Also in *Italian* in *30 Giorni*, June 2000, pp. 88–93; and in the *German, English, French, Spanish*, and *Portuguese* editions of *30 Giorni/30 Days*.
German: in *Die Tagespost*, June 27, 2000, pp. 5–6; *OR(D)* 26 (June 30, 2000).
English: in *Origins* 30 (2000): 120–24; also in *Inside the Vatican*, special supplement, June–July 2000, pp. 10–14.

"Un corpo mi hai preparato: L'Omelia in occasione di sacerdoti e diaconi della Fraternità sacerdotale dei missionari di San Carlo Borromeo". *Tracce—Litterae Communionis*, no. 7, 2000, pp. 83–86.

"Il mio amico Pavan". In *Sussidiarità: Pensiero sociale della Chiesa e riforma dello Stato*, edited by P. Licciardi, pp. 17–22. Rome, 2000.

"Musica e liturgia". *Communio* 29 (2000): 37–48.

"Dichiarazione 'Dominus Iesus': Contesto e significato del documento". *OR*, September 6, 2000, p. 9; also in *Tracce—Litterae Communionis*, no. 9, 2000, pp. 97–99.
German: in *Die Tagespost*, September 9, 2000, p. 5.

"Es scheint mir absurd, was unsere lutherischen Freunde jetzt wollen: Ein Interview mit Christian Geyer zur Erklärung 'Dominus Iesus' ". *Frankfurter Allgemeine Zeitung*, September 22, 2000, pp. 51–52. Also in *"Dominus Iesus": Anstößige Wahrheit oder anstößige Kirche? Dokumente, Hintergründe, Standpunkte und Folgerungen*, edited by M. J. Rainer, pp. 29–45. Münster, 2001.
Italian: in *OR*, October 8, 2000, pp. 4–5.
English: in *Inside the Vatican*, January 2001, pp. 112–18.

"Konsens über die Rechtfertigungslehre?" *IKaZ* 29 (2000): 424–37.
Spanish: in *Communio* 22 (2001): 93–106.
French: in *Communio* 25 (2001): 41–57.

Foreword: Alice von Hildebrand, *The Soul of a Lion: Dietrich von Hildebrand*, pp. 9–12. San Francisco, 2000.

"Wiara i Teologia" (*Glaube und Theologie*). *Wrocławski Przegląd teologiczny*, August 2000, no. 2, pp. 7–13.

"Dem Menschen helfen, das Leiden zu erlernen und anzunehmen: Predigt in Sankt Paul vor den Mauern, Rom, 6. 3.1999". *Selige Anna Schäffer von Mindelstetten/Bayern* (Regensburg, 2000), Brief 38, pp. 10–17.

"Europas Kultur und ihre Krise". (Slightly abbreviated version of the lecture given November 28, 2000, in the 'Bayerische Vertretung' in Berlin.) *Die Zeit*, December 7, 2000; in *Die Tagespost*, December 16, 2000; abbreviation of the *Die Zeit* version in *Kirche heute*, no. 1, 2001, pp. 10–12. Extract from this lecture in: . . . *unterm Himmel über Berlin: Glauben in der Stadt*, edited by A. Herzig and B. Sauermost, pp. 88–95. Berlin, 2001.

Spanish: in *Nueva Revista* 73 (2001): 67–88; also in *Communio* 22 (2001): 238–53.

Portuguese: in *OR(P)* 13 (March 31, 2001): 2–4, 10; and in *Humanística e Teología/Faculdade de Teología*, Porto, 22/2 (2001): 159–75.

Italian: in *In Cristo nuova creatura: Scritti in onore del Card. Camillo Ruini Gran Cancelliere della Pontificia Università Lateranense*, edited by N. Reali and G. R. Alberti, pp. 375–92. Rome, 2001.

Polish: in *Niedziela* 41 (*Dodatek Akademicki*, no. 14), October 14, 2001, pp. i–iv.

"La nuova evangelizzazione". *OR*, (December 11/12, 2000, p. 11; also in Congregazione per il Clero, *Catechisti della nuova evangelizzazione*, edited by M. Piacenza, pp. 58–70. Genoa, 2001. In *Divinarum Rerum Notia: La teologia tra filosofia e storia: Studi in onore del Cardinale Walter Kasper*, edited by A. Russo and G. Coffele, pp. 505–16. Rome, 2001.

Spanish: in *OR(E)*, January 19, 2001, pp. 7–8.

English: in *Inside the Vatican*, August–September 2001, pp. 20–23.

"Per un nuovo inizio del movimento liturgico: Dal libro: Introduzione allo spirito della liturgia". *30 Giorni*, December 2000, pp. 48–54; also in the *German, English, French, Portuguese*, and *Spanish* editions of *30 Giorni/30 Days*.

"L'eredità di Abramo dono di Natale". *OR*, December 29, 2000, p. 1; also in *30 Giorni*, December 2000, pp. 58–59; and in the *German, English, French, Portuguese*, and *Spanish* editions of *30 Giorni/30 Days*; in *Il Regno—documenti*, no. 3, 2001, pp. 96–97.

German: in *Heute in Kirche und Welt*, no. 2, 2001, pp. 1–2.

"I movimenti, la Chiesa, il mondo: Dialogo con il cardinale Joseph Ratzinger". In Pontificium Consilium pro Laicis, *Laici oggi: I movimenti ecclesiali nella sollecitudine pastorale dei* *vescovi*, pp. 223–55. Vatican City, 2000. Appeared at the same time in *English*, *French*, and *Spanish*.

"Lectio Doctoralis und Bibliographie". In *LUMSA, Collana della Facoltà di Giurisprudenza: Per il Diritto: Omaggio a Joseph Ratzinger e Sergio Cotta*, pp. 9–14 and 27–87. Turin, 2000.

— 2001 —

"Hirt und Vater des Erzbistums: Erzbischof Degenhardt—75 Jahre". *Der Dom: Kirchenzeitung für das Erzbistum Paderborn*, January 28, 2001, p. 18.

Prefazione: J. Lozano Barragán, *Teologia e medicina*. Bologna, 2001. *Spanish*: in J. Lozano Barragán, *Teología y medicina*, pp. 9–10. Santafé de Bogotá, 2000.

Introduzione: M. Camisasca, *Comunione e Liberazione: Le origine (1954–1968)*, pp. 5–11. Cinisello Balsamo, 2001.

"Conclusion". In Cardinal Christoph Schönborn, Mgr. Michel-Marie-Bernard Calvet, Cardinal Christian Tumi, Cardinal Francis Eugene George, Mgr. John Chang, Cardinal Joseph Ratzinger, *Quel avenir pour l'Église? Perspectives dans les cinq continents: Conférences Notre-Dame de Paris 2001*, pp. 161–88. Paris, 2001.

"Ein Briefwechsel zwischen Metropolit Damaskinos und Kardinal Ratzinger". *IKaZ* 30 (2001): 282–96. *Slovenian*: in *Communio* 3 (2001): 207–23.

"Glejmo na prebodeno srce". (From *Schauen auf den Durchbohrten*; see under I.) *Communio* 3 (2001): 103–18.

"Weisheit: Unsere eigentliche Berufung". In *Was kommt. Was geht. Was bleibt*, edited by M. Schächter, pp. 357–59. Freiburg, Basel, and Vienna, 2001.

"Dank an unsere jüdischen Brüder". *Freiburger Rundbrief*, no. 4, 2001, pp. 241–47.

"Een nieuw en eeuwig Verbond: De gedachte van het Verbond in de teksten van het Avondmaal". *Emmäus* 32 (2001): 92–96.

Vorwort: *Compendio di Semantica del Dolore: Dolore, Fede, Preghiera,* edited by P. Zucchi, pp. 20–21. Florence, 2001.

"Das Archiv der Glaubenskongregation: Überlegungen anläßlich seiner Öffnung 1998". In *Inquisition, Index, Zensur: Wissenskulturen der Neuzeit im Widerstreit,* edited by H. Wolf, pp. 17–22. Paderborn, 2001.

"Il Vescovo maestro e custode della fede". In Congregazione per i Vescovi, *Duc in altum: Pellegrinaggio alla tomba di San Pietro e incontro di riflessione per i nuovi Vescovi nominati dal 1° gennaio 2000 al guigno 2001,* pp. 32–45. Vatican City, 2001.

"El problema de fondo". (= two interviews for *Mercurio,* Santiago de Chile, 1987 and 1994.) In *Crónica de las ideas: En busca del rumbo perdido,* edited by J. Antúnez Aldunate, pp. 148–59. Madrid, 2001.

Geleitwort: Franz Mußner, *Was hat Jesus Neues in die Welt gebracht?* pp. 7–8. Stuttgart, 2001.

" 'Let God's Light Shine Forth': Interview with Robert Moynihan". *Inside the Vatican,* August–September 2001, pp. 14–19.

"Das Wort ist Fleisch geworden". In *Friede auf Erden den Menschen seiner Gnade,* edited by H. Nitsche and J. Nabbefeld, pp. 81–82. Bad Honnef, 2001.

"Il 'munus docendi' un servizio al Vangelo e alla speranza". (Decima Assemblea Generale Ordinaria del Sinodo dei Vescovi/Interventi dei Padri Sinodali.) *OR* October 8/9, 2001, p. 5; also in *30 Giorni,* October 2001, p. 20, and similarly in the **German, English, French, Portuguese,** and **Spanish** editions of *30 Giorni/30 Days.*
   German: in *OR(D)* 43 (October 26, 2001): 8.

"Retrouver l'esprit de la liturgie: Entretien avec le Cardinal Ratzinger". *L'Homme nouveau,* October 7, 2001, pp. 9–11.

"La Théologie de la liturgie". *La Nef* 120 (October 2001): pp. 18–24 (with extracts from *Der Geist der Liturgie;* see under section I).

"Vom Rosenkranz: Joseph Kardinal Ratzinger im Gespräch mit Peter Seewald". *Stimme der Legion: Legio Mariae* 53 (December 2001): 54–56.

"The Local Church and the Universal Church: A Response to Walter Kasper". *America: A Jesuit Magazine* 185, 16/4548 (November 19, 2001): 7–11.

"Un secondo Illuminismo: Conferanza durante 27a edizione del Seminario Ambrosetti (7.–9.9.2001) a Villa d'Este e a Cernobbio". *Il Regno, documenti*, no. 19, 2001, pp. 650–52.

" 'Exclure la religion, c'est mutiler l'être humain': Un entretien avec le cardinal Ratzinger". *Le Figaro Magazine*, November 17, 200), pp. 58–60.

"Um die Erneuerung der Liturgie: Antwort auf Reiner Kaczynski". *StZ*, 2001, pp. 837–43.

"Les Figures de Marie et de Marthe". In *Autour de la question liturgique: Avec le Cardinal Ratzinger: Actes des journées liturgiques de Fontgombault, 22–24 juillet 2001*, pp. 6–9. Fontgombault, 2001.

"Théologie de la liturgie". In ibid., pp. 13–29.

"Bilan et perspectives". In ibid., pp. 173–89.

Préface: Pontificia Commissio Biblica, *Le peuple juif et ses Saintes Écritures dans la Bible chrétienne*, pp. 5–13. Vatican City, 2001. Also Paris, 2001, pp. 5–13.

" 'Chi ha visto me ha visto il Padre' (Gv 14,9): Il Volto di Cristo nella Sacra Scrittura". In *Il Volto dei Volti Cristo*, edited by Instituto Internazionale di ricerca sul Volto di Cristo, pp. 11–18. Gorle, 2001.

Prefazione: Angelo Montonati, *Fuco nella città: Sant'Antonio Maria Zaccaria (1502–1539)*, pp. 7–9. Cinisello Balsamo, 2002.

IV.
ARTICLES IN WORKS OF REFERENCE

LThK (2nd ed.):
"Auferstehung des Fleisches" I, VI, and VII: 1:1042, 1048–52.
"Auferstehungsleib": 1:1052f.
"Benedictus Deus": 2:171–73.
"Donatismus": 3:504–5.
"Ewigkeit" II (theological): 3:1268–70.
"Gerhard von Borgo San Donnino": 4:719–20.
"Haus, Haus Gottes": 5:32f.
"Heil": 5:78–80.
"Himmel": 5:355–58.
"Himmelfahrt Christi": 5:360–62.
"Hölle": 5:446–49.
"Joachim von Fiore": 5:975f.
"Kirche" II and III (doctrine of the Magisterium and systematic): 6:172–83.
"Leib Christi" II (dogmatic): 6:910–12.
"Leichnam": 6:917f.
"Liebe" III (historical): 6:1032–36.
"Mittler" II (dogmatic): 7:499–502.
"Neuheidentum": 7:907–9.
"Primat": 8:761–63.
"Schöpfung": 9:460–66.
"Sterben": 9:1055.
"Sühne" V: 9:1156–58.
"Ticonius": 10:180f.
"Tradition" III: 10:293–99.

RAC:
"Emanation": 4:1219–28.

RGG (3rd ed.):
"Protestantismus: III. Beurteilung vom Stadpunkt des Katholizismus": 5:663–66.
"Katholische Theologie": 6:775–79.

Der Große Herder (Freiburg, 5th ed., 1956ff.):
"Gottesbegriff und Gottesbild", vol. 12 (supplementary vol. 2), 1087–90.

HThG:
"Licht": 2:44–54.
"Stellvertretung": 2:566–75.

DSp:
"Fraternité": 5:1141–67.

SM:
"Auferstehung" II: 1:397–402.
"Himmelfahrt Christi": 2:693–96.

Meyers enzyklopädisches Lexikon:
"Christentum": vol. 5 (1972), cols. 669/671.

NOTES ON TEXT SOURCES

With the exception of the article "Der Heilige Geist als Communio [The Holy Spirit as Communion]", which was taken from the collection *Erfahrung und Theologie des Heiligen Geistes*, edited by C. Heitmann and H. Mühlen (Hamburg and Munich, 1974), pp. 223–38, all the other pieces have been published on the basis of the original texts put at our disposal by the author, even if they have in the meantime already been published elsewhere. This is the origin of minor variations in the text. This is true in particular of the article "Die Ekklesiologie der Konstitution *Lumen gentium* [The Ecclesiology of the Constitution *Lumen gentium*]" (compare *Die Tagespost*, special supplement, March 2000), to which the footnotes 7 and 12 have been added.

"Was ist das eigentlich—Theologie? [What in Fact Is Theology?]" appeared under the title "Was heißt Theologie?" in *Die Weite des Mysteriums: Christliche Identität im Dialog: Festschrift für Horst Bürkle*, edited by K. Krämer and A. Paus (Freiburg, Basel, and Vienna, 2000), pp. 14–19.

"Communio, Eucharistie—Gemeinschaft—Sendung [Communion: Eucharist—Fellowship—Mission]" appeared under the title "Kommunion—Kommunitat—Sendung", in J. Ratzinger, *Schauen auf den Durchbohrten: Versuche zu einer spirituellen Christologie* (Einsiedeln, 1984; 2nd ed., 1990), pp. 60–84. We are grateful to the Johannesverlag, under the management of Frau Cornelia Capol, for permission to reprint this.

For "Eucharistie und Mission [Eucharist and Mission]" see *FoKTh* 14 (1998): 81–98.

"Dienst und Leben der Priester [The Ministry and Life of Priests]" appeared in *Eucharisteria: Festschrift für Damaskinos Papandreou*, edited by M. Brun and W. Schneemelcher (Athens, 1996), pp. 125–37.

"Kirchliche Bewegungen und ihr theologischer Ort [Church Movements and Their Place in Theology]" appeared in *IKaZ* 27 (1998): 431–48; also in *Lebensaufbrüche: Geistliche Bewegungen in Deutschland*, edited by P. Wolf (Vallendar and Schönstatt, 2000), pp. 23–56.

The "Briefwechsel mit Metropolit Damaskinos [The Exchange of Letters with Metropolitan Damaskinos]" appeared in *IKaZ* 30 (2001): 282–96.

"Zur Lage der Ökumene [On the Ecumenical Situation]" appeared in *Perspectives actuelles sur l'œcuménisme*, edited by J.-L. Leuba (Louvain-la-Neuve, 1995), pp. 231–44.

"Das Erbe Abrahams [The Heritage of Abraham]" appeared in *Heute in Kirche und Welt*, no. 2, February 2001, pp. 1–2.